W ***main***

When Memories Remain

Karen Emilson

Nordheim Books

Box 670 • Ashern, Manitoba Canada • R0C 0E0

(204) 768-3312

Published by Nordheim Books, Box 670, Ashern, Manitoba, Canada, R0C 0E0 (204) 768-3312.

Editor: Roger Newman, Gimli, Manitoba.
Copy-Editor: Nancy Hall, Gimli, Manitoba.
Cover design & layout:: Andrea Dyck, Moosehorn, Manitoba.

Frontispiece: David Pischke at 15 years of age

Cataloguing in Publication Data

Emilson, Karen, 1963 -
When Memories Remain

ISBN 0-9681242-1-6

This book was written in cooperation with David Pischke, based on his recollections. Numerous neighbours, friends, family members also provided information for this book.Whenever possible, information has been substantiated by government files, records or documentation.

Printed and bound in Canada

For Bruce Snively

A wonderful father and a truly good man

Acknowledgements

Writing non-fiction requires the assistance of many people. Over the past four years, I received help from the following:

Sharon Cote, Ernie Arns, Lorne Park, Nick Kolansky, Dave Asmundson, Helmut Neufeld, Bob McAfee, Alan Thomson, Robert McMillan, Walter Pischke, Karen Makowski, Dwight Cook, Margaret Shiells, Riane Lee, Mike Leitold, Jean Clearwater, Ken & Jane Price, Sheila Shiells, Phyllis Klingbell, Diane Price.

Sincere thanks for all your help.

Thanks

A very talented writer and editor, Roger Newman. His patience and hard work makes me a better writer.

Nancy Hall the copy-editor who helped me turn a manuscript into a polished book.

Ken Malenko whose critical eye made this into a better story.

Andrea Dyck who scanned the photos and designed the cover.

Mary Alards-Tomalin, a wonderful friend who provided the encouragement and assistance I needed to get this book finished.

And finally to the wonderful men in my life - my son Laurie and husband Mark for their love, support and faith.

Prologue

When I finished *Where Children Run,* I thought that my contribution to the Pischke story was over. However, because the first book covered a span of 12 years of the twins' lives, it left a lot of unanswered questions for the reader. The three most frequently asked questions were:

"Why did the twins contact you in the first place?" and

"What happened to the twins after they left the farm?"

Readers wanted more than what the epilogue provided. They wanted to know what *really* happened to the family. What readers asked for was a second book. One that answered those questions and:

"What was their mother thinking?"

I'm hoping that this book demonstrates how a person's circumstances in life helps to shape and influence their behaviour and their decisions.

But I had to wait. Answering these questions was not enough reason to write a second book. What would the focus be? I couldn't write an aimless series of stories. I needed a reason, a very good reason to write a sequel. Then the phone rang.

David and Dennis were asked to take a polygraph test in the Mike Kalanza murder investigation.

It raised once again why the twins had come to me in the first place. First thieves, now murderers?

And so the book began.

"The measure of a man is how well he cares for his children."

\- Sidney Poitier

Chapter 1

"DID YOU KILL MIKE KALANZA?"
The immensity of the words were shocking even though he'd been expecting the question. He tried to hide the alarm he was feeling.

"Did you kill Mike Kalanza?" the officer asked again.

The man said nothing.

"Are you comfortable answering this question?"

He nodded that he was.

"Are you sure?" the officer asked.

"Y-yes," he stammered.

Sergeant Robert McMillan was relieved that the suspect had finally calmed down.

An officer with the Royal Canadian Mounted Police for 21 years, Robert McMillan had interviewed many suspects. He'd worked as a plainclothes investigator for three years and in the Regina Drug Unit for six. He'd spent eight years in three different detachments in Saskatchewan before training as a polygraph examiner at the Canadian Police College in Ottawa the year before. Now he handled all cases in rural Manitoba—which meant traveling to small communities and remote areas across the province.

Tonight he was in Ashern, eliminating suspects in a 12-year-old murder investigation. It was his job to determine if David Pischke was telling the truth.

"Are you comfortable with all of the questions we've reviewed?" he asked. "Remember, I'm not here to find you guilty."

"S-sure you're not," David scoffed. "If that's t-true then why did you read me my rights?"

The officer hesitated. He'd explained this already. He wasn't sure if David had misunderstood or was baiting him for another argument. Maybe Pischke was stalling. Or maybe it was an effort to intimidate. Either way, it was McMillan's job to keep the upper hand and not let the suspect take control of the interview. Men like David were exhausting to deal with. In fact, he was one of, if not the most difficult suspects McMillan had ever put through the rigors of polygraph questioning.

People who agreed to take the test usually exhibited some degree of anger, fear and annoyance at the procedure. But this man was different. He was downright belligerent and his anger seemed to originate from somewhere far beyond the Ashern detachment walls. McMillan had learned a bit about David from his twin brother Dennis, who'd been in to take the test seven months earlier. He'd also been difficult, but not as angry as David.

"While the result of the polygraph machine is not admissible in court, whatever you say in this room is," McMillan explained, using a different analogy this time. "Let's say you tell me that no, you didn't kill Mike, but that you killed somebody else. We need to make it clear that what you say to me can be used in a court of law. There is no client privilege here. Not like with a lawyer. While I am a polygraph examiner, I am also a peace officer and any confession of a punishable crime will be taken seriously. Do you understand?"

David nodded.

"Do you trust me?" the sergeant asked. "Do you believe that I'm not trying to trick you?"

"No," he chided. "I don't t-trust n-none of you guys."

"Well then we have a problem," he said. "We can't do the test until we establish a level of trust."

David shrugged. "How am I s-supposed to t-trust you?"

McMillan was curious. "Why don't you?" he asked.

David laughed. "Because you guys have done n-nothin' but accuse us our whole lives! An' the assholes around here did n-nothin' to help us w-when we was kids, n-nothin'!"

"Well, why did you come in here then?" McMillan asked. "If you don't want to be here—there's the door."

David exhaled. "I got no choice."

"Yes, you do," he said softly. "You don't have to be here."

David laughed. "I gotta take the test to clear my n-name. Otherwise, everyone's gonna say I'm a killer."

McMillan raised his eyebrows. "Well, then it's up to you, isn't it?"

David grimaced.

An inconclusive result on tonight's test would mean that Bob would have to come back to Ashern for a retest. This was one suspect he didn't want to test again. It was important that David be calm, rational and comfortable with the questions before being connected to the machine, to avoid an inconclusive result.

"Okay," the officer began. "I'm going to leave the room and I'll come back in 10 minutes. You think about it and when I get back, we'll decide if you're ready to proceed."

David looked away.

This is going to be a challenge, McMillan thought as he got up from the desk, stepped out of the room and quietly closed the door behind him.

David glanced at his watch. He'd been there answering questions for more than two hours. The officer had called them "background"questions. David still couldn't understand why they needed to know so much personal information. It was embarrassing and seemed to make no sense, really.

"Just hook me up an' ask me what you need to know," David had said as soon as he walked in.

The officer tried to explain that it didn't work that way.

"W-why do you have to ask me all that s-stuff?" David hollered. The cop . . . what was his name? He'd said something about determining if he was physically and psychologically able to take the test. He'd mentioned something about "safety valve" questions, too. They were the bad ones—the ones David didn't want to answer. That interrogation made him feel lower than he'd ever felt before.

An' that's pretty low, David chuckled to himself.

One of the first things David had to tell the officer was that his dad died when he was only three years old.

"And so who raised you?" the Sergeant had asked.

"You mean who beat the hell out of me," David corrected.

He recalled one of the last summers that he and Dennis had been together on the grain and cattle farm where they'd grown up. It was a typical July afternoon in Manitoba—the sky was deep blue and cloudless. The warm southeast wind carried dust through the air and it stuck to their sweat-soaked skin. The breeze smelled of the freshly mown hay that lay curing under the hot sun.

In February of that year the twins had celebrated their 13th birthdays at a neighbours' home on the other side of the small lake that separated the two farms. The boys had fled into the bushes the previous night, with gunfire overhead. Their stepfather Boleslaw 'Bob' Domko had tried to shoot them in a fit of anger. Too afraid to go home and thankful for a place to stay, David and Dennis lived with Leon and Anna Koch for nearly two weeks. The Kochs were kind people who were as generous as their modest circumstances would allow.

When the twins' mother Caroline arrived to pick them up, they were delighted to discover that their stepfather, who everyone called "Domko," had been taken by the RCMP to a mental hospital more than 100 miles away. To them it was like he'd been transported to the other side of the earth—they rejoiced!

The twins, along with older sister Eunice and younger sister Rosie, worked their mother's tiny, isolated farm without complaint. The boys, who weren't afraid of hard work, became the men of the house. They began attending school regularly, slept without fear and everyone resumed eating together again. Half-siblings, eight-year-old Kathy and three-year-old Raymond, missed their father who was always kind to them, but soon became accustomed to his absence as everyone embraced the relaxed atmosphere at home.

Then, one day in the middle of June, Domko returned. Their mother had gone to the nearby town of Moosehorn to pick him up at the bus station. He'd been discharged from the mental hospital due to good behaviour.

For the first few weeks, the twins noticed that his temperament had improved. Unfortunately, little Raymond got into the pills that Domko was taking, and thinking they were candy, ate some. The rest were spilled on the floor. Domko refused to buy more medication and soon he returned to his old ways of overworking, starving and beating his stepchildren. He also appeared to derive great pleasure from pitting little Raymond against the twins. This fostered a mutual hatred and competition among the three.

But on this particular July afternoon, the twins received some respite. They met on the path between two adjoining fields as their horse teams greeted one another with a whinny then fell into a side-by-side trot. The boys had been out cutting hay for winter feed.

"Look!" Dennis said with a cheer as he pointed towards home. "Domko's gone!"

David squinted in the direction of the farmyard, a good half mile away. He couldn't see their stepfather's car which was normally parked beside the house. This usually meant that he and their mother had gone to town.

Dennis stood recklessly holding the reins as the hay mower clanged behind him. He held back the team, skinny arms straining with effort. His T-shirt was too big and dirty from wear while his pants were too short—exposing tanned ankles and bare, calloused feet. The bruise on the boy's upper cheek, which last week had been deep purple, was fading to a sickly yellow. David knew from experience that once a few more days passed, the tell-tale signs of his brother's beating would be gone altogether.

"Whatcha lookin' at?" Dennis smirked.

"Oh nothin'," David said, forcing a smile. A pang of guilt washed over him as he watched his skinny twin as the mower wheels bounced over hard bumps in the ground. It was the first time he'd been relaxed in days.

The week before they'd been out raking hay when Dennis stopped to pick Saskatoon berries growing in the bush at the edge of the field. David continued raking, glancing over his shoulder at his brother who had been happily gathering the ripe, purple berries in a basket he'd made by folding up the bottom hem of his shirt. Picking berries was forbidden by Domko, especially when there was work to be done, but the starving children couldn't resist. Dennis popped every second handful into his mouth, and put the remainder in his cupped shirt.

The wind had been blowing hard, which muffled their hearing. Seagulls squawked hungrily overhead as they waited patiently just out of reach. David's rake turned the windrow and he watched passively as a gull swooped down and grabbed a mouse in its beak. Another bird followed, biting the back end of the squirming rodent and in a tug-of-war, ripped it in half. Other gulls, seeing the opportunity for a meal, joined in the furious fight over the mouse.

There were times that David felt like a hungry gull. So little food was given to the Pischke children that they went to bed most nights with nothing in their stomachs but a dull ache. It made David wonder what a mouse tasted like. He shuddered. Thoughts of the juicy berries that Dennis was daring to take made his mouth water. He hoped the ones saved in the shirt were for him.

Glancing over his shoulder, his stomach lurched as he noticed their stepfather quietly approaching Dennis from behind. Naively, the boy continued to pick berries, jamming handfuls into his mouth. David had to quickly decide whether or not to shout a warning to his brother. He knew from experience that he'd be putting himself in danger by alerting Dennis. Domko had no tolerance for loyalty, especially between the twins who he believed were conspiring against him. It was frustrating that he couldn't turn them against one another.

Turn around, Dennis! David silently implored.

And then, as if his brother could read his mind, Dennis suddenly turned to look over his shoulder—but it was too late. Domko delivered a blow that caught the boy in the head, knocking him backwards against the bushes. The impact sent the berries flying into the air, then scattered them on the ground beside the youngster. Instinctively, Dennis' arms came up over his head and his knees curled towards his chest.

David was thankful for the strong wind that muffled Dennis' cries. His heart beat heavy and fast in his chest and the strange sensation of time halting overtook him—the same feeling he got each time one of his siblings received a beating. This unnerved David who counted the blows silently to the beat of the blood pounding in his head. Three, four, five . . . David dared to look again and was relieved to see that Domko was slowing—six, seven and then one more unmerciful kick to Dennis' back. He then took a step back and ordered the boy to get up.

Scrambling to his feet, the boy limped towards the waiting horse and mower. Domko lunged at him once more, but the teenager avoided the kick by veering to one side. He then jumped on the mower seat and slapped the reins hard against the horses' backs. The animals, always tense in Domko's presence, bolted. Domko stood at the edge of the field for awhile watching the twins work until he became bored. He then walked back to his tractor which was concealed behind a nearby brush pile. He'd administered his "daily beating," so the rest of the children would be safe for another day—unless they did something seriously wrong. David was thankful it hadn't been his turn. Tomorrow he might not be so lucky.

"Where's Eunice?" Dennis called out. The question brought David out of his trance.

"I don't know," he said, shaking his head gently. The horses began to slow as they approached the yard fence. "She's prob'ly 'round here somewhere."

The twins jumped off the mower seats and led the horses into the yard, halting them by the chicken coop. The cows would need to be milked later on, but for now the boys were free to do whatever they wanted.

Picking up the glass sealer he carried on the mower, David dropped the reins across the drawbar. They strolled to the well and took turns pumping water from the well onto the ground. The cold, clear water cascaded onto their bare feet. They slipped off their shirts and splashed each other with the water, a welcome relief to their overheated bodies. As they filled their jars, a little dog ran into the yard and began barking. Looking up, David recognized the mongrel that Domko had brought to the farm a few weeks before. The dog had absolutely no farm sense and David was surprised that the animal hadn't been shot by Domko like so many others that he'd stolen from unsuspecting owners in town. David speculated that little Raymond's attachment to the dog might have bought it extra time.

The dog scampered towards the twins who ignored the animal's pleas for attention. David watched as Eunice and Raymond strolled into the yard, each carrying a pail of berries. Two years older than the twins, their sister was a tall, thin, attractive girl with dark blonde hair and bright blue eyes. Usually friendly and talkative, Eunice had been subdued lately. She motioned for Raymond to stay outside as she took both buckets into the house.

The dog, looking for something to play with, ran towards the chicken house. He barked and yapped at the clucking hens that foraged in the dirt. The sudden appearance of the dog sent them into a frenzy which in turn startled the horses.

"Get away from there!" David scolded. The dog paid no attention. Like little boys, he seemed to believe that chickens were meant to be chased.

The horses whinnied and began backing up to get away from the yapping dog. Dennis' team reared then took off in a trot towards the safety of the barn. David's team, however, continued to back up. By the time he realized what was happening, the reins had become caught in the drawbar and tangled around one mower wheel. As the horses' retreated, the reins wound tighter around the wheel, pulling their heads back even further. The animals were beginning to panic.

David dropped his jar and ran towards the team. Grabbing the reins, he tried to untie the knot but it wouldn't budge. By now, the horses heads were pulled so far that their front feet were beginning to lift off the ground.

Getting behind the mower, David pressed his hip against the coop wall for leverage and tried to hold the implement so it wouldn't roll any farther.

"Go get a knife!" he screamed to Dennis who immediately turned and ran into the house. The horses' hind legs banged against the mower bar as the animals continued to resist the unknown force pulling their reins. David jammed his feet and legs against the wall, but could feel himself weakening from the strain. Suddenly, the horses reared together and the mower slammed back against his legs, causing him to slip part way to the ground. His chest was pinned to the coop and it looked as if the horses were going to fall back on top of him as the frothing animals stomped and fought to free themselves. David could feel the edge of the mower cutting into his chest and the poorly constructed building was giving way under the strain. Dennis arrived moments later with Domko's butchering knife in hand.

"C-cut the reins!" David screamed. "Hurry, Denny, they're killin' me."

Dennis found what looked like a worn area on a rein, then sawed furiously. It took all his strength to keep the horses from crushing his brother while he cut a deep slash into the hardened leather.

David sobbed as Dennis worked.

"I got it!" Dennis panted as the knife broke through one rein, then the other. This freed one horse, whose first instinct was to run. This helped free the trapped teen as it dragged the other horse and mower away from the chicken coop as well.

David crawled a few feet across the grass then collapsed on the ground.

"You okay?" Dennis asked, panting as he dropped to his knees.

David laid face down on the grass for a long time before slowly turning over.

"I almost got killed," he choked. Then shading his eyes from the bright sun, he squinted them open enough to see chubby, dark-skinned Raymond standing over him. The boy's lips and cheeks were stained purple with Saskatoon juice.

"I tell Ta-Ta," he taunted, then turned and ran to the house.

David was too disoriented to care whether his little brother tattled or not.

"Denny, let's get outta here," he said.

The brothers got up and Dennis helped David stagger into the safety of the bush just a short distance from the house. David thought that they should continue through the trees to where the St. Thomas Lutheran Church sat in a nearby clearing.

The building had been a sanctuary for the twins who'd spent many a winter's night huddled on the floor wrapped in the minister's robes. The thick, white candles used during Sunday church services threw just enough heat to keep them from freezing to death. For some reason, Domko wouldn't come after them if they were hiding in that church.

But this was summer. The building would be too hot and stuffy and besides, there were members of the parish irritated that the boys spent so much time there, and they didn't want to be caught inside. Their kindly neighbours, Gus and Emma Harwart, had defended the twins on more than one occasion, saying that if it weren't for the church, the twins would surely be dead. This shamed the less charitable parishioners into silence, but David knew that it wouldn't take much of an excuse for them to lock the back window that was always mysteriously left open.

The boys lay under the shade of the poplar trees beside the ashes of one of their old campfires, chatting until David fell into a deep sleep. He awoke at dusk to find Dennis gone. He dozed off again, sleeping intermittently until his twin returned. Once he knew that Dennis was safe, he slept soundly.

David awoke early the next morning to the annoying buzz of mosquitoes near his face. He casually swatted the pests and listened to the sounds of morning. The rooster crowed and the chickens clucked happily, bragging that they'd just laid an egg. A chipmunk twittered to its mate high in a tree not too far away. The air was still and David sensed it was going to be another hot day.

Sitting up, his aching limbs protested as he recalled what had happened the day before. Still hidden, he could see the house, barnyard and the cows standing patiently at the far gate—waiting to be led into the barn for milking. He decided it would be best to wait until Eunice emerged from the house before limping to the barn to help.

Dennis stirred beside him. When he awoke, he explained that he had slipped into the yard and unharnessed, fed and watered the horses while David slept. He'd helped Eunice milk the cows, then hidden the cut reins so that Domko wouldn't find them. He reported that Domko and their mother had arrived home late at night, so they wouldn't have noticed that David was missing and that the haying wasn't finished. Dennis sat cross-legged with his hands relaxed on his knees, as he waited patiently for David to thank him for his efforts.

Dennis, thought David, his twin and his salvation.

The two could barely stand to be apart. The quieter of the two boys, Dennis' mannerisms were gentle. The injustices of their lives weighed heavier on him, and his vulnerability showed. He was caught and beaten by their stepfather at least twice as often as David, who in contrast was gregarious and quick. He was the leader of the two, and because of this, felt it was his responsibility to keep them both alive.

Domko loved to beat Dennis, not only because the boy was easily fooled and would cry out in pain, but because the harder-to-catch twin would stand nearby and suffer as well. Domko knew it hurt David terribly to watch Dennis being beaten.

Now that they were in their early teens, the boys could endure the beatings with stoicism—unlike when Domko first came to the farm. Their father, Bill Pischke, had died of tuberculosis shortly before the twins' third birthday. Bill had been an easygoing man, never spanking the children or losing his temper. Domko's strictness and erratic behaviour came as a surprise to the children whose disobedience was no longer met with a firm word, but with a closed fist. It didn't take long before the seven happy-go-lucky, mischievous children became fearful and withdrawn.

Self-preservation became a daily objective and it often came at the expense of the other children. Within a few years, the three older boys, Walter, Stephen and Norman, moved away given the first opportunity. That left only four young Pischke children to do all the work.

David watched from the bushes as the door opened and Eunice stepped out carrying three clean milking pails. At 15, she was tired of the family's dismal living conditions and anxious to start her own life. Like the older boys, she was awaiting her chance.

Quietly, the twins emerged from hiding and Dennis ran ahead to get the cows. David fell into line beside his sister, then he pulled open the heavy barn door. Eunice didn't even ask where he'd been. The boys had spent so many nights in the bush that she was accustomed to their absence.

They stepped into the dark building. The air was heavy with the pungent smell of livestock manure and urine. It took a few moments for their eyes to adjust as the bright sunshine filled the barn. A chorus of screeching and chirping came from overhead as their sudden appearance disrupted the peaceful existence of the barn swallows whose nests were built high in the rafters. A pair of adult birds swooped threateningly at the teens, a warning to ignore the nests filled with tiny chicks. Another pair of birds came from a different direction and did the same thing, then continued out the barn door. Soon they were back, and the children swung their arms overhead to fend off the birds, thoughts elsewhere.

The cows streamed in bellowing as they found their stalls. The children began working immediately to fill their buckets and then dump the warm, frothing milk into a large cream can near the door. It took nearly an hour to milk the dozen cows. Eunice and Dennis each took a handle of the heavy can then carried it to the house so the cream could be separated from the milk. David chased the cows out of the barn and back into the pasture. He returned to harness the horses that waited in larger stalls at the back of the barn. Their tails swished as they tried to brush away the annoying flies that buzzed around. They whinnied as David approached, anxious to be let outside.

The boy whispered a stream of meaningless, softly spoken words to the animals, hoping they would remain calm while he worked quickly to get the harnesses in place. Luckily he'd found an extra set of reins. Backing the animals out of their stalls, he emerged through the doorway, leading a horse in each hand.

Suddenly he stopped.

Domko was standing directly in front of the open door, the pair of cut reins hanging loosely at his side. He'd been watching David the entire time.

Domko stood only five foot three inches, but what he lacked in height, he made up for in width. His broad shoulders were muscular and his stocky limbs powerful. He stood with legs spaced a shoulder's width apart, and his muscles twitched with anger. He wore army boots, gray work pants and a dirty, plaid shirt. A week's worth of butts were stashed in one pant cuff. A greasy cap sat atop his head, pushed far enough back that David could clearly see the four-inch scar that ran across his forehead. It was just below the hairline over his left eye where the metal plate had been inserted.

The stub of a hand-rolled cigarette was pinched in the corner of his thinly lipped mouth. He didn't bathe or shave regularly and smelled of body odour and manure. When angry, his almond-shaped eyes flashed in a wicked way and he seemed to lose control of his senses. As he lashed out, he would yell obscenities in Polish and broken English, which revealed one gold tooth in the front of his mouth.

Some people claimed that Domko could be friendly and talkative—even helpful—but David only saw this when Domko was interacting with his own children or in the company of someone he was trying to impress.

His sheer intensity and aggressive demeanour caused people to fear him. A Polish war veteran, Domko had a hatred for German people. He bragged many times about killing, torturing and maiming prisoners during the Second World War. This terrified the children who'd spoken Low-German at home when their father was alive.

At first it appeared that Domko was trying to beat the bloodlines out of them. Soon it appeared that the beatings had become a habit. Now, it looked like Domko was enjoying it.

Strong for his age and determined, the boy had grown taller than Domko over the past year, but he was still intimidated by the man who had used fear as a weapon for nearly a decade. David had never once considered fighting back.

Their eyes met and David realized today it was his turn.

"You soneebeech bastard," Domko seethed, stepping forward, thrusting the reins towards the boy. "You's be cuttink it some!"

Letting go of the horse, David tried to run, but Domko blocked the doorway knocking him to the ground.

"I's be showink you bastard!" he screamed as he swung the leather reins at David, catching him on the bare back. The scrambling boy wailed as Domko thrashed him again.

"Sauger!" Dennis yelled.

David saw his twin hop over a fence and disappear into the bush. The secret word told him where Dennis would be hiding.

Instinctively, David covered his head with his arms. Each time the tip of the reins seared his bare back it felt like a razor slicing through his skin. His mind whirled as he remembered Raymond saying he would tell Ta-Ta. The boy likely followed Dennis when he hid the reins, then reported everything to his father who would have rewarded him with a chocolate bar.

David's mind reeled. It was so unfair that his own father had died so young, but even worse that the brutality they suffered had erased most of the memories of what life was like before his father's death.

David hated crying out, but knew that his screams pleased Domko. If he didn't yell, the next whip of the reins was delivered more carefully, to be sure that it elicited the desired response. The pain across his back was excruciating and he writhed on the ground, but was careful not to turn over. He knew that a blow across the chest would hurt even more and across the face could be disfiguring. He felt himself scream again and again as the flogging continued.

Whipping was something that Domko had wanted to do for quite some time. David could sense the man was enjoying himself. He'd often bragged about how much pain he could inflict and grunted with the delivery of each lash.

When he felt like he just couldn't take the pain any longer, an odd sensation came over him. He felt detached from his body as his mind floated far away from the man who swore with the delivery of each blow. It was almost as if somebody else was taking the blows for him as his mind drifted to another place.

He thought about the few people who cared about him. He could hear Emma's voice repeating over and over again: "You're a good boy."

I should have put on my shirt, he scolded himself. Next time I'll wear my shirt. He stared blankly at the ground less than an inch away and tried to focus on the dirt and pebbles. He knew that the circumstances of his life were wrong and unfair. He knew that not all children suffered as he did.

David lay on the ground fading in and out of consciousness for a long time before he realized that Domko had stopped whipping him. It took a few minutes for his mind to clear and comprehend that he was still alive. His back throbbed, gently at first, and then painful waves rippled from his shoulder blades to the back of his knees.

It had been his own carelessness that had caused the near-accident the day before, resulting in this beating. He knew it was his fault. But he also knew that what he'd just experienced was more than Domko punishing him for the cut reins. It was about control and power. It was about how much Domko enjoyed the pain, blood and fear he inflicted on the helpless children. It was about trying to break the spirit of boys who were growing into men. The trouble was, David refused to be broken.

Chapter 2

THE DOOR OPENED AND SERGEANT McMillan stepped back into the room.

"Shall we continue with the questions?" he asked.

David looked up at him solemnly.

"I got all n-night," he said.

McMillan sat down on the other side of the desk.

Was David Pischke physically capable of committing murder? he wondered.

Yes, without a doubt. David appeared as strong as an ox. Years of physical labour had built thick muscles across his arms and chest. Standing nearly 6 feet tall, David would be a formidable adversary to most men.

McMillan had heard that the man was quite likable. Unfortunately on this night, he'd only seen that side of David a few times. On the odd occasion that he did forget his anger and made a joke, his blue eyes shone with merriment. He was a tidy, clean-shaven man whose thick blonde hair was short and neat. Whether David realized it or not, he had a strong physical presence.

"Do you have any fears or questions about the polygraph machine itself?" McMillan asked.

David thought for a moment.

"What about my s-speech problem?" he asked. "How's that g-gonna affect it?"

David hated the stutter that he and his brothers Dennis and Walter had. Some people said it was a condition inherited from their father's family, while others believed it was the result of the trauma they'd suffered growing up. Either way, it had caused each of them a lifetime of embarrassment.

The stutter seemed to worsen when they were excited, nervous, angry or tired. David worried that the polygraph machine might interpret the speech problem as an indication of guilt. He hoped that the machine was better than that.

He also hoped that his difficulties expressing himself wouldn't influence the test results. The secret 'twin language' that he and Dennis had spoken carried into their early teen years and affected his vocabulary.

Words like "puck, puck," and "sauger," "mucktork" and "wee wa" thwarted Domko's attempt to understand their plans. They also called everyone by nickname, adding to his confusion. Their strange speech had caused people in the community to think they were "retarded" but the secret language was actually quite clever.

As they matured and Domko learned to decipher the language, they simply changed the meaning of words. At the time, David hadn't realized it, but their secret language had caused their stepfather to think they were conspiring against him.

"Your speech impediment shouldn't cause a problem when you're on the polygraph machine," he explained. "All we require is a 'yes' or 'no' answer. As long as you don't have trouble saying those words, you'll be fine."

David sat quietly for a moment. He wasn't sure what to believe. A retired RCMP officer had warned him against taking the polygraph saying it was unreliable. Other people told him that he should take the test to halt rumours circulating about his involvement in Mike's murder.

"Earlier you said someone beat you," the officer said. "Who was that?"

"The ol' bastard," David answered. "An' he didn't beat just me. All us kids s-suffered."

"Your stepfather?"

"Oh, yes."

"So I take it you didn't get along with him very well then?" McMillan noted.

"Y-you g-got that r-right," he stammered.

"And how about your mother, did you get along with her?" he asked.

"Yes, but M-Mom . . . you see, the thing about M-Mom is that she never knew what to do," he explained. "There was so goddamned many of us. An' she had a h-horrible childhood too, so she g-gave up."

"How many brothers and sisters do you have?" he asked.

David had to stop and think.

"There was seven Pischkes an' . . . four Domkos," he said.

"How did you get along with them?"

"Good, good," he said adding, "Well, I got along good with my-my real b-brothers an' sisters, but not them other kids."

"How do you get along now? Are you close?"

"Close? No," David replied. "People think it brings families together, but it don't."

"What brings families together?" the officer asked.

"The a-abuse," he said. "People assume that because you l-l-lived through hell an' torture that you get close, but all it does is bring up bad memories. It a-actually rr-rips you ap-part."

David remembered the few times that social workers had come to the farm. One was Martha Jeske, a big woman of German descent. Domko despised her. On one occasion there had been a complaint filed by neighbours that the Pischke children were being neglected. It had been her job to assess the situation.

David remembered most of her visits, but he was an adult before he was reminded of the story of Martha's arrival at the farm when the twins were about six years old. Of course the boys were very shy and when they saw the strange car ran into the bush. This time, however, Martha saw where they'd entered. She got out of her car and followed them to the edge of the dense poplars and undergrowth. Pulling back the branches, she could see the two little boys hiding like frightened rabbits.

"Come on out of there!" she said firmly.

To David, Martha looked like an angel—her hair framed her face in soft curls. He didn't dare disobey this woman for fear that when he died he wouldn't go to heaven. He grabbed his shy twin by the arm and led him out of their hiding place.

"Well, well," she said, her voice softer, "what have we got here? Twins?"

The boys were shabbily dressed and dirty from head to their bare toes.

They appeared identical, blonde hair bleached white from the sun and blue eyes shining like sapphires. They were a cute sight, in spite of their shabby appearance.

"What are your names?" she asked.

It took some coaxing, but finally it was Dennis who spoke.

"I be s-soneebeech," he said pointing a dirty thumb to his chest. ". . . an' he's be bastard."

People in the community had "tsked" and some even laughed as stories like this about the Pischke children filtered into the kitchens of neighbouring homes. Social activities of the time centred around going to church and the occasional picnic or community dance. For the most part, people were hardworking and honest with little free time. Unfortunately, gossiping was also commonplace in small communities where everyone knew everyone else's business.

The nearest neighbours to the Pischke farm were Gus and Emma Harwart and Jim and Ruby Deighton. Both couples had frequently intervened on the children's behalf and were disturbed when they heard unpleasant stories about the family.

David didn't know how much Martha had discovered that particular day about the children's living conditions, but he concluded that she must have had very little power since nothing was done for them. It was obvious by the way she talked to Domko that she knew the children were being abused, but domestic violence laws were vague at the time and enforcement near impossible. Martha threatened him once, saying that if anything ever happened to the twins she'd hold him responsible.

Eventually, she was transferred to a different government office. A new social worker came by the farm but still nothing was done to help the children. Unfortunately, most people were reluctant to become involved in domestic matters which were usually kept private.

In this case, people either liked Domko and felt sorry for him for having such an unruly bunch of stepchildren to raise or they thought he was a thieving maniac who had been a terrible influence on the children. Either way, it was Caroline and her brood who suffered as people whispered, then turned their backs. Fear silenced mostly everyone.

David remembered the last time Jim Deighton took them to the RCMP detachment in Ashern, approximately 16 miles southeast of the farm. The officer had scowled at them before putting the 11 year olds in the back seat of the cruiser. He drove them back to the farm, had a short conversation with Domko in the kitchen, then left.

"Yous soneebeech bastards!" Domko screamed once the officer was gone. "I's not be doink nothink ant they's be comink!"

Grabbing David first, he threw him against the wall and then kicked him. Opening the door to the crawl space beneath the house, he grabbed the boy and shoved him through the trap door. David landed on the soft earthen floor and could hear Dennis being beaten above him. David looked around the crawl space which was dark except for the light that came through the above opening. He hoped that Domko would toss Dennis down too, so that he wouldn't have to stay in the dark place alone. Dennis was crying now, he could hear Domko stomp closer to the opening. David rolled out of the way as his brother dropped to the ground beside him.

"Ant yous bastards be stayink there!" Domko yelled as the door crashed shut.

The twins sat silently in the dark until they heard heavy footsteps overhead round the corner of the front room, move into the kitchen and then the faint sound of the outside door being slammed behind him.

"He's gone," David whispered.

Their eyes quickly adjusted to their dark surroundings. The crawl space was framed by the worn foundation of a house that was far from air tight. Tiny streams of light penetrated where the cement was cracked and giving way. David could see Dennis sitting beside him with his knees pulled up to his chest.

Dennis rubbed his eyes with his palms, then crossed his arms over his knees resting his head on his forearms. He sat like this for a long time, staring into the dirt. He wiped his nose on his sleeve. David knew his twin would be ready to talk once the sniffling stopped.

The crawl space was familiar to the boys. Whenever Domko wanted to keep the children from running away, he'd lock them in the cold, spooky spot. It smelled of wet earth, mould, rodent droppings and rotting vegetables. The only consolation in being there was that they were safe from beatings.

"How does he think we can stay down here an' not eat nothin'?" David asked, trying to divert Dennis' thoughts from pain. They'd spent two days there recently and had eaten a jar of pickles. Domko had flown into a rage when he discovered the missing preserves.

"I dunno," Dennis said, wiping his eyes again. "I don't know how we can work if he starves us to death first."

David laughed. He could sense his brother was starting to feel better.

"Yeah, we could be lyin' there dead in the ground and he'd dig a little hole and yell in, 'Hey, yous be cleanink out but-a-some barn.'"

The boys chuckled together.

"An' did you hear him?" Dennis asked, turning his head slightly to face David. "Just as he pushed you down here, he let out a big fart."

"That pig!" David laughed. "I bet it stunk."

"Did it ever!"

"What did it smell like?"

"I dunno . . . maybe like pig shit."

"'Cause he's a pig."

"That's for sure."

They sat quiet for a moment, then both chuckled. Laughing always helped make them feel better.

"So how long do you think we gotta stay here this time?" Dennis asked.

"I dunno," David thought. "When was the last time we cleaned out the barn?"

"A few days ago."

"It'll be gettin' deep soon."

"He won't do it. He'll have to get us to."

"Then he'll let us out."

"But he still won't give us nothin' to eat."

"I'm starvin' already," David said.

"Me too," Dennis added.

The twins chatted until nightfall.

"Is it October yet?" David asked, now surrounded by darkness.

"I dunno, maybe."

"Is tomorrow a school day?"

"Um, I think so," Dennis said. "We was s'posed to go today."

"Yeah."

"It don't feel so good bein' with those little kids," David said as he crossed his legs.

"Yeah," Dennis added. "Maybe if we didn't have to stay home we could pass."

"I can pass," David said indignantly.

"No, you can't," Dennis teased.

"Yes I can."

"No you don't read any good."

"Yeah, but I know 'rithmetic."

"Okay, then what's two plus two?"

"Four."

"Four plus four."

"Eight."

"Eight plus eight."

David hesitated. "Sixteen."

"Sixteen plus sixteen."

"Um, I dunno. Do you?"

"No, 'member? I didn't pass!"

David reached over and punched his twin on the arm and they both rolled on the dirt laughing. The ground was cold on their backs and it was then David noticed that the air was starting to cool. As he stared at the dusty, cobwebbed ceiling, he could hear noises coming from above. They'd spent enough time in the hole to know what was happening by listening to footsteps crossing the floor.

It sounded as if their mother was making supper and Eunice was separating the cream. Raymond was running back and forth between the kitchen and the front room. Domko had come in and was likely waiting for supper in his chair in the far corner of the kitchen. Kathy was right beside him, running on the spot and pounding her little fist against the wall. The boys listened to the methodical sound.

"How come she does that all the time?" Dennis asked.

"I dunno. Maybe 'cause she's stupid like him."

"Is it 'cause she's blind?"

"Maybe."

The twins were quiet for a few minutes.

"I heard Jim tellin' Ruby that Domko blinded her when he threw her against the wall," David said. "Mom told him so."

"I don't 'member that. All I know is she used to be able to see an' then one day she couldn't."

Shivering, David moved a little closer to his twin. "Where do you s'pose Rosie is?"

Their eight-year-old sister had learned at a young age how to make herself virtually invisible. She was a small girl who had suffered at least as many beatings as the twins.

"She prob'ly ran away," Dennis said, squirming on the cold ground. "Domko hates her most."

David almost disagreed, but stopped himself. It would only hurt his brother's feelings if he told him the truth—Dennis was at the top of Domko's hate list. The quiet, introspective boy had been there for quite some time.

Dennis had been alone in the house one cold, winter morning. The rest of the children were out milking cows. Dennis pushed a chair up to the window to look outside. Distracted by the beauty of the frost inside the window, he began scratching patterns with his fingernails. Each time his fingers became cold, he would put them in his mouth to warm them. He hummed to himself and stuck his tongue on the window, gradually melting an opening so he could see out. Suddenly, Domko's face appeared on the other side. The boy was only six years old, but knew instantly by the man's expression that he was angry. Jumping down from the chair, Dennis ran into the front room. The sparsely furnished house provided him with few places to hide. Scrambling, he squeezed his thin body between the chesterfield and wall. He heard the door slam and Domko's heavy boots move across the floor. He covered his eyes.

At first Domko called his name gently, but when Dennis wouldn't reveal himself, his stepfather became angry. He demanded that the boy come out of hiding. Paralyzed with fear, Dennis knew that continuing to hide would make Domko angrier. He gambled that he wouldn't be discovered.

Suddenly, the couch was pulled back and his stepfather stood over him.

"You's not be comink, I's be giving you some!" Domko roared as he pulled his belt from his pant loops. Grabbing Dennis by the hair, he hoisted him onto the chesterfield. The boy screamed for his mother as the belt pounded against his body. He wasn't sure why he was being beaten. Was it because he didn't go out to help milk the cows? Or because he'd hidden?

Somehow, between the blows, he managed to scurry between the other end of the chesterfield and the wall. This made Domko even angrier as defiance was a fuel that seemed to incite him further. It was then that their mother came inside. She'd been milking cows in the barn with the older children and hearing Dennis' screams, dropped the pail and ran to the front room.

Caroline Pischke was an average-sized woman with dark hair and a handsome face. She'd grown up on a nearby farm, the only daughter of Polish immigrants. She and her two brothers were forced to leave school at a young age to help with chores around the farm.

During that era, many men and women believed that it was the woman's obligation to obey the dominant man in the household—first their fathers, then their husbands. Children were to be seen and not heard and stepchildren were often held in low regard. The word "abuse" wasn't commonly used when Caroline was growing up.

It would be unfair to say that all men treated their wives and children brutally during this time in history. However, there was a strong mind set that the best way to discipline a child was with a belt, willow switch or fist at the discretion of the parent. Whether it was from a lack of education, lack of intelligence or patterns learned in childhood, some men ruled their households by dominance and fear.

Caroline had resigned herself that this was her lot in life. She could argue and fight back, but to expect to win respect was ludicrous. Her limited experiences and lack of a good education left her with few choices and feeling empty inside. Caroline wasn't brilliant—but she was kind-hearted, patient, attractive and well-liked. As a teenager she liked to go out, dance and flirt. She left home at 15 and had met and married Bill Pischke by the time she was 18. Baby Walter arrived less than a year later and six more children were born over the next 10 years. She was widowed by the time she was 29.

Her father, Walter Kolodka, complained that she and Bill had been far too lenient with the children. After Bill died, Walter's matchmaking intentions were obvious when he and Caroline's brother John, brought Domko to the farm. They'd said on numerous occasions, "Now she has a good man."

The perception existed in the community that because the farm was more successful after Domko's arrival, that life must have improved for them all. The trouble was, the farm wasn't being worked by him but by the children. Complaints on Caroline's part were met with the attitude, "You made your bed, now you lie in it."

"Boleslaw!" she yelled. "You're hurting him!"

Strong from years of physical labour, it took all she could muster to pull Domko from her son. As he let go of the boy, he turned and punched her hard knocking her backwards across the floor. The other children who'd come into the house behind Caroline, turned and ran back outside. Domko's anger transferred from Dennis to Caroline and the boy watched helplessly as his mother received a beating for defending him. David had not run outside with the others but had stood by and watched.

The remembrance caused tears to well in his eyes. He decided that watching a loved one being beaten was almost as bad as being beaten yourself.

He glanced at Dennis lying on the cold ground beside him.

"Next time we go to Jim's I'm gonna tell him not to take us to the cops no more," David said. "They just get mad at Jim an' it don't do no good anyhow."

"Yeah," Dennis agreed. "Nobody can help us anyways. It just makes ol' Satan madder."

As the noises overhead subsided, the boys knew it was getting late. The last time they'd been in the crawl space, they'd found a spot under the stove that felt warmer. They'd placed a board along the wall and an old burlap bag on the ground to make a bed. They crawled to that spot again then lay down. David pushed his back up against the board. At first, it felt cold but gradually it was warmed by his body heat. Dennis pulled part of the burlap bag up around his back, and facing one another, the boys fell asleep.

The next morning they awoke to the sound of footsteps overhead and the faint smell of cooking. They lay quiet for a moment, then Dennis spoke.

"Hey Davey, I'm hungry," he whispered.

"Me too," David said, rubbing his eyes. "Do you think we should eat somethin'?"

"I dunno," Dennis answered.

Sitting up, their eyes were drawn to the sealer jars filled with vegetables and pickles on a makeshift shelf of old boards along the wall. Burlap bags of carrots and potatoes were on the ground nearby. The crawl space was less than five feet high, so the boys had to sit most of the time. Crouching and stiff-legged, they made their way over to the tempting jars of ready-to-eat food.

"How 'bout a carrot?" Dennis said, reaching into a bag and pulling out a large one. Wiping it on his pants, he took a bite and crinkled his nose.

"My favourite is the pickles," David said.

"Me too," his brother agreed.

They looked longingly at the jars of dills lining the shelf.

"How 'bout if we ate 'em an' then hid the jar?" Dennis suggested.

"No, I think he counts 'em," David said.

Sitting down on the ground, they stared at the jars.

"Well, we can't just sit here," Dennis complained. "We gotta eat some."

"I know, I know," David said impatiently. "But we gotta think of a plan."

He thought for a few more moments, then smiled.

"Okay then, how 'bout we take a pickle out of each jar?"

"Do you think he'd notice?" Dennis asked.

"How? He don't count each pickle!" David said, stomach growling in anticipation. He couldn't remember the last time he had sat down to a meal. Mostly, he and his siblings just grabbed food when Domko wasn't looking.

"I'm thirsty too," he said, his voice trailing off.

Dennis took one of the jars from the shelf and put it on the ground in front of them. He tried to lift the metal spring-action lid but the heavy glass was sealed tight. It took some prying before it gave a little "pop." He lifted back the lid and each boy paused for a moment before reaching in and pulling out a fat dill.

"Eat it slow," David whispered.

They savoured the sour taste, first licking the pickle and then taking small bites. They took turns sipping the juice and then held up the jar to see if the amount they had consumed was noticeable. They put the jar aside, then did the same with a few more. Soon, their digestive systems were working again.

"I gotta pee," David said. "How 'bout you?"

Dennis nodded in agreement.

Looking at the open jars, a thought struck them at the same time. They drank half the juice from each jar and then unbuttoning their pants, refilled the sealers.

"There," David said satisfactorily. "He'll never notice now."

They spent that day in the crawl space. They were careful not to eat too many pickles and were even more careful to place the refilled jars away from the unopened ones. Because of what they'd done, they wanted to avoid mistakenly eating pickles from a wrong jar.

Early the next morning, the crawl space door opened and the musty space filled with light. The boys shielded their eyes from the sudden brightness. Domko grunted and told them to climb out. He turned and walked into the kitchen. Squinting, David grabbed Dennis around the hips and lifted him up high enough that he could hoist himself the rest of the way out of the hole. Dennis then lowered a stool for David. He glanced over his shoulder hoping that Domko wouldn't lose patience because they were taking too long. David stepped on the stool and pulled himself up.

Cautiously, the boys went into the kitchen. Their mother was doing dishes and Eunice was in her usual spot, separating the cream. The boys were still squinting from the sudden brightness of the kitchen when Domko instructed them to go out and shovel manure out of the barn. He warned them against running away. The boys nodded and quickly went outside.

After working all day, the twins came inside to find Domko sitting at the table with his children. Their mother had made a meal and there seemed to be a lot of food. The twins could smell cooked chicken and were glad to see the pots were full, as this meant they'd be able to eat the leftovers once Domko and his children had finished.

Noticing a jar of pickles on the table, the twins looked at one another but said nothing. They crouched on the floor by the door and watched as Domko served himself a large portion of meat and potatoes. Their mother filled Kathy's and Raymond's dishes and then served herself. She looked blankly at the boys. It was obvious to them that she'd given up long ago trying to include them at meal time.

The twins stared at the pickles. David thought the liquid looked off-colour in the jar which didn't seem to be packed very tight. He guessed there were at least two pickles missing from the jar. Just then, Domko reached across the table, picked up the jar and popped open the metal latch. He pulled back the top, then frowned slightly.

"She's be smellink it some," he said, mostly to himself as he sniffed the contents again. "Hmmm?"

Reaching in, he pulled out a pickle. The twins cringed as he took a big bite. His expression lightened as he bit into it again.

"But she's be tastink goot!" he said happily, passing pickles to Kathy and Raymond.

Autumn was a pleasant time in most rural communities. Farmers began to relax with the pressure of harvest over. Pantries and root cellars were stocked for the winter. Now that the summer's work was behind them, they also began visiting again.

Members from the local Jehovah's Witness congregation resumed house visits, spreading their beliefs and leaving behind Watchtower magazines. Caroline had become a Jehovah's Witness shortly before Bill died, rejecting her Catholic upbringing. She found the Jehovah's Witnesses to be a more loving, caring group. People who knew her at the time rolled their eyes at this suggestion—saying that her switching religions was an act of defiance and a way to "get attention." Nevertheless, Caroline wanted to become a devout Jehovah's Witness, much to the chagrin of church members from both congregations.

Visits from the group were met with mixed reaction by Domko. Sometimes he'd use the opportunity to dress up and show off his children, after first chasing his stepchildren away so that people wouldn't see how dirty and neglected they were. Other times, he'd force the twins to sit at the table and listen to Bible readings.

Whether he was studying to convert to the religion himself, nobody knew. He would welcome them one minute, then swear behind their backs the next. This was very difficult for Caroline who never knew what her husband's reaction would be.

Late one afternoon a car drove into the yard. A woman from the church was behind the wheel and she had another church member with her. The twins recognized Mike Kalanza immediately. Mike was a well-driller who lived in Steep Rock. He had two sons, Nicky and Teddy. They were close in age to the twins and the boys were disappointed that he hadn't brought them along. David and Dennis watched in the yard as the visitors got out of the car and walked to the house.

Mike carried a briefcase that contained his Bible and Watchtower magazines.

He turned and smiled at the boys. He was a short, stocky man with dark hair and a tanned complexion. He possessed rugged good looks and a straightforward gaze that left no question that he was in charge of every situation he found himself in. He was the eldest child of Ukrainian immigrants, Onufry and Christina Kolansky. Mike's parents were poor dirt farmers who came to Canada in the early 1920s and settled first in the Sundown, Manitoba area and then relocated near Steep Rock in the early 1920s. The Kolanskys were English illiterate but they ensured that their children attended school on a regular basis. Because of this, nine of their 10 children received a good education. This was a bit unusual at the time. Most immigrants spoke English poorly and as a result their children did not do well in school. The Kolansky children, however, earned above-average grades and boasted excellent attendance. All except for Mike. He was not interested in school, but wanted to earn a living instead. He worked alongside his father at Steep Rock's cement plant and during the Depression, Mike helped pay the household bills. He's been credited with keeping the family together during those difficult years.

Now in his mid 50s, Mike was considered frugal but honest. He was a very hard worker and extremely strong-willed. He cared nothing about what people thought of him and his overbearing nature was sometimes offensive. At some point, he began spelling his surname Kalanza, while the remainder of the family continued to use Kolansky.

On this particular afternoon, Mike was dressed in his best suit and his face was cleanly shaven.

"Hey, kids, how are ya' doin?" he called out to the twins. His voice had a high-pitched, squeaky sound that belied his rugged appearance.

The boys nodded shyly. It wasn't often that an adult spoke to them in a favourable way—but Mike always did. They followed the visitors into the house and sat on the kitchen floor. David stared at Mike's right hand, at the baby finger which had been severed at the top joint. He wondered how that had happened.

The boys were at the age where they liked listening to adult conversation and knew that if Mike was there, it was going to be lively.

"How ya doin', Bob?" Mike said, extending his hand in greeting.

It was obvious by Domko's disheveled look that he'd been caught napping on the chesterfield. Grunting, he took Mike's hand and offered a polite smile. The adults sat at the table and exchanged pleasantries before they began studying. Soon, the twins could see that Domko was searching for things to say. He liked to outdo other men, but had a difficult time bettering Mike.

Domko bragged about the farm for a while and then gossiped about the neighbours. Then, as the visit was starting to wind down, he began flirting playfully with the female visitor. He commented that a beautiful, smart woman like her and a man as wonderful as himself would have exceptional children together. The woman was obviously embarrassed by the suggestion.

Caroline became furious at his flirtation and began clearing the coffee cups from the table.

Mike, who was sitting at the end of the table, burst into laughter.

"You've gotta be kiddin' Bob," he said, in his squeaky voice. He then pointed at Raymond. "Any kids you'd ever have would end up stupid and lazy, just like you."

David and Dennis had been fidgeting and whispering in the corner and the unexpected comment caused them to snicker with delight. Domko shot them an angry look and they covered their faces with their hands so that he wouldn't see how much they were enjoying his embarrassment.

Domko was incensed.

"Vat?" he yelled. "Vat's be wrong with mine keets?"

Kathy was chattering to herself in the front room, oblivious to what was happening around her. The poor girl suffered from brain damage that reduced her comprehension level below that of other children her age.

Raymond was chubby and his teeth were rotted black from too much candy and poor hygiene. The visit had caught Caroline off-guard so there had been no time to wash and change the boy who looked almost as grubby as the twins. His speech was a combination of baby-talk and Domko's strange interpretation of English.

"Nothing's wrong with your kids," the woman interjected, trying to smooth things over. "They're just fine. Cute, even."

Caroline agreed.

Domko stared at Mike who just sat there grinning.

The twins got up and hurried outside to the chicken house. Once safe, they burst into laughter.

"Did you hear him?" Dennis whooped. "Did you hear what he said about Domko's kids?"

David laughed until his sides hurt.

"I like that Mike," he giggled. "He's a good guy."

"Yeah," Dennis grinned. "He can come around here anytime."

The twins waited until the visitors left before returning to the house. By now, everyone had gone to bed. Stepping inside, they could hear their mother and Domko discussing the evening's events from their bedroom. The twins silently crept by and climbed the stairs to their attic room. Rosie and Eunice were asleep on the only bed, so the twins decided to sleep in their usual hiding spot—a crawl space along the eaves of the attic walls.

While in this spot, they could see into their mother's bedroom as light from downstairs shone up into the eaves. Lying down, they could hear the conversation from below.

"Why did you have to say that to her," Caroline admonished. "You know that she likes to be better than me."

"Vat? I's be sayink it to Mike," he argued. "He's be thinkink he's be such a goot man."

"Well, I don't like it," she sniffed.

"He's be thinkink he's got a goot job and be makink so much mooney."

"Well, he does make good money," she said.

Domko grunted. "Then, why's his wife be leavink if mooney so goot?"

Caroline sighed. How was she going to explain Mary Makowski to her husband?

Mary had been the eldest daughter of Ludwik "Louie" and Bernice Makowski from Faulkner. The Makowskis were neighbours to Caroline's family when she was growing up. She and the Makowski children attended Carn Ridge School together. Mary attended for only part of one year, when she was 11 years old.

In 1943 she married Mike and her first son, Nicky, was born. Two years later Teddy arrived. Mike was an extremely hard worker who demanded no less from his wife. He'd married 17-year-old Mary when he was 38 and was well-known as a jealous, possessive husband.

It was rumoured that Mary was being pressured into becoming a Jehovah's Witness, the religion that Mike had adopted a few years earlier. Like Caroline, she'd been raised Catholic but unlike Caroline didn't want to switch religions. No one knows for sure why she left, but she did one day, leaving her two young sons behind. It appears that nasty small-town gossip about the woman and the drudgery of her life became too much for Mary.

Mike went to Winnipeg and found her, bringing her back to the farm. She left again soon afterwards, this time taking one son with her. The boy somehow arrived back in the area and both were minded by their grandmothers until Mike was ready to assume responsibility for their day-to-day care. Members of both the Kolansky and Makowski families respected him for taking on the task. Those who knew him say he loved his boys and that they loved him in return. Not only did Mike raise his sons, but he provided for his siblings and mother when his father left the family to go traveling after retirement from Canada Cement in the mid-1940s. Mike was considered both solid and reliable.

"If you think you're going to make Mike jealous by flirting, then you've got the wrong idea," Caroline said. "He's not interested in women our age. He likes younger girls."

"Every man likes girls!" Domko exclaimed.

The comment caused Caroline to pause. She'd caught Domko on more than one occasion leering at her daughters. Her experiences suggested that he was right—men did like young girls. She just didn't want to believe that her husband might harbour the same thoughts that Mike was rumoured to have.

"Thinking that way about young girls is not right," she shot back, watching for a reaction. She was relieved when he ignored the comment, and hoped that her fleeting thoughts were nothing but that—thoughts.

Chapter 3

"**HOW WOULD YOU DESCRIBE YOUR** general physical condition?" Sergeant McMillan asked.

David frowned. "You mean am I sick?"

"Well, more like, how do you feel?"

"Good, good," David said. "I feel good."

"Do you have any chronic problems?"

"Ch-rronic?"

"Yes, anything that bothers you all the time," he explained.

"Well, I got arr-thritis but everything else is good."

"What time was your last meal?"

"Oh yeah . . . an' I get gout sometimes, too," David remembered.

"Alright," McMillan said writing it down. "What time did you last eat?"

"Wh-at time is it now?"

The officer glanced at his watch. "8:30."

"I ate at 6:00," he said. "Why?"

"Because I need to know your general physical condition," he said.

"Well, if you're wonderin' if I can eat lots, the answer is yes," David laughed.

The officer smiled.

"What is the best thing that ever happened to you?" the Sergeant asked.

David chuckled.

"The best thing? Are you kidding? That's easy. The day I left the farm."

David spent his last year at the farm without his twin. Dennis had been successful in finding a place to live in the small nearby town of Grahamdale. A nice Jehovah's Witness couple, Herman and Crystal Bray, needed a farm hand. They also felt sorry for the boy so Dennis went to live with them.

David worked for a few different farmers, but when his mother located him and begged him to return home, David relented.

Then in the spring, just three months after his 15th birthday, David fled from Domko once again. As he sat around a campfire in one of their well-used hiding spots, he looked up to see his older brother Norman walking along the path towards him.

"Hey, Norman," he said. "Whatcha doin' here?"

"Came to find you," he said.

Norman sat down and David told him how Domko had tried to stab him with a pitchfork the afternoon before.

Norman shook his head. "Well, I see nothing has changed around here," he laughed. They talked for awhile longer then Norman suggested that David move to Moosehorn to live with him.

"R-rreally?" David stammered. "I c-can c-come l-live with you?"

"Sure," Norman said.

They got up and walked back to the house. David couldn't believe his luck. Living with Norman would be like a dream come true!

Everybody loved Norman. The 20 year old was charismatic and popular. He had a quick wit and friendly disposition which gave every person he met the sense that he was their best friend. He had a handsome face, with perfectly straight teeth that flashed each time he offered his ready smile. Norman wore his dark blonde hair "James Dean" style—short along the sides and long on top. In the summer it lightened to the colour of young corn. His bright hazel-coloured eyes had a mischievous glint that revealed a passion for life and risk-taking.

Norman was ambitious and worked long hours as a heavy equipment operator, truck driver and general labourer. At five-foot-eleven, 190 lbs., he was sturdier than most young men his age and could work as hard as those in their prime. His bull-like strength, daring nature and self-confidence made him a daunting adversary. Fearless was the best way to describe Norman.

They stayed at the farm that night, helped with chores and then the following afternoon David stuffed his few possessions into a bag and stepped out into the sunshine. Norman's car sat in the driveway—a 1956 Ford Meteor convertible. The car was white with a black vinyl roof. David had admired the car the afternoon before and now was barely able to take his eyes off it. He threw his bag into the back seat and went back into the house to say an angry good-bye to his mother. For a brief moment he hesitated. He'd been on the farm for so long, he wasn't sure how he'd manage elsewhere. It was an odd sensation and one that couldn't be rationally explained. The pang of guilt he felt about leaving Rosie behind disappeared once he climbed into Norman's car.

"W-what a great s-sset of wh-eels!" David exclaimed, running his hand across the leather seat and admiring the chrome accents. His thoughts spun as Norman started the car and with a grin, stepped hard on the gas pedal. He left a spray of dust and gravel as they turned onto Bayton road, accelerated first past the church, then the school, and finally Harwart's house.

"You wanna buy it?" Norman asked casually.

David was shocked. "I don't got no money 'cept for the b-bond I won in the art con-test," David said.

"How much did you say it is?" Norman asked.

"Fi-fifty d-ddollars," David said.

"Fifty dollars," Norman mused. "Not enough to buy the car but it'll help with your share of the rent."

David smiled. Of course the only thing he was concerned about was food.

Norman chatted casually about the different things they'd do. David's mind whirled with excitement as his older brother described life off the farm.

David was free! The day he'd dreamed of for so many nights had finally arrived.

He'd heard Domko talking to his mother about the concentration camps in Europe and believed he understood how those people must have lived.

He'd suffered too.

Life had become nothing but a series of days and nights that all ran together in a meaningless sequence and it had whittled away part of his spirit. His only objective had been survival and now he realized he'd survived a hell on earth. But he'd lived! And now he was gone from there and vowed never to return.

At that moment he felt no one on earth could be happier than him.

"In a few weeks, they're gonna need some guys to build the floodway," Norman began. "I worked there last year and made real good money. I figure we can move the trailer to the city and get jobs."

"Sure," David exclaimed. "I w-wanna get a good job."

Norman reached for a package of Colts on the dashboard and pulled one out. Balancing the steering wheel with his elbow, he reached for a lighter, flipped back the top and lit the end of the cigar.

"You want a smoke?" he asked, chewing the plastic end. He was enjoying being the big brother as much as David was relishing the attention.

"Oh, no," David said, "I don't touch them things."

Watching Norman sucking on the cigar made David shudder. He remembered the summer before, shortly after he'd returned to the farm. With Dennis living at Brays' farm, Rosie became David's companion. It was David's first opportunity to get to know his younger sister, who he discovered was funny and quite bright. Rosie had stubbornly decided years before that she wouldn't give into Domko and refused to cry out when he beat her. It amazed David how she could take a licking in silence.

It was early one fall afternoon and David and Rosie watched as Domko rolled a cigarette, smoked it down and then stashed the tiny stub in the cuff of his pants.

Occasionally these butts would spill out of the cuff onto the ground or floor in the house. To amuse themselves, David and Rosie started gathering up the butts. They decided to save enough to make their own cigarette. When they felt they had the right amount, David told Rosie to go outside and wait for him behind the house. Rosie nodded and ran out the door.

David needed to find some rolling paper. He didn't dare touch anything that belonged to Domko, so wouldn't even consider using real rolling papers. He needed to find something similar though. There was nothing in the house that could be used for this purpose. It was then he noticed his mother's Bible. It was sitting on a chair, tucked under the kitchen table. Picking it up, David opened it and wondered if a page would be missed. The old Bible had become quite worn over the years, suffering through rough treatment from ignorant children and a trip into the stove's firebox during one of Domko's violent outbursts. Their mother had managed to fish it out before it caught fire. Miraculously, the delicate pages had escaped with no damage, though the cover was a bit charred.

The idea of taking a page didn't make David feel bad. Firstly, he didn't believe in God. No loving God would allow the torture that Domko was inflicting on them. Secondly, the members of the church who did believe in God and who preached from the Bible, had never done a thing to help them—at least not that David had witnessed.

Lastly, he hadn't been allowed to attend much school and so his reading skills were underdeveloped. Books about history and literature weren't allowed in the house so why should his mother's Bible be important to him? Nobody had ever respected his desires or possessions so in an act of defiance, he tore out the first page. He reached for the box of matches sitting on a shelf above the stove then hurried to the door. He opened it, stopped for a moment to see if his stepfather was anywhere in sight, then joined Rosie at the back of the house where she was sitting cross-legged in the grass waiting for him.

"Where's the ol' squeezer?" David whispered.

"Dunno. He's not in the barn," she whispered.

David scowled. It was disturbing not to know where Domko was.

"His car there?" he asked.

"Yep," she said.

"Hmmm," he thought, deciding what to do. "Where's Mom an' the other kids?"

"Dunno?" she shrugged.

David looked around once more. Believing it was safe, he pulled the butts from his pocket that he'd collected. He sat down in front of Rosie and placed the Bible page on the ground between them.

"We'll just h-hide if we hear s-someone comin'," he said. "Wh-where are your butts?"

Rosie reached into her pants pocket and pulled out a handful as well. Giggling, she held out her hand.

"Okay, put 'em here," he said, pointing to the paper. He lined his butts in a straight row on the page. Rosie dropped hers on top.

"Bleeech!" she said, rubbing her hands on her pants.

David was also repulsed by the grimy, little butts but was intrigued at the same time by the prospect of smoking. Domko seemed to enjoy it so much that David wanted to know what the attraction was.

"Okay," he said, "but you go and w-wwatch to make s-ssure nobody's c-ccomin'."

Rosie jumped up and went to the far corner of the house. When she returned, David had the butts rolled into a big, fat cigarette.

"Nobody's comin'," she whispered.

"Good," he said, holding up the cigarette. "Well, whadda ya think?"

Rosie giggled. "Are you gonna put your lips on it?"

"Yeah, why?"

She shuddered, her whole body vibrating at once.

"It's yukky," she said.

David didn't care. He held the huge cigarette to his mouth with both hands.

"Okay, Rosie, you light it," he said.

Concentrating, the girl struck a match and then held it to the end of the homemade cigarette. Smoke rose from the paper for a moment and then it caught fire. The flames grew big enough that David pulled it away from his face.

"Ho, ho!" he exclaimed, blowing it out.

He stared at it for a moment. Knowing what to do, he moistened his fingers with his tongue and rubbed the saliva on the charred end.

"There," he said, pleased with himself. "Now it'll burn slower instead of like a grass fire."

Laughing, Rosie lit another match, holding it this time to the damp end. It caught a bit and started to smolder. Seeing this as his opportunity, David inhaled. The smoke traveled through the tube and filled his mouth. He coughed it out and then inhaled again. He did this a few times and soon started to feel lightheaded.

Engrossed in what they were doing, they didn't notice Domko approaching from the other side of the house. He had been in the barn loft feeding his pigeons. He heard the children laughing and came to see what they were doing.

"Ahhh, you's be smokink!" he said, startling the pair. "Vere's yous be gettink it, eh? You's be stealink it?"

David dropped the cigarette on the ground, and rubbed his hands on his shirt.

"Uh, no, just some butts, that's all," he said.

Stepping between the two, Domko picked up the odd-looking cigarette.

"So, yous be vantink to smoke?" he taunted. "Yous tink it be but-a-some goot?"

Ripping the cigarette in half, he handed one piece to David and the other to Rosie.

"Yere," he said, smiling. "Yit."

A feeling of dread came over David. Most of his life he'd listened to their stepfather berate and taunt them and yell that they were 'goot for nothin'k' and that they were "peesink ant sheetink and yittink all day long." It had taken him a few years to figure out what Domko was saying, but now he knew. "Yit" meant eat.

Domko was telling them to eat the cigarette.

"Yit!" the man said firmly and with a wicked smile. He took a step closer to the cowering children, then crossed his arms. David hesitated and began whimpering. Domko took another step forward, so David took a tiny bite. The taste of the stinky butts made him gag.

"I say yous be yit!" Domko yelled, grabbing the boy by the hair. Rosie saw this as her opportunity to flee, and ran around the house, disappearing into one of her secret hiding spots.

Domko pulled the cigarette out of David's hand and drove it into the boy's mouth, pushing David's head back against the ground. Instinctively, the teenager's jaw clamped shut. Domko laughed as he covered David's nose with his filthy hand, and the boy had no choice but to open his mouth in order to breathe. He turned his head to the side and gagged as the dirty hand stuffed the cigarette inside. David choked as Domko slapped his face and forced him to swallow. Once David had most of the cigarette down, Domko stood up, satisfied that he'd taught the boy a lesson. He strode into the house and slammed the door shut. David ran a few steps then vomited in the grass.

"No," David said firmly to Norman, "I d-ddon't s-ssmoke."

His brother shrugged. "Yeah, well, whatever."

Norman accelerated with a jolt and smiled. David was enjoying the rush of the wind on his face through the open window. Norman knew all too well what this day meant to his brother. He recalled it was the most liberating feeling in the world.

With mixed feelings and jumbled thoughts about leaving the farm, David wondered what was waiting for him in the future.

"There are people around Moosehorn who say he's crazy and then there are those who think he's the cat's ass," Norman said, as if reading David's thoughts. "They say it's you kids who are driving him around the bloody bend."

"Us?" David exclaimed, "Us! That ol' bastard was nuts l-long before he ever got to our p-pplace."

"That's for damn sure," Norman agreed.

"What did we ever do?" David asked.

"Just bein' there, I guess," he said thoughtfully.

"He d-ddidn't hafta s-sstay," David said, struggling to finish his sentence. It was times like these that he and his twin would work together to communicate. One would start the sentence while the other would finish. It was an odd feeling to be carrying on a real conversation with someone other than Dennis. Especially without his twin there to do half the talking.

"It's d-ddad's f-ffarm, not his an' Mom sh-oulda kic-ked him out a long time ago. We belonged there, n-not him."

Norman smiled. David had said exactly what he needed to hear. He'd been listening for years to the town gossip about "poor Domko having to look after so many kids," and it had affected him. He'd begun questioning whether they really were bad kids who deserved Domko's brutal treatment. He began wondering if he'd deserved the beatings, too.

But Norman didn't like dwelling on the past and lately felt quite removed from what was happening at the farm. He felt a touch of guilt over not helping sooner, but believed there was little else he could do.

"Don't ever go back," he said quietly. "Don't get trapped again."

"Don't worry," David laughed. "I ain't s-sstupid."

Norman laughed and they rode for a few minutes in silence.

"We did get h-him b-bback a few times," David said, his mood brightening. "N-nobody got him better than you did—'member when you 'mooned' him?"

Norman laughed, then coughed lightly. He covered his mouth with his fist, coughed hard once more and then took another drag from his cigar.

"He kicked my ass for that one."

"Yeah, but it w-was worth it, w-wasn't it?"

"Every goddamned second of it."

They laughed and then each lost himself in thought as they drove along the dirt road towards town.

"Yeah, he deserved every bit I ever gave him," Norman said quietly. He stared in a far-off way that David recognized.

The brothers didn't discuss the small, silver handgun that Norman had tucked inside the front of his pants. David knew his brother had brought it to the farm for a reason. There was no doubt in his mind that Norman wouldn't stand by and watch his mother or siblings receive another beating.

David wanted to be that kind of brother someday. Right now, though, he was too excited by what was ahead to dwell on what would happen at home once Domko realized that the primary farm worker was gone.

Norman turned onto the highway and within a few minutes they were in Moosehorn. Built along the Canadian National rail line during the early 1900s, Moosehorn was a bustling community of approximately 200 people. It was the main service centre for neighbouring farmers—where they shipped their products and purchased supplies.

Like most of the small prairie towns of the day, Moosehorn had a grocery store, a dry goods/hardware store, an auto repair shop, car dealership, gas station, café, creamery, grain elevator and a hotel. Originally built as a rail stop, Moosehorn was beginning to change with the advances in transportation. As rail service declined and provincial highways improved, trucks and buses became more economical ways of moving goods and people. As a town, Moosehorn was holding its own and so was Ashern, the next community, less than 10 miles south.

As Norman drove down the main street, David soaked in the details of each building and every person he saw. He'd been in town a few times before, but now he saw things from a different perspective.

"So, wh-here do you live?" he asked. He'd overheard his mother say that his brother had a trailer in town, but couldn't imagine what it would be like.

"Over there," Norman said, pointing ahead.

Looking ahead, David could see an older white stucco house with a tiny trailer in the yard. As they got closer, David pointed to the house.

"Who lives there?" he asked.

"The Mathesons," Norman said as he pulled into the driveway.

"What are they like?"

"They let me stay here, don't they?"

Shutting off the car and opening the door, he threw the cigar to the ground and stepped on it.

"C'mon," he motioned to David as he started towards the trailer. "Bring your stuff."

David stepped out of the car and hurried to catch up to his brother who opened the trailer door and went inside. David followed and it took a few moments for his eyes to adjust to the dimly lit dwelling.

Looking around, he could see that Norman wasn't exactly living in style. The 12-ft. trailer was old and run down. There was a set of bunk beds at one end and a table at the other. A wood stove sat in the middle of the trailer with a small pile of wood stacked nearby. Two chairs were on either side of the table and a small lamp sat in the middle. A toaster and hot plate were collecting dust on a shelf behind one chair. To Norman's credit, he kept the place tidy and if he was embarrassed by his modest living conditions, it didn't show.

"Whew, it's stuffy in here," Norman said, reaching over the table. He slid open the window and pushed back the heavy hemmed curtains. A light breeze blew in.

"There's nothin' to eat," he said casually. "Mostly I work odd jobs and people feed me."

"Oh," David said, disheartened. He'd been looking forward to a meal.

"The bank's closed so we'll go to Ashern tomorrow and cash the bond," Norman said over his shoulder as he went back outside. "That will give us some money to buy food and pay the rent."

He opened the door wide and leaned it flat against the outside wall of the trailer. Picking up a heavy board, he jammed one end into the soft ground and pressed the other against the door.

"The trailer is leaning a bit so I gotta do this to keep the door open," he said as he hopped up the stairs "You can sleep on the top bunk. Get rid of your stuff."

Nodding, David made his way to the back of the trailer. He tossed his bag onto the floor at the foot of the bed. Norman was using the top bunk as a storage area.

"W-what should I do with all this j-junk?" David asked.

"Throw it on the floor," Norman said.

David shrugged and began stacking his brother's belongings beside the bed.

The two sat at the table and caught up on each other's lives.

"So, w-what's with M-mmom?" David asked after a lengthy silence. "How come she picks him over us kids?"

Norman shook his head. He'd always been close to his mother and had heard that the girls and the twins were giving her a hard time.

"She's the one who called me, you know," he said. "She called saying that Domko had stabbed you and that you were dying somewhere in the bush. She begged me to come out and find you."

David was surprised.

"Well, it's a g-ggood thing you did," David said. He felt a twinge of guilt over arguing with his mother before he left. "'Cause I wasn't goin' back to get shmashed again."

"Yeah, well, anyway it's not so easy for her with all you kids and that crazy ass too," Norman explained. "Her life's been hell."

David thought for a moment and agreed. "But h-hhow come she left us a-alone w-with him?"

"Well, what else was she gonna do?" Norman asked. "If she took you kids to town she'd have to feed you and then he'd come roarin' down and take you back anyway," he said sadly, "And he beats her, too, you know that."

"Not so much now," David said.

Norman scoffed.

"I know, but she only thinks about herself," David complained.

"And you don't?" Norman chided. "Where is Rosie right now?"

David was silent. He hadn't thought of it that way.

"We all did it. Walter did. Stephen did and me too. We got the hell away from there as soon as we could and didn't look back. We only go home when we know the bastard isn't gonna be able to keep us there. It was like a goddamned prison. We just hoped he wasn't killing you guys. Mom always called us when it got bad."

"Not always," David argued.

"Yeah, well often enough. You and Dennis were in the bush so much you didn't know half of what was going on," Norman said.

"Yeah, well you don't know either—'cause you weren't there."

The brothers were quiet for a few minutes. David hadn't expected that on his first day off the farm he would spend so much time thinking about it.

"I was there enough," Norman said quietly. He stared vacantly at the table, then winced as an unspoken memory ran through his mind.

"And we aren't the only ones who had it bad," he said blinking away the thought. To make his point, Norman motioned to the open door.

"Look at those poor guys," he whispered.

David glanced out and saw two teenagers sitting on the stoop of the white stucco house. Around the same age as David, they were dressed in ragged clothing, were barefoot and wore solemn expressions.

"Who are they?" David asked.

"They're two of the Mathesons—one of them is Johnny and the other is Jimmy, but I don't know which is which. One of them talks okay and the other talks like you and Dennis," he smirked.

David laughed and reached across the table and gave his brother a playful punch. "Shuddup!"

Norman and David watched as the side door opened and Johnny and Jimmy jumped up. An older woman handed something to the boys and motioned them towards the trailer. Timidly, they walked across the lawn to the driveway carrying a loaf of bread and jar of jam.

"Yeah?" Norman asked when they arrived at the open door.

"G'here," the boy grunted, holding out the food. "M-ma s-sez 'tis f-fer yous."

"Thanks," Norman nodded taking it, then whispered to David as he put the food on the table, "he's the good talker."

David was amazed by his speech. He also noticed the boys weren't in a hurry to leave.

"S-should we ask them to come in?" he whispered. Fascinated to meet someone else with strange speech, he wanted to talk to these boys longer. They made him feel "normal."

"Nah," Norman said, turning to the brothers, "we'll see you guys tomorrow, eh?"

The Matheson boys nodded sheepishly then made their way slowly back to the house. It was starting to get cool outside so Norman got up and closed the trailer door.

"Do ya think they're hungry?" David asked, watching them through the window.

"Of course they're hungry," his brother answered. "I don't know why old Mrs. Matheson gave us this bread, but I'm sure not gonna argue with her."

Opening a drawer, he pulled out a knife, cut eight slices and then popped the lid off the jar. He brought it to his nose and sniffed.

"Chokecherry, I think." Digging in with the knife, he spread a glob on four pieces of bread before passing it to David.

Realizing how hungry he was, David started to shake as he dug into the jar. It had been at least two days since he'd eaten, his last meal being nothing but a handful of boiled potatoes—which he'd scooped out of the pot when Domko wasn't looking.

Folding the bread in half, David took a huge bite. It tasted wonderful! The brothers continued cutting slices of bread and slathering on jam until there was none left.

Norman watched David sweep the bread crumbs into a pile with his hand and lick them off the table.

"C'mon, man," he exclaimed, "we'll have more to eat tomorrow."

Getting up, he took wood from the pile and made a fire in the stove.

"It's getting cold," he muttered.

That night, David climbed onto the top bunk and covered himself with an old blanket. It wasn't long before he could hear his brother breathing heavily beneath him. David stayed awake for awhile wondering why Mrs. Matheson had given them something to eat. He concluded that people were the same everywhere. Those who had enough to give, sometimes kept everything for themselves, while generosity sometimes came from the poorest people. He fell asleep thinking about the people who'd helped him over the years and pushed away thoughts of those who hadn't.

Chapter 4

"**SO, DAVID I'D LIKE YOU** to describe yourself to me," McMillan said as he leaned back in his chair and crossed his legs. David noticed the man's shoes were shiny black. At one time, he found tidy men dressed in nice clothes intimidating.

"De-scribe myself? Now or before?" he asked.

"How about now?"

"Well, I'm a hard worker an' I'm honest an' I pay lots of income tax," he said, anger boiling to the surface again. "S-so that guys like you can go around an' let guys like him get away with it. An' then try to arrest me an' Dennis."

"Guys like who, getting away with what?" McMillan asked.

"A-abuse!" he said. "Domko, who else?"

"All right, well, as painful as all that was, and I really do sympathize with you, there is nothing I can do about that now. What I am here for is to help clear your name in this murder investigation," McMillan said, uncrossing his legs and leaning forward. "Do you understand?"

David nodded but refused to make eye contact.

"Okay, so I know what you're like now," he said. "What were you like before?"

David laughed and shrugged his shoulders. He looked at his fidgeting hands.

"We was bushed," he said, voice cracking.

"Bushed?" he asked.

"Yeah, you know, hillbillies."

Cruising down the highway in Norman's convertible was, in David's estimation, the greatest way to spend a morning. The car was heavy on the road and his brother drove with confidence. It was a little early in the year to have the top down, but on a sunny morning like this, the rays felt warm on David's bare skin. The chill of the wind was tempered by the exuberance David was feeling.

Ashern was less than 10 miles south of Moosehorn so it took only a few minutes and they were there. David was slightly disappointed by the short trip, since he felt free, traveling down the open highway. He vowed to someday have a car of his own.

As they turned onto Main Street, David recognized a few buildings but none of the people. His family had lived there for awhile when he was about six years old, but their mother was forced to return to Domko and the farm after only 18 months. The other times he and Dennis had been in Ashern, they'd been taken to the police station by neighbours.

Norman was much luckier than the twins. After he left the farm, he'd lived with a family on the outskirts of town. He went to school, made friends and worked in the area for a few years, so he knew a lot of people. There were some government offices and a handful of businesses in the town, so it always seemed busy. People came from the smaller communities when they needed a lawyer, justice of the peace, or to apply for social assistance. In this instance, David needed to go to the bank to cash his bond—winnings from a provincial art contest. He'd won the contest a few years earlier when he was a student at the Bayton school.

Norman parked the car in front of the bank.

"You go in and I'm gonna go over to the supply store and look around a bit," he said, as he opened his door to get out. He waved to someone down the street and his mood visibly brightened at the prospect of socializing with acquaintances.

Just then David panicked. His survival instincts were acute from living in the bush but he had little experience doing much else. He could build shacks, make fires, put up hay and shovel manure—but had no idea how to deal with people.

"C-ccan you d-do it?" he asked, grabbing his brother's arm.

"What do you mean?" Norman scoffed. "It isn't my bond, you go do it."

"No, c'mon," David pleaded, "I d-ddon't know w-wwhat to do."

Exasperated, Norman shook his head.

"Just go in, tell them who you are and say you want to cash it in. It's simple."

"In th-ere?" he stammered.

"Yeah," he nodded as he stepped out and slammed the car door. He started across the street. "That there is the bank."

David got out of the car and stepped onto the sidewalk. He stared at the flat-fronted, wooden building. The door opened and a man came out. David turned away, pretending he'd forgotten something in the car. When the man was clearly out of sight, he turned back to the building and tried to work up enough courage to go inside.

Stepping onto the stoop he slowly pulled open the heavy wooden door. Entering the bank, he saw both men and women working at desks behind the long, tall counter. He stood for a moment by the door, not sure what to do. A woman looked up from her desk and then went to the counter.

"May I help you?" she asked. Others gazed up from what they were doing to see who had come in.

David noticed immediately that the workers were dressed in crisp suits and dresses, making him very aware of his own grubby appearance. David was tall and gangly, having grown out of his hand-me-down clothes months earlier. He could feel the teller's eyes moving over his tan-coloured cotton pants that were too short and ripped at the knees. His hands moved instinctively to cover his crotch where he'd fixed the broken zipper with a pin. The long-sleeved shirt he wore was both too short in length and too warm for the season. His thick blonde hair hung heavy over his ears. He was a handsome boy whose thin face revealed dimples when he smiled.

The bank smelled of wood, documents and nicely scented women. He hadn't bathed in weeks and could smell his own body odour. It was a familiar odour that he didn't find offensive. He wondered if others in the bank noticed this as well.

The image of the Matheson brothers sitting pathetically on the porch flashed briefly through David's mind. All the confidence that he'd found before walking into the building left him, and he stood shyly in the doorway. He considered turning and running, but knew that Norman would throttle him if he left the bank without any money. He reached into his pocket and pulled out the thick, folded piece of paper.

"Can I help you?" she asked again.

"Uh-mm," he said quietly. "Y-yyes." David took a few steps forward then stopped. He felt like a Matheson offering bread. Trying to summon courage, he swallowed hard and made his way to the counter. It only seemed like everyone was watching him.

"I-I n-nneed to get m-my bond," he said, handing her the paper.

"Pardon me?" she asked politely.

"I-I n-n-need t-to g-get my b-b-bond."

"I'm not sure what it is you want," she said, clearly embarrassed for him. She took the paper and unfolded it.

By now, David's pink cheeks had turned scarlet. The harder he tried, the worse his stutter became. He couldn't lift his eyes from the counter top.

"Oh, I see," she said. "Do you want to cash this?"

"Y-yes."

"What's your name?"

"D-David Pischke."

"What's your account number?"

"I-I d-ddon't know."

"Do you want me to look it up?"

"Okay," he nodded.

The woman pulled out a ledger and turned a few pages quickly and then with a pencil, moved her way down the page.

"Pischke . . . Pischke," Puzzled, she looked up from the book. "You don't seem to have an account here."

David stared back. He didn't know what to say.

"Do you have any identification?" she asked as she returned to the counter.

"Huh?"

"Identification. You know, something with your name on it."

He pointed to the bond.

"No, I mean something to prove that you're you."

Reaching into his back pocket this time, David pulled out his crinkled birth certificate then handed it to her.

It was obvious to the teller that the young man in front of her was in desperate need of money. He was behaving strangely, staring blankly at the counter and jumping each time she spoke. These were warning signs of someone acting dishonestly.

"Just a moment," she said, taking the certificate and bond with her. David watched solemnly as she went into a small office and spoke to the man behind a desk. The older gentleman looked up from his papers and slipping on his glasses, stared intently at David. He then nodded at the teller.

She returned to the counter and opened the cash drawer.

"The manager says you look like your brother Norman," she said cheerfully. "Unless you have a twin, you're probably you."

David opened his mouth to tell her about Dennis but simply smiled instead.

The woman counted the money and handed it to him. Sheepishly, he took it and put it in his pocket. He felt like he needed to explain how he earned the bond, but knew the words would never come out straight.

"If you ever want to come in and open an account, we'll be here," she said.

He nodded and left the bank. He instantly felt rich because he'd never had more than a few dollars in his pocket at one time.

Norman was waiting by the car.

"What took you so long?" he asked. "Did they give you a hard time?"

David shrugged.

"You got the money?"

"Yep, an' they g-ggave me . . . m-mmore than fifty d-ddollars."

"What do you mean?" Norman asked.

"She gave me an extra s-sseventy-two cents," he said. "It's n-nnot called s-stealin' if they g-give it to you, r-rright?"

"No, stupid, it's called interest," Norman laughed, giving David a playful punch. "Let's go get something to eat."

David nodded eagerly as the pair walked across the street to the café. Norman opened the door to the small restaurant and the warm scent of grilled food and french fries greeted them as they stepped inside. Norman nodded hello to a few men drinking coffee as he guided David through the maze of tables. They found a booth near the front window. Because it was lunch time, the small café was filled with customers. The waitress approached after a few minutes carrying menus.

"Hey, Norm, how are you?" she asked as she handed one to each brother. She gave the table a light wipe with a damp cloth. "Where have you been?"

"I'm living in Moosehorn right now," he said smiling at the girl and lighting a Colt. "But I spent most of the winter takin' flying lessons in Portage la Prairie."

"Flying lessons?" she exclaimed. "You're going to be a pilot?"

"Yep," he said, taking a drag from his cigar and blowing the smoke into the air beside her. "They say I'm a real natural."

"I bet," she laughed. "Coffee?"

"Sure," Norman said.

David nodded. He was too timid to order what he really wanted—a glass of root beer.

The waitress returned a few minutes later with a coffee in each hand. Placing the cups down, she pulled out her order book.

"What would you guys like?" she cooed.

"Well . . . I know what I'd like, but I'll have to settle for a burger and fries," Norman flirted. The waitress giggled then turned to David. "And you?"

David was still staring at the menu.

"Oh, and by the way, this is my brother David," Norman said casually.

"Brother? Another one? How many do you have anyway?" she laughed.

"I don't know," Norman smiled, "I kind of lost track."

David's face turned red. He wasn't feeling any more comfortable in the café than he'd been in the bank.

The waitress waited for him to answer.

He felt his throat constrict. His tongue seemed heavy in his mouth and his mind raced. He feared that whatever he tried to say would come out as garble, so he just pointed to a picture of a hamburger platter on the menu.

"Same then?" she asked.

David nodded.

"Okay," she said. "It'll be about 10 minutes."

Norman followed her with his eyes back to the kitchen. "Cute, eh?"

David shrugged.

"C'mon," Norman teased. "You think she's cute, right?"

"I dunno," David whispered.

"What? You're not a faggot, I hope," he said more seriously.

"No!" David exclaimed, not exactly sure what a faggot was.

"Good, 'cause if you were, you'd be sleeping outside tonight."

"What about you?" David asked.

"Me?"

"Yeah, d-do you think s-she's cute?"

Norman looked at the girl who was taking an order from another table.

"Nah," he said, chewing on the plastic tip of the cigar. "She's not my type."

As much as he liked flirting with girls, Norman had only one young woman on his mind. Sharon Russell. He was head-over-heels in love with the pretty, popular teenager from Moosehorn. Norman's single-minded pursuit of the 16 year old caught her attention, but he wasn't sure yet if he'd captured her heart.

Nobody knew what Sharon's parents, Hugo and Freda Russell, initially thought of the blossoming relationship. Some guessed that Hugo saw shades of himself in the young man, as both he and Norman were smart, handsome and charming. Each liked to socialize and had a daring, adventurous side. Hugo channeled his passions into business while Norman took to the skies.

David had heard about Norman and Sharon's relationship from Caroline and it made him wary since Hugo was friends with Domko. He told Norman his fears—that Hugo might side with Domko and believe the worst concerning the Pischke children. But his brother just laughed. He explained that Hugo was someone who didn't judge people on hearsay. Because Hugo's only dealings with Domko had been pleasant, he had nothing bad to say about the man. The two got along well—which likely worked to Norman's advantage in the pursuit of Hugo's daughter. Norman was confident that Hugo would judge the twins on what he saw, not by what he heard. David wasn't so sure.

Their discussion was cut short as the waitress emerged from the kitchen carrying a plate of food in each hand.

David's thoughts switched from Hugo Russell to the steaming plate now sitting in front of him.

"Ketchup?" she asked.

"Thanks," Norman nodded.

The waitress placed the ketchup on the table.

"Enjoy your meals," she smiled.

Norman thanked her while David ignored everything but the wonderful plate of food.

Half of his plate was filled by a fat hamburger and the other half with golden brown, homemade french fries. It was the most food he'd seen at one sitting—since he stayed with the Koch family over a year earlier.

"I hope you're gonna leave her a tip," Norman said as he poured ketchup over his fries. He handed the open bottle to David.

"Whadda ya mean?" he asked.

"A tip. You leave extra money on the table when the food and service is good," his brother explained. "That way, when we come back she'll remember us and be sure that we get the most fries or the biggest piece of pie."

"We gonna order pie?"

"Oh, yes!" Norman exclaimed.

David laughed as he poured ketchup over his fries then dug his fork into the pile. He'd tasted ketchup only twice before and loved it. He blew hard on the steaming food, but couldn't wait for it to cool. Shoveling the fries into his mouth, he had to suck in air to cool his burning tongue. He took a big bite of the hamburger. The taste was incredibly good.

As he happily ate, David was relieved that they'd stopped talking about Domko and Hugo. He didn't want to argue with his brother, who also seemed to welcome the diversion when the food arrived.

Norman chatted about the job he'd had the past summer, explaining he'd been a heavy equipment operator building the Red River Floodway. The project was the brainchild of Premier Duff Roblin in response to the devastating flood in 1950 that crippled the City of Winnipeg. Roblin decided to build a diversion that would start at the south end of the city and run in a semi-circle around it. The theory was that during high-water years, the floodway would divert water away from Winnipeg.

Construction began in 1962 and it was estimated it would take another four summers of work before it would be finished. Norman had worked for Ramsey-Bird Construction and was promised by the foreman that they would hire him again in the spring. It appeared that the company was always looking for workers, and that David might get a job there as well.

"They pay really good," he assured his brother. "You'll be able to eat like this all the time."

David popped the last bit of hamburger into his mouth. "W-when do we start?"

Norman chuckled. "We'll go into Winnipeg in a few weeks."

David nodded and then whispered, "I want another one."

Norman motioned for the waitress, pointing at David. "He wants another hamburger."

She shook her head in amazement. "Another burger?" she laughed. "What are you, starving or something?"

David blushed as he tried to cover his skinny arms with his big hands.

"Y-y-yeah," he laughed, trying to sound relaxed. The waitress looked at him again. This time her eyes moved over his body. Her cheeks turned pink when she realized there was some truth to the boy's statement.

"I'll get you another burger right away," she said quietly.

David took a sip of water to soothe his scorched tongue. He watched Norman eating french fries and for a moment felt envious. Then he realized he didn't need to envy Norman. He wasn't on the farm anymore. As long as he had money in his pocket, he wouldn't have to worry about being hungry ever again. There was lots of food for everybody behind the swinging café door. His life had changed overnight, but the memory of hunger, jealousy and competition remained vivid.

His thoughts drifted to the worst time of year at the farm—winter. With the fall's harvest of fresh vegetables nearly gone, there was less food to share. Domko's mental state always deteriorated as the days became shorter and he was at his worst during the dark, cold months of December and January.

One afternoon the twins had emerged hungry and cold from a neighbouring barn. With the exception of some food from the Harwarts and peanut butter sandwiches from a kindly teacher, they'd had nothing substantial to eat in weeks. Cowering at the door of their mother's house, they waited to see their stepfather's mood before entering.

Domko grunted and waved them in, just as the family sat down to eat chicken, dumplings and potatoes. The boys waited on the floor for the leftovers, which amounted to a few boiled potatoes and the chicken carcass. The food was nothing but an appetizer that left a hollow ache in their stomachs for the rest of the night.

The next morning, the twins awoke in foul moods. They were sent outside by Domko to do chores in the chicken house. They were expected to collect eggs, shovel manure and then feed the hens. Opening the door of the small building, they stepped inside where the warmth from the roosting birds was a welcome relief to their sparsely clad bodies. Each had been able to scrounge a coat, pants, shirt and shoes from the box of used clothing Domko had bought at the Goodwill store, but the boys were never warm enough, no matter what they had to wear.

The hens clucked quietly in their roosts, sitting content. While Dennis carefully reached under each bird and gathered eggs into a basket, David began shoveling manure out the door making a pile beside the building. Dennis carried the eggs to the house and returned with a pot of boiling water to thaw the water troughs.

"Hey, Denny," David called, his tone suddenly bright. "Come look!"

Dennis joined his brother in the open doorway of the feed bin. They were delighted to see that it was full of freshly boiled chop—a mixture of grain, chopped fish and molasses that had been cooked on the kitchen stove into an oatmeal-type mash. It would be used over the winter to feed the chickens and fatten pigs that were fenced in behind the coop. As well, an open five-gallon pail of livestock-grade molasses was in the corner by the door.

"Food!" Dennis exclaimed.

"Shhh!" David whispered. "He might be outside. Go look."

Dennis' eyes widened.

David gave him a slap on the chest and pointed towards the door. "You go watch out the window an' I'll feed the chickens. Then I'll get us some food." He grabbed a small plastic container and filled it with chop while Dennis ran to the door, opened it and peeked out.

"Don't see him," he whispered back.

David's legs could hardly move fast enough. His hands shook with anticipation as he dumped chop for the chickens into flat wooden boxes on the floor. He knew that if he didn't hurry, they'd miss their opportunity for a meal.

"Is he comin'?" he whispered back towards the door.

"No, not yet."

"Good."

David ran back to the feed bunk and filled the container to the top with chop.

"Go outside and find a jar," he instructed his brother.

Dennis quietly opened the door and slipped out. He was back within a few minutes carrying an old sealer.

"Good," David said, grabbing it from him. "Go watch the door."

Obediently, Dennis went back to his post. "Whatcha doin'?" he whispered.

"Ssshhh!"

Pulling the lid off the molasses pail, David pushed the open end of the jar onto the stiff surface. Grunting, he poked and dug with a stick until he was able to pull off a small hunk of molasses. Using the stick and his fingers, he dug into the pail again, kneading it until he was able to pull off another large piece. He dropped both pieces into the jar and then holding it up, tried to visualize how much would be there once it was warmed.

"He's comin'!" Dennis whispered as loud as he dared.

Holding the jar under one arm, David picked up the container of chop.

"Go stand behind the door!" he commanded to Dennis. A look of panic came over the boy's face, but he followed his brother's orders without question.

Grabbing the lid, David pushed it down on the molasses pail until it sealed with a pop. Quickly closing the door to the feed bin, he darted to the coop door and pushed himself close to Dennis. He placed both containers on the floor and blocked them from sight with his legs.

The brothers felt oddly exposed, standing there along the wall, not appearing to be hiding at all. Experience had taught them, however, that Domko never looked behind a door. Once it was opened, they hoped to be perfectly concealed.

Their hearts leapt as the coop door opened and swung towards them. The sound of Domko's heavy boots entered the tiny building. The chickens were startled by the sudden draft and clucked wildly. The twins held their breath and pushed their backs tightly to the wall. David curled his toes as the door tapped gently on his growing feet. He let out a small sigh, feeling his warm breath bouncing back from the bare wood that was just inches from his nose. Dennis was trembling beside him.

Domko moved through the hen house, grunting as he counted the number of chickens sitting on nests. Pleased that the total corresponded to the number of eggs Dennis had brought into the house, he continued checking the boys' work.

Opening the feed bin door, he stood for a moment. David closed his eyes, hoping that nothing was out of place. His mind raced as he tried to remember what he'd done with the stick. Domko grunted again. Satisfied that the chores had been done to his liking, he left the coop and pulled the door shut behind him.

The twins stood paralyzed for a few moments, still afraid to move. Then, cautiously, they stepped away from the wall. Dennis picked up the containers. He followed David who opened the door slowly in time for them to see Domko entering the house.

"C'mon!" David said excitedly as he swung the door wide. The cold north wind stung their faces as they ran around the coop, away from the house and into the nearby bush. They kept running along a path until they came to one of their many campfire sites concealed in the bushes.

Then without a word, they began making a fire, gathering up deadfall and sticks. David had stolen a package of matches from the kitchen which he kept hidden deep in his pants pocket. Conserving matches was as important to him as finding food.

"Don't throw no dead leaves in there 'cause they make too much smoke," he cautioned. "We don't want ol' squeezer findin' us."

Dennis nodded.

Once the fire was roaring, David sat down and placed the containers of molasses and chop in front of himself.

"Whatcha doin'?" Dennis asked eagerly.

"Well, 'member that time Walter brought us those candy bars?"

"Yeah," Dennis answered. "They was called Eat Mores."

"Right, well, we can make our own Eat Mores right here."

Dennis smiled. "Ya think?"

"Yeah," David said, tilting the molasses jar so that the bottom was over the fire. "We gotta melt this first."

Using a stick, he stirred until the molasses began to thin. He then sat the jar down at the edge of the fire so it would stay warm. Scooping a handful of chop from the other container, he examined it closely, picking out the mouse droppings. Dennis grabbed handfuls as well and when they had all the chop cleaned and in a pile on the ground in front of them, David spooned a glob of molasses into his hand and juggled it back and forth until it began to cool. He kneaded it, then molded it first into a ball and then rolled it between flat hands to make something that looked like a small log. Dennis followed his lead and soon the molasses logs were ready to be mixed with the chop. They rolled the molasses over the chop, then flattened the logs until they resembled the shape and consistency of Eat More® candy bars.

Pleased with themselves, they admired their creations before taking a big bite. Neither boy wanted to admit that this didn't taste anything like the delicious candy bars they'd remembered. So they kept chewing and eating, their spirits dampening with each bite. Their mouths and throats burned from the unrefined molasses.

David's eyes filled with tears as he stared into the fire and tried to choke down the food. He didn't know what was worse—the raw feeling in his mouth or the disappointment in his heart. As he tossed the last bit of the bar into the bush, he longed for the day when he could go and buy a real Eat More®, unwrap it and not be disappointed.

The waitress placed the second burger in front of him and he quickly picked it up.

"Be careful," she cautioned. "You don't want to burn your tongue."

David grinned.

"Either of you boys want dessert?" she asked.

"Sure," Norman said. "What kind of pie have you got?"

"We've got cherry, apple, raisin, banana cream, coconut cream, chocolate cream and lemon meringue . . ." she said, thinking while her pencil tapped on the edge of her order book.

"Hmmm," Norman muttered. "I'll have apple."

She wrote down Norman's order then looked at David, whose bony elbows were resting on the table while he held the burger with both hands.

"D-don't m-m-matter," he said, his mouth full. "I l-like 'em all."

"Pardon?" the waitress said.

"Pick one," Norman said.

"I c-can't."

"You have to."

"You pick."

"Okay," Norman said rolling his eyes. "He'll have apple with ice cream. You bring us big pieces and there'll be a nice tip waiting for you."

"I'll do my best," she laughed.

"I'm sure you always do," Norman said slyly.

"Norm . . . honestly," she laughed as she trotted back to the kitchen. She emerged a few minutes later with two large pieces of warm pie, each with a scoop of ice cream.

"How's that?" she asked.

Once again, David was speechless. He moved closer and inhaled deeply, filling his senses with the smell of warm cinnamon, brown sugar and buttery-soft cooked apples. He'd never eaten apple pie and couldn't imagine anything tasting as good as this smelled. He dug in his fork and took a big bite of the hot pie. The melting ice cream helped cool his tongue.

"Good, eh?" Norman said, as if reading his mind.

"G-ggood thing there's ice ccc-rream to cool it off," he laughed, fanning his mouth.

When the brothers finished their meals Norman asked for the bill. The waitress slipped the little piece of paper onto the table and picked up the plates that had been wiped clean.

"Gimme some money," Norman whispered to David. "You leave the tip."

David reached into his pocket and handed over a twenty-dollar bill. While Norman went to the cash register, David dug out all his change. Not knowing what else to do, he left the full amount on the table.

Norman met him at the door, glanced back and then elbowed his brother in the side. "That's too much!" he whispered. They stood for a moment and watched the table, unsure whether to go back and retrieve some of the change.

"Ah, what the heck," Norman said. "There's lots more where that came from!"

Giving each other a shove, the boys stepped out onto the street. It was a glorious warm day and the sun was high.

"C'mon," Norman said. "Time to go."

The brothers climbed into the Ford and drove slowly down the main street. Both were relishing the fact they were young, with full stomachs and in an eye-catching car.

Norman turned into the service station and pulled up to the gas pump. A young attendant came out and filled the tank while David followed Norman inside. The business was owned and operated by 53-year-old Emil Maurischat, a senior member of the Jehovah's Witness congregation in Ashern. He was a friend of their mother and was also Norman's former employer. While Emil was friendly to Norman, he scowled at David for reasons the young man didn't understand.

He had been told that after their father's death, neighbours had pressured their mother to sell the farm and move to town. She had stubbornly refused and that fall there had been incidents of vandalism and theft at the farm. Unfortunately, Caroline had taken someone's advice to sell most of the cattle to raise enough cash to pay bills. This had been a short-sighted decision, leaving her with little future source of income. David didn't know whether the advice given to their mother had been in her best interest or not. Emil had been one of those people.

"So, I see you've got one of the twins with you," Emil said. "Which one is this?"

"Dave," Norman said. "He's living with me now and we're going to get jobs on the floodway."

"Oh yes," Emil smiled. "Good to keep you young boys working. I take it the other one is still at Herman Brays' farm?"

"Yes, he's still there."

"Good, good," he said, taking the cash from Norman and ringing in the sale. "Herman needs the help and it'll keep the boy out of trouble."

David was surprised by the comment, although Norman didn't seem to notice.

"Yes, yes," Emil continued as the brothers made their way to the door. "We want to keep those twins out of trouble."

David squinted as he stepped into the bright sunlight. Norman pulled sunglasses out of his shirt pocket and slipped them on.

"W-what did he m-mmean by that?" David asked, trotting beside his older brother. "About us g-ggetting into trouble?"

"Ah, don't worry about that," Norman scoffed as he opened the driver's door and climbed in. "You're always going to run into guys like that."

Frowning, David slid into the other side. "I s-ssure hope not."

Chapter 5

"DO YOU HAVE ANY loans or debts?" McMillan asked.

"Par-don?" he asked, turning his head slightly.

"Do you owe any money?" he asked.

"I got a m-mortgage just like everybody else," David said. "I know they say how did the Pischke boys get those n-nice houses an' I tell you, I worked hard for every goddamned thing I ever got. Nobody ever gave me n-nothin'."

McMillan nodded. "Do your debts cause you worry?"

"No," he said. "My wife takes care of the bills."

"Yes, but you are the primary wage earner, correct?"

"I'm the only one," David said.

McMillan wrote that down on the sheet.

"Do you know right from wrong?" he asked.

David was stunned. He stared for a moment then slammed his hands down on the table. Then he stood up.

"Do I know right from wrong?" he hollered. "Do I? Of course I know right from wrong! Do you know regular people from criminals?"

"I have to ask you that question," McMillan said. "Do you know right from wrong?"

"What the hell do you think?"

"I don't know, I'm asking you," he said calmly.

"Of course!" he yelled. "I'm not in jail, am I? 'Cause I'm sure you guys woulda been there ready to arrest us if we did do s-ssomethin' wrong. You've been tryin' to put us in jail ever s-ssince we were kids."

"That seems hard to believe," McMillan stated. He did not want to antagonize David but doubted his claim.

"Oh, yes," David glared. "Let me tell you, it's been hell," he said. "Pure hell."

"So how has society treated you then?" he asked.

David scoffed. "Like d-dogs," he said. "Actually, worse than d-dogs. At least guys get charged with cruelty to animals, you know what I mean? But us kids, we was treated worse than d-dogs."

Norman and David kept themselves busy during the next few weeks, earning a daily wage by doing odd jobs. They fixed fences and tackled other manual labour. Most times, the farmers they worked for fed them a noon meal, and the farms with kindly wives gave them supper, too. They earned enough money to make the monthly loan payment on the trailer and considered themselves lucky that the Mathesons allowed them to stay rent free in their yard.

One Monday near the end of April, the brothers hitched the trailer to the back of Norman's car and drove south to Winnipeg. Turning off Hwy. #6 onto the Perimeter Highway, they followed the circular road around the city to the southeast side where the floodway was being built.

"Now let me do the talking," Norman warned as they got out of the car in front of the Ramsey-Bird Construction office.

David nodded. He was relieved by Norman's suggestion as he followed close behind his brother. Norman knocked lightly on the trailer door, opened it and the brothers stepped inside.

Two men were standing beside a desk talking. Norman recognized one as the supervisor, Jack McGuiness. Turning to Norman, Jack smiled. He recognized his former employee immediately.

"How are you doing, Norm?" the short, husky man boomed. His normally stern expression was absent for the moment as he ran his hand through his cropped hair. His gruff voice filled the trailer.

"Fine," Norman said, extending his hand. "This here is my brother David."

David nodded shyly then looked away.

"You boys looking for work?" Jack asked. "I just fired some guys and need two replacements."

"Yes sir, we are," Norman said. "You got anything we can do?"

"That all depends," Jack said, crossing his heavy arms across his chest. "Let me finish up with this other fellow first."

The brothers nodded and casually made their way to the other end of the trailer. When Jack had finished, he called them back.

"Can David here drive my machines?" Jack asked as he moved to the other side of his desk.

Norman looked at his brother. "He's never done it, but he's operated farm machinery. That's pretty close."

Jack looked at David. "How old are you, son?" he asked.

"Fffi-ffif," David stammered, unable to get the word out.

"Just came in from the country," Norman joked, trying to make light of David's speech impediment. "Only the second time he's been out of Moosehorn."

Jack smiled as he looked the teen over. He'd seen "bushed" kids before—uneducated, poor talkers and naive as hell. Usually the eldest boy would come in and start working, then one by one the other brothers would show up. For the most part, these kids turned out to be good, honest workers. Sometimes he got burned, but Jack had a soft spot for kids like this. With a constant need for diligent, hard workers, he'd hired many inexperienced boys from the country.

"Driver's licence?" he asked.

Norman winced.

"Gotta have a driver's licence," Jack said, picking up a pen, examining it and tossing it back on the desk. "You're not 16, are you?"

Norman hesitated. He'd told David that he'd do all the talking, but he didn't want to bullshit and risk the chance of not getting hired himself. Jack was a fickle man and hard to read.

Unable to lie, David spoke up.

"Nnn-oo s-ssir," he said.

"But he can do other stuff," Norman said confidently, "and he's honest. You wouldn't want him answering the phone—" Both men laughed. "And he might be skinny as a stick, but he's strong. He can work the pumps and dig holes, you know, all that shitty work you had me do last year."

David's face flushed. He'd never heard Norman express confidence in him like that before.

Jack snickered and shook his head. Norman could tell he was getting through to the man.

"You work half as good as your brother?" Jack asked David.

"I w-wwork b-better," he answered timidly, but with a grin.

Jack threw back his head and roared with laughter.

"Well, he's definitely your brother," he said to Norman.

"Yeah, but he's not as smart as me," Norman chuckled.

The men shared a laugh and then Jack's tone turned serious.

"Okay, you guys are on," he said. "I pay the same as last year—

$1.30 an hour and paycheques are issued every second Friday. You get extra for overtime work."

"That sounds fair to us," Norman agreed. "When do we start?"

"Tomorrow," Jack said. "You start work at 7 a.m. If you don't show up or come in late, stoned or hung over—you're fired."

"Yes, sir," Norman said again while David nodded in understanding.

Jack looked once again at David. "And you wreck anything, I'll take it out of your paycheque."

"Y-yes sir," he said quickly.

"And don't tell anybody you're 15."

"N-no sir . . . I mean, y-yes sir," he nodded again.

"Alright, we'll see you tomorrow at seven," Jack chuckled.

"See you tomorrow," the brothers echoed. "At seven."

"Hey Norman," David asked, as they turned off the highway into the Shangri La trailer park, "what's 'stoned' mean?"

Norman chuckled.

"Well that all depends," he answered. "Jack's an old bugger so stoned to him probably means drunk. To us guys, though, stoned means high on grass or coke or pills."

"Oh," David said. He was still not entirely sure what his brother meant, but was too embarrassed to press further. "This is where we're gonna live?" he asked.

"Yes," Norman answered. "It's great 'cause they got showers we can use. I phoned the guy and he said we can stay in my trailer until one with a toilet comes up for rent."

"Then we g-gotta pay?" David asked.

"Yes, we have to pay," he said. "You don't live in the bush no more. You can't just go wherever you want."

"I know," David said, defensively. "It's just . . . we gotta have enough left over for food."

"Don't worry," Norman said. "You heard Jack. We're makin' $1.30 an hour. We'll be loaded. We'll split the rent and you buy your food and I'll buy mine."

"You got any more money left?" David asked.

"A little bit, why?"

"'Cause we g-ggotta work two weeks before we get paid. How we g-ggonna eat?"

"That's easy," Norman smiled. "Most of the guys eat at the Birds Hill Café and charge it. Then we go in and clear up the tab on pay day."

"So we can eat tomorrow?" David asked, his tone hopeful. "I'm gettin' sick of bread an' jam."

"God, is that all you think about?" he asked.

David nodded. "Pretty much."

Norman scowled. "Bread and jam is better than what you got at the farm. You didn't get shit there."

"I know, it's just the b-burger and f-ffries was so very much good."

Norman smiled at his brother's description. He searched for a vacant spot. "Don't worry, Davey boy," he said, giving him a nudge, "starting tomorrow you'll never be hungry again."

The brothers found a spot for the trailer and got settled in. Norman went to take a shower. David ate another meal of bread and jam, climbed into the top bunk and fell into a deep sleep.

They got up early the next morning and went for breakfast at "The Spud Stop," a nearby restaurant. They ate a hearty breakfast which Norman paid for with the last of their money. Then they drove to the construction office and were told to find George Rentz, the company foreman. George was standing beside a large machine shed.

"Hi, Norm," he said. "Good to see you back."

"Good to be back," Norman said. "What do you want me to do?"

"See that work crew over there?" he said pointing along the banks of the floodway. "Go join them and they'll put you to work."

Norman nodded and then hurried off towards the other workers.

George, a small, thin man with short hair and rubbery features, turned to David.

"You the kid?" he asked.

"Uh-huh."

"What's your name again?" he asked, motioning for David to follow.

"Dd-david."

"Okay, David," he said as he pushed open the big door on a machine shed. "Come with me."

David followed George into the dark building. Switching on the light, the foreman explained that the mechanic would be there soon and it would be David's job to tidy the place and organize tools.

Looking around, David could see this was going to be a big job. There were huge pieces of equipment in various stages of repair throughout the building.

"Just watch you don't throw out anything they need," George explained. "If you're not sure, ask."

David gulped. "Asking" was not what he did best.

"Okay," he said quietly.

"And if anyone gives you a hard time, come see me," he smiled.

David nodded but felt a little surprised. George looked too kindly to be of any help, but David was happy nonetheless to have someone he could go to with problems.

David worked all morning and by noon, was covered with grease. As the hours ticked by, he mentally calculated how much money he'd earned. As he was scooping up a pile of spilled nails to put back into a box, he heard his brother's voice echoing through the building.

"Hey! You hungry?" Norman called.

"Course!" David called back as he ran to the door.

The brothers climbed into the car and drove a short distance to the Birds Hill Café.

"Hey, Norman," David said, as they stepped out of the car and made their way to the restaurant, "I got my pay figured an' I made $6.60 already."

Norman didn't answer. He was noticeably distracted as he pulled open the café door. Stepping inside, he began looking for an empty table. The small diner was filled with labourers from different crews, most working on the floodway. There was a haze of cigarette smoke overhead.

The din of chatter was suddenly interrupted by a loud voice.

"Hey, look who's back," a man called out from across the diner. "It's 'whiskey.'"

Norman stiffened as he looked in the man's direction. He instantly recognized Bryan—the company bully who constantly picked on young, new or timid workers. Norman had received his fair share of ribbing the year before. Bryan was one person he wasn't looking forward to seeing again.

"Hey 'whiskey,'" Bryan repeated, "where you been all winter? Crashing planes in Portage?"

The other men laughed.

Norman's expression turned serious. "Don't say anything," he whispered to David through clenched teeth. He then switched on his familiar charm.

"Hey! How are you guys doing?" Norman asked, feigning interest in the men. He immediately told them a joke, which caused everyone to laugh. He avoided looking at Bryan as he tried to win over the man's table mates. They were all drinking coffee and ordering lunch.

Norman waved and returned to David, who stood awkwardly waiting by an empty table. He'd chosen a spot far enough away that they wouldn't be included in the conversation.

"Who you got there," Bryan called out to Norman again, "your girl-friend?"

The men laughed and made a few comments to themselves.

"My brother," Norman called back, as the Pischkes pulled out their chairs and sat down.

"Aren't you gonna introduce us?" the bully asked.

"This here's David," Norman replied. Turning away, he picked up the menu and muttered between clenched teeth to David, "and that's a fuckin' asshole."

Intimidated by Bryan and the other men, David stared solemnly at the paper menu in front of him.

"Another 'whiskey' boy," Bryan said, taking a gulp of coffee.

"Whiskey?" David whispered, his face red with embarrassment.

"Yeah, you know, Pischke - whiskey," Norman snickered. "He thinks it rhymes."

"Oh."

David didn't see the waitress approaching and jumped when she spoke. She gave him an odd look and then asked what they wanted to order.

Politely, Norman asked if they'd be allowed to run a tab and pay at the end of the week.

"You guys with Ramsey-Bird?" the middle-aged woman asked.

"Yes, ma'am," Norman said.

"No problem," she said. "But don't run out on me, 'cause it comes out of my pay."

"We won't," he promised.

She took down their names and Norman ordered two lunch specials each with a large glass of cola.

The waitress left and Norman turned to David.

"Quit jumping every time someone talks to you," he scolded. "Bryan just loves shit like that."

David nodded and glanced over his shoulder at the bully eating lunch.

"The only time the bastard's quiet is when he's filling his fat face," Norman said.

David giggled and turned back quickly.

Bryan sensed he was being watched and looked up from his plate.

"Whatcha lookin' at?" he sneered.

"Nothing," Norman said innocently. "Just waiting for our lunch."

"Don't fuck with me, 'whiskey,'" Bryan said. "And tell 'shitskey' there the same thing."

David watched as Norman stiffened. His brother could take a fair amount of teasing and seldom lost his temper, but when pushed too far, Norman didn't hesitate to fight.

Bryan had teased the younger man so much the year before that his tolerance for the bully was at a low point. Norman was a year older, wiser and stronger—he wasn't going to take guff from anyone.

"Maybe we can tell George," David whispered.

Norman looked at him, but he had a faraway look in his eyes. He paid no attention to the comment.

"Oh, don't worry there Bryan," Norman said loudly, the words rolling sarcastically off his tongue as he pulled out a cigar, "nobody would want to fuck with you."

The men sitting at the table behind Norman laughed. Bryan, however, was chewing and hadn't heard properly. He wasn't sure how to respond and just stared back. This caused the group to laugh even harder.

The waitress appeared a few minutes later with lunch, and that helped ease the tension between tables. As they ate, David watched Bryan's movements out of the corner of his eye. He jumped slightly when the man pushed back his chair and got up.

If Norman noticed, it didn't show. He continued eating his lunch and making small talk with David who was so frightened that he wasn't hearing a word his brother said. He didn't relax until the café door closed behind Bryan and his friends. David had naively thought that once he got away from Domko, he'd never feel fear again. He was dismayed to discover that bullies exist everywhere.

The first two weeks went by quickly and David did everything possible to avoid Bryan. Still, the man picked on him relentlessly. Because of this, David stayed close to Norman who was irritated by the bully and tired of being shadowed by his brother.

They received their first paycheques one Friday afternoon and David signed his over to Norman to cash at the bank. He mentally calculated how much was needed to pay the trailer rent and buy a few amenities, and gave the rest back to David before they went to the café to pay their food bills. This left David with a little bit of cash in his pocket.

The following week, Jack McGuiness showed up at the work site during lunch hour. The casual talk stopped and the workers stiffened as Jack approached. His expression was serious.

Jack pointed to Norman, David and two other men. "You want to make a little extra cash?" he asked. "I need men to stay until 10 p.m."

David eagerly nodded.

"Sure, we'll work," Norman said, concealing his delight from the other men.

"Good," Jack said. "And the rest of you guys, pick it up a little. We're running behind schedule."

Bryan and the other men continued eating their lunches while David jumped up and with lunch bag in hand, trotted back towards the machine shed. He'd been given a bit more responsibility and was now assisting mechanics who were fixing broken-down machines.

Jack stood and watched for a moment.

"That poor bastard can't talk worth a damn, but he sure can work," he said to no one in particular. Then turning to Bryan, he said, "and that's what we need around here—more work and less talk."

Jack started back towards his truck and Norman took this as his cue to return to work as well. He wasn't worried about keeping up to David but he wanted to avoid Bryan. Once in the driver's seat, the roar of the diesel motor made the bully's comments inaudible. That's how Norman liked it—that way he didn't get angry and wasn't tempted to react.

The weather was good and the brothers worked until 10 p.m. for two weeks straight. They took a break at 4 p.m. Friday to pick up their second paycheque.

"So, h-hhow much do you think we're g-ggonna get?" David asked as they walked towards the office. "I lost track. I think it'll be lots 'cause we w-wworked so very much overtime."

Norman had calculated their hours but wasn't sure what the government deductions would be.

"Hard to say. It's gonna depend on how hard they ding us for income tax."

"Oh," David frowned. "That don't seem fair that we gotta pay tax for workin'."

Norman laughed. "Yeah, well welcome to the real world, Davey boy. But it doesn't matter. We're paying unemployment too, and that's going to come in handy this winter when we get laid off."

David was so happy to be working that he'd forgotten this was seasonal work that would come to an end. He pushed the thought out of his mind.

The brothers opened the door to the office and stepped inside. It was full of employees who'd also taken a break to pick up their pay. George was sitting behind Jack's desk handing out cheques. The brothers got in line.

"So, how are you liking the work?" George asked David when it was his turn.

"G-gggood," the teen stammered quietly. He looked at the floor as George pressed him for more details.

"You think you'll stay until freeze up?"

"Oh y-yyyes, s-sir."

"Good," he said, handing David the cheque. "You're doing a good job."

David nodded, took his pay and began walking toward the door. He stopped when he noticed out of the corner of his eye that Bryan was watching him. David glanced over his shoulder at Norman who was entertaining George with one of his many jokes.

"Hey, 'shitskey,'" Bryan called out.

David knew who 'shitskey' was, but pretended he didn't hear.

"Hey, 'shitskey,'" the bully said again, this time louder, "I'm talking to you."

David looked at the big man who was standing near the door.

"How much overtime did you get?" he asked.

David looked at the floor and said nothing.

"How many hours?" he asked again, forcing David to acknowledge him.

"T-ttt," David stuttered. "T-tttw."

As the word "twenty" stuck behind his teeth, David's face warmed with embarrassment. He felt all eyes on him as he struggled to say the word. This, of course, only made matters worse.

Bryan laughed and then rolling back his eyes, began mimicking David's stutter. The teenager hung his head and tried to walk past, but Bryan blocked the door.

"Hey, 'shitsky,' when was the last time you took a shower?" he taunted. "You stink."

Some of the men chuckled while the others just watched as the bully teased David. Too shy to look at anyone, David glanced nervously over his shoulder for Norman. George was still talking but Norman was no longer paying attention to the conversation. He noticed what was happening near the door and politely nodded at the supervisor. His eyes were on Bryan who continued to taunt David. Devastated, the 15 year old could do nothing but wait for his older brother.

At first glance Norman looked like just another handsome, young man. But a maturity borne of many experiences, not all pleasant, was evident when people took the time to look into his eyes. He'd seen more in 20 years than most men in that trailer had seen in their lifetimes. To them, the Pischke brothers were bushed kids from the country—the current butt of jokes to lighten long days of boring, manual labour. Like chickens in a coop, one always had to be picked on.

The look on Norman's face was one that few people had seen before, but David recognized it well. It was the same look Norman had as a youngster when he realized he couldn't fly his siblings away from the farm in his homemade airplane. David had seen the look again when Domko punished Norman by shooting the boy's faithful dog. And the last time he'd seen Norman with a clenched jaw and rigid gaze came after a horrific beating he'd taken from Domko. After Norman regained consciousness, he got up, walked away from the farm, and never returned.

But that had been when Norman was only 13 years old. Now he was a young man who feared no one. It was in these moments that Norman moved with a fluidity and purpose that was quick, sure, and frightening. He strode across the room no longer reluctant to make trouble with a fellow worker. He stopped just inches from Bryan, then looked up at the man who stood more than an inch taller. Surprised, the bully took a step backwards.

"How much overtime we've worked is none of your goddamned business," Norman said flatly.

"Yeah, well it is my business when you're taking work away from the rest of us," Bryan sneered.

"You don't like it, talk to McGuiness," Norman said calmly.

"What's the point? I'm not going to kiss anybody's ass," he said. "Why do you think your brother over there is called 'shitsky'? It's from all that ass-kissing that's going on."

Norman grabbed Bryan by the front of the shirt and rammed him backwards against the wall. The bully tried to swing but Norman had him pinned, lifting him slightly off his feet. Pressing his strong forearms against Bryan's chest, he pushed his elbows up under the man's armpits and held him tight against the wall.

"Take it outside!" George yelled as he came around from behind the desk.

In a fluid motion, Norman pulled Bryan towards him and the two men struggled towards the open door. Norman instinctively knew Bryan's weaknesses and he pushed the heavy-set, out-of-shape man out backwards. Norman pounced on Bryan who lost his balance when he missed the step and he hit the ground hard. Before Bryan realized what had happened, Norman's knee was pressed firmly into his back. Norman twisted Bryan's arm back and forced his wrist towards his shoulder blades until the bully cried out in pain.

The other workers followed and jumped down onto the grass to watch. David noticed the men who'd been picked on by Bryan were smirking at the man's predicament.

This was the first time David realized how truly strong his brother was. He could see the muscles on Norman's back, shoulders and arms bulge under the thin T-shirt. Bryan kicked a bit but in spite of his size was no match for the solid young man.

"It's Pischke," Norman said in a soft but commanding tone as his forearm pressed Bryan's face into the ground. "Say it."

Bryan refused.

Teeth clenched, Norman forced the bully's wrist higher. "Say it, or I'll break it." The coldness in his voice was unsettling and David wasn't the only one who noticed.

"Don't do it Norm," someone said softly from the crowd.

"Yeah, he's got a family to support," another added.

And with that single-minded intensity that David recognized once again, Norman ignored the pleas of those watching. His resolve seemed even stronger.

"Say it," he said softly, giving another twist.

"Pischke."

"Louder."

"Pischke! Now will ya let me up?" Bryan squealed.

David held his breath hoping Norman would release his grip. Slowly, he did—and then he got up. The men's eyes followed Norman as he went back into the trailer to pick up his cheque, which had dropped to the floor during the scuffle.

Angry and embarrassed, Bryan got up but didn't dare look at anyone. He made a comment to the foreman before storming towards his truck. He got in and sped away.

"All right," George said, a little shaken and probably feeling guilty that he hadn't stopped the scuffle before it got out of hand, "get back to work."

The crowd dispersed with some men going home and others returning to their equipment to log more overtime hours. David stuffed his cheque in his pocket and waited for Norman who stopped in the doorway to talk to George. He could only hear part of what the men were saying.

"I know . . . bully . . . tired, too . . . McGuiness wouldn't like it . . . at work . . . take with a grain of salt . . . hope it won't happen again."

Norman turned, then giving George a backwards wave, stepped out of the trailer and walked towards his brother.

"C'mon," he said. "We gotta cash our cheques and get back before they start docking our pay."

"Okay," David said excitedly. "That was g-great. You shmashed that guy."

"Yeah, well, whatever," Norman said quietly.

"You shoulda seen everybody, Norman, them guys he picked on was glad," David smiled.

"Yeah, well he's picked on a few," he replied.

"An' his friends was scared of you too," David said proudly. "He won't be pickin' on us no more."

"Guess not," Norman said casually, adding, "but do me a favour, will ya David?"

"What's that?" the boy asked.

"Take a shower when we get home, okay?"

Chapter 6

"**DO YOU TAKE ANY MEDICATIONS?"** McMillan asked.

"No, none," he said, "except for my gout pills."

"Have you ever taken any non-medicinal drugs?" he asked.

"You mean like marijuana?"

"Yes."

"No, not ever," he said.

"How often do you consume alcohol?"

David thought for a moment.

"I dunno, s-sometimes on the weekend," he said. "An' on special occasions, or w-when people come over."

"How about in the last 24 hours?" McMillan asked.

"No, I had n-nothin' to drink since . . . Fri-day."

"Do you have any other problems like diabetes, ulcer, epilepsy?"

"No . . . my gout acts up s-sometimes when I drink or eat food that's got too much fat in it," he said.

"Is it bothering you now?"

"No."

"Are you sure?"

"Yeah, why?"

"Because any physical discomfort you might be feeling can affect the test," he explained.

"How 'bout bein' pissed off that I'm here?" David asked. "Does that count as fiscal dis-comfort?"

One evening after work, Norman and David arrived at the trailer to discover a note stuck to the door. A trailer with a toilet was available for rent and if they wanted it they could pick up the keys from the park office. The next day they paid the first month's rent and moved in. Now they had a toilet, sink, shower and a kitchen plus more room to sleep. They also had hydro and a small fridge. They went grocery shopping and stocked the cupboards.

The following weeks went by quickly. They settled in at work, ate two brown bag meals a day on the job site and one meal a day at the café. Bryan avoided them and found someone else to tease. The bully was always careful what he said when Norman was around.

The brothers had been working 15 hour days, six days a week. It became obvious they were spending too much time together as they were beginning to argue. Late one Friday afternoon, while David was busy pumping water, Norman drove up in his car and motioned for him to come over.

"I'm not workin' late tonight," he said, his tone brighter than it had been in awhile. "I'm goin' to Moosehorn to see Sharon."

"How am I g-ggonna get back to the trailer?" David asked, obviously offended.

"I don't know," Norman said. "Get someone to give you a ride."

David thought for a moment. "Who?"

"Who else is working late?" he asked.

"That George Klingbell guy, I think."

"Okay, then ask him," Norman said.

"W-what if he w-won't?"

"I don't know," Norman said, exasperated. "I guess you'll have to walk."

"Cc-can you ask h-hhim for me?"

"No," Norman said, putting the car in reverse. "I have to go. See you Sunday."

For the rest of the evening, David worried about how he'd approach George Klingbell to ask for a ride to the trailer park. What exactly would he say? They'd spoken occasionally—and while the young man seemed nice, he didn't know him well.

When his shift was over, David hurried back to where the men parked their vehicles. He could see George talking to another man and approached quietly. After the other fellow left, David came out of the shadows.

"H-h-hey G-ggeorge," he said, "c-ccan I g-gget a ride?"

George looked at him and smiled. He was a few years older than

David. He had blonde hair, a round, pleasant face and an easy demeanour.

"Sure," he said. "You're Norm's brother, right? You live with him?"

"Uh-huh," David nodded.

He began walking towards his car and motioned for David to follow.

They climbed inside then drove in awkward silence along the highway until they came to the trailer park. David knew his stutter made people uncomfortable, but didn't know what to say to lighten the mood in moments like this. He certainly couldn't talk about his problem, so he just sat there and said nothing—staring out the window as they drove past the houses and small businesses that lined the highway.

"Do you need a ride back in the morning?" George asked, mercifully breaking the silence. He came to a stop at the trailer park lane.

"S-ssure," David replied. He thanked George quickly, got out and ran to the trailer.

The next morning, David was waiting for his ride at 6:30 a.m. along the highway. George smiled as he stopped and motioned for David to get in.

After a few minutes on the highway, they fell into a comfortable conversation as George waited patiently for David to finish his sentences. That in itself relaxed the boy, and his speech improved considerably. They became instant friends and soon a ritual developed. Whenever Norman couldn't give David a ride either to or from work, George would. To keep his supervisor and friend straight when talking, he began referring to them as "old George" and "new George."

After working a regular shift and picking up their paycheques one Friday afternoon, Norman dropped David off at the trailer.

"I'm goin' to get Sharon," he said. "We'll be back in a little while."

David nodded and watched as his brother drove away. He felt a bit jealous that Sharon was taking so much of Norman's time and occupying most of his thoughts. That's when David started thinking about Dennis. He missed the closeness they once shared and wondered what his twin was doing. He decided that soon he'd find a way to pay his twin a visit.

It took Norman just over an hour to pick up Sharon, cash their paycheques and drive back to the trailer. David was sitting at the table when the door opened and his brother stepped inside. Sharon was behind him.

David was stunned by the teenager who was one of the prettiest girls he'd ever seen. She had large hazel eyes that peeked out from behind long bangs. Her hair was the colour of honey, cut in a fashionable bob. Her face was slim, but revealed dimples when she smiled. Femininity flowed from her every movement. She was wearing tight pants and a fitted blouse with a pink sweater draped casually over her arm. Her features were delicate and her figure stunning.

Sharon stood in the doorway, purse slung over her shoulder, as she surveyed the inside of the trailer.

"This is David," Norman said, pointing to his brother but not taking his eyes off his girlfriend.

"Hi," she said shyly. "So this is where you two live."

"Yep," Norman said. "We just moved in."

"It's all right," she said, smiling. "The colours are a bit ugly, but it could be fixed up pretty good."

The three sat at the table and began discussing their weekend plans.

"Beer?" Norman asked as he pulled one out of the case. David took one and drank it, even though he didn't like the taste. He enjoyed the feelings alcohol gave him though—it made him feel happier and relaxed. It was a pleasant experience that helped his speech and enhanced his gregarious nature.

"So, do you want to buy my car?" Norman asked his brother.

"What? You w-wanna sell it?" David asked.

"Not right away, but when I get together enough cash," he said looking at Sharon, "I'm gonna buy an even better car."

They discussed the possibility of David buying the convertible plus the little trailer that Norman had taken back to Moosehorn the weekend before.

"I really don't need it any more," Norman said. "You should buy it. That way you'll have your own place and I'll have enough money for flying lessons."

David thought this was a fine idea. He wanted to visit Moosehorn but was prevented from doing so because he had nowhere to stay.

They negotiated a price, and David agreed to pay Norman a portion out of each paycheque until the debt was paid.

"And I figure I'll be ready to sell the car in the winter time," Norman said.

"W-winter time!" David exclaimed. "That's so long away."

"Well, you can't drive it until then anyway 'cause you don't have your licence," Norman teased.

"I know but you'll sell it to s-someone else."

"No, I won't," he promised.

"Good, 'cause I'll buy it now if you w-want," David said.

They continued the discussion and then asked Sharon for an update on news from Moosehorn.

"I've heard that things aren't going well out at your farm," she said.

"Whadda ya m-mmean?" David asked.

"Well, Domko's been complaining that there's nobody there to help and that you twins abandoned the family when they needed you."

"W-wwe did not!" David argued. "How can you say that?"

"I didn't," Sharon said defensively. "I said, that's what Domko's been saying."

"Well, I'm not goin' back to sh-ovel shit!" David lamented. "I got a gg-good job now. What about Dennis? Is he still at Brays'?"

"I don't know," she said. "I haven't heard."

"Well, th-ey'll be tryin' to get him bb-back," David continued. "Domko can't do the work. Not never. We always been doin' it."

"Well, anyway, I just thought you should know," she said.

Norman was working staggered hours at a separate job site and his brother's absence left David feeling vulnerable around the bullies at work. Fortunately he and new George had become good friends, and the young man came to David's defence when other workers poked fun at him.

The months went by quickly. Norman and Sharon continued to date and it became apparent that their relationship had reached a serious point when Sharon started assuming household duties around the trailer. She began paying bills, doing laundry and buying groceries. She also purchased household items like towels, blankets and dishes.

This pleased Norman but David resented it because he was expected to pitch in financially but wasn't entirely certain how his money was being spent. After all, he was saving to buy Norman's car and purchasing anything but food was unimportant to him.

One Friday afternoon new George asked David if he wanted to go with him to Libau, a small town near Beausejour. He planned to visit friends there, and offered to take David along. Not too keen on meeting new people, David declined saying he was going to Moosehorn with Norman instead.

"Do you need a ride to work on Monday morning?" George asked before he left for the weekend.

"S-sure," David said. "I'll meet you in the usual spot."

George waved as he drove off.

David and Norman arrived in Moosehorn on Friday night. David stayed in the trailer which was parked once again in the Matheson's yard. Unfortunately, he couldn't find anyone to give him a ride to the Bray farm so he was unable to visit Dennis. He spent the weekend walking around town with Jimmy and Johnny Matheson, suggesting at one point that they go to a restaurant.

"We d-don't got no m-money," Johnny said quietly.

"That's okay," David said. "I got money."

He treated the teens to a meal at the café as other patrons watched. A few men poked fun at their appearance, but this didn't bother David who had grown accustomed to being teased. He felt far removed from people in suits and dresses so their opinions meant nothing to him. He knew how it felt to be judged by appearances and vowed he wouldn't do the same thing. He was comfortable with the Matheson brothers, even if they were a bit different. Still in a state of euphoria over having a good job and enough money to buy food, he gladly paid for their meals.

Monday morning arrived and David was waiting on the highway for new George, but his friend didn't arrive. After 20 minutes passed, David started walking to work. Realizing that he was going to be late, he started jogging. He glanced over his shoulder occasionally, expecting to see George's car pull up, but it never did. By the time he'd traveled the full five miles on foot, David was tired, late and angry at his friend for forgetting him. Almost everyone in his life let him down, and he became despondent that he could count on so few people. He burst into the construction site trailer worried that tardiness had cost him his job.

Jack was standing by the desk talking to old George.

"S-ssorry I'm l-llate," David panted, his eyes focused firmly on the ground. "G-ggeorge was s-s'posed to pick me up b-but d-ddidn't."

The men looked at one another, then Jack spoke.

"That's okay David," he said softly. "You're not in trouble. Actually son, there's been an accident."

As David stood there trying to catch his breath, he noticed his boss's eyes were puffy and red.

"George was killed in a car accident on the weekend," Jack said, his voice breaking. "We just got the call."

David was dumbfounded. His mind emptied of all thoughts and a feeling of disbelief washed over him. He was left speechless by the churning emotions that made it difficult for him to think. Slowly, he turned and left the trailer. He walked across the muddy lot without saying a word. Every noise around him seemed loud as his senses struggled to understand what this meant. As he felt the warm morning sunshine on his cheek, he couldn't believe how life could so quickly change from one minute to the next. He walked to a ditch that had been excavated the week before. The pump he'd been using Saturday was still sitting at the edge, but it had rained all night and the ditch needed to be pumped out again. Dropping his lunch bag onto the ground, he fell to his knees.

George—dead? He couldn't believe it. Except for his father, David had never known anyone who'd died before. He remembered that he was invited to his friend's house that weekend. David was filled with guilt as he realized that it hadn't crossed his mind that something terrible might have happened to his friend. His first instinct was that he'd been let down.

But he was just here! he thought. *How can this be? Why did George, of all people, have to die?*

And then, glancing around, he shook his head. He hadn't thought about the farm much in the last few weeks, but now the memories came flooding back.

It had been a crisp fall afternoon and the twins were bringing the cows in from the field for milking. The animals' pace picked up as they approached the fence separating the area where they grazed from the barnyard. As soon as they passed through the gate, however, they slowed and began eating grass. They also searched for fresh hay to eat. Tired of feeding on dry pasture, the cows were looking forward to being closer to home where they could laze all winter and eat hay. Their appetite made chasing them into the barn difficult, but with the help of their little dog, "Sporty," David and Dennis usually managed to get the job done before the cows got into the hay stack reserved for winter feeding.

Sporty was a little black and white Border Collie who was quick and smart. Someone on a nearby farm had trained the dog to work with cattle and Sporty enjoyed the work. Domko had stolen the dog and brought it home that spring. The twins had become attached to Sporty who followed them and slept by them at night.

Domko had been so impressed by the little dog's work with the cattle that he'd stolen another dog, hoping for the same results. Unfortunately, this dog came from town and the big, mixed-bred animal barked too much and lacked any farm training. It only took a few days for it to become obvious that Domko had been hasty in picking up this dog. Embarrassed and unable to admit he'd made a mistake, he said that the little dog should be able to train the big dog to help out.

Days passed and the twins could see that the big dog was nothing but a nuisance. Domko was growing increasingly angry as he watched the twins moving cattle. David had made a comment, to nobody in particular, that the big dog was "useless" and it caused his stepfather to seethe.

On this particular afternoon the twins ran into even more difficulty when they'd finished milking. When it was time to take the cows back to the field, the cows were not interested in returning to grass that had been grazed so low. They bawled and complained, fanning in all directions as the boys tried to chase them through the open gate.

Sporty ran and nipped the heels of the errant cows, trying to herd them into a circle. He was doing a good job on the side of the barnyard he chose to take. He understood how to chase the cows toward David and Dennis who were in the middle of the pack, leading the animals toward the open gate. Sporty yapped and chased in a zig-zag motion, understanding the need to keep the lead cow within sight at all times.

The other dog ran barking into the bawling cattle and did nothing but cause confusion. The cows, thinking the dog was a predator, turned and started back toward the safety of the barn. The twins tried desperately to counteract the dog's actions. In the distance, they could hear Domko swearing obscenities at them as a few cows settled into eating hay from a nearby stack. The twins panicked, knowing that if they didn't get the cows through the gate soon, they would receive a beating for taking too long and wasting hay. It took over 15 minutes, but with Sporty's help they were able to get the animals all going in one direction. As they closed the gate behind the last animal, they turned to see Domko approaching from the barnyard with a 303 caliber rifle in his hands.

The dogs, having chased the cattle a safe distance from the gate, were now doubling back towards the twins. Sporty was in the lead, slowing to a trot as he approached the yard with his tongue dangling loosely in his open mouth. The big dog, loping close behind, stopped briefly to smell something along the fence line. As the dogs neared, Domko lifted his rifle, took aim, and shot the big dog. The animal let out a startled yelp and crumpled to the ground. It struggled and gasped for a few moments before its body lay still.

The sound of the shot startled Sporty whose ears flattened close to his head. Seeing the twins, he hurried towards them for safety. A second later, Domko took aim and shot Sporty, too. The little dog was killed instantly when the bullet pierced his skull at the temple. His soft body slid to the ground and lay lifeless on the other side of the gate.

Fearing that Domko might shoot them as well, the twins trembled in silence as they stared intently at the ground. Afraid to cry, David let his mind clear and felt a loud rushing sensation in his head. In that moment, he understood that the big dog had embarrassed Domko and that everyone involved must be punished before the man could regain power over the situation. A comment by Domko that both dogs were useless, confirmed David's assessment.

The brothers stood frozen until their stepfather turned and walked back to the house. When he was a safe distance away, they walked over to their dog to see if he was really dead.

"Why'd he shoot Sporty, too?" Dennis asked, his voice trembling with emotion. "He didn't do nothin'."

David's heart ached as he looked at the lifeless form.

"He was helpin'," David said quietly in defence of the dog.

Grief-stricken but unable to cry, David lifted the little body at the shoulders while Dennis slipped his hands under the dogs hips. Carrying Sporty around the edge of the barnyard, they disappeared into the bush near the church.

Unfortunately, this wasn't the first pet that the twins had buried on their property near the church grounds. They had made a pet cemetery that was filled with the bones of numerous murdered animals. Each grave had a stick or rock to mark it and the twins knew which animal was buried in each location.

They found a spot close to the fence between two trees. Using the blade of a broken shovel they started to dig. They placed the dog's body in the shallow hole and then covered it with dirt. Both sat beside the grave for a long time in silence.

David stared at the church and asked God why these terrible things were happening to them. He listened hard for an answer, but all he heard was the gentle breeze in the trees and the rustling of leaves.

Standing up, he climbed over the fence and walked towards the graveyard behind the church. As he strolled through, he read the names on the markers of neighbours buried there. Some had nice headstones while others were simply marked with a cross. He wondered what would happen to him when he died and morbidly played the scene in his mind. He visualized his mother standing at his grave sobbing uncontrollably among mourners who all regretted he was gone. A part of him wanted to die as he was overwhelmed with feelings of hopelessness.

Stopping at a fresh grave, he looked at the soft earth and the flowers that surrounded it. He bent and picked up the plastic wreaths and carried as many as he could to where Dennis sat by Sporty's grave.

"Look what I got," he said.

Dennis smiled. "Now we can bury them for real."

The twins took the wreaths and placed them on the graves of their pets. They went back to the church graveyard for more—until every pet had a wreath to symbolize it had not been forgotten.

The traffic along the highway at Birds Hill echoed meaninglessly in David's ear. It seemed so unfair that everyone was going about their daily business when his friend had just died. He could hear the roar of diesel engines in the distance and a small plane flying overhead. He felt his eyes fill with tears as he stared into the water-filled ditch. He said a silent thank you to George and made a promise that he would never forget him, and someday would tell people what a good friend he'd been.

Standing up, David took the pull cord in hand and started the pump's engine with a brisk tug. He stood there in the deafening roar as tears streamed down his face. He felt completely alone as he mourned the senseless death of his first real friend.

Chapter 7

"**ARE YOU DONE? MCMILLAN ASKED.** This time it was his turn to be sarcastic.

"I don't know," David mimicked, "what do you think?"

McMillan stared back. He wasn't sure how to interpret David's misuse of words. He'd be glad when this interview was done. While David wasn't an articulate man, he wasn't a stupid one either. Taking a deep breath, McMillan held back his anger.

"Do you attend church?" McMillan asked.

"No, n-not since I was a kid."

"What religion are you?" he asked.

"N-no re-ligion."

"What church did you attend when you were a child?"

"My m-mother was a Jehovah's W-witness," he said.

"So why don't you attend church then?" he asked.

"I had enough of that goddamned outfit," he said. "I vowed that when I walked out the door, I'd never go back. Ss-ome of the guys around here were n-nothin' but a bunch of two-faced bastards."

McMillan was startled by the intensity in David's voice.

"But that doesn't make the whole religion bad," McMillan said.

"Don't matter," he stated. "They never helped us so why should I help them now? You know what I mean? Everyone has to help build the Kingdom Hall an' pitch in, but there's no way I'm g-gonna help them. No, sir."

Work on the floodway continued that year until the ground froze in

November. David and Norman were laid off and moved back to Moosehorn where they applied for unemployment insurance and lived in the little trailer now owned by David.

Norman needed cash to pay for flying lessons so David gave him what he'd saved for a down payment on the car. He had nearly a hundred dollars in his pocket the afternoon his older brother Stephen arrived on his doorstep. Stephen, who had been working at odd jobs, had heard there was plenty of work in British Columbia for young men who didn't mind hard work. Short of cash, he was looking for someone to accompany him west and help fund the trip.

David agreed to go. Throwing a duffel bag with most of his belongings in the back seat of Stephen's car, the teenager was off on another adventure.

This time it was with 21-one year-old Stephen, the quietest of David's male siblings. Regrettably, the two had never gotten along as children. Stephen had the same tough exterior the Pischke boys were known for, but he kept his opinions to himself. He was well-liked by most people and also admired for his fearless nature.

The trip to British Columbia started on a high note. The brothers laughed and joked, got plenty of take-out food and slept in motels most nights. By the time they hit the B.C. border, however, they'd had a number of disagreements and were thoroughly sick of each other. They'd run out of money and both were hungry and tired by the time they reached the outskirts of their destination—100 Mile House, a logging community in central British Columbia. When David discovered Stephen had driven there on speculation, he became furious. While he hadn't asked, David had assumed that his brother had jobs waiting for them upon arrival.

The uncertainty of where their next meal was coming from caused David to lose his temper. He was reminded of the times he'd looked to his older brother for protection from Domko, but Stephen had been unable to help. David's resentment towards his brother had tempered after Stephen left home, but the childhood wound hadn't completely healed over.

The brothers got into a roaring fight on the outskirts of 100 Mile House. It ended when Stephen kicked David out of the car. The door was slammed and David stood there, with his duffel bag at his feet, watching his brother drive away. Feeling like an unwanted dog, he waited for a few minutes hoping Stephen would return once he'd cooled off. Regretting a few—but not all—of the things that he'd said, David looked first at his watch then at the sky. It was mid-afternoon and the sun wouldn't be visible much longer.

After 45 minutes he concluded that his brother wouldn't be returning. He had to decide what to do next. It appeared to him that the town's main street was a few blocks away. David picked up his bag, swung it over his shoulder and walked toward the sounds of downtown.

He roamed the streets for a few hours, familiarizing himself with the community and the businesses there. Nestled in a valley surrounded by rolling, tree-covered mountains, 100 Mile House was a town with a "gold rush" feel to it—built up to serve the logging industry. The streets were busy. People he met nodded politely as he glanced in store windows and lingered at the entrance to a restaurant. The delicious smell from the cooking vent at the back of the building caused David's stomach to vibrate with hunger. He secretly hoped that someone would come to his aid after recognizing that he was alone—with no money. Unfortunately for him, the area saw a lot of transients during the 1960s and residents paid little attention to strangers.

The sun moved quickly through the western sky, disappearing behind a rolling mountain top. David began dreading the thought of spending the night outside. Remembering a bank of trees that seemed sheltered from the cold wind, he started back to the spot where Stephen had dropped him off. The frozen ground crunched under his worn work boots and he shivered as the temperature begin to drop. The cold wind swooped down and swirled around him.

The outcrop at the edge of town turned out to be a good choice for shelter. The trees were spaced close enough to deflect the wind. David smiled ruefully realizing he was once again using the outdoor survival skills he'd learned as a child.

He dropped his bag and cleared debris from the warmest spot in the trees. Reaching into his pocket, he pulled out a book of matches. There were enough twigs and deadfall to make a fire. He knew that keeping his spirits high was going to be a much more difficult task than staying warm. As he piled twigs and gathered a few sticks, he scolded himself for agreeing to come to this place with Stephen—he should have known better!

He cupped his hand around the lit match and crouched over the kindling he'd piled in the centre of the clearing. The dry leaves ignited easily and a small puff of smoke rose from the fire. Once he was confident that it was going, he unzipped his duffel bag and pulled out two old sweaters. Slipping off his leather jacket, he stretched the sweaters over his shivering body and then put the jacket back on. He sat for a while, feeding the fire and watching the flames grow as each stick burned.

Before long the town was enveloped in complete darkness. As he lay on the needle-covered ground surrounded by huge spruce trees, he looked up at the clear, dark sky and remembered advice that his mother had given him. She had said if he ever found himself in trouble or in need of help, to seek out the closest Kingdom Hall. She assured him that Jehovah's Witnesses were linked across the country and would help him if needed.

He slept soundly until he shifted position. The cold ground underneath jolted him awake. He lazily pushed a few heavy sticks from the edge of the fire to the centre of the smoldering ashes, watching as the smoking embers grew into orange flames when they caught the dry branches. Satisfied that the fire would burn most of the night, he nestled closer to it and again fell asleep. This time, however, it was a fitful rest filled with dreams of strangers, movement and fear. He awoke in the early hours to find a dusting of white powder across the ground and snowflakes falling gently.

As he slowly sat up, he brushed the snow from his chest and legs. His limbs stiffly protested movement including his fingers which felt blunt from the cold. The thought occurred to him that many people die from exposure and he wondered why the cold nights had never claimed him. He thought it an odd contradiction that the human instinct is to fight for survival at all costs and yet the body's reaction to cold temperatures is to slow down and stop moving—a recipe for certain death.

Many times, too terrified to go home, the twins had slept huddled together beside a fire in the bush. David wondered how they awoke so many times after falling into a deep, quiet sleep under the crisp cold sky.

Not a bad death, he thought, shaking his head and then laughing out loud. Hypothermia sounded better than being beaten to death. At least it was peaceful.

David's stomach complained of hunger and Norman's words, "you'll never be hungry again," caused him to wince. Easy for Norman to say! He was driving part-time for Hugo Russell back in Moosehorn. David, on the other hand, was sleeping outside, somewhere in British Columbia. He mentally chastised himself for not taking care of the little money he'd brought along.

I look like a hobo, he thought. It was one thing to be a child hiding in fear, but there was no excuse for a working man to be sleeping outside in the bushes. He remembered how Domko had said that the Pischke children would "amount to nothing" and be "useless" or "hobos."

Deciding to take his mother's advice, David stood up, stripped off his coat, removed the extra sweaters and packed them in his bag. He slipped on his jacket and kicked the fire until it was out. Stepping out of the bushes, he surveyed the street and wondered how to find the nearest Kingdom Hall.

The sun was coming up but the town was still quiet. Slinging his bag over his shoulder once again, he started toward a nearby coffee shop he'd noticed the night before. He opened the door to the smell of fresh coffee and toast which nearly brought him to his knees. His stomach growled as he sat at the table closest to the entrance.

When the waitress approached, he said he had no money for food but wanted to find the nearest Kingdom Hall. She gave him an odd look, and disappeared through a swinging door into the kitchen.

A moment later the door swung back open, and a man—obviously the cook—stuck his head out.

"Whadda ya want?" he asked.

"I'm l-llookin' for the K-kkking-dom H-hall," David stammered.

"Well, that's a first," the cook laughed. "Usually they're the ones bangin' on your door. You a Jehovah?"

"M-mmy m-mmother is."

"Oh," he said. "Here, I'll draw you a map."

Ripping a page from his order book, the cook flipped it over and sketched the route to the hall, handing it to David.

"You drivin'?" he asked.

"N-nno," he answered. "W-wwalkin'."

"Oh well, it's not too far, good luck," the cook said with a smile before disappearing back into the kitchen.

"Thanks," David called back as the door swung shut again.

Looking at the map, David stepped outside and calculated where he was in relationship to his destination. According to the drawing, it was at the opposite end of town. What David didn't know was how long it would take him to walk there. Luckily it was Sunday morning and he felt that if he hurried, he could still make it in time for the service.

He'd always had a keen sense of direction which was proving useful as he navigated his way through the unfamiliar town. Hurrying, he found himself in front of the Kingdom Hall with plenty of time to spare before the service was scheduled to begin.

Timidly, and unable to make eye contact with anyone, he approached the building and watched as families filed into the hall. He waited until most everyone had gone in before following. The people in front of him glanced over their shoulders and, with furrowed brows, talked among themselves. They turned into the cloak room and still watching him, removed their jackets. David rejected the thought of hanging up his old coat for fear of losing it. He continued down the hallway towards the meeting room still wearing the black leather bomber-style jacket. It wasn't worth stealing, but Norman's old coat was the only thing David had to keep himself warm. He wasn't taking any chances with it or his duffel bag.

He continued into the meeting room and found himself a seat in the middle of the hall. Keeping his eyes on the floor, it took some time before he was able to relax enough to look around. Feeling that all eyes were on him, he was self-conscious, especially since the hall filled with people, but no one took the seats next to him. He took a deep breath and stared straight ahead.

One of the elders of the congregation walked to the front of the room and gradually the murmur of conversation quieted. The elder addressed the crowd and began giving the week's lesson about the need for more kindness in the world to reduce suffering and poverty. Feeling that the sermon had been written especially for him, David's face turned scarlet. He silently pleaded for the man not to look in his direction as his ears burned with humiliation. The feeling reminded him of why he didn't like church.

As the lesson progressed, David began to relax. Soon he had enough courage to glance around the room. He watched as members nodded at the elder, obviously agreeing with the man's plea for charity. The elder was stressing that spreading "the word" about helping the less fortunate should be every member's mission.

This all sounded very good to David, but he secretly wondered if anything the man said mattered. After all, did this man understand the needs of the suffering? Preaching about giving help was one thing, but actually doing something useful was not an easy task. David knew this first hand.

None of the people here looked like they were suffering. It was impossible for David to believe that they had an understanding of how it feels to be alone and desperate. Did these people really wanting to help others or were they just making themselves feel better by talking about the plight of the less fortunate? Or maybe this was a way of getting to the New Order—the religion's name for a heaven-like place.

And then David felt his heart soften. Looking at these strangers, he could see a gentleness in their expressions—the same humble look he'd seen before when people are in church, sitting before their God. David wanted to believe that they were good people who would help him.

He suddenly brightened as he thought of the opportunities before him. This, as awkward as it was, could be an excellent opportunity for him. His mother had talked about a Witness family at 100 Mile House that had a huge ranch. Maybe he could find this place and be hired as a worker there.

He daydreamed through the remainder of the service, picturing himself in cowboy garb, rounding up cattle on a horse. He thought this would be a very glamorous way to make a living but was jolted back from the rolling hills of his imagination to the stuffy Kingdom Hall by a chorus of comments indicating that the lesson was finally over.

He waited in his seat until most people had started milling about and visiting before shyly inching his way toward a friendly-looking family. He stood for a moment saying nothing until the man offered his hand in greeting.

"Hello," the stranger said, introducing himself.

"H-hhello," David stammered extending his hand.

"Are you from around here?"

"No," he began. "From M-mman-itoba."

"Visiting friends?"

"N-nno, I'm l-llookin' for w-wwork," he said. David managed to tell the man about his mother's advice that he should go to a Jehovah's Witness congregation and they'd do what they could for him.

The man nodded, saying a church member did have a large ranch in the mountains that employed people year-round. He thought for a moment before motioning for David to follow him. He took the boy over to meet the ranch owner and explained David's plight.

The well-dressed man looked both intelligent and confident. His eyes bore into David.

"What skills do you have?" he asked.

Stammering his way through, David explained that he could do most farm work, that he understood horses and had worked with cattle.

"I'll w-wwork f-ffor food an' a p-pplace to s-ssleep," he said, proving that a hungry man is a poor negotiator.

The man looked him over. His expression didn't soften and the teenager could sense that his speech problem had made the man uncomfortable. He'd seen that "look" before.

"I don't think so," the rancher said. "We're not hiring right now."

David nodded as he looked at the floor. His face was warm and he wanted to run away. Trying to be polite, he stood for a few minutes before slipping out of the meeting room. He felt anger boiling in him as he strode down the hallway, then exploded out the door.

The cold November wind hit him hard, whipping his hair away from his face. He stood looking at the gray sky and felt as if he were being swallowed up by the gloom. Tears welled in his eyes as he stormed down the steps onto the sidewalk. He vowed he'd never again step into a Jehovah's Witness hall. He pounded the palm of his hand against his forehead to make sure he never forgot.

Stupid! he thought, shaking his head as the tears slipped down his cheeks. He didn't dare wipe them away for fear that someone would notice. Once he'd distanced himself from the hall, he brought his shoulders up and one at a time, quickly rubbed his cheeks against the cold leather of his coat.

He made his way to the downtown district and wandered the streets for hours, looking for "help wanted" signs while he tried to make sense of his situation. The day wore on as he roamed the streets, peering in shop windows and sniffing the air hungrily near restaurants. His mind whirled as he tried to think of what to do. The only idea he had was to call Norman who, he hoped, would come to save him from this awful place.

He looked up and down the street for a phone booth. Soon it would be dark and he dreaded the thought of spending another night alone in the bushes. He found a booth and sighed as he stepped inside and pulled the door shut behind him.

He stared at the phone. He'd seen Norman make a collect phone call but had never actually done it himself. Carefully, he lifted the receiver and pressed "0" for Operator. A woman's voice came on the other end.

"Operator, may I help you?"

"Yes," David began, and then following a long pause, the words became stuck in his throat. "Ccc . . ."

"May I help you?" she asked again, this time not so friendly.

The words whirled in his mind. What should he try to say? What would come out?

"I n-nneed to mmm . . ."

The woman "tsked" and probably thinking it was a prank call, hung up.

David pressed the receiver down and tried again. Feeling even more pressure than before, his stutter worsened and he couldn't utter a single word.

Calm down! he thought, but frustration made him unable to speak. The operator hung up again. Slamming down the receiver and stepping out of the booth, David looked around. The streets were quiet and a quick glance at his watch told him it was the supper hour. He decided to go back to the café where he'd been that morning, reasoning that the cook there had been friendly and maybe someone would help him call home.

Crossing the street again, he began walking to the south end of town. Preoccupied with hunger and worry, he was startled by the opening of a heavy wooden door. Music, voices and cigarette smoke rolled out onto the sidewalk in a stream of light and warmth. Suddenly, a man hurling insults at the angry voices behind him came tripping out the door. He stumbled onto the sidewalk and fell hard, letting out a stream of curse words. He shook his fist at the door as it slammed shut, muffling the noise and cutting off the light. The street was quiet again, in the gathering dusk.

David stood silently watching the man, then tried to slip past without being noticed.

"Whatcha lookin' at?" the older fellow asked as he struggled to stand.

"N-nnothin'," David said casually. He'd chosen the street side of the sidewalk so he wouldn't be caught between the man and the building.

"Those bastards," the man swore under his breath as he reached into his pocket and pulled out a pack of cigarettes. "I'm not goin' back in there again."

David nodded.

"They don't want my money, then fine, I'll spend it some place else," the man slurred. "This ain't the only joint in town where a guy can get a drink."

Staggering slightly, he fumbled with a match. His hands shook and his brows furrowed in concentration as he lit the end of the cigarette. David wasn't sure if the man was drunk, angry or a combination of both.

He watched the small, thin man and wondered if he should be afraid. The gaunt face was covered by a recent growth of beard, mostly gray. The stranger's nose and close-set eyes made him look like a hawk which David found unsettling. Terrible at guessing ages, he decided this man was probably in his 40s. In the man's drunken state, outrunning him would be easy so David stood there, waiting for the man to say something else.

"Hawk-eyes" took a long drag on his cigarette, sucking the smoke deep into his chest and holding it for a long time before blowing it out. He coughed a little and then took another puff. This seemed to calm his nerves.

"You look lost," he said to David, appraising the teen quickly. "Where ya from?"

David was shocked. He didn't realize his predicament was that obvious.

"M-mman-itoba," he said.

"What's your name?"

"David."

"David, eh?" he said, taking a step closer and extending his hand. "Mine's Roy—Roy Hollingsworth."

David cautiously took the man's hand, surprised by the strength of the grip.

"Yeah, we get lots of lads from Manitoba comin' here," he said, letting go of David and taking another drag. "Lookin' for work, they are. You lookin' for work too?"

"Uh, y-yeah," he stammered.

Roy stood quietly finishing his cigarette. His eyes darted quickly from David's face to his arms and then his legs. He grunted when he'd finished scrutinizing the teen's six-foot frame.

"You come up to see me tomorrow morning," Roy said, dropping the butt on the sidewalk and stepping on it. "I got a job for you."

David stared at him in disbelief.

"W-wwhat?"

"I got a job for you," Roy said again as he turned and began walking down the sidewalk. "Come up and see me tomorrow."

"Okay," David replied, somewhat shocked. "W-wwait! W-wwere do you l-llive?"

"Well, up on the hill, of course!" Roy laughed, pointing ahead in the direction he was walking. "You come on up tomorrow and we'll talk."

David nodded and watched as Roy hobbled down the sidewalk out of sight.

David spent another night alone in the bushes. He awoke early, feeling tired and light-headed from hunger. Once a wave of nausea had passed, he stood up and began looking for the hill Roy had pointed to the night before. Since the town was in a valley and Roy had been a little drunk when giving directions, David had no idea which hill the man lived on.

Crossing the street in the cool morning air, David retraced his steps to the café. He entered to find the faces inside were becoming familiar. It was a good feeling for David who'd seen nothing but strangers for over a week.

The waitress yelled to the cook, "the guy who can't talk is back," and the man stuck his head out the kitchen door. "Yeah?"

"Uh, I'm l-llookin' for R-rroy H-hhauling W-wwood," David said.

"Did you say Roy?"

"Yeah."

"He lives up on the hill."

"W-what hill?"

The cook came out of the kitchen and wiping his hands on his apron, motioned for David to follow him across the restaurant. When they reached the front with the big window, the cook leaned across the table and pointed to a huge hill.

"See that road up there?"

"Uh-huh."

"Okay, you follow that to the top of the hill and you'll come to Roy's place," he said. "You can't miss it."

"Thanks," David said, hoisting his duffel bag over his shoulder.

The walk up the hill was long and difficult. Since he was from Manitoba, his hill climbing experience was limited to having to go over the occasional snow drift. His calves burned as he stopped to rest for a moment. He swung his heavy bag to his other shoulder and started up the hill again.

Cars and trucks passed, but no one stopped to offer David a ride. Too apprehensive to stick out his thumb, he pretended to know where he was going. His smile masked a fear deep in his gut. What if Roy was nothing but an old drunk who didn't have a job for him after all?

Pushing the thought from his mind, David paused as he reached the top of the hill and turned around. For the first time in days, he felt his heart lighten and a feeling of renewed faith swept over him. Overhead the sun shone brightly. Puffy white clouds drifted aimlessly across a deep blue sky. The light wind was a relief as it cooled his sweating brow.

The town lay stretched below him—long and narrow in a valley surrounded by hills and mountains. David stood there and listened to the sound of his breathing as he absorbed the crisp, clear beauty of the mountains. He had never seen anything like it before and the thought occurred to him that this was a place of opportunity. Anxious to reach his destination, he felt he should keep going, but his eyes were reluctant to leave this beautiful sight. He thought about Dennis and wondered what he would think about the mountains.

Trudging on, he soon reached the top of the hill and there, as the cook had promised, sat a house not too far away. It was a good-sized home with sheds, garages, a trailer and machinery all around it. David hurried his pace as he turned up the long driveway.

Stepping onto the front porch, he suddenly had the disconcerting thought that Roy might have forgotten meeting him the night before. He pushed the worry from his mind then knocked on the door. There was no answer and he leaned forward, straining to hear movement inside. Banging again, this time a little harder, he heard a woman's voice answer. Carefully, David opened the door and stuck his head inside.

"C'mon in," a woman called as she appeared from the back of the house. David could smell the excruciatingly wonderful scent of warm bread baking.

Nodding, he stepped inside and took off his boots.

"Roy's in the kitchen," she said, coming closer. "I'm his wife."

When she was in full view, David could see that Roy had married for reasons other than physical beauty. The woman, who stood as tall as David, looked as though she'd have no trouble putting in a full day's work herself. Dressed in blue jeans and a man's thick plaid work shirt, she was the most rugged woman David had ever seen. She had a kind voice, though, and David warmed to her immediately.

"You hungry?" she asked in a motherly tone.

"Yes, ma'am," he said, sounding just like Norman. He thought it would be wise to borrow some of his brother's charm.

"Well, I got fresh bread and tea," she said motioning for him to follow. "C'mon in and set down."

David followed her to the kitchen where Roy sat at the table, drinking tea from a mug. He looked up from his Saturday paper and gave David a wide smile.

"Good morning," he said. "You found your way up here I take it?"

"Y-yes, s-ssir," David replied, returning the smile.

"Set down," Roy said, pushing out a chair. "Mother, this here's the boy I was tellin' you about."

David sat down and looked around the kitchen. It was modestly furnished, cluttered, but seemed clean. David felt comfortable in these casual surroundings and the padded chair was a welcome relief to his stiff back. He noticed that Roy had shaved and looked a little younger in the bright, yellow-walled kitchen than he did on the street the night before.

Roy's wife set a loaf of bread and a large knife on the table along with a slab of butter. She gave David a cup and filled it with tea. Searching the table, he helped himself to a spoon in a jar beside the sugar bowl. The tea looked dark so he scooped in two spoonfuls of sugar before stirring slowly. He couldn't take his eyes off the bread.

"So," Roy said, laying the paper down, "you're lookin' for a job."

"Y-yes, s-ssir."

"Well, I'll tell ya," he began, taking a sip of tea, "I got the contract to widen the road around Canim Lake. It's a loggin' road an' it's lots of work."

David nodded, glancing up at Roy but his eyes fell again to the steaming loaf in front of him.

Roy seemed to notice and pointed. "There's plenty more where that came from—help yourself."

David cut himself a thick slice and slathered it with butter. Roy started describing the area around Canim Lake, but David was so engrossed in eating the bread he barely heard what was being said.

"I got a job for you, but you ain't gonna like it," Roy said loudly and in a matter-of-fact tone.

"I d-ddon't mind workin' h-hhard," David said, taking another bite.

"It's not just that," Roy answered after another sip of his tea. "The hours are long and the two guys you gotta work with are miserable. Been working for me most of their lives. Anyway, the job's dangerous, too. Like I said, you ain't gonna like it."

David smiled and shook his head in disagreement. He would have said something, but his mouth was full of bread. He remembered the worst job he'd ever had as a child. It was the fall after he and Dennis had turned 12.

Domko had planted a wheat crop that spring and when it was ready to harvest, he had asked the neighbours to come and bring equipment to bind straw into sheaves. It was a huge field to be harvested but after a few hours, the machinery broke down. The neighbours tried for two days but were unable to repair the equipment. They gave up and hauled the machinery home, much to the boys' disappointment.

When Domko had finished ranting about the neighbours' incompetence, he instructed the twins to scythe and tie the sheaves by hand. They were kept home from school and forced to work from sun up until dark every day for more than a week until the job was done. Domko stood by and supervised, not allowing them to rest or eat all day. They scavenged what food they could at night and as best they could, nursed the blisters and cuts on their bare feet and hands at bed time.

This job had been the most painful David had ever undertaken. By the time the boys were finished, the prickly straw had rubbed their calloused skin raw.

David shuddered at the memory.

"I'll d-do it."

"But you don't even know what the job is!" Roy laughed.

"Don't matter," he said, swallowing hard. "I done w-wworse."

Roy laughed. "You've done worse?"

"Yes, s-ssir."

"An' you think you know how to work, do ya?" Roy laughed again.

"I w-wwork good."

"Yes, but can you run?"

Now it was David's turn to laugh.

"Runnin's my m-mmiddle name!"

"Okay, then if you can work an' you can run, then we have a deal."

Roy looked at his wife, shook his head and smiled. If the boy worked half as well as he ate, then Roy would end up ahead on the deal. He waited until the loaf was gone before pulling on his boots.

"All right, let's go," he said, standing up. "I'll give you a ride back to town."

David jumped up and ran to the front room for his boots and bag. He put them on, darted out the door and ran around to the back, just in time to see Roy step outside.

"See!" he said. "Told ya I c-ccan r-rrun."

"Well, maybe you don't need a ride into town then! Maybe you'd just like to run?"

The smile left David's face and Roy burst into laughter.

"Just kiddin' ya boy," he said, pointing toward an old truck parked nearby. "Just kiddin'."

David climbed into the passenger side and gripped the door and dash as Roy backed up quickly. He put the truck in gear and sputtered forward.

Once they were on the road, Roy explained the plan for the day to David.

"Now, I want you to go into the dry goods store and get yourself some supplies," he explained. "Get yourself food that ain't gonna go bad—you know, rice, flour, sugar and stuff like that. Be sure you get toilet paper an' a writin' pad and pencil. An' get some soap . . ."

Roy could tell from the boy's face and hair that cleanliness had never been a priority. "You're gonna be up there a long time. You charge it up to me."

"W-wwhat?" David said, unsure of what he was supposed to do.

"I said, charge it up to me. Tell them my name an' they'll know what to do."

David nodded.

"We'll go out there this afternoon, but there's no point in goin' without food. It's a long ways," he said. He shook a cigarette out of the package he kept in the front pocket of his lined work shirt. "Get yourself some work clothes too. Get enough provisions for four months."

David nodded and watched out the window as the truck rumbled down the hill and into town.

"Good," Roy said, satisfied with the plan. "I'll pick you up at four in the afternoon. I got a few more things to do before we head out."

"Okay," David said.

Roy stopped the old truck in front of the local dry goods store.

"You go in there and get yourself what I told ya," he said. "Tell them to charge it to me. Got it?"

"G-ggot it," David said.

"You can leave your bag here."

David opened the door and got out.

"Wait," Roy hollered as David started towards the store. "aren't you even gonna ask what it is I'm gonna get you to do?"

David shrugged. "You g-ggonna f-ffeed me?"

"Sure, why?"

"Then it d-ddon't m-mmatter."

Roy chuckled. As he drove away he shook his head and wondered why David spoke in such an odd way.

David walked into the store and was instantly reminded of his home town. There were groceries stocked on one side and supplies and clothing on the other. He approached the counter and waited for the clerk to look up from what he was reading.

"Yes?"

"I'm s'posed to c-ccharge to Roy H-hhhauling W-wwwood," he said importantly, "for Canim L-llake."

"Roy Hollingsworth?" the clerk asked, smiling.

David nodded yes.

"Okay, go ahead," the man said, turning back to what he was doing.

Looking around, David was unsure where to begin. He started by picking up a big bag of rice and putting it on the counter. Slowly moving down the aisles he looked at everything and selected tea, sugar, ketchup, oatmeal, lard, salt and flour. He added a big bag of potatoes, a large bunch of carrots, margarine, bread, peanut butter, canned meat and a jar of pickles. He had the clerk cut a large hunk of bologna and some cheese as well. Looking the pile over, he hoped that this is what Roy had in mind when he said to buy food. The clerk rang the items through and stacked them in boxes.

Next David moved to the dry goods section. He'd discovered the joy of toilet paper while living at the trailer court with Norman—before that, he'd just gone in the bush and had never been taught about cleaning up afterwards. He grabbed the biggest package of toilet paper the store carried.

He also picked up a note pad, pencils, matches, candles, work pants, work shirts, socks, gloves, a toque and a pair of work boots. Satisfied that he had everything he needed, he started looking at items he knew he couldn't have. There were small toys and comic books on the shelves, displays of candy bars, soda, and ice cream in a freezer. He stared for a long time at the case with penny candy—so long that the clerk asked if he needed help. As much as he would have loved a treat, he didn't dare pick out a thing for fear Roy would get angry.

He paused at length to look at a coat, but wasn't sure if he would be taking advantage of Roy's generosity. He also wasn't sure if extra items would be deducted from his paycheque or not—Roy hadn't explained. He reasoned that if he was paying for it in the end, he might as well have a good coat. It was cold out and the last thing he wanted to do was freeze.

He found what he thought was his size, took it down from the rack and tried it on. Zipping it up, he gave himself a pat on the chest. Unbuttoning the pockets he put his hands inside and wallowed in the comfort of the big, warm coat.

Just then the store door opened and Roy walked in. As Roy chatted with the clerk, David quickly unzipped the coat and tried to replace it before Roy noticed. He turned around quickly, trying to act like nothing was out of place.

"What are you doing?" Roy asked.

"N-nnothin," David said nervously, looking at the floor.

"You're not stealin' anything are you?"

"No!" David exclaimed. "I'm not a s-sstealer!"

By the look on the boy's face, it was obvious that it bothered him to be called a thief. Glancing at the rack, Roy could see an empty hanger and a coat out of place—shoved into the pant shelf.

"You got everything you need?" he asked casually.

"Yep."

"Are you sure?"

David nodded yes.

"All right, then let's go."

David followed Roy to the counter and winced as his boss neared the big pile of provisions he'd picked out. Half expecting Roy to turn and yell at him, David braced himself and began to think of an apology for being so greedy. Instead Roy picked up one of the boxes and pulled open the door.

"I'm surprised at what you bought," he said. "When I send most young guys for provisions, they buy candy bars and soda."

David beamed. He lowered the bag of flour he was carrying into the truck box.

"I like f-ffood," he exclaimed, following Roy back into the store. "I like c-cccandy bars too, but I l-llike f-ffood better."

Roy smiled and then motioned for David to pick up the rice. He lifted another box high on his shoulder and they left the store again.

"Did you buy yourself a coat?" Roy asked.

David shook his head shyly that he hadn't.

"What?" Roy asked. "I'm not gonna be payin' you good money so that you can stand around shiverin' all day. Now go back and pick one out."

David dropped the rice bag beside the supplies in the truck box and hurried back into the store. Roy followed. Pretending he was interested in items at the end of the aisle, Roy watched as David ignored the rack and instead of taking a coat from a hanger, picked up the one he'd tried to hide. Roy smiled. The boy had been just admiring it after all. Turning, he quickly made his way back to the counter.

"Got it?" he said asked gruffly as David appeared.

"Yes, s-ssir."

"Okay, mark it down," he said to the clerk, "now let's get going."

❖

Chapter 8

"I REALIZE THAT YOU'VE HAD a traumatic childhood," McMillan said. "Your brother told me a lot about your lives when he was in here."

"An' he passed the test, didn't he?" David noted.

"Well, I'm not allowed to discuss another's test results," he said. "That's confidential."

"Well, he said he passed," David argued. "He must've, otherwise, you'd have locked him up, r-rright? You guys are always ac-cusin' us, so if he passed, then I must be in-nocent, too."

McMillan waited until David's rant was over.

"So, I know what you don't like about people," McMillan said. "What do you respect the most in a person?"

"Par-don?" David asked.

"What character traits do you respect the most in a person?"

"Re-sspect the most?" he asked. "I re-sspect guys who give us a chance. Guys who look at us an' don't just write us off like a piece of garbage."

The ride to Canim Lake in Roy's old truck was long and arduous along a narrow, twisting, muddy road. The old beast groaned its way up the mountain side and Roy rode the brakes most of the way down before beginning another climb. The truck jolted each time he shifted gears and they jammed hard before catching. The roar of the interior heater drowned out all other sounds. David found it oddly comforting listening to the noise and feeling the warm air on his face. He kept looking out the back window to check on the supplies that were bouncing around in the truck box. Roy noticed his preoccupation and glanced in the rearview mirror.

"Smart boy," he chuckled. "Didn't buy eggs."

David smiled. "I s-ssee why you d-ddrive here in the d-ddaytime," he said, peering out his window at the guard rail that offered peace of mind but no real protection from the 100-foot drop on the other side of it. David rested his head on the window and closed his eyes.

Roy was astounded by the boy's lack of concern about the steep inclines and the absence of a shoulder on the road. It was obvious that one miscalculation and they'd slide down the side of the mountain. Most boys held on and chatted nervously, but this teenager barely noticed. Roy wondered where the kid had come from. He guessed that life must have been pretty hard since he seemed to have no fear of the unknown.

"How old are you, David?" he asked over the roar of the heater as he lit another cigarette.

"Fif-teen," David mumbled, and then his eyes slowly opened, "but I'll be s-ssixteen in F-ffebruary."

"How long you been away from home?"

"Since s-ssspringtime."

"How'd you get way out here?"

"My brother," he said. "But we's be gettin' into a f-ffight an' he k-kkicked me out."

Roy laughed. "Where is he now?"

"Dunno," David answered.

"What about your parents?" Roy asked, inhaling deeply and filling the cab with smoke. "They know where you are?"

"My dad's d-dddead . . . an' M-Mom's on the f-fffarm," he said. It was hard for him to explain without Dennis there to add words.

"The ol' bastard . . . . he's got n-nnobody to shmash now. Denny's at Brays'."

Feeling like he'd missed half the conversation, Roy was quiet for a few minutes.

"Who's Denny?"

"My b-bbrr-rother," he smiled. "Me an him's like lookin' in a m-mmirror."

"He's not the brother who brought you here?"

"No, that's S-Stephen," he said.

"What's your last name?"

"Pischke."

"Pisshkee?"

David nodded.

This kid is naive as hell, Roy thought, realizing the boy had no idea about the roughness of life in a bush camp. Some men were up there because they didn't fit in anywhere else. The boys in the camp were often escaping a bad situation at home. Sometimes, the younger boys became the objects of an older man's desire—causing problems. It had chased more than one kid home and cost Roy some good workers.

The two drove a few more miles before David started giggling to himself.

"What?" Roy asked.

"I thought your n-nname was H-hhhauling W-wwood," David said with a wide grin.

"Where'd you get that from?"

"Dunno, just how I heard," he said, remembering someone making a joke about traditional Indian names. "I thought m-mmaybe you was an Indian."

Roy threw back his head in laughter. The pair enjoyed the joke, chuckling for a while, before Roy's tone turned serious.

"You don't have anything against Indians do you?" he asked.

"Oh no!" David said quickly. "Any I m-mmet is g-ggood . . . it's the Polacks I don't l-llike."

Roy snickered and shook his head. "Yeah, well, it'll be best if you keep that to yourself, all right?"

David nodded and turned to stare out the window again.

It was dusk when they arrived at the camp deep in a valley. David had dozed in the truck and awoke to hear Roy's gravelly voice. He jumped out of the truck and was immediately overwhelmed by the sound of rushing water. Grabbing an armful of supplies, he closely followed his boss.

"What's that n-nnoise?" David asked, looking all around.

"Waterfall," Roy said, as he paused at the doorway of an old trailer. "You'll get used to it."

Balancing a box on his knee, he turned the knob on the trailer door. "We don't keep it locked 'cause there's nothin' to steal."

David nodded and followed him into the dark, musty interior.

Roy lit a kerosene lantern that quickly illuminated the room.

"This here is your place," he said.

David brightened as he put the box he was carrying on the table. "It ain't no ch-chicken coop."

Taking the comment as a strange compliment, Roy shrugged.

The pair went back to the truck until all supplies were in the trailer.

"The last guy who was here needed to get out," Roy said. "Been here since spring. He was gettin' a little bushed."

David nodded in understanding.

"There's wood for the cook stove piled outside and you can get water from the stream," Roy said, pointing at everything as he spoke. "There's a crawl space below where you can store stuff that needs to be kept cold. It might freeze later on, but that's the chance you'll have to take."

David glanced at the small door on the floor and shuddered. It reminded him of the crawl space at home.

"You get settled and I'll be by first thing in the morning," Roy continued. "We get goin' pretty early."

David nodded, and then timidly looked at all the provisions on the trailer floor.

"Is this f-fffood all for m-mme?" he asked.

Roy nodded that it was. "I guess I don't have to tell you to pack a lunch, now do I?" he laughed.

"No, s-sssir!"

"Well, I'll see you tomorrow," Roy said, pointing as he opened the door. "My trailer's over there."

The door shut behind Roy and David immediately began digging through boxes to find the food he'd been dreaming about the entire ride from 100 Mile House.

He chattered to himself in anticipation as he pulled bread from a bag and made three big bologna and cheese sandwiches. He sat at the table and ate them while surveying his surroundings.

The trailer was one big open room. Half of it was a kitchen, with cupboards, an old wood cook stove, a table and chairs. The other half was a living area with a few easy chairs and a vinyl-covered chesterfield that unfolded into a bed. There was a table in the living area and a stack of old blankets were piled on a chair. A rusted oil heater sat in the middle of the trailer along the back wall.

When David finished his sandwiches, he began organizing his thoughts on how to keep house. First he lit the oil heater before unpacking the rest of his supplies. He put the food in cupboards and stacked the boxes and paper in a corner so he could use them to light a fire in the cook stove.

There were pots on top of the stove and he noticed that they contained the remnants of a meal. His nose wrinkled as he smelled the crusty contents. Picking up the pots, along with a few empty whisky bottles, he opened the trailer door and put them outside on the stoop.

The roar of the waterfall filled his senses and he stood for a few minutes outside listening to the sound of water rushing past. He was anxious for morning so that he could see what was making that magnificent noise.

With his hunger satisfied it suddenly occurred to him that he was thirsty. Lifting a pail that sat by the door, he slipped on his boots and stepped outside. He carefully made his way across the slippery, snow-packed ground toward the sound of the rushing water. He glanced over his shoulder many times before he reached the river bank. His eyes slowly adjusted to the darkness.

The unfamiliar surroundings looked a bit threatening. What he could see didn't frighten him as much as the pounding of the rushing water. The noise overtook his senses, leaving him feeling vulnerable. Shaking, he dipped the pail and turned to go back. The lamp shining through the kitchen window of the trailer was a welcome sight. Off in the distance he could see lights dotting the valley—an indication that more trailers and bunkhouses were nearby. He made his way back to his new home and opened the door to find that it had warmed up nicely.

He poured himself a glass of water and sipped it as he stacked his new clothes on the table in the living room. Turning the heavy, padded chesterfield, he positioned it so that he'd be able to see the oil heater without turning his head during the night.

Pulling the top towards him, it unlatched and he was able to lay it flat to make a bed. He spread out blankets and, satisfied that it was late enough to go to sleep, blew out the kerosene lamp. He slid between the blankets fully clothed and studied his surroundings for awhile until he was oriented to the dark. It was a habit he'd acquired after being attacked by his stepfather while asleep. When he finally did close his eyes, he had an escape route mapped out—just in case.

The next morning David woke early. He changed his clothes, leaving the dirty ones in a heap in the corner. He put on clean pants from his duffel bag, pulled on a new pair of thick socks and one of the new flannel shirts he'd bought the day before. He touched his arms gingerly. He liked the smell of new clothes and kept sniffing his shoulder and cuffs as a reminder that he was wearing something store-bought.

He made porridge for breakfast and ate quickly. He wasn't sure how early "early" was, and didn't want to be late. He made himself a large lunch and packed it in the cloth sack he had brought along in his duffel bag. He pulled on his new work boots and thought about wearing his new coat, but decided to save it for colder weather. He slipped on his leather jacket and stepped outside.

The sun was not up yet but he could see its glow in the sky behind a mountain top to the east. To the west was the base of the waterfall—less than 50 yards from his trailer. Huge trees towered over the little trailer which was nestled in a small alcove against the mountain. He could easily see the waterfall through two big cedar trees that acted as buffers to the spray and noise. He estimated it was a 50-foot drop and shuddered at the thought of plummeting over from the top.

He was astounded by the beauty of this place. Stepping down from the stoop, he walked toward the wide stream that flowed by the edge of camp. The water was clear to the bottom. It was then he realized that it was more of a stream than a river and that the waterfall was not too terribly big. Gazing up, he guessed that the noise was amplified by the sound bouncing off the mountain walls.

He looked around camp for a while, then went back to wait on his stoop. He wasn't there long before Roy's truck appeared, with the little man driving and a passenger in the cab. Stopping at David's trailer, the pair got out and he was introduced to his new supervisor.

"When I'm not here, you take orders from Tom," Roy said, motioning for David to follow them to the next closest trailer. "The guys you're working with live here."

Just then the door to the trailer opened and two older men stepped out. They grunted at Roy and eyed David suspiciously. Introductions were made, but David immediately forgot their names. He was frightened by their scruffy appearance and unfriendliness. David rode with these men in the back of the truck, in silence, to the work site up the mountainside. When they arrived, Tom explained to David that they were widening the current road so that it would accommodate logging trucks traveling to the sawmill at 100 Mile House.

To do this, they were having to chip off part of the mountainside. David's job was to dynamite the area and then clear away boulders, stumps and debris. Sometimes this was done with the caterpillar tractor, bulldozer and loader. Sometimes it was done by hand. David was pleased to discover that the job paid even better than Ramsey-Bird. He was anxious to get started.

During that first week, Roy and the supervisor felled trees and showed David how to drill holes for the dynamite. He was also trained to operate the equipment and the two bosses took him ahead to explain plans for the rest of the road. They worked from daybreak until dark, six days a week.

Before Roy and the supervisor left the three of them to work alone,

David had a solid understanding of the job at hand. He began taking the lead and oddly the two older men didn't seem to mind him giving them instructions. He discovered they were bachelor brothers who had been working in the bush most of their lives. They never smiled, seldom spoke and worked slowly. David sometimes found himself becoming impatient with their dawdling, but was thankful they weren't nasty to him.

One afternoon, the trio had cleared up to a spot where it was obvious they would have to blow up a huge piece of rock. Up to this point, David had only watched Roy do it. He was excited about having the chance to light the dynamite himself.

He was a diligent, fast worker who didn't stop for a rest until a job was finished. He quickly hammered cylinder-shaped holes into the rock face as he'd been shown. Taking the sticks of dynamite, he inserted them in the holes while the brothers sat and watched. After checking he'd done it right, he pulled a small box of matches out of his pocket.

"You guys ready?" he asked as he lit the match. Tentatively, he held it to the first fuse until it began burning and then to the second. Confident that both were lit, he turned and began running.

"C'mon, let's go!" he yelled as he ran past the old brothers plodding down the road. David was a good distance from the dynamite before he realized he was running alone. Glancing over his shoulder, he could see the men struggling slowly toward him, their faces strained with effort as they hobbled along the frozen mud road.

"Run!" David yelled, helpless to do anything more than yell. Suddenly, sensing they were out of time and with few places to hide, the brothers veered off the road and took refuge behind a rock pile. David continued running then darted off the road and crouched behind a tree. He covered his ears and waited.

The explosion was deafening as it ripped through the mountainside, sending rocks of all sizes in the air. The next sound was of stone hitting stone as the flying rocks landed and bounced along the road and down the mountainside. David waited until all was quiet before emerging from behind his tree.

His heart pumped hard as he ran back up the hill. Dodging rocks, he made his way to the brothers' hiding place. Slowly, one brother looked out from behind the rock pile and then stood up. He brushed himself off and then the other brother appeared. Relieved that they were not hurt, David stopped and sat down for a moment to regain his composure and calm his nerves.

The brothers, still panting, came down the road and scolded David for not giving them fair warning.

"Just 'cause you run like a jack rabbit, don't forget that we're just a bunch of old goats," one said. David apologized profusely.

When he was alone, he laughed at the memory. It was the first time the men had ever spoken to him and the quickest he'd ever seen them move, too.

Later that afternoon they prepared to blast a piece of rock that had survived the first try. David sent the men a quarter mile down the road to wait by the equipment. From that day forward, he ignited the dynamite by himself.

David was thankful the work days were long because it helped quell some of the loneliness he felt in the evening. The other men would get together to drink, play cards and talk about women. David participated for awhile, but lost money playing poker and felt that he had nothing to add to the conversations about women.

When the men started looking for extra potatoes for the mash for their home brew, he quickly slipped away, not wanting to donate his food for their alcohol. He spent most nights alone in his trailer, writing letters to Dennis and his mother. He also daydreamed about what to do with his money when he left Canim Lake.

Over Christmas, Roy made a trip back to 100 Mile House and David asked his boss to bring him a calendar when he came back. Roy did and David crossed off each day. He was consumed with the promise of spring and the day he could leave the beautiful, but lonely place.

Near the end of January, while walking back to his trailer at dusk, David noticed a light coming from inside. Smoke curled from the chimney into the cold, still evening sky. Panicking, David immediately thought that Roy must have given his trailer to someone else!

Worried that he'd done something wrong and had been fired, David started running toward the trailer to retrieve his belongings. He was thankful to be wearing the big, warm coat which he'd carefully guarded since the day he got it. A few of the men had made snide comments that Roy didn't buy them a coat—and he was fearful that someone would steal it. Hurt, he wondered why Roy would do this to him.

Hurrying up the steps, the thought suddenly occurred to him that maybe someone was robbing him. What should he do? Looking around, he realized that he was the only man out on this cold night and suddenly felt vulnerable.

He hadn't made a plan for a situation like this. Listening at the door, he could hear the intruder going through the cupboards, probably looking for his money! Well, they wouldn't get that—he'd made arrangements for Roy to deposit it in a bank account at 100 Mile House. The very little money he did have was in his pocket.

Glancing back at the rest of the camp, he saw the old bachelor brothers walking slowly to their trailer. The sight of them was a bit of a relief. While they never spoke to him, David felt they didn't dislike him and would come to his aid if he was in serious trouble. He waved, and when confident that he had their attention, burst into the trailer ready for a fight.

There, standing by the stove, was Dennis.

The smell of boiling potatoes and roasting luncheon meat filled the trailer. The two stared at each other for a moment before speaking. Then, as usual, they spoke at once.

"Denny!"

"Davey!"

David shut the door and hurried toward his brother. "How'd you get here?"

"I took the bus," Dennis said proudly.

"The bus? The bus don't come here," David quizzed.

"No, I took the bus to 100 Mile House an' then asked where the camp was. I started walkin' an Roy picked me up an' gave me a ride. When I got here, I saw your trailer right away."

"How'd you know?"

"The waterfalls, 'member? You told me in the letters."

David laughed with delight. He'd written Dennis and told him all about the place, with no thought that he would come.

"What about Brays?" David asked. "Don't they need you?"

"I'm only gone for a while," his brother answered. "I told them I'd be back in the springtime to help with chores. They knew I wanted to take a little trip an' so they got another guy until I get back."

"How long are you stayin'?"

"Dunno. When are you goin' back?"

"Prob'ly end of February."

"I can stay 'til then."

"Good," David said looking around the kitchen. "What you cookin'?"

Dennis smiled broadly. "You said you ran out of meat so I brought some."

"You brought meat!" David exclaimed. "I can smell it."

"Yeah, but only a little."

"What is it?" David said, sniffing the air around the stove.

"Klik®."

David smiled. “I love Klik®!”

“I know,” he beamed. “An’ I cooked up the last of the potatoes.”

“Good, we’ll have a cel’bration supper!”

Turning back to the stove, Dennis started fussing over the meal. Taking an old sock that David was using for an oven mitt, he opened the stove to check the meat.

“Crystal taught me to cook,” Dennis said, referring to the woman of the house where he’d stayed the past few years. “But she got an ‘lectric stove, not like this old devil.”

As they ate, the brothers chatted about what each had been doing for the past two years. David noticed that Dennis had matured and concluded that living with the Brays had been a good experience for his brother who had been allowed to regularly attend school and Jehovah’s Witness meetings.

The Brays were clean, honest people and David felt a bit envious as he looked at his twin who seemed more tidy and refined than the last time they were together. David felt conscious of his own grubby appearance.

That was soon forgotten though. His mind whirled with excitement as he thought about the prospect of Dennis living with him again. He began making plans for the rest of the winter.

“I’ll talk to Roy t’morrow an’ see if you can work too,” David said.

“I was gonna ask him, but I was too scared,” Dennis confessed.

“Yeah, Roy’s got a growly voice, but he’s a good guy,” David assured his brother.

“He won’t mind?”

“’bout what?”

“Me livin’ here too.”

David hadn’t thought about that. After all, Dennis was eating food that Roy paid for and would be living in the trailer for free. “I’ll ask him,” he said.

“What if he won’t let me?”

“He will.”

“What if he won’t?”

“Then you can go live next door,” David joked.

“What? With those two old guys?”

David laughed. As they sat down to eat, David updated Dennis on all the happenings since the last letter he wrote. He felt like a real grown up as he talked about his job and the people he worked with. He was also very proud of the trailer and the fact that he could provide a place for his brother to stay.

They talked late into the night, stoked the fire and then crawled between the blankets on the fold-down chesterfield. Both had slept alone for more than a year and a half and it seemed odd, yet comforting, to feel each other's warmth again.

The next morning they awoke and cooked oatmeal for breakfast.

"The food is gettin' low," Dennis said, shaking the bag to get a sense of how many more breakfasts were inside.

"I know."

"What happens if we run out?"

"Well, that all depends if Roy's goin' into town. I think I gotta pay for my food now, an' I don't wanna buy too much. I heard rumours that we'll be gettin' laid off pretty soon."

Dennis nodded. "Well there's still lots of rice and ketchup."

"An' that's good," David said. "'specially together."

"Yeah, when everything's done we can eat that."

"Sure."

Their conversation was interrupted by a rap at the door and the turning of the door knob. David quickly unlocked the door. Roy stepped inside. Glancing around the trailer, he noticed Dennis and smiled.

"So David you glad to see your brother?"

"Yes, s-ssir," he answered.

"I'm guessing this isn't the brother you fight with?"

"No, this is D-dd-dennis," David said.

" . . . an' he be Stephen—the one we fights with," Dennis said.

"Well, I can see that you're twins," Roy said. "I saw Dennis on the road and thought it was you, David."

"But how could you think that?" Dennis joked, pointing to the nail on the wall where their coats hung. "He's got that nice coat, an' look at me."

Dennis' old two-tone blue poly-filled coat was dirty, too small, with worn-out elbows.

"An' look at what I'm w-wwearin'," David bragged. His brown, canvas-type coat was down-filled, double stitched and had a corduroy collar and quilted hood. "Big shot, eh?"

"Yeah, big shot!"

Roy listened in amazement as the brothers finished each other's sentences in quick, chirpy tones that seemed to be fueled by each other's presence. Roy struggled to understand what they were saying and was amazed by the change in David. Alone, he was quiet and calm, but the boy became surprisingly extroverted when his twin was there.

Roy laughed at the interplay.

"We was w-wwonderin' if you got any work f-ffor Dennis?" David asked, tone serious.

Roy cringed. He'd come to the trailer to tell David that he'd be getting laid off in a month. Hiring someone else, when guys were starting to get laid off, was bad for employee morale, especially since he hoped some of the guys would return to work for him again.

"Actually, boys, the work is winding down and David, you'll be getting laid off soon," he said. "I don't have anything for Dennis to do right now."

"That's okay," David said quickly. "It's all right if he s-ssstays?"

"Sure, no problem."

"Thh-anks."

The next four weeks passed quickly. The days were growing a little longer and it was pleasant for David to return to a warm trailer in the evening. Dennis did the cooking, cleaned up and washed their clothes in the stream.

Just days before they were scheduled to leave, David stopped Roy in front of the trailer and asked him what he should do with his money. Mentioning that he and Dennis would be catching the bus to Winnipeg, he said he didn't want to carry his cash on the bus. Roy suggested wiring the money to Manitoba, and they decided to send it to the Ashern bank.

"How much money are you going to need for the trip?" Roy asked.

"For t-tttwo bus tickets an' s-ssome f-ffood," David said.

"Okay, I'll do up your last paycheque tomorrow and keep some back for your bus tickets" Roy said. "How does that sound?"

"G-ggood," David nodded.

"I think the bus leaves on Saturday afternoon," he said. "You can catch a ride out of here that morning."

"You can't take us?" he asked.

"No, I have to go tomorrow morning to get the payroll," Roy said. "And there's clean up that needs to be supervised here over the next few days. I won't be goin' back until next week."

"Oh," David replied, disappointed. He stood looking at Roy and realized how much he was going to miss the man.

They both stopped talking to listen to the sound of an approaching car. They watched until the vehicle came into view. The lights on the top indicated that it was a police cruiser. The car bumped along the rough camp road. It stopped for a moment and the officer rolled down the driver's window and spoke to a worker standing at the far end of the camp. The man pointed to Roy and David who, by now, were curious about what the police wanted.

The car drove up to the trailer. Hearing the engine, Dennis stopped what he was doing and opened the door to see what was going on. The officer turned off the motor and got out. Glancing at his note pad, he paused a short distance away before speaking.

"I'm looking for David and Dennis Pischke," he said.

"W-wwe be them," David said. "W-wwhy?"

"I have a few questions I'd like to ask the two of you."

The twins looked at each other. David's face turned scarlet with embarrassment. He was ashamed that Roy would see them being questioned by the police. It reminded him of the many times they'd been blamed for stealing things that either their stepfather had stolen or forced the children to take. Dennis pulled on his boots and followed his twin to the police car.

"Where were you last Saturday night?" the officer asked.

"We w-wwas here," David said.

"Can you prove it?"

David looked shocked.

"Because," the officer began, "we've had a complaint that a Caterpillar tractor owned by a Mr. Charles Ratz was vandalized in the Moosehorn area of Manitoba. Do you know anything about that?"

The twins shook their heads.

"We b-bbeen here the whhh-hole time," Dennis said.

"When the vandalism was reported, the RCMP in Ashern were told that you boys were in the area and that you'd fled to B.C. afterwards."

The brothers were astounded.

"R-rrroy," David called out. "Me an' Dennis we be here, r-rright?"

Sensing the trouble in David's voice, Roy approached.

"What's the problem, officer?" he asked.

"Who are you?"

"This is my outfit and I've been David's employer since November," Roy said, annoyed. "Why?"

"Can you vouch for their whereabouts last weekend?" he asked, pointing to the twins.

"Certainly," Roy said. "They were here. Where else would they be?"

"There was some vandalism in Moosehorn, their home town, and an eyewitness said it was them."

"Then that person had better get some new eyes," Roy said, "'cause both of these boys were here, I can guarantee that."

"You're sure?"

"Well, where else are they gonna go?" Roy said sarcastically.

"They've got no car, no way out of here and certainly haven't had the time to get from here to Manitoba, back again and put in a full week's work."

"Well, we're just checking," the officer said. "We have to follow up all leads."

"I'd say this one's a little ridiculous, don't you think?"

"I had no way of knowing that they've been here all winter," the officer said. "As far as I knew, they committed the offense then skipped the province."

Roy could see the officer's point, but the twins were still insulted that they'd been questioned.

"Who said it was us?" Dennis asked.

"I'm not sure," the officer answered. "The only thing I know is it was someone in the area who knows you boys and your reputation."

"What r-rreputation?" David asked.

"For getting into trouble," he said.

"What?" they said simultaneously. "When?"

"I don't know," the officer said defensively. "All I know is that I was told to question you."

"We n-nnever did n-nnothin," David stammered. "People think we's bad 'cause of Domko, but we n-nnever did n-nnothin' wrong."

The officer looked confused.

"Are you satisfied with what we've told you?" Roy interrupted.

"Yes, I think so," he said, brows furrowed.

"Good," Roy said walking the officer toward his car. "I don't know what your sources have said, but I haven't had a bit of trouble with these boys. I wish I had more workers like David."

The officer nodded. "Sorry to trouble you."

A few days later, David and Dennis said good-bye to Roy and hitched a ride to 100 Mile House with a truck driver. When the twins mentioned where they were going, the driver asked if they were traveling by train or bus.

"By b-bbus," David said.

"Bus? Really? How come you don't just take the train?" he asked.

"Dunno," David answered.

"It's faster and just as cheap," the trucker said. "Personally I don't like riding on either, but given the choice, I'd pick the train any day."

"Oh," David said, looking at his brother. "How c-ccome?"

"Well, like I said, it costs the same and it's a lot faster," the driver continued. "You'll be sitting on the bus for what seems like a week, but it only takes a couple of days by train."

"Only two?" Dennis asked.

"Yeah, something like that. And another good part about the train is the dining car where you can eat all you want."

"Really?" the twins chimed.

"Yeah. On the bus you have to wait for scheduled stops and places rip you off 'cause they know you don't have a choice."

Dennis nodded that the trucker was right. The bus had taken a long time and the food along the way was more expensive than at home.

"And on the train there are sleeping cars where you can lie down. You go to bed at night and you're halfway home by the time you wake up. Yep, if you can't afford to fly, the train is the way to go."

The twins discussed the issue quietly and made their decision.

"We w-wwanna go by train," David said.

"All right, well you'll have to take the bus to Prince George first," the trucker said. "Then catch the train from there."

The twins looked at one another. The idea of free food on the train was too tempting to resist.

"We don't care," David said. "We w-wwanna take the t-ttrain."

"Okay, I'll drop you guys at the bus station, and you tell them you want to go to Prince George," he said.

David nodded in understanding.

They pulled into town just before noon and the driver swung his rig toward the bus station. Thanking him for the ride and the advice, the twins waved good-bye. Hoisting their duffel bags over their shoulders they walked into the bus station.

They stood for a few minutes looking around before it became obvious where the tickets where sold. Dennis sat down with their bags while David got in line. He worried what he'd say to the woman behind the wicket and played it over in his mind so he wouldn't get mixed up.

"May I help you?" she asked.

David stepped forward.

"T-ttwo tickets for Pr-rince George," he said.

"One way or return?"

"One w-wway," David said, handing her his wad of cash. She counted out the money and gave him the change. "You can board at gate three in 10 minutes."

Soon they were on their way to Prince George. They got off at the train station and David stood in line once again to buy tickets.

"May I help you?" the woman behind the counter asked.

"T-ttwo tickets for W-wwinnipeg," he said.

"One way or return?"

"One way," David said.

"First Class or Coach?"

David shrugged.

"What c-ccosts less?"

"Coach."

He nodded, handing her the rest of his money. She rang in the sale, gave him two tickets and ten cents change.

David stared at the dime and then looked back at her.

"The train leaves at 1 a.m., but you can begin boarding any time."

David took the tickets and walked back to his brother who was sitting happily on a bench.

"You got 'em?" Dennis asked. "When do we leave?"

"Not 'til one in the mornin'," David complained. "An' they cost me all my money."

"What?"

"It took all my money."

"How come? The guy said it was the same!"

"Well, it's not."

They stood quietly for a moment, glancing out the train station window.

"How much money you got left?" Dennis asked.

"Ten cents."

Dennis winced.

"But it's okay," David said. "They got food an' a place to sleep on the train. So we don't got no more money left, but it don't matter."

Dennis shrugged. "I guess so."

The brothers waited all afternoon and evening in the train station. When it finally came time to board, they made their way to the loading ramp. Showing their tickets to the conductor they were pointed in the direction of the coach car they were to ride in. Excited about being on a train, they looked all around the inside of the car before taking a seat.

"So, where's the food?" Dennis whispered. "I'm hungry."

The conductor walked slowly through each car, checking passenger's tickets and answering questions. The brothers listened as he explained the rules of the dining car to a couple in front of them. It didn't take long for the twins to realize that the dining car was not free and neither were the sleeping bunks. The bunks were reserved for passengers with first class tickets. Everyone had to pay for their food.

They sat in stony silence as the train pulled away from the station. Looking out the window, they watched as the town disappeared from sight. The track paralleled the highway, and at times the winding road disappeared all together, only to appear again around a mountainside. Then they saw an eastbound bus accelerate, pass a long dark blue car on the highway, and disappear out of sight.

For the teenagers, the train ride to Winnipeg was torture. They had to sit for three days without food, smelling what was being served in the dining car and watching the people around them eating bag lunches. They had to sleep sitting up and David had a horrible fear that he'd lose his last dime.

When they finally did get to Winnipeg, they were grouchy as they approached a pay phone. Dennis used the dime to call their brother Walter.

Walter was living in Winnipeg and working as a pressman for Union Carbide where he imprinted plastic bags and other items. Known for his cheerful disposition, he arrived at the train station to pick them up.

"Hey boys!" Walter called as he waved, stepping out of his car.

The sight of his older brother reminded David of the time that Walter ran away from the farm as a youngster, only to be returned a week later by the police. He emerged from the back of the police car, stone faced, wearing new clothes and shiny rubber boots. He'd been taken in by a family named Ruchotzke and these people had treated him like a member of their own family. This gave Walter hope that life could be good. Beneath the flushed cheeks of a shy, awkward child, a steely determination had built.

The twins hurried to his car carrying their duffel bags.

"Hi, Walter," David said, relieved to see the familiar face. Walter had always been something of a father figure to him. He had dark hair, blues eyes and sharp features reminding everyone of Bill, their father, and this made David admire his older brother even more.

They drove across town to Walter's house where he was living with his new wife, Lorie Kirkland, originally from Plumas, Manitoba. On the way, Walter asked them about the trip and what it was like living in the bush camp.

David explained the work he did and brightened when he talked about the money awaiting him in Ashern. They told Walter about the long, arduous train ride and asked for something to eat the minute they stepped through the door.

"Yeah, all we ate the last few weeks was r-rrice with ketchup," David said.

". . . an' when we got tired of that, we had ketchup with rice," Dennis added.

Everyone laughed as Lorie made sandwiches. As fast as she put them together, the twins wolfed them down. Everyone listened as the teens retold the story of the terrible trip home.

"So boys, it sounds like quite the adventure," Walter laughed.

"It sure w-was," David sighed. "And I learned one th-ing for sure."

"What's that?"

"Truck d-ddrivers don't know n-nothin' 'bout trains."

Chapter 9

"**SO YOU LIKE PEOPLE WHO** are kindhearted, generous and trusting?"

"Yes," David said.

"I understand why you respect people who have given you a chance," McMillan said. "That makes a lot of sense."

David nodded.

"So do you have many friends?" he asked.

"Yes. I got lots of friends."

"Who is your best friend?" McMillan asked.

"My best friend . . . I dunno, let me think," he said. "Well, I wish I could say Dennis, but I can't. We've been fightin' our whole lives, off an' on. But we were gettin' along real good an' then this polygraph came up, well then, the fight was on."

"Why?" McMillan asked.

"Why?" he mimicked. "Why? Because all this Mike business brings back all the bad memories an' the times that we've been accused of things."

"What things?" the officer asked.

"Everything!" he said. "Anytime there was somethin' wrong, it was 'the Pischke boys' who did it. An' we never did, not once!"

"But what's that got to do with you and Dennis fighting?" he asked.

The twins had celebrated their 16th birthdays while in 100 Mile House. When they arrived back in Moosehorn, David asked his mother to take him to get his driver's licence.

They were told they could find the tester at the Moosehorn Hotel. They drove there and David went inside while his mother waited in the car.

David asked an employee where the tester was sitting. He approached the man who was sitting with a few others at a table.

"C-ccan I get my dr-river's licence?" David asked.

The man looked him over.

"How old are you?" he asked gruffly.

"S-sssixteen," David stammered.

"Did you drive here?"

David nodded that he had.

"Did you bring your birth certificate and an application with you?"

David reached into his pocket. He pulled out a folded wad that he handed over to the man. The fellow took it, unfolded it then slipped on his glasses.

"Hmmm," he said as he wrote across the bottom.

"There," he said, handing the papers back to David. "You got your licence."

David smiled as he left the smoky room.

That was easy, he thought.

At the beginning of April, Dennis went back to Brays' farm and David rode into the city with Norman. The pair resumed working on the floodway for Ramsey-Bird Construction.

Jack was happy to see the brothers, putting them to work again right away. They rented another trailer at the same park and after a week felt as if they had never left.

One Friday night in early July, David and Norman went around by Selkirk to pick up Sharon from work, then they drove to Moosehorn for the weekend. They spent the evening socializing with friends. The next morning, David asked to borrow Norman's car.

"It's gonna be my car soon," David chided. "Usually guys get at least one test drive."

Norman laughed at his brother's wit.

"Yeah," he conceded. "I guess you deserve to drive it at least once."

Norman handed his brother the keys with a warning.

"But don't bugger off for too long," he said. "Me and Sharon are going out later and I don't want to be looking all over for MY car."

"Yeah, okay," David said as he climbed into the driver's seat. "But it won't be yours for long."

David slowly backed out of the driveway and drove through town and onto the highway. He enjoyed the sensation of the wheel in his hands and a feeling of anticipation surged through him. Someday soon this car would be his!

He could hardly believe it. Just a year earlier he'd been stuck on the farm like a prisoner, working like a slave. How his life had changed. Now he was earning his own money and driving, too. His mind whirled with excitement as he followed the highway toward Grahamdale.

Remembering the way to the Bray farm, David turned off the highway onto a dirt road. Within a few minutes he saw the modest, tidy farm. David pulled into the driveway and a barking dog ran around the corner of the house.

"Hey, boy," he said, extending his hand as he got out of the car. "'member me?"

David walked to the door and knocked. Crystal Bray, a large-boned woman with dark hair, answered.

"Yes David?" she asked.

"Is D-dennis h-hhere?" he asked. They'd been separated for nearly six months but it felt like a lot longer.

"Yes, come on in," she said. "He's in the kitchen."

As David rounded the corner, he noticed that another man was visiting with Herman as Dennis sat passively at the table listening.

"David's here," Crystal announced and the men stopped talking. David suddenly felt very self-conscious interrupting their conversation and his eyes fell to the floor.

"H-hhi everyone," he said.

"Hey, David," Dennis exclaimed, jumping up from the table. "how are ya' doin?"

"Good, good," he said. "How 'bout you?"

"Good."

The twins made conversation with the men for a while and then Crystal suggested they move to the front room so they could talk privately. David followed closely behind Dennis.

"So you're workin' on the floodway?" Dennis whispered. "You still like it?"

"Oh, yeah, Denny, it's great," David said, his voice filling with excitement. "I got this great job. You should see me Denny, I'm drivin' these big road con-struction machines, all different kinds an' it's great work."

Dennis was impressed. "How much money do you make?"

"A hundred and fifty bucks every two weeks," David said proudly.

Dennis' mouth gaped wide, then he slowly repeated the figure.

"That's right an' guess what the best part is? I asked the boss if he needs anybody else, an' you know what he said? He said, 'If your brother works half as good as you do, then he can start on Monday.' Hear that Dennis? You can come work for Ramsey-Bird too."

"I can?"

"Sure, I can take you back with me today," David whispered. He hoped the Brays hadn't overheard because he didn't want to be the one to tell them. "We can stay in Moosehorn tonight then go to Winnipeg tomorrow."

Dennis was speechless. He knew that this time his departure would be for good.

"I gotta talk to Herman an' Crystal first," he said quietly. "They're gonna be sad I'm goin'."

"Sure, I get it," David said. "Oh yeah, do you got your licence yet?"

"Driver's licence?"

"Yeah."

"No, not yet."

"Crrrist, man, you're missin' out!" David said, sounding just like Norman. "We gotta get you a licence. I've got your birth certificate in my wallet—I took it when I got mine."

Dennis nodded cheerfully and asked David to wait outside while he told the Brays. As he'd expected, they were upset about his decision. They were sorry to see him go since he'd become like a son to them over the past two years. He was also hard-working and reliable.

Dennis packed his duffel bag and climbed into the car beside David. As the vehicle slowly backed out the driveway, Dennis waved goodbye to the Brays who stood together at the front room window. Looking back, Dennis could see Crystal crying.

"So, Denny, whadda ya think of this car?"

"It's great," Dennis said a bit distracted. "Is it Norman's?"

"Yeah, but I'm buyin' it," he said. "I already made a down payment an' I gave him some of my money from Canim Lake."

"How much money you got left?"

"A couple hundred."

"So, you an' Norman are gonna have cars to drive but I'm gonna have nothin'," he said.

"You don't even have your licence yet," he shot back.

Dennis thought for a moment. "Hey, I got an idea. How 'bout after I get my job, I can save up an' we can buy it together. We'd get it faster."

David was so excited about having his own car that he didn't want to share it with anyone—not even Dennis.

"We'll see," he replied.

That Sunday evening on their way to the city, Norman and Sharon dreamily discussed their future together while David and Dennis sat together in the back seat.

"How's Rosie?" David whispered.

"Not so good," Dennis said. "I went to visit Mom a little while ago and she begged me to come back. Rosie got so sick that they had to take her to the doctor."

"Who's doin' the farm work now?"

"I dunno, Rosie I guess," he answered.

David shuddered. There was far too much work for their sister. David knew from experience that one young girl could not handle the labour required for a farm of that size, especially one that had few modern conveniences.

"Poor Rosie," he said. "We're gonna have to get her away as soon as we can."

The brothers sat quietly for a minute as they remembered how difficult their lives had been.

"I'm never goin' back," Dennis said quietly. "Never!"

David nodded.

Norman turned into the service station at Ashern and got out to fill the tank with gas.

"An' Raymie's too little to help. How old is he anyway?" David asked.

"Six?" Dennis guessed.

"When's his birthday?"

"In April, I think."

David thought for a moment. "Mom hasn't brought any more babies home, has she?"

"Not that I saw," Dennis replied.

"Good," David said. "She don't need no more babies. Why do you s'pose she keeps bringin' 'em home from the hospital?"

"I dunno," Dennis answered. "Crazy I guess."

"She just can't leave one there," David said, remembering how two years earlier their mother had gone to the doctor because she wasn't feeling well and came home with baby Mark. "Maybe some other women will start takin' the babies home."

"What are you guys talking about?" Sharon asked. "Babies? Who's having a baby?"

"N-nnobody," David said.

Norman paid for the gas and they continued driving south. He and Sharon became immersed in their own conversation once again.

"Do you 'member when we picked up Raymie an' Domko said,

'He's be forty dollar—mooney out of but-a-some pocket'?"

The twins giggled.

"Yeah," Dennis said, "too much mooney."

"I wouldn't wanna pay $40 for Raymie either," David whispered.

They laughed.

"What's so funny?" Norman asked.

"N-nnothin," David said.

The twins rode for awhile in silence.

"So you're sure they're gonna want me?" Dennis whispered. "At work."

"Yeah, I think so," David said, tone serious. "An' if you can't get on right away, then you can stay at the trailer an' as soon as there's a spot, then you can start."

Dennis was having second thoughts about leaving the Bray farm.

"Maybe I shoulda got the job first," he said.

"Don't ya trust me?" David asked, his feelings clearly hurt. "I told ya what the boss said."

The next morning Norman dropped the twins off at the construction office and then continued on to his job site.

David was feeling confident about his abilities and his responsibilities at work. He wasn't nearly as shy as when he'd first started working there. He knew that his diligence was paying off since he was getting overtime shifts and the boss and foreman were kind to him.

He loved his job and felt he'd finally accomplished something in life. He wanted to be the conduit for helping Dennis to experience the same thing.

His heart raced at the thought of being able to do something truly worthwhile for a sibling. There would be a side benefit of course. For the first time in his life he would be a "big shot." A good job, lots of money, and he might just be able to show-off a bit.

Taking a deep breath, he stood up straight and puffed out his chest.

"Okay Dennis, follow me," he said. "An' let me do all the talkin'."

Dennis nodded and trailed closely behind his brother. Boldly, David opened the trailer door and stepped in, with Dennis stuck to his heel like a piece of chewing gum.

Looking around, David could see a few men standing at the end of the trailer, sharing a morning coffee and talking about what they'd done on the weekend. The boss was sitting behind his desk, reviewing plans for the week with a few men around him. The sun was streaming in the window, creating a kaleidoscope of colour across the top of the desk. Looking up, Jack McGuinness focused on David standing just inside the doorway.

"Morning, David," he said, smiling. "What can I do for you today?"

David's face turned bright red and his courage suddenly left him. Dennis' skinny body was totally hidden behind his brother and as he peered over his twin's shoulder the illusion made Jack blink and then chuckle to himself. It appeared that David had grown an extra, nearly identical head on his shoulder over the weekend.

"T-ttthis here's m-mmmy br-rrother Dennis," David stammered. "He's l-llookin' f-ffor w-wwwork, too."

Jack looked at Dennis whose eyes were on the ground.

"What experience do you have, Dennis?"

Dennis' face was pale as he shot a glance at Jack who had a gruff, straightforward way of speaking. He'd never been talked to like this before.

"H-hhe's d-ddone some f-ffarm work," David said, "just like m-mme."

"Dennis," Jack said emphatically, "have you ever driven heavy equipment before?"

The boy looked quickly at David and then back at the ground. "N-nnno."

By now everyone in the trailer had stopped talking and was listening to the brothers.

"Pardon?" Jack said.

"N-nnno, s-sssir," Dennis said a little louder. Jack couldn't believe it. They looked like identical twins—and they both stuttered. How on earth was he going to tell them apart?

Oh well, he thought, *that's why I've got a foreman.*

Standing up, Jack came around to the front of the desk. Instinctively, the twins took a step back in unison. Jack sensed he was frightening them and lowered his voice.

"Your brother David here is a good worker," he said. "Are you a good worker too?"

Dennis looked up from the floor and for the first time, Jack saw a glint of mischievousness in the boy. Dennis started to say something, but the boss interrupted him.

"You're better, right?"

The boys smiled.

"I've heard that story before," Jack laughed. "Okay, David have you told him the rules?"

"Y-yes s-ssir."

"Good," he said. "The guy we hired last week buggered off to go work for someone else, so I guess we'll hire Dennis. I take it you can start today?"

The twins nodded.

"Okay," he said, turning to George Rentz. "Take Dennis out and show him how to run the pump."

George nodded and put down his coffee cup.

Jack started toward his desk and then remembered something.

Turning he said, "No driver's licence, right?"

"N-nno, but I g-ggot *my* licence," David said proudly adding "we w-was borned at t-tthe s-same time."

"I gathered that," Jack chuckled.

"So he can just use mine," he offered.

The room erupted in laughter.

"Help him get his driver's licence, okay David?" Jack said, trying not to laugh.

The boy nodded and the brothers scurried out the door with a stream of chuckling behind them. When they were a few feet from the trailer, David turned to his brother and punched him in the arm.

"See! I told ya I'd get ya a job," he said.

George chuckled as he followed behind.

"Judas Priest!" he exclaimed. "I got both of them Pischke boys to look after now."

Dennis gave David a quizzical look.

"His wife is religious so he don't swear," David whispered. "He says that 'stead of Jeezus Crrrist."

Dennis nodded.

"I gotta go," David said as he waved to Dennis and trotted off. George took him for training on the job David did the year before.

David worked happily, knowing that Dennis was in the city and they were together again. He thought about how great this would be, especially since Norman was spending so much time with Sharon.

Besides, Norman and Sharon kissed and held each other which made David feel uncomfortable. He found himself dreaming about girls and the thought of having one close to him excited and confused him. He decided it was better to have Dennis around because then he didn't daydream so much and he wasn't as lonely.

At lunch time David drove his machine over to where Dennis was working, and shut off the engine.

"C'mon, let's go to the café," he said. "We gotta get a seat before Bryan gets there."

"Who's Bryan?" Dennis asked, as he followed David across the road. They hurried through the small parking lot to the café door.

Glancing over each shoulder, David was confident that they'd arrived before the bully.

"I tole you 'bout him," David said. "That mean guy."

"Oh, yeah," Dennis said.

David would have preferred a table in the corner, but they ended up close to the door of the café. The waitress came over and wiped the table. They studied their menus closely. She did a double take and then smiled.

"So what will you boys have?"

Still unable to converse with people he didn't know, David pointed to the dinner special. He said something unintelligible to Dennis.

"N-nno!" Dennis whispered back to his brother. "I d-ddon't want that."

The waitress waited as Dennis studied the menu further. He held up the laminated paper and pointed to a hamburger platter.

"To drink?" she asked.

"C-ccoke," David said, pointing first to himself and then at Dennis across the table.

She left and David leaned across toward his brother.

"Burgers are too slow!" he whispered. "The special's best 'cause it comes fast."

"But I want a burger," Dennis said. "I'm payin', so I'll get what I want."

"You're not payin! You don't got no money," David corrected.

Dennis thought for a moment. "Okay, well you're payin' then, but I'm the one whose gotta eat it."

"Yeah, well you'll find out," David argued. "I'll be all done an' leave you sittin' here for big ol' Bryan to pick on. You gotta eat and get out fast before he gets here."

Dennis scoffed.

The waitress brought their pop and then came back a few minutes later carrying a dinner special.

"Yours will be a few minutes," she said to Dennis as she put the plate in front of David.

"Told ya," he said under his breath.

The door to the cafe opened and a crew of workers entered. David surveyed the faces and quickly looked away. As the men filed past, Bryan was suddenly standing over them laughing.

"Holy shit!" he roared, pointing at the twins. "Will you look at this! There's two of them stuttering bastards."

He stood by their table waiting for the boys to look at him. The embarrassment was awful. David could feel his cheeks turn red and heat radiated from his ears. He felt certain that everyone in the café could hear his heart pounding. He continued eating, refusing to look up. Dennis studied the inside of his Coke glass.

"What's your name, boy?" Bryan asked, looking around the restaurant first to be sure Norman wasn't there. Confident he could pick on the twins without retribution, he gave Dennis a poke in the arm. "I'm talkin' to you."

"D-ddennis," was the whispered reply.

"DDD-dddddennnnnnnis," Bryan imitated. "So, DD-dddennniss, what's your momma think about havin' two retards in the shitsky family?"

Dennis was aghast. Over the years, his speech problem had caused him some embarrassment, but nothing as cruel as this. People had sometimes pointed and chuckled at the twins, but never before had he encountered a stranger so blatantly malicious and unkind.

The other men had seated themselves at a large table in the far corner. George came in last and gave Bryan a nudge as he passed him.

"C'mon," he said, "let the boys eat their lunch in peace. I need them to get back to work."

"Two of them," Bryan repeated as he followed George to the corner table. "I still can't believe my eyes."

David sighed and gave Dennis a disapproving look.

"I tole you!" he rasped.

"I didn't know," Dennis argued.

Glancing around, they could see strangers at other tables staring at them. The waitress arrived a few minutes later with Dennis' meal.

David finished his lunch a few minutes later and got up to go.

"Wait!" Dennis whispered. "What about me?"

"Bring it!" David scolded, reaching into a pocket to find a quarter for the waitress.

He walked to the cash register and asked the cashier to add the meals to his tab. Dennis unfolded a napkin and dumped his fries on it. He watched Bryan and the other men out of the corner of his eye as he wrapped the fries and then picked up his hamburger. He trotted out of the restaurant after David.

"Wait up!" he called. He wasn't sure what had angered his brother—him or Bryan.

David muttered profanities about the bully and how he wished he could make wisecracks back, but he knew the words would never come out quick enough. He directed a comment to his brother instead.

"Well, I didn't know!" Dennis yelled back.

David checked his watch.

"T'morrow we'll go in a bit earlier an' maybe we won't see him at all."

Dennis nodded as he bit into his hamburger.

The twins walked back to the trailer after finishing work that day. They had nobody to give them a ride the next morning so they walked to the job site. At 11:30 a.m. David signaled to Dennis and they once again trotted to the café. They surveyed the little restaurant for Bryan and then sat down quickly. They were served by the same waitress.

"Good morning boys," she said, "what can I get you today?"

David looked at the menu and pointed to the special.

"And how about you?" she said turning to Dennis.

"S-ssame," he answered. "An' f-fast."

Dennis' first two weeks of work passed quickly and he was quite proud the day he picked up his first paycheque. The twins cashed their cheques then gave their share to Sharon who was paying the bills. The brothers decided to go grocery shopping.

"Look at all this food, Davey," Dennis said, his eyes wide with wonder as they entered a grocery store.

He'd shopped in the small stores of Grahamdale, Moosehorn and Ashern, but had never been to a grocery store in Winnipeg. Taking a basket each, the twins started buying the things they wanted.

"Don't pick too much," David warned. "We gotta have enough to pay our café bill an' don't forget—we gotta carry it all back to the trailer."

Dennis laughed.

"It's food Davey—I can carry it!"

They bought chocolate bars, bananas, cake, cheese and a dozen cans of luncheon meat. When they got to the check-out, David handed over a big wad of cash for the cashier to count out. They each left carrying a brown paper bag. When they got to the highway, they put the bags down.

"I'm havin' a banana," David said. "An' I'm gonna eat more than the stub that ol' bastard used to leave me."

"An' I'm havin' a chocolate bar," Dennis said.

They stood and ate the banana and chocolate bar, discarding the garbage along the highway. They each picked out another snack and started walking. By the time they arrived back at the trailer, their stomachs were full and there was a trail of refuse littering the road behind them.

"The best part 'bout livin' here is I can eat whenever I want," David said.

"Yeah," Dennis agreed, sighing. "Isn't it great?"

Norman and Sharon got married that September. Everyone gathered at the Baptist Church in Moosehorn for the ceremony. Jalmar Erickson was asked to officiate.

Jalmar was a big, friendly minister with a jovial laugh. He never missed an opportunity to say a kind "hello," to friends and strangers alike. A jack-of-all-trades, Jalmar had done many jobs and performed countless hours of community work for families and organizations. He'd been a school bus driver and worked for the local funeral home. He performed many marriage, baptismal and funeral ceremonies.

He gave away most of his time and resources and devoted his life to helping others. In exchange, there was nothing he liked better than a good meal. Jalmar spent many hours smoking fish and preparing elaborate meals during the holidays. Anyone who had no place to go would attend. His home and his heart were always open.

Jalmar began the habit of greeting people whose first name he couldn't remember as "Mister" or "Missus." It had worked so well for him that as a prominent member of the community who didn't want to forget people's names, he started using it with everyone—whether he knew their first name or not. That way, nobody was ever offended.

"Hello, Mr. Pischke," he called out to David as they approached the church together. Jalmar grasped the young man's hand in his own. "Good to see you, my boy."

"Hi, Jalmar," David replied. He was glad this man was performing the ceremony as he wasn't overbearing or preachy. Jalmar was the only person David knew who could bring together Jehovah's Witnesses, strict Baptists, atheists and agnostics and deliver a sermon that didn't offend anyone. When someone asked what religion Jalmar preached, David replied, "the good one."

When the ceremony was over, a reception was held in Eric and Hilda Nachtigall's barn. Eunice was a bridesmaid and the 18 year old had been thrilled by the honour. She was dating a young man named Mel Bullerwell who was in the Canadian Armed Forces and stationed at the Gypsumville base, approximately 40 miles north of Moosehorn.

There were rumours that they, too, would get married. Mel was a nice man, although very quiet and difficult to get to know. Eunice, on the other hand, was vivacious and bubbly. It was never a secret what she was thinking. Eunice had blossomed into a lovely young woman and she and Mel made a very attractive couple in spite of their obviously different personalities.

Norman and Sharon's wedding reception brought the family

together for the first time since the older children had left home. It felt odd for David, especially with Domko and Caroline in the same room. David felt as though he hadn't yet been forgiven for abandoning his mother and the farm. He avoided meeting Domko's gaze

David was both shocked and dismayed to see his mother was holding a newborn baby. By this time he had overheard the men at work talking about sex and Norman had furnished the rest of the information in a lesson late one night. It was still a mystery to David how having sex could create a baby, though. Shuddering, he pushed the idea of his mother with Domko far from his thoughts. The sight of the new baby caused him to frown. Jennie, his half-sister, had been born just days before.

At only 42 years of age, Caroline looked tired. She'd borne eleven children and had had at least one stillborn birth in the past 23 years. When other people looked at Caroline, they saw a kind, patient, non-judgmental woman with simple tastes and few aspirations.

David, of course, saw someone else. He saw a mother he loved deeply and the woman who had been given the responsibility to nurture and care for him. But she'd become so overwhelmed with her own problems she had no energy left for the task. Caroline also had diabetes, a condition requiring daily insulin injections. He'd overheard other adults telling Caroline she should take better care of her health, but his mother had laughed off the suggestion.

Looking around the room, he saw his younger sister standing alone.

"Hey, Rosie," David called, "c'mere."

Rosie was shyly watching the other guests at the wedding and she welcomed the chance to talk to her older brother.

"How are you?" he asked.

"All right," she said quietly. "How 'bout you?"

"Good, good," he said. "I'm makin' big money workin' for Ramsey-Bird Construction. I got Denny a job there too," he bragged.

"Can ya get me a job?" she asked.

"You?" he said, trying not to sound too harsh. "I dunno. They don't got no work for girls."

"How 'bout cleanin'?" she asked. "I can clean good."

"Not much needs cleanin'," he said.

Rosie was clearly disappointed by this. David tried to reassure her.

"But I got an idea . . . as soon as I can, I'll come get you an' you can come live with me an' Denny," he said.

Rosie's eyes brightened. "When?"

"Well," he said, thinking, "how old are you?"

"I'm 13."

David winced. Thirteen was quite young. He wondered if it was called kidnapping if he took a child away from home without the parent's permission. He knew that Domko would never let her go willingly.

"I'll keep lookin' for a job for ya," he reassured. "An' whatever you do, don't tell Domko."

"I won't," Rosie said.

"Good," he smiled. "So how are the other kids?"

"Well, Kathy gets her own way an' Raymie makes Domko so mad now," she said, "sometimes he hits him."

David was shocked.

"Y-yyou're kk-kiddin', right?" he stammered. "He never got mad at Raymie before."

Rosie shrugged.

In all the years that David had lived on the farm, Domko had done nothing but praise his own children while beating the Pischke kids.

"An' Markie's just cute," Rosie continued. "Domko treats him like he used to treat Raymie."

"Has ol' Satan been to the hospital lately?" David asked.

"No, not for a long time," Rosie said. "But he an' Mom are fightin' lots. I hear her cryin' sometimes."

David felt the flesh on the back of his neck start to tingle. Instinctively he froze. This was a reaction borne of intuition, not fact, and within moments the feeling became all too familiar. His nostrils flared slightly, and his senses became acute.

"Okay, Rosie," he said stiffly, "'member what I said. Don't say nothin' to nobody."

His sister immediately understood what was happening. Her expression flattened and she slowly turned and slipped into the crowd.

David casually moved in the opposite direction. Once he felt protected amidst the group of guests, he glanced over his shoulder to see Domko standing on the other side of the room—glaring at him. The man, clean-shaven and dressed in a black suit, had been watching him talk to Rosie. Although David had a sudden, urgent need to use the washroom, he didn't dare leave the safety of the crowd for fear Domko would follow him.

"Did you see him?" Dennis ranted as the pair walked to work on Monday morning following the wedding. "Did you see him talkin' to Hugo Russell?"

"Yeah," David said, "I saw him."

The brothers had already discussed at length how friendly Domko had been to Sharon's family, especially her father. The twins believed Domko had been "schmoozing" in an effort to impress the in-laws. They angrily discussed the wedding present that Domko and Caroline had given to Norman and Sharon.

"Six cows!" Dennis exclaimed. "Can you believe it?"

"I know, an' he had no right givin' those cows away," David added facetiously. "They weren't his to give! They's ours. We're the ones who made the hay that fed 'em all winter. Those cows woulda died if it weren't for us."

Dennis agreed. "He's just bein' a big shot."

"That's for sure. He just wants Hugo Russell to think he's rich."

"He's jealous," Dennis added. "'Cause Hugo's got a business an' Domko's got shit."

"But now he's a biiiiig maaaan!" David exaggerated.

That evening while they were walking home, they discussed what Domko's motivation might have been for giving Norman and Sharon cattle.

"Betcha he wants them back on the farm," David said. "He prob'-ly thinks if he gives 'em cattle, they'll go home."

Dennis pondered this for a few minutes.

"You're right, but it ain't gonna work," he said. "Why would Norman want to go back to that hell hole?"

"He won't, but Domko don't know that," David laughed. "He's tryin' to bribe 'em."

"Well it won't work. I overheard Norman an' Sharon talkin' an' he's gonna get his pilot's licence for sure."

"I know, he's almost got it already," David added. "He's just gotta do a bit more flyin'." The twins enjoyed a few minutes of silent satisfaction that Domko had given up six head of cattle but would receive nothing for them in return.

Life for the twins changed drastically after Norman and Sharon were married. At first the newlyweds lived in the trailer, but quarters were cramped and it became clear that Norman and Sharon wanted to be alone. One afternoon, not long after the wedding, the four had a meeting.

"We've found a place to rent in Winnipeg and we're moving," Norman said. "You guys can stay here in the trailer, but you'll have to pay the rent yourselves."

The twins nodded.

"And what about the car?" Norman asked David. "Have you got the rest of the money to pay for it?"

"Yep, I do," David said proudly. He hadn't spent the money he made in 100 Mile House and kept it hidden from everyone. He had learned the hard way how important it was to have enough money to pay the bills when their motorcycles were seized the year before.

"As soon as you pay me, the car is yours," Norman said.

While the twins were just learning how to budget, they agreed that they'd continue living in the trailer and that David would buy the car. The twins were ecstatic that they could drive back and forth to work since it was difficult finding someone to give them a ride.

That day Sharon and Norman moved out and the twins were on their own. David took his money out of the bank, gave it to Norman and became the proud owner of the beautiful car that had whisked him away from the farm.

The joy that David felt was unbelievable. The next morning he went outside and stared at the car. *His car!* It was then he noticed that it looked different. Now he was seeing it through the eyes of an owner. He'd paid for a new paint job a few months earlier and was proud of its cherry red colour.

Funny, though, all the times he'd looked at it, he'd never noticed the shape of the lights or the amount of chrome it had. The roof was up and he noticed some marks on the top. It had rained a few days earlier and mud had splashed the sides and dirtied the fenders and hub caps. David moved closer and carefully opened a door.

Surveying the inside door panel, he noticed it was also dirty. The driver's seat had a few marks and there was some dirt and sand on the vinyl-covered floor. Dirt had accumulated on the steering wheel and, mixed with sweat from Norman's hands, had caked in the crevices. The ashtray was open and held ashes and butts from his brother's cigars. There were a few pennies on the bench-style seat, a pay stub and a worn, black comb. The dash was dusty and a collection of finger prints marred the smooth surface of the front panel.

David's senses were heightened as he stood there on that warm, sunny morning and stared at his car. A squirrel, gathering nuts for winter, scurried past into a nearby clump of trees. A few birds chirped, and he could hear the occasional car coming down the highway and then fading in the distance as it passed.

For a moment, he felt as if he'd stepped into someone else's body, that he was living another man's life. He had choices! Domko wasn't standing over him telling him what to do. It was Saturday morning and he was in front of his very own car!

Then he realized that he'd never cleaned anything before. It took a few minutes of thought before he knew where to start. Closing the heavy door firmly, he went in search of a bucket. Looking inside the trailer he couldn't see anything big enough to hold the amount of water he needed. He did however find some towels, rags and liquid dish soap that Sharon had bought and left behind. Quietly, he made his way to the trailer park office and went to a maintenance shed. Sitting on the ground was a metal bucket. He picked it up and carried it to the outdoor tap. He filled the bucket with water and took it back to the car. Squirting the detergent and dropping in a rag he swished the water until it made bubbles. He began massaging the hood of the car with the rag which felt warm on his chilled hands. He stared into the bright red paint and watched his reflection as he worked to remove a week's worth of dirt.

Norman had kept this car clean, but David decided right then that he would keep it even cleaner. He worked his way down the hood and cleaned every inch of the grill before moving to the sides. He made his way slowly around the car, rubbing every bit of tar and dried bugs with the wet rag. He filled the bucket with water and soap many times before he'd come all the way around.

Squirting soap directly on the roof he started scrubbing the stains, which were more stubborn than he'd first anticipated. Inch by inch, he removed each and every one. Water streamed down the front, back and sides of the car, leaving behind soapy tracks. He wasn't upset by this as he refilled his bucket and rewashed the soapy sections making a mental note to do the roof first next time.

Hours later when David was satisfied that all the dirt was removed from the car's exterior he pried the lid from a tin of car polish that Norman had left in the trunk. With a damp cloth he dug out a glob of wax. Starting at the front of the car, he spread the wax across the hood in a gentle swirling motion. He pondered the best way to wax the car—to cover the entire body in wax and then start polishing? Or to wax and polish one section at a time?

David decided the best way was to cover the car in wax and then once it was dry, begin polishing. He let his mind wander and hours later when the job was done, the finish on the car was like a looking glass. He polished the chrome, digging out every speck of dirt from the crevices. He buffed the hub caps until they shone. Careful not to splash, he began washing the windows. He rubbed the glass and mirrors until there were no marks to be seen.

It took all morning and part of the afternoon, but when he stood back, he was pleased with the results. Filling the bucket with fresh water he started cleaning the interior. He first considered the best place to start and spent the rest of the day gradually scrubbing down every inch inside the car.

As he cleaned he thought about Domko. The image of the man's dark, dirty face came to memory in an instant. He'd smelled the man's odour so many times that he believed it was permanently embedded in his senses. Trying to think objectively, David couldn't be sure if his stepfather had always been as he remembered. It seemed that over the years his inattention to hygiene increased with his rage. Because of this, it had been impossible for his mother to keep things nice in the house. It seemed that things had deteriorated around them at the same rate as Domko's mind.

David recalled the times Domko had belittled Caroline, whittling away her self-confidence and pride. One time, Domko had berated her as she lay on the bed, overwhelmed by depression. He called her terrible names and she responded by saying, in a lifeless voice, how she wanted to die. She welcomed the thought of leaving this world. She believed strongly in the Jehovah's Witness' teaching, that when she died there would be justice and she'd be resurrected to a New Order.

This talk frightened the children who could not imagine their lives without her. Eunice had valiantly grabbed a cloth and pail of water and had begun cleaning. Seeing this, Domko praised the girl, saying that Caroline should be more industrious—like Eunice. This only made the children resent him more. Eunice had done this to help her mother, not to earn praise from him.

Frustrated, David ran helplessly from the house. He didn't want his mother to die, but he didn't know how to help. He angrily lashed out at Dennis who stood nearby. Hating each other in that moment, the twins began to fight, their dirty fists pounding each other's flesh until both boys were lying on the ground crying. They convulsed until their guts ached and tears became dry sobs. David was on the ground beside his twin for a long time afterwards, ashamed of how he'd acted. Looking at his dirty fist, scraped and swollen from fighting, a small voice in his head told him that the same forces that controlled Domko were gaining control of him. It was the first time he ever recalled knowing in his heart that he had a choice. He could be like Domko—or he could be his own man.

Standing up, David tossed the dirty rags into the pail. The sun was fading, sending golden streams of light across the western sky. It was then he realized the day was gone. David could see his reflection in the red paint. Walking around the car, he looked it over carefully, not wanting to lose the satisfaction of the moment. Finally he gathered up the cloths and began putting things away. As he walked toward the maintenance shed to return the pail, he glanced over his shoulder to admire the job he'd done on his car.

If anyone had spoken to him that day he didn't remember it. The gnawing pains of hunger tightened his stomach and he realized that he hadn't eaten. He laughed out loud. It didn't matter, really! These hunger pains were different from the ones he'd felt on the farm. He knew that after this satisfying day of work, there would be something for him to eat and that he'd never go hungry again—not ever. It was a wonderful feeling of directing his own life and one he vowed to never lose.

Stepping into the trailer, he turned on a lamp. As the light brightened the room, the sight of his hand shocked him. For the first time in his life it was absolutely clean. He glanced at the other hand too. Then, bringing one up for closer inspection, he noticed the cuticles on his fingernails were a clear pink. The skin under his fingernails was white. He examined his other hand too. He couldn't find a speck of dirt on either. He looked past his hands to his wrists then forearms. The skin on his arms was lightly tanned with pinky undertones. But as he inspected further up his arms, the stains of deeply embedded dirt were apparent. Holding his hands out once more, he was repulsed by the dirt on his arms.

He went to the tiny bathroom and grabbed a towel hanging on the rack and a half-used bar of soap. He left the trailer and strode purposefully toward the trailer park shower room. Glad to find no one else there, he stripped off his clothes and turned on the stream of water. At first it was cold, but soon it warmed and he stepped under it. Taking the bar of soap, he began to wash himself. He started with his hair and face before gradually working his way down his body. He used his fingernails to dig out the dirt embedded deep in his skin. He scrubbed hard as the water at his feet turned brown and swirled down the drain. He rotated the tap until the water became almost too hot to stand—but he stood there anyway, scrubbing his skin until it burned in a surprisingly pleasant way.

And then he began to cry, first softly and then uncontrollably as he raked his soapy hands over his body. He wished the memory of his childhood could be washed down the drain as easily as the dirt that covered him. He scrubbed himself until the water ran clean.

Chapter 10

"LIKE I SAID, WHEN things like this come up, me an' Dennis don't always agree and then we argue," David explained.

McMillan was surprised.

"You wanna talk about ulcers?" David chuckled. "I'll give you goddamned ulcers."

David could tell by the officer's expression that he hadn't understood what he meant. He slowed down to explain.

"You know what I mean, all this crap we've been though is enough to give anybody an ulcer," he said. "The things that happened to us . . ."

The officer stared at him.

"You would not beeeelieve what we saw," David said quietly. He paused for a few moments before continuing. He stared at the table as a memory played through his mind.

"I've seen a lot too," McMillan said.

"Why don't you guys do something about it then?" David snapped.

Monday morning, when the twins drove to work, their fellow workers were standing around and the sight of them in the car raised a few eyebrows. The men, who hadn't seen the new paint job, looked it over. For the first time David felt that he and his brother were accepted by the men. This car, he decided, was the ticket to leading a life of normalcy.

Later that week, David took it to a garage at Birds Hill. The engine was running a little rough and David thought it needed to be looked at. He drove it up to the garage and got out. A teenager standing talking to the mechanic let out a long, slow whistle.

"Nice car," he said, walking towards David. "Where did you get her?"

David was shocked. A stranger was talking to him in a kind way. He tried hard not to stutter.

"M-mmy br-rother," he said casually.

"Oh yeah?" the guy said. "In for a tune up?"

"Yeah, she's r-rrunnin' a l-llittle rough."

"Well, you picked the right garage," the teenager said. He introduced himself as Gord. "My brother here owns the shop and he's a great mechanic."

A man in his early 30s came over to greet David. He wiped his hands on a rag as the three men made small talk. David decided to leave the car in their care.

"Gimme a day," the mechanic said.

"Sure, no p-pproblem," David said.

He walked back to the trailer and the next day he and Dennis got a ride to the job site with a fellow worker. He had the man drop him off at the garage on the way home. David was pleased to see his car sitting in line with the other vehicles that had been fixed.

Opening the door to the garage, he went in. David had been paid that day and hoped to have enough to cover the bill.

"I'll be with you in a minute," the mechanic called out from under the hood of another vehicle.

David looked around and his eyes fixed on a calendar hanging on the wall by the door. It was illustrated with a picture of a naked woman. Blushing, he looked away, but then glanced back hoping nobody noticed.

The mechanic walked towards him and then veered off towards the area he used as an office. David approached the grease-covered desk and watched as the man thumbed through a stack of bills.

"Okay," he began, handing David the invoice. "We got her fixed. Just needed a little work, made a couple of adjustments, a tune up, oil—you know. She's ready to go."

David reached in his pocket and pulled out a wad of bills. He carried his whole cashed paycheque with him. Counting slowly, he peeled off enough bills to cover the total and handed it to the mechanic.

"Thanks," the man said, opening his cash register. He reached for the keys to the car which were hanging on the wall behind him.

Just then Gord came in carrying two bottles of Coke. He recognized David, and followed him back outside to the car.

"So, I bet the chicks really dig this car," Gord said, handing one bottle to David. "You got a girlfriend?"

David shook his head "no."

"Have you taken any women out in the car yet?" Gord asked, taking a gulp from the bottle.

He indicated that he hadn't. The two stood and made small talk for a while, and it seemed that Gord didn't want David to leave.

"Hey, I got an idea," he said. "I have a girlfriend and she's got a friend who'd be perfect for you. You want me to set you up?"

David blushed. He'd been thinking about girls but was too shy to ask anyone out. He shrugged as he took a sip of pop.

"Would you go on a blind date if I arranged it?" Gord asked.

"B-bbblind?" David asked.

Gord laughed kindly. "Yeah, it means that you go out with someone you've never seen before."

"Oh," he said, blushing some more. "S-ssure, I guess s-sso."

"All right. I'll talk to my girlfriend. Stop by in a couple days and we'll see if we can get something set up for the weekend."

David nodded, got into the car and drove back to the trailer.

A few days later while Dennis was working overtime, David went back to the garage to find Gord waiting for him. This was the third time he'd seen the teenager and noticed that each time Gord was covered from head-to-toe in grease. He silently dubbed him "Greasy Gord."

"Well, I got dates lined up for Friday night," Gord said. "Can you make it?"

"Sure," David said. "S-sso where's she f-ffrom?"

"Her name's Barb and she's a friend of my girlfriend's. They live out in Beausejour. She's a real nice looking girl with red hair, a pretty face and . . ." he said cupping his hands in front of his chest while raising his eyebrows, "big tits."

David nodded shyly as Gord's brother approached.

"You're not tryin' to fix up that ugly, four hundred pound friend of Nancy's again, are you?" the mechanic joked.

David's eyes widened. "I d-ddon't want no f-fffour h-hhhundred pound g-ggirlfriend," David said quickly, "She'd eat too m-much."

Gord and his brother roared with laughter.

"Yeah, but there's nothin' like a fat girl on a cold night," the mechanic said.

"Well, you'd know," Gord laughed as he dodged a playful punch.

"I bet David here doesn't even know what to do on a date," the mechanic said.

David shrugged.

"You have to take her out to a movie or for something to eat," he began, motioning for the teens to follow him inside. "And then if you guys seem to get along okay, you take her somewhere and park the car so that you can talk for a while."

"Talk," Gord whispered, "yeah, right."

"Ssshh," the mechanic said, "I'm giving him some pointers."

Gord chuckled again and the brothers proceeded to offer dating advice, most of which David did not understand. He knew from conversations at work that getting the girl to take off her clothes was supposed to be his main objective. He glanced up at the picture of the nude woman on the wall and wondered exactly how he was supposed to do that.

As Friday night approached, David started to get nervous. He showered, combed his hair and put on his cleanest clothes. He stood in front of the mirror in the trailer park shower room and for the first time in his life, gave his body a good inspection.

His hair was too long and he immediately regretted not getting it cut earlier that week. His clothes did not fit properly—the arms on his shirt were too short.

Just then Dennis entered the washroom. "Whatcha doin'?"

"I'm gettin' ready," David said, feeling self-conscious. He moved away from the full-length mirror.

"For what?" Dennis asked.

"I'm goin' out, 'member?"

"What do I do about this?" he asked, pointing to his sleeves, which were too short.

Dennis thought for a moment.

"I seen guys roll 'em up like this," he said, undoing his own cuffs and turning them over.

David unbuttoned his, flipped them back, and rolled them up to just below his elbows. Stepping back in front of the mirror, he looked at himself again.

"How's that?" he asked.

Dennis moved in front of the mirror and looked at his brother's reflection.

"You need a haircut," he said.

"I know, stupid, but I don't got no time," David replied.

Looking at himself in the mirror, he saw a very frightened teenager wearing a "farmer" shirt that was buttoned up past his adam's apple.

"Okay," he said, loosening the button. "How's that?"

"Better," Dennis said.

"How 'bout my pants?"

"What about 'em?"

"Are they too long?"

"Yeah."

"Yeah?"

"Yeah, but that's okay 'cause draggin' is better than too short."

"No it's not."

"Yes it is. Norman's drag."

"That's just 'cause Sharon don't sew," David laughed.

The brothers laughed and shoved each other.

"No, really," Dennis explained. "Short is bad, I know 'cause some guys asked me if I was workin' on the floodway an' when I said yes, they laughed an' said they could tell 'cause of my pants."

Normally David would have laughed at a joke, but he was too nervous. He picked up his towel and toiletries from the shelf.

"Hey," Dennis said, holding up a plastic, pencil-sized object. "What's this?"

David grabbed it from him.

"You bought a toothbrush?" Dennis teased.

"Yeah!" David said. "One guy said that if I tried to kiss a girl, she'd fall over dead 'cause I never brush my teeth."

"No, you don't wanna kill your first date!" Dennis laughed, adding, "I brush mine."

"No you don't."

"Yes I do," he said. "Crystal bought me a toothbrush when I lived there so I brought it with me."

"I never seen you use it," David said.

"You never see me take a crap either, but I do," he said.

David was too nervous to make jokes.

"You're startin' to sound like Norman," he said as he walked out of the shower room.

"Yeah, well you smell like him," Dennis said.

David scowled back. He'd taken a small bottle of Norman's aftershave and splashed it on. He realized that he didn't need to use so much on clean skin.

"Peee-uuww," Dennis said holding his nose while they made their way back to the trailer.

"I'm goin'," David said as he tossed his towel and dirty clothes on the bed. He grabbed the car keys from the counter and went outside. He felt nervous about leaving, but didn't want Dennis, who was standing in the doorway, to tease him any more.

"See ya' later," Dennis called out. David smiled and waved to him as he drove onto the highway.

David picked up Gord who was waiting for him at the garage. The young man had cleaned up a bit, but his "greasy" moniker still applied. David cringed when the teen got into the front seat and hoped that no grease would rub off on the upholstery.

"Hi!" Gord said. "I'll show you where to go."

David followed Gord's directions to a girl's house in Beausejour. Nancy was waiting outside on the step and waved cheerfully as they drove up. She got into the back seat and gave them directions to her friend's house. When they pulled into Barb's driveway, she too emerged from the house and approached the car. Greeting Nancy in the back seat, she smiled at the boys and climbed in beside her friend.

"This is David," Gord said making the introduction. "And this is Barb."

"Hi," she said smiling.

David was too nervous to say anything so he just nodded.

Gord instructed him to drive to a restaurant and the guys talked about cars while the girls gossiped and giggled in back. David kept staring at the girls in the rearview mirror, but averted his eyes each time they caught him staring.

The girls had been warned that David had a stuttering problem, but were told that he was a nice, sincere guy—and quite funny when relaxed.

They drove to a local café where they ordered burgers and fries. Gord did most of the talking as David sat listening. He couldn't help but stare at Barb's hair. It was a dark red—similar to a teacher he once had a crush on. Barb flushed when she caught him looking at her. The pair listened to stories told by Gord and Nancy avoiding each other's gaze.

After eating, they walked around town for a while before driving to a secluded spot on the outskirts of Beausejour. Gord and Nancy sat in the back while Barb moved into the front with David. They became very uncomfortable when their friends in the back started kissing and groaning. David tried to talk to Barb, but couldn't concentrate and made the excuse that he had to get home.

They had a few similar dates and then one evening David arrived to pick up Gord to discover that something unexpected had happened and Gord was unable to make it. It would be just David and Barb.

Afraid he wouldn't know what to say, David considered canceling the date. To do that, though, he'd have to phone her and that would be more torture than stuttering his way through funny stories all evening. He decided to take her out without Gord, arriving at her house only a few minutes late. Barb climbed into the front seat and smiled.

"Nancy called and said they can't come," she said. "But I'm glad you still did."

David smiled weakly as his heart pounded heavily in his chest. He was glad to have the distraction of driving because he had a hard time looking at the girl without blushing. He wanted to talk to her, but words stuck in his throat.

Sensing how uncomfortable he was, she began to talk. At first she told stories about school, then about her family. They drove to the same café where David and Dennis ate meals most days. It wasn't very fancy, which didn't matter to David, and luckily it didn't seem to bother Barb either. As they waited for their meals, she chattered about many topics.

"You're pretty shy, aren't you?" she asked.

David was caught a bit off guard by the comment.

"Uh, yeah," he answered.

"Well, I've dated shy guys before," she said smiling, "you don't have to worry. I can talk all night!"

By the time they'd finished their meal, David was starting to warm to her. He began telling a few stories himself, mostly about his adventures with Dennis, but soon ran out of things to say. Most of his stories involved Domko and he wasn't ready to talk about life on the farm. Whenever he felt himself veering in that direction, he stopped or switched to something else. He told her about Bryan from work and how he'd made fun of the brothers. He was surprised to discover how sympathetic she was. He proudly told her how Norman had stood up to the bully, and she listened intently to the dramatic story.

"Norman sounds like a great guy," she gushed. This made David feel good, but he felt a pang of jealousy over his brother's popularity.

David paid for the meals and the two strolled casually out to the car.

"What are we going to do now?" she asked.

"Well," he said. "we c-ccould d-ddrive around a little."

"Sure," she smiled, as she climbed into the car.

"It's g-ggettin' c-ccold," he said as he slid in beside her, started the car and turned on the heat. Pulling onto the highway, he drove around, and they talked for at least an hour.

"If you'd like to stop for a while, I know a good place," she suggested. David nodded and followed her directions. They ended up along a dirt road near her house. He pulled off to the side and shut off the engine.

They talked for a while, and as they talked and laughed their bodies gradually worked their way closer until they were pressed up against each other. David felt like a sissy with his hands folded in front of him, so he reached out and put his arm across the back of the seat. His hand rested on her shoulder. She looked up at him, her blue eyes twinkling, and both stopped talking. David's heart raced wildly with anticipation and he bent down and gave her a kiss on the lips. She responded, and soon the two were kissing passionately.

The feelings that flowed through his body were overwhelming! For a while as they kissed, he felt good, thinking about Barb and the wonderful sensation of lust that had overtaken him. He'd experienced arousal before, but had always felt guilty about it.

Domko had once threatened to castrate him and that fear had stuck with him. It was a terrible time for the memory to return, just as he and Barb were warming to one another. Sensing his hesitation, Barb reached over and her hand brushed against the front of David's pants.

All of a sudden he pushed her away and pulling the keys from the ignition, jumped out of the car. He ran like a scared rabbit through the ditch and into the bushes. He crouched down out of sight. He could see Barb's outline in the dark car. She waited patiently for him to return, and when he didn't, she opened the door and began calling for him.

"David!" she yelled. "David—where are you?"

He didn't answer.

"David! Are you all right?" she called again. A few minutes later, the door opened again. "David! This isn't funny, you're scaring me."

Too afraid to go looking in the bushes for him, she closed the door.

By now he was no longer rattled, but extremely embarrassed about what had happened. There was no way he was going to be able to explain all this to her so he sat in the bushes deciding it would be easier to wait her out. Finally, an hour later, she got out of the car and sobbing, ran down the dark road back to Beausejour.

Once David was satisfied she had gone, he crept from the bushes, got quietly into the car and with the lights off, drove away in the opposite direction.

Word of David's odd behaviour must have got back to Gord and Nancy, because David never heard from them again. He saw Gord once, but pretended not to notice the strange look the teen gave him.

One day shortly before freeze-up, David's foreman asked David to help him move to Khedive, Saskatchewan. David agreed to spend his last week at work moving George's belongings, while Dennis stayed and finished up at the job site.

It took a day to load, and a day to make the drive with two trucks and trailers. In the morning David awoke with a horrible pain in his hand. Each time he lifted something while unloading a trailer a sharp pain ran up his hand.

"Did you bang it?" George asked.

"No," David winced. "But I can b-bbarely m-mmove it."

"Huh?" George mused. "How about when you slept? Maybe you cut off the circulation. Here, lemme see."

David stuck out his hand. "Ouch," he yelped as George touched the top.

"I'll be danged," he said. "I don't see nothin'."

The next day they drove back to Manitoba to discover that Dennis had broken his finger the day before.

"Well, Judas Priest!" George exclaimed. "I ain't never heard anything like it as them Pischke boys feelin' each other's pain."

When the brothers were laid off that fall, the twins left Birds Hill and moved back to the little Moosehorn trailer, parked in the Matheson's yard. Norman and Sharon moved back as well and lived with Sharon's parents Hugo and Freda. Norman worked part-time for his father-in-law driving trucks.

One morning late that fall, the twins awoke during the first snow storm of the season. Heavy wind whipped against the thin trailer walls. Dennis hurried across the cold floor to make a fire. They were sitting warming themselves by the stove when a car drove into the driveway, leaving the first track of the day in the freshly fallen snow. They recognized the car as Norman's and watched from the window as their brother walked quickly toward the trailer. They opened the door before he knocked and stepped back as the cold wind blew their brother inside.

"Whew!" Norman exclaimed, pulling the door closed. "Windy out there."

"Hey, Norman," David said. "whatcha doin'?"

"Got a call from Ma," he said, shaking the snow from his head. "She needs someone to go out there and move her and the kids to the old Kolodka place."

"Today?" David asked. "In this storm?"

"Yep," he said. "She wants to go today."

David thought for a moment. "What are you doin'?"

"I'm working today," he said. "What are you guys doing?"

"Nothin'," they chimed together.

"Okay, then you guys can do it," Norman said. "She wants you to go right away because Domko's having a fit."

"You sure?" Dennis asked.

"What do you mean?" Norman frowned.

"They're not trickin' us?" David asked.

"No, Domko's off his rocker again," Norman said, opening the door and stepping back into the storm. "Quit being so paranoid."

The twins pulled on their heavy jackets and went outside. They drove out to the farm in David's car, but didn't dare pull into the driveway. They sat for a moment with the engine running while they talked. The heater blew hotly on their legs.

"You go see what's goin' on," David suggested.

"No way, you go," Dennis said.

"No, I gotta watch the car an' make sure it don't stall."

"I can do that."

"No you can't," David said. "It's my car."

"Yeah, well she's your Mom."

"She's your Mom too."

"Yeah, but you always go first."

David winced. All his years of "being first" was backfiring on him. He thought for a moment and decided that Dennis was right.

"All right, I'll go but don't drive away an' leave me here," he warned.

"Okay, I won't," Dennis said.

"Promise?" David asked.

"Promise."

"I'll signal if it's safe to come in," David said as he got out of the car. He walked cautiously up the driveway looking around to see if Domko was waiting outside for him. Rounding the corner of the house he was hit in the face by the cold wind blowing hard from the north. Head down, he paused for a moment at the back door. He could hear Domko and his mother arguing.

At first, the sound of Domko's voice made him want to run. The adrenaline began flowing through his veins and his stomach knotted with fear. His legs felt like they were being weighted down with cement, refusing to move from the doorstep. There was a quiet voice within himself telling him to stay and to open the door—to stand tall and face Domko.

Two years of hard work and regular meals were beginning to show on his body. While he was still terribly skinny, he no longer had the gaunt signs of malnourishment. His cheeks were rosy, his eyes bright and his movements swift. Sometimes, lying in bed at night after a day of hard work, he cleared his mind of all thoughts and could almost feel every cell in his body thriving and growing. Physically, David had become strong.

Grasping the door knob, he turned it and stepped into the kitchen. Caroline was standing there facing her husband. Domko sat in his usual chair in the corner. The children were somewhere else—David suspected that Rosie had herded them upstairs to safety.

The man glowered as his gaze met David's. The boy's eyes dropped to the floor and his shoulders slumped slightly. This submissive reaction wasn't something he could outgrow overnight.

"Vat?" Domko questioned. "So, yous be here? Vat for? Yous be takink her?"

David said nothing, thankful for his mother's presence.

"Yes, David has come to take us to John's," she said. "You say we're all lazy and good for nothing so what difference does it make if we go?"

Domko snorted as he rose from his chair. Anticipating that he'd storm in David's direction, the boy instinctively stepped aside. He glanced over his shoulder for an escape route. Caroline stood her ground as her husband grunted and walked past them out the door. For a brief instant, David sensed that Domko was losing his power over their mother.

David watched Caroline as Domko left. She seemed a bit stronger than he'd remembered her and she also seemed older. Was she finally summoning the courage to defend herself and the children, he wondered?

"Hi, Ma," he said quietly.

"Hi David. Where's Dennis?" she asked.

"I'll wave him in," he said.

David went outside then reappeared a few moments later. Soon the door opened again and Dennis stepped into the kitchen.

They made small talk for awhile as the twins updated her on what they'd been doing with their lives. When they got around to the difficult subject of Domko and the farm, Caroline started to cry.

"Help me get out of here," she begged. "I can't take it anymore. He's getting worse and there's nothing I can say or do to please him."

The twins well understood that feeling.

"What do you w-wwant us to do?" David asked.

"Move us out to John's," she suggested.

The sound of the twins' voices brought the children down from upstairs.

"David! Dennis! Is that you?" Kathy called as she groped her way down the stairs. Rosie smiled as Raymond and Mark stood quietly watching the twins.

"Yes, it's us," David said, his heart warming at the sight of his half-sister. He'd always been jealous of the attention Domko gave the girl, but felt sorry for her at the same time. Feeling her way towards the twins, she grabbed David's arm and jumped with excitement.

"You're back!" she exclaimed.

"Not for long," David said. He scowled at baby Jennie who was sleeping contently in Rosie's arms. He didn't think his mother needed another mouth to feed. "We're helpin' Mom move you guys outta here."

"What?" Kathy asked, clearly disappointed. "I thought you was back for good."

"Nope, I'm workin' at a good job in construction," he said.

"You're not working right now," Caroline corrected.

David shook his head. "No way Ma, I'm not movin' back. I said I'd help you move but that's it."

Caroline shrugged as she went into the other room to begin packing.

"Besides, Norman's talkin' about goin' west," he called after her. "Me an' Denny are thinkin' of goin' too."

"I don't know why you boys want to do that," she said.

"Because," David began, "there's lots of work an' the money's good."

"You can get a job here," she argued.

"Here?" David asked, "Where? In Moosehorn?"

"Yes, I'm sure you could find a job here."

"Not as good as in B.C.," he said. "It'll work out. I can go to B.C. an' come back to work on the floodway again next year."

Caroline shrugged again switching her thoughts to the job at hand. She handed David an old suitcase full of clothes and pointed to a few kitchen items she wanted him to load into the car.

"I'll go get it," Dennis offered.

Gathering up boxes of pots, pans, dishes and clothes that Caroline had packed, the twins carried them outside and piled them in the trunk. When they'd finished loading the car, they stood surveying the farm while they waited for their mother and siblings to come outside. It was obvious that little outside work was being done. The fences were in need of repair and the buildings were beginning to look rundown. Caroline stepped outside leading a child with each hand. She shook her head in despair as she anticipated what the twins must be thinking. Defensively, she pointed to the cattle in the hay yard.

"I can't do it all myself!" she said, her eyes filling with tears.

"We know Ma," Dennis said.

"Then don't look at me like that," she said. "I'm doing the best I can with no help from you."

Believing the comment was critical of them, the twins began arguing with her until her tears turned to anger. The discussion stopped abruptly as the children were herded into the car.

David winced as his snow-covered siblings piled into his clean back seat. Caroline sat in front with the twins while Rosie and the rest of the children fought and whined as they jockeyed for a place to sit in the back.

"Ma, Markie's squashin' the baby," Rosie called out.

"Sit down!" she scolded as she reached into the back and grabbed the rambunctious two year-old. She moved him away from Jennie who had been sleeping but now was fully awake and fussing.

"Where's Ta-Ta?" Mark whine for his dad.

Nobody answered.

"Where's Ta-Ta?" the boy persisted.

"Shhhh!" Caroline hissed. "We'll be there soon."

David drove slowly out of the driveway turning north towards Faulkner. The wheels of the heavily laden car packed snow as it went, and David was relieved to see that it had stopped snowing. The wind continued to blow, however, making visibility poor. David drove twelve miles along the back roads to the abandoned homestead. Caroline's brother, John, had been living there with his family but moved to Winnipeg after his wife took her two daughters and moved away.

David leaned forward wiping the steam from his windshield as he struggled to see the approach. He slowed, turned off of the main road and began making his way down the tree-lined path that led to the house.

"We gotta get out here," he said, halting the car, "or we're gonna get stuck."

Everyone climbed out of the car and pulling on their mitts and toques, began trudging through the snow. The twins led the way in, carrying Raymond and Mark. Rosie was close behind with the baby. Caroline led Kathy through the snow, which by now had settled knee-deep in the shelter of the trees.

A feeling of despair washed over David as the barn, and then the house, came into view. He had no fond memories of this farm, and remembered it only as a dreary place they had fled to occasionally when he was younger. He'd never developed a meaningful relationship with his grandfather or uncles, and in fact had always felt shunned by his mother's family. He wondered how she could so willingly come back to a place that held so many unhappy memories. They'd discussed her childhood on a few occasions, but it usually ended with Caroline's thoughts wandering and her eyes staring in a far-off way. She'd usually change the subject when pressed for details about what life was like for her growing up.

Stepping up to the door of the old house, Dave grasped the knob and was relieved to find that it was not locked. He pushed open the door and the family filed in behind him. The tiny, three room house hadn't changed much over the years and they were heartened to find that it was still being used occasionally by family members. It was completely furnished with old, but still serviceable, chairs, tables and beds.

The first task was to find wood to make a fire. The twins stepped back into the storm, and as they walked past the hydro pole, David reached up and flipped on the switch. They went around the house to where their uncle had kept his wood pile. Fortunately, there was a small stack of wood covered with an old tarp. They brushed the snow off the top and flipping back the canvas were able to pull out a dozen dry pieces of split wood. They made two trips to the wood pile, stacking the pieces indoors alongside the stove.

"C'mon," Dennis said to his brother, "we gotta unload the car."

David nodded as the two pulled their toques on tight and stepped back into the wind. Glancing to their right, David stared at the big barn that sat at the edge of the farmyard. It was a well-made building that towered over everything as if it was standing guard.

"The barn's better than the house," David snickered. "Figures, eh?"

"I wonder if that ol' mattress is still up there?" Dennis pondered, pointing to the loft.

David shrugged. "Prob'ly."

David recalled the time his mother had defied Domko and taken the children to a Jehovah's Witness convention in Winnipeg. When they returned two days later, he flew into a rage. While he was running to get the shotgun from the granary, the children and their mother fled north into the bushes. Once a safe distance from the farm, Caroline decided they should go to the homestead where she grew up. Her brother John was living there at the time with his wife and two young daughters.

It had been the middle of summer and the sun was hot as they tramped across fields of uncut hay that scratched their bare ankles and calves. David and Dennis found an old cotton-stuffed mattress on the way and they decided to carry it so they'd have something soft to sleep on. That night, they stayed in an abandoned barn and then by early afternoon of the next day arrived at John's farm. As they walked up the laneway, they saw both the barn and the house in the distance. When they got closer, they noticed movement in the yard near the house.

"What's that?" David asked. As they got closer, they saw their cousin's head bobbing up and down.

"It's the baby," Caroline said. "What's she doing outside by herself?"

"Let's go see," David said, grabbing Dennis by the arm. The twins ran toward the two year-old girl, who stopped playing in the dirt and looked up at them. She stood, and it was then they noticed she was wearing only a diaper. She brushed away the flies that were buzzing around her dirty nose and mouth. She was flushed from being in the sun and was sobbing. The girl was tethered to a stake by a thin rope that was tied around her ankle. She'd worn away the grass under foot from many hours in the same spot.

"Ma, come here!" David called out.

Caroline approached and then let out a gasp.

"It's too hot for a child to be out in the sun like this," she said. "Boys, untie her."

Obediently, the twins approached the little girl who backed away from them and started to whimper. They untied the rope at her foot, and as soon as she was loose, she darted towards the bushes.

"Catch her!" Caroline yelled. "Don't let her get out of sight or we'll never find her."

The twins ran after the little girl and caught her at the edge of the trees. Picking up the crying child, they brought her back to Caroline.

"Let's take her over there and wash her off," she said, pointing to the outdoor pump. "The poor little thing probably has heat stroke."

They led the girl to the well and Caroline held her while Dennis began pumping water onto the ground. They stuck her dirty hands and arms under first, and then coaxed her under the cool stream.

"How come she's tied up?" David asked.

Caroline thought for a moment. "Everyone's out haying. They probably don't have anyone who can stay back to watch her."

"Oh," he said, adding "you never did that to us, did you Ma?"

"No," she said. "I'd have one of the Harwart girls come to babysit or take you along."

The little girl splashed under the water.

"How's that?" Caroline cooed. "You feeling a little better?"

"Me JeeJee," she said.

"JeeJee?" David said. "Is that your name?"

The little girl giggled as he picked her up. David stared into her bright eyes and noticed that with a clean face, she had beautiful skin and a row of straight, white teeth. Her chubby arm wrapped around his neck and he suddenly felt protective towards the little girl as they walked back to where the other children waited.

Opening the barn door, Caroline instructed the children to climb into the loft. She knew there was no room in her brother's small house for them and that they'd be sleeping in the barn. She went to the house for a few minutes and came back with clothes for the little girl. David and Dennis managed to pull the mattress up the loft ladder and put it on top of some leftover straw.

By late afternoon they heard voices in the yard and went outside. Caroline explained why they were there. That evening they overheard Caroline suggest to her brother and his wife that Eunice and Rosie were old enough to do some babysitting for them, if needed.

Caroline and the children stayed in the barn for a few days and then one morning she decided it was time to go home.

"Try not to make Domko so mad," she said to the twins. "Why do you always run away? That's what makes him so angry with you."

"No, it don't," David said. "If we don't run then he catches us an' shmashes us."

"But if you kids behaved yourselves, he wouldn't punish you," she said, trying to find a way to make her children, and herself, more acceptable to Domko.

"We do!" David said. "Sometimes he gets mad for nothin'."

"When?" she asked, picking up Raymond and walking towards the loft opening. The other children were waiting for them outside.

"When we's asleep," David said. "How come he shmashes us at night?"

"You're not asleep, you're making too much noise," she said. "You know he can't stand noise."

"He don't mind Kathy," David stated, as he followed her down the loft stairs.

Just then, little JeeJee trotted into the barn.

"We have to go now," Caroline said to her. "You have to stay here."

JeeJee looked up at her. “JeeJee too?” she asked.

“No, you have to stay here,” she said.

“JeeJee too!” she said, stomping her bare foot. “Go.”

The little girl had become quite attached to her cousins and enjoyed the company of the older children. David looked down at the little girl who had a firm grasp on the bottom of Caroline’s dress.

“Can we take her with us?” one of the children asked.

Everyone fell silent as they looked at the little girl.

“What do you kids think?” Caroline said, “She could come stay with us for awhile.”

David cringed. He thought about how Domko would react to having another child to feed. He visualized Domko beating the little girl and it made his insides ache.

“Ma, we can’t,” he said. “We gotta leave her here.”

Caroline sighed. “All right, but it’s not going to be easy. She wants to come with us and is going to follow,” she said. “You boys take her to the house, me and the kids will start walking and then you catch up.”

The twins nodded.

“C’mon JeeJee,” David coaxed. “Let’s go.”

“JeeJee go,” she said happily as the twins each took a hand and led her towards the house. They distracted her as Caroline and the other children hurried down the lane. When they got to the far side of the house, David could hear voices coming from inside.

“Okay, now you stay here,” he said, letting go of her hand. He looked at Dennis and on cue, they bolted around the house towards the lane.

“No!” JeeJee cried out in shock. “JeeJee come!”

The brothers easily out ran the girl, who in childish determination, ran after them.

David glanced back over his shoulder and the sight of the little girl running with her arms outstretched, sobbing and screaming for him, tore at his insides. It didn’t take much to outrun the girl, whose sobs could still be heard when they reached the road. David wanted to go back and get her, and looked to his mother for comfort. Caroline had also been troubled over deceiving the child and had lost herself in her own thoughts.

David’s eyes burned as he stared at the ground which passed quickly beneath his feet. Soon he couldn’t hear the girl crying anymore. Had they done the right thing?

Yes, he resolved within himself. *A kid is better off dead than livin’ with Domko.*

But the image of JeeJee stayed with him for the rest of the walk home and for many weeks to come.

"How long do you think she'll stay this time?" Dennis asked as he ran a gloved hand across the window of David's car, sweeping away the heavy wet snow before opening the door. He hoisted a box of his mother's belongings onto his shoulder.

"Who?" David asked, lost in his thoughts.

"Ma," Dennis replied. "Do you think she'll stay here all winter?"

"I dunno," David said as he reached into the car and pulled out an armful of blankets. "If she does, she'll need more wood."

The brothers trudged back to the house through the deep snow. When they had finished unloading the car, their mother rewarded them with a bowl of soup and a piece of bread. They talked late into the night and listened to the storm howling outside. The small cabin was cramped, but it was warm and peaceful. Even the young children were content as everyone sensed how calm life was without Domko lurking nearby.

The next morning the twins had to ask the neighbour to give the car battery a boost. They also needed help digging out the car from the snowbank that had blown around it in the night. That afternoon they returned to the trailer in Moosehorn.

Chapter 11

"**YOU GUYS NEVER DID** n-nothin' for us," David snorted. McMillan could see there was no point arguing with the angry man—so he changed the subject.

"Where do you work?" he asked.

"I've worked all over the place," David said. "I've worked in W-winnipeg, Lu-lumsden."

"Do you ever take time off work due to illness?" he asked.

"Almost never," he said. "The last time was just before the book came out, I fell off the roof of the garage an' broke my ribs. I had to take about a week off then."

McMillan continued to write on the note pad.

"The book?" he asked.

"Yeah, you know, the one that was w-wrote about our lives," he said.

McMillan nodded then looked back at his question sheet.

"Have you ever had a head injury?" he asked. "How about when you fell?"

"I shmashed my teeth," he said.

"How about any other times?" he asked.

"Yes, I twisted my n-neck when I was a kid," he said. "The doctor said I was l-lucky I didn't end up in a wheelchair."

"Were you knocked unconscious?"

"Yes, I was out for a little while," he said.

"Do you ever have any blackouts?"

"Not that I remember," he chuckled.

The weeks went by quickly. One afternoon the twins were talking with Norman and Sharon who outlined their plan to move to B.C. Bored with living in Moosehorn and collecting unemployment insurance, the twins asked if they could go along. David told the newlyweds about the job he'd had with Roy Hollingsworth the winter before and felt quite confident Roy would help them find jobs. Norman wasn't sure what he wanted to do, but had heard that working in the mines paid well. The brothers made plans to leave the following weekend after collecting their next unemployment cheques.

The twins arrived at the Russell house, where Norman and Sharon were staying, to find them packing last-minute baggage in the car.

"Ready to go?" Norman asked, excitement spilling over into his voice. "We want to get a good start."

"Yeah, we're r-rready," David said as he opened the car door. Peering in, he was startled to find that the back seat was filled with boxes. "What's all this?"

"Oh, we're bringin' some stuff for the house," Norman said.

"Can't we put this in the t-ttrunk?" David asked pointing to the contents of two large, open boxes.

"There's no room," Norman said. "We've got a butchered pig back there."

"A what?" David asked.

"A pig."

"What for?"

"What do you think?" Norman said. "To eat."

"Well, where are me an' Denny s'posed to sit?"

Norman looked inside the car.

"We left you a spot there," he said, pointing to a foot-wide space in the back seat behind the driver.

The twins scoffed.

"And one of you can sit in the front with us," Norman added.

The teens tried to protest, but Norman interrupted them.

"Someone go get Sharon," he said. "It's time to go."

Dennis shrugged and disappeared into the house as Norman got into the car and started it. A high-pitched squeal, followed by a loud "thunk" under the hood, startled David who was standing in the snow-covered driveway.

"What the . . .?" Norman said as he opened his door. He slid around to the front of the car and lifted the hood.

Sharon and Dennis came out the door carrying the last things that were to be packed into the already-crammed car.

A cat jumped out from under the hood and dragging a ripped tail and broken leg, staggered behind the house and out of sight.

"My cat!" Sharon exclaimed, dropping her bags and running after the poor animal.

"Ah shit," Norman said as he examined the motor. "The cat got caught in the fan belt and it looks like it broke the power steering case."

Slamming down the hood, Norman began muttering to himself. Following him into the house, the twins waited quietly by the door while Norman called a local mechanic to explain their plight. He arranged to have a tow truck pick up the car and transport it to the garage for repair.

"Well, I guess we won't be leavin' until later," he said to his brothers. "Come back this afternoon."

The twins nodded and hurried off to a local café to wait for the car to be fixed.

"So what kinda car is that anyway?" Dennis asked after ordering something to eat.

"Home made," David snorted as he took a sip of his coffee.

"What if they can't get it fixed?" Dennis asked.

"Well, we're not goin' in my car," David said. "They're not puttin' no dead pig in my trunk."

Dennis laughed. "What if it starts leakin'?"

David shook his head in disgust. "I don't know an' I don't care," he laughed.

Dennis nodded.

"I'm gonna be sittin' in the front," David said casually.

"Hey!" Dennis said.

"Hey, what?"

"I don't wanna sit back there all squashed," Dennis laughed. "An' besides—I'm not skinny enough." He sucked in his stomach and turned sideways.

"Where'd ya go, Denny?" David whispered as he bit into his hamburger. "Ya look like a stick with a head."

The twins giggled as they ate their lunch and continued discussing Norman's car.

"So why do you think he bought it, anyway?" Dennis mused.

"I dunno," David said. "It's not as good as the car he sold me, but I'm not complainin'!"

"No or he'll take it back."

"No, he won't!"

The brothers sat in the café drinking coffee until mid-afternoon. When it felt like enough time had expired, they sauntered back over to the Russell house. Norman wasn't there; Sharon explained that he had gone to pick up the car.

The twins stood outside and waited. The sun was low in the sky by the time Norman drove up the street. He pulled into the driveway and left the car running as he motioned for the twins to get in.

"Hey, ya got only one tail light," David said as he walked around the back of the car.

Norman got out to look for himself. His brow furrowed. The repair to the power steering casing had cost more than he'd expected.

"Ah, don't worry about it," he said.

Sharon stepped outside and waved good-bye to her parents. She reminded them to take care of her cat, which had a broken leg but was in surprisingly good condition following it's accident in the motor.

"Ready to go?" she asked cheerily.

"Yep," Norman beamed. "It's all fixed."

David stood firmly at the front passenger door and motioned for Dennis to get in the back seat. Dennis reluctantly squeezed in beside the boxes. His initial annoyance with the seating arrangements gave way to excitement. Soon they were laughing and joking as Norman turned onto the highway.

"We'll take the Trans-Canada," he said.

David argued that it might be faster to travel west via the northern route, on the Yellowhead Highway, but Norman had already made up his mind.

"Nope, the roads are better down south," he said.

David shrugged. He squirmed closer to the door in an effort to make more room between himself and Sharon. Not that he didn't like Sharon—he just didn't feel comfortable with his left arm and leg touching her. But an hour of sitting stiffly was more than he could take, and he soon became accustomed to close quarters. He began to relax.

The four of them fell into casual conversation. After a while David sat mesmerized, watching as fat snowflakes began beating against the windshield. The road ahead was illuminated only by Norman's headlights. They met few vehicles as the car moved south on the highway. Norman said that the roads were becoming slippery. He slowed slightly and frequently switched between high and low beams to give his eyes a change of focus. His forearms flexed as he held the car on the road.

"That's one strong wind," he muttered as he turned west off the highway at the southern tip of Lake Manitoba. He planned to cut across to Marquette and then drive south to the Trans-Canada at Elie where he'd then go west. What the group didn't know was that they were driving into a prairie storm.

"Damned cat," he said, shooting a playful glance at Sharon. "We should have been on the road hours ago. We'd be in Medicine Hat by now."

Sharon rolled her eyes and gave him a nudge.

"It wasn't the cat's fault," she said. "You should have hit the hood first."

"I shoulda hit the cat first," he said, nudging Sharon back.

She gently slapped his arm and everyone chuckled.

Norman looked for Dennis in the rearview mirror.

"How are you doing back there?" he laughed. "Are you still alive, or what?"

"Huh?" came a sleepy reply.

They laughed.

"He w-wwants to know if you're still a-live back there," David asked.

"Yeah, but I'm not happy about it," Dennis replied.

The car filled with laughter again as it rolled along the deserted highway.

"S'pose we're the only ones out t-ttonight?" David asked.

Norman nodded as he lit a Colt. "I think that may be so."

The wind blew hard from the southwest, churning snow on the road and reducing visibility. Norman chatted quietly, lulling David to sleep. Suddenly, as they wound around a curve in the road, a gust of wind caught the hood. The force slammed it up against the windshield, startling David from his slumber.

"Hold on!" Norman hollered as he fought to keep the car on the road. All he could see was the hood banging in the wind.

Norman applied the brakes, sending the car fishtailing across both lanes. He regained control of the car and slowed to a stop.

David's body throbbed from the sudden adrenaline rush. His ears were pounding from shock as he inhaled deeply to calm himself.

"I have to fix the hood," Norman said as he pulled on his gloves. He slammed his door and they watched as he pulled the hood down.

"That s-scared the shit out of me," David said.

"Me too," Sharon gasped.

"But at least we don't got to worry now about no more cats hidin' under there," David teased.

"David!" she joked, giving him a playful punch in the arm.

David could see his brother illuminated by the headlights. Norman was studying the hood, which had been severely bent by the wind. A few moments later he went to the back of the car and opened the trunk. He returned carrying a rope. Norman tied the hood down.

"There," he said as his door opened and the wind pushed him back into the car. "All fixed."

David stared out the windshield. The hood was noticeably twisted.

"What's gonna happen if snow gets in there," he asked.

"Ah, you worry too much, Davey boy," he said. "It'll be fine."

They drove for a few more hours in the blinding snowstorm.

"Norm, can we stop soon?" Sharon asked sleepily.

"Stop?" he asked. "I don't think so, honey. We've got to keep driving. We don't have any money to waste."

Everyone agreed, but glanced with worried eyes at the snow that seemed to get deeper and heavier the farther west they traveled.

As they crossed the Manitoba-Saskatchewan border, Norman and David exchanged a knowing look over Sharon's sleeping head. Visibility would decrease even more as they traveled across the flat terrain and open fields of Saskatchewan—known to have the most unforgiving weather in all Canada.

David noticed the challenge didn't deter Norman who ploughed ahead. They drove all night, arriving in Medicine Hat, Alberta, before sunrise. Norman pulled into a gas station. He was told by the attendant that the roads ahead were treacherous. He advised them to stay in Medicine Hat to wait out the storm.

Weary from traveling and exhausted from fighting drifting snow, Norman took the advice. He got back in the car and drove to a motel along the highway.

"Duck," he told the twins as he stopped in front of the motel office. "I'm only paying for two."

The twins crouched until Norman halted in front of the motel unit. Stiff from the long ride, everyone groaned as they got out of the car.

Norman opened the door and they clambered inside.

"Sharon and I get the bed," he said in a tone that left no room for discussion.

The twins were too drained to argue. After removing their coats, they each grabbed an extra pillow and blanket from the bureau drawer and lay down on the carpeted floor in front of the baseboard heater. David groaned with relief. It felt good to stretch out, even if it was on the floor. Within minutes, all four were sleeping soundly.

They awoke late that afternoon to find themselves snow bound.

Norman reluctantly agreed to spend that night in Medicine Hat. They watched television and played cards while waiting out the storm.

They arose early the next morning. Norman sent David out to start the car.

David returned a few minutes later. "I think the car don't got no b-brakes," he said.

"What did you do to it?" Norman asked, as he pulled on his thin jacket.

"Nothin'," David said. "I just started backin' it up, an it kept goin'."

"Probably froze up," Norman muttered. "We'll get it checked. Let's get going."

Although the snow had ceased, a damp wind met the travelers as they emerged from the motel. The sky was still overcast but the morning sun was sending pink streams through breaks in the clouds. All was silent except for the roar of snow-clearing equipment in the distance.

The car sat idling against a post in the parking lot. David again explained how the car had reacted when he tried to brake in front of the motel.

Norman stood for a moment examining the vehicle.

"You hit a post?" he asked.

"How else was I gonna stop?" David replied. "I didn't shmash it, just shmooshed up against it."

Norman thought for a moment. "Half the time I don't know what the hell you're saying," he chortled. They climbed into the car and squealed with discomfort.

"Aren't leather seats nice?" Norman laughed, as he put the car in gear. "Whoever invents ass-warmers for cars is going to make a fortune."

They all snickered at the thought.

"Hold on," Norman said cheerfully as they slid across the parking lot. The brakes definitely needed checking so he drove slowly to a nearby garage.

"That's one thing about traveling in a storm," Norman said, waving cheerfully at the mechanic standing in the doorway. "There's nobody else around."

They climbed out of the car and stood in the drafty garage while Norman explained the problem to the mechanic who hoisted the vehicle and examined the brakes.

"Well, you popped the rubbers," he said after the inspection. "How far are you going?"

"Shit . . . " Norman said, "we're going to B.C."

"B.C.? You're gonna need brakes. You can't go anywhere like this," the mechanic said, eyeing the bent hood. "Actually, I wouldn't even put this car on the road . . ."

"Yeah, well, whatever," Norman said glancing at the twins and then back again. "How much is it going to cost?"

The man suggested he buy a used pair of brakes from the local auto wreckers. That would cost $50.

"Well, we have no choice," Norman said.

Pooling all their money, he paid for the brakes and stuffed the rest into his pocket. It took all morning to get the brakes replaced, leaving everyone in a foul mood by the time they started for Calgary. By late afternoon, it had resumed snowing and the highway was drifted in places.

Just past midnight they found themselves in the mountains west of Banff. Sharon and the twins dozed as Norman hummed along with the radio. Suddenly, a tire blew. Norman fought to keep the car on the road as he braked and guided the hobbling car toward the shoulder.

Jolted awake, David could hear Norman muttering to himself as he got out of the car. He returned a moment later, letting in a frigid blast of air as he opened the driver's door.

"Get out, we have to change the tire," Norman sighed.

Reluctantly, everyone stepped into the cold, dark night. It wasn't until the trunk was half open that David remembered it was packed full.

"Where's the tire?" David asked stupidly.

"Where do you think?" Norman said as he stared at the neatly packed trunk. "Under the pig."

They all groaned.

"Please don't get any of my stuff wet," Sharon pleaded. "I don't want it wrecked."

Dennis cleared snow along the shoulder with his boots while David and Norman started unloading. They had to stack everything on the ground before they were able to lift out the spare tire. Feeling around the bottom of the trunk, Norman swore again.

"Damn!" he exclaimed. "No wheel wrench, do you believe it?"

Jamming his hands in his pockets, he looked around. "We've got to flag somebody down," he said.

"I'm waiting in the car," Sharon said.

Norman and the twins stood by the roadside waiting for another motorist to come along. Fortunately, only a few minutes elapsed before a car approached. Norman moved into the middle of the road and began waving his arms. The car swerved around him, slowed, then pulled off to the side of the road.

A man in his early 40s stepped out.

"What's the problem?" he asked Norman who hurried to meet him.

"Flat tire," Norman said cheerfully. "And see that gorgeous doll sitting in the car there?"

The man nodded.

"She packed every goddamned thing except a wheel wrench," he joked.

The man laughed. "Where you headed?"

"B.C.," Norman said.

"I've got one you can borrow," the motorist said hurrying back to his car.

Norman motioned for Sharon to hop out. He began jacking up the car as the stranger returned with a wheel wrench and flashlight.

"This should work," he said, handing the wrench to David. "What happened to your hood?"

Norman chuckled. "Marquette is one helluva windy place."

The man glanced at the licence plate. "You from Manitoba?"

"Yep, but we're going to work in 100 Mile House," Norman smiled.

They finished changing the tire and Norman handed the man his wrench.

"Thanks a lot," Norman said, shaking his hand. "I'd offer to pay you, but we're pretty short of cash."

"No problem," the guy said raising his hand as he turned to leave. "I've been there."

"Thanks again," Norman said, adding, "and if you're ever in Marquette, watch out for your hood!"

The man laughed as he hurried back to his warm car.

"All right," Norman said, clapping his hands in excitement as they began repacking the trunk, "let's get the hell outta here."

David offered to drive but Norman shrugged off the suggestion. Sharon's head rested comfortably on his shoulder as they pressed on through the night.

The next morning, they all fought to keep their eyes open as the sun emerged from behind a mountain, reflecting brightly on the side mirrors. David scanned their surroundings and was amazed once again by the majestic beauty of the tree-covered wall ahead.

The highway wound around the side of the mountain until it reached the peak and emerged near the top. David held his breath as he listened to the car's engine labouring under its heavy load. He relaxed as Norman rounded a curve and began the descent. Despite the tension of the ride, David felt reassured knowing that he'd be living in the mountains again.

As they neared the town of Golden, B.C., the severity of the slopes began to increase. While everyone was tired, spirits were high as they chatted and joked.

Once again the car suddenly jerked to one side.

"Hold on!" he hollered as he hit the brakes while the car jolted down the highway. "Another flat!"

David closed his eyes and braced himself, expecting this time that they'd slide down the mountainside. Norman managed to wrestle the car under control and when David opened his eyes, they were stopped on the shoulder. Everyone sat in silence.

"This bloody car's going to give me a heart attack," Norman said as he got out to look at what had happened.

"W-what are we gonna do now?" David asked, following his brother outside. "We don't got no s-sspare."

"I know," Norman said, deep in thought. He glanced at the blowout on the rear driver's side. "C'mon and help me."

Norman opened the trunk and began unloading the frozen meat once again. Unsure what his brother was planning, David silently helped.

"I'll hitch to the next town and get the spare fixed," Norman said, as he lifted out the tire and put it on the ground. Holding it between his knees, he lit a cigar, squeezed the plastic tip into the corner of his mouth and started rolling the tire up the road. He paused and turned back to David.

"We're almost out of gas, so you guys have to shut off the car," he yelled back.

"We're gonna freeze!" David yelled back.

Norman shrugged as he began shuffling up the highway again. Hearing a car approach from behind, Norman turned, stood upright and stuck out his thumb. David stood beside their car looking quite pathetic. The oncoming driver accelerated first past the stranded car, then past Norman who raised his middle finger in response. David could hear his brother muttering, but couldn't grasp what he was saying.

David climbed back into the car.

"Where's he goin'?" Dennis asked.

"To get the tire fixed," David said. "We gotta wait here."

The three chatted for awhile watching Norman's image shrink and eventually disappear. David looked at the gas gauge. "We gotta shut off the car," he sighed. "Norman said."

Sharon reached over and turned off the ignition. "He'll be back soon," she replied confidently.

The twins nodded. They had total faith in Norman's ability to solve any problem. So many times when they were children they'd looked to their older brother for hope. Sometimes, all he had to offer were a few humorous words or a defiant look, but it was always enough. David had a solemn expression as he thought about their past. He suspected Dennis was remembering as well.

It wasn't long before a car approached from the opposite direction. David watched as it slowed, made a u-turn on the highway and pulled in behind the Pischke car. Norman got out and it was apparent he was telling jokes to whomever had given him a ride. Both men were enjoying the punch line as the twins got out of the car.

The anonymous driver waved, got back in his car and drove away. Norman's mood was cheerful as he rolled a new tire toward the car.

"I got a good deal on a couple of tires from a garage in Golden," he said, holding up a wheel wrench. "The guy there loaned me this."

They quickly changed the tire and were once again on their way. Their moods were bright as they drove into town.

"We have to stop and pick up the other tire," Norman said.

"We really need gas," Sharon whispered to her husband who glanced at the gauge and nodded. He drove to the garage and waved to the mechanic who was standing in the window. The man smiled, disappeared for a moment and then the overhead bay doors slid open. He motioned for Norman to drive inside.

The teenage travelers piled out of the car in the warm garage. They watched as the mechanic made his way around the car.

"How long you been driving with your hood like that?" he asked, raising his eyebrows.

"Not too far," Norman shrugged.

"Where did you say you were going?"

"100 Mile House," he replied.

The man sucked in a deep breath. "I don't know . . ." he said slowly exhaling. "You got chains for the back tires?"

"Huh?"

"Chains," the mechanic said. "You gotta go through Roger's Pass to get to 100 Mile House, and if I were you, I wouldn't attempt it without chains."

Trying to hide his frustration, Norman reached into his pocket and pulled out some change. He gave it to Sharon. "Go get us something to eat, okay?"

She took the change and quickly left.

"Okay," Norman said turning back to the mechanic. "How much are chains going to cost?"

The pair negotiated a price, then Norman said he couldn't afford to have the mechanic put them on.

"No problem," he said. "You can do it in here, but we only got one hoist and I'm using it over there."

Norman nodded as he took the chains. He began looking for a jack.

"And you better fix that tail light," the man added. "I got lights in stock too."

"Thanks," he grumbled. "Goddamned car, anyway. If I had a plane, we could just fly there."

David hunched down beside Norman as he jacked up the car.

The twins stepped forward and helped their brother as needed.

"Yep, Davey, one of these days I'm gonna buy a plane," he said, mood suddenly optimistic, "and then we'll just fly wherever we want to go."

"We got any money left?" David whispered, spoiling Norman's daydream.

"A bit, why?"

"We got enough for gas?"

"Yeah—barely," he whispered back.

Sharon returned and passed around a bag of chips.

"Are we almost there?" she asked.

"Not far now," Norman said as he wrapped the chains around the tires. "We should get there this afternoon."

He finished fastening the chains and the mechanic appeared. He handed Norman a new taillight bulb.

"Give me a hand, will you?" Norman said handing the bulb to David. "Here, hold this."

As Norman hastily tried to snap off the broken taillight cover, his hand slipped—slicing the palm on the sharp glass.

"Oh hell," he said, grasping his cut hand with the other. Blood trickled down his arm.

Blood.

The sight of it made David woozy. He'd seen so much blood in so few years that it now caused him to panic.

"Aaaah," he moaned as his stomach heaved. "Norman," he whispered covering his eyes with his hands.

Falling back against a tool box, David's knees buckled and he slid to the ground. He fought to keep down the food he'd just eaten.

Norman grabbed a rag from a nearby pile, wrapped it around his injured hand and tied it tight.

"Maybe you should go to the hospital to have that checked," Sharon suggested.

"Nah, I'm fine," Norman said as he continued to fix the light. "Take him," he chuckled pointing to David.

Still sick from the sight of Norman's cut hand, David lay motionless on the cold, cement floor.

"All finished," Norman said a few minutes later as he wiped his good hand on his pants. "Are you all right?"

David groaned again. "I'll be okay."

"Well, then let's go," Norman said.

They helped David into the car. Norman backed out of the garage and pulled up to the gas pumps. He gave the attendant the last of their money

"I sure hope this Roy guy gives us jobs," he said glancing at David.

David smiled bravely, but inwardly felt his stomach churn. The fact they had traveled nearly 1,300 miles on blind faith in David's word was something he didn't want to think about just then.

In keeping with the trip's bad luck, another tire blew—this time near Revelstoke. Norman was livid when he discovered it was one of the new back tires. For the third time, he flagged down a motorist to borrow a wheel wrench. A young man stopped to help.

"Who was the idiot who put the chains on?" the motorist asked as they examined the tire.

"Why?" Norman asked.

"Well, he put them on backwards," the man said. "See how they've worn through right here?"

"Some asshole back in Golden," Norman said lamely.

David fought to keep from laughing.

"Well, it's a good thing you got a spare," the man said cheerfully. "You wouldn't believe how unprepared some guys are." He then helped them rearrange the trunk for the seventh time in 24 hours.

"Yeah, I know what you mean," Norman replied through clenched teeth.

"He lives right up there," David said, pointing to the hill on the edge of 100 Mile House. Norman drove slowly through town as they took in their surroundings.

For the first time on the trip, Norman was looking to David for advice. The twin stepped into the leadership role, pointing out landmarks he remembered from his first stay in the quaint town. He felt like he'd come home.

"An' that's where I charged up my groceries an' the coat," he said. "An' over there, that's the hotel where Roy got thrown out . . . an' them people in that café over there is real nice . . . an' if you go down that street there an' turn, there's the bus station—'member that Denny? Ten cents! That's all we had left after takin' the train."

"Okay, shuddup," Norman chuckled. "We got the idea."

David blushed, pausing for a moment. "Okay, turn here to go to Roy's."

The car climbed the hill and everyone was quiet as Roy's yard came into view. David was relieved that nothing had changed. When they got out of the car, he tried to look confident as he led the way to Roy's door.

He hid the fact that his stomach was queasy and he was filled with uncertainty. What if Roy didn't want to hire them after all? He felt as if he might be sick again and decided that if he fainted, he'd blame it on the blood stains that had soaked through the rag on Norman's hand.

David knocked on the door. It opened a few moments later and Roy recognized David and Dennis immediately.

"C'mon in boys," he said stepping away from the door and giving them a wide smile. "I was hopin' I'd see you two again."

David stammered through introductions as Roy and Norman shifted uncomfortably, embarrassed for the teen. Roy mercifully cut David short, asking if the young men were looking for work.

They nodded that they were.

"Well," Roy began, turning toward the kitchen and motioning for them to follow. "I don't have anything for you guys right now, but I know they are hiring at the sawmill in town."

"Oh," David said, "do you think they'll w-wwant to hire all th-three of us?"

"Well son, with the way you work, and I'm sure your brothers are the same, you Pischke boys will have no trouble at all."

David beamed.

"Are you hungry like usual?" Roy asked.

David nodded and everyone laughed. Roy put together a makeshift dinner for them while he updated David on news from 100 Mile House. He said that nobody was staying in his cabin located a few miles away—he'd show it to them. It overlooked the sawmill.

They thanked Roy for lunch and after putting on their boots, followed him to the cabin.

"It's not pretty, but it's warm," Roy said opening the door. He glanced at Sharon as he spoke. Her striking beauty shone even though she hadn't bathed in a few days. All eyes were on her as they opened the door to the dingy, dirty space.

"This looks great, Roy," she said charmingly.

The young men were relieved that she was making the best of the situation. Roy left them to unload their belongings and promised to put in a good word for them at the lumber company. He also loaned them enough money to buy food.

The next day they were hired by Canim Lake Sawmills to work on the "green chain" with men who sorted lumber into boxcars as it came off conveyor belts. The work was difficult and dangerous as they had to stand in the boxcars and manually stack each plank according to size. If they didn't move quickly, they were hit by 12 foot planks which hurtled along the conveyor belt. During each day of the first week, the twins returned to the trailer bruised and blistered. It took a while for them to "toughen" to the job but soon they were comfortable with the work.

Being an older, more experienced worker, Norman wanted a better job. After a week, he and Sharon left 100 Mile House to find work elsewhere.

The teens walked back and forth to the sawmill after that, hitching rides whenever they could. They were well paid and soon could afford to buy food again. Most of their meals consisted of sausage, sauerkraut and potatoes.

A month after their arrival, the twins moved into shack-like row housing beside the sawmill. This cut down the distance to work, but it also meant they had to live in a community of transient labourers. This made the twins nervous. A fear of being bullied kept them from socializing as did their dislike for spending money on alcohol, drugs or gambling.

They became more out-going after they got to know the men next door. The Oslin brothers were big men in their mid-20s who had worked at the sawmill for a few years. The brothers visited back and forth and one day while chatting in the Oslin cabin, the twins noticed that the brothers had a radio with speakers. They remembered seeing a similar luxury before and commented on how fortunate the Oslins were to own the radio. In an amicable moment, a hole was drilled through the adjoining walls and speaker wire strung through. Mutual agreement was made that one of the speakers would be loaned to the Pischkes on the condition that they paid $5 a week rent. The twins now felt they were in heaven. Feeling quite grown up and independent, the boys settled in nicely at 100 Mile House.

One evening there was a knock at the door. The twins were surprised to see Roy standing there with Eunice.

"Got a surprise for you guys," he said.

"Eunice!" David exclaimed. "Whatcha doin' here?"

"I came to see you two," their sister laughed, "and Norman and Sharon, too."

Eunice explained that she wanted to do some traveling and thought 100 Mile House would be a good place to visit.

"How did you find us?" David asked.

"From your letters," she said. "I didn't know where you were, but it wasn't hard finding Roy."

David snickered. "Did I ever tell you guys how I met R-rroy?"

Of course, the whole family had heard the story many times.

"Good ol' R-rroy H-hhauling Wwwood," David smiled.

Roy had an obvious soft spot for the Pischke boys and after realizing Eunice was their sister, he hired the teenager to do cleaning work.

"Now we're all here!" Dennis exclaimed.

They knew that Stephen was also in the area, but so far, they hadn't seen him.

The following week there was another knock at the twins' door. They opened it to find Norman on the stoop, sporting a wide grin.

"Hi guys," he said, stepping inside. He carried a big wooden box.

"Tracked you down," he said, explaining that he found a well-paying job at a uranium mine near Canim Lake. He and Sharon were living at the Canim Lake resort.

"What's in the box?" David asked.

Norman put it on the table, then opened the lid.

"Dynamite," he smiled.

The twins stared at the explosives at the bottom of the box.

"Dynamite?" David asked excitedly. "Whatcha gonna do with that?"

"You know all the rocks and stumps around home, well this will come in handy for clearing the runway I have planned at the farm," he said. "I can just blast them out."

The twins stared at the dynamite. David knew that purchasing it required a permit. He also knew that men his age were fascinated by it.

"Where did ya get it from?" he asked.

"From work," Norman said. "But don't tell anybody. I have to leave it here. Where can you guys hide it?"

The twins offered to store it under their bed.

Norman carried the box into the small bedroom and looked around.

"You guys are still sleeping in the same bed?" he scoffed.

The boys shrugged.

"Gees, we have to find you guys some girls," Norman said. "Aren't there any women around here?"

David blushed at the suggestion. He hadn't had a date since abandoning Barb in Beausejour six months before.

"Girlfriends cost too m-mmuch m-mmoney," he said. "Besides, we can't find n-nno girl for Dennis be-cause he's too ugly."

Dennis punched him playfully in the arm. "I look like you!" he exclaimed.

Norman chuckled as he slid the box under the bed.

"Now don't tell nobody it's here," he warned. "And whatever the hell you do, don't burn the place down."

Feeling important that their brother trusted them, they nodded their heads eagerly.

"Don't worry Norman, we'll watch it g-ggood." David said.

One evening the Oslin brothers arrived for a visit and the four young men started bragging about what they were going to do when they left 100 Mile House. Proud of Norman, the twins swore the Oslins to secrecy, then told them about the dynamite—and how he hoped to use it when they returned to Manitoba.

Another evening while the twins were discussing Eunice's recent decision to return to Manitoba, the music from next door began blaring. The Oslins were having a party that lasted all night. The twins had to unhook the speaker wire so they could fall asleep.

This started happening regularly and soon the twins were sick of the radio station selected by the Oslins. The friendship began to deteriorate and the twins decided to renege on the deal to pay rent for the speaker. Behind in rent, they put the Oslins off for a few weeks, telling them to come back on payday and they'd square up. Just before the brothers returned the following Friday, David and Dennis shut off the lights and pretended they weren't home. Thinking they were quite clever they went to bed, only to be awakened hours later by the sound of splitting wood. They jumped out of bed to find the angry, drunken Oslins had broken down the door.

"Give us our money," one brother demanded.

"H-hey, you busted d-down our d-door," David yelled as he clambered out of bed. "Who's gonna f-ffix it?"

"Give us our money," the other brother said swaying across the room, "and our speaker." He reached up and pulled one off the wall.

"S-stop t-that!" Dennis yelled.

"Who's gonna make me?" the man said, giving Dennis a shove.

"Hit him!" David said. "Hit him, Dennis!"

Never having been in a fist fight before, except for the occasional fight with his brother, Dennis danced around the bigger man, gathering courage. The Oslins thought the scene was quite comical and taunted Dennis, encouraging him to fight.

Dennis wound up and punched one brother in the chest—a blow that barely registered. The man laughed and quickly retaliated by punching Dennis hard in the face. The teen went down, but quickly scampered past the Oslin. Within seconds, the twins were out the door. Once they were a safe distance away, they hid out of sight.

They returned to their cabin a few hours later to find the Oslins had smashed most of the furniture. The bed was overturned and the dynamite was gone. The Oslins taunted them all night through a broken window, saying they were going to "blow up" the cabin.

The twins didn't sleep the rest of the night and decided to go to the local RCMP office the next morning. They told police what had happened and said they wanted to press charges. They returned home and watched out the window as a police cruiser pulled up in front of the Oslin cabin. The officers, carrying guns and small billy clubs, went inside. Feeling that they'd been vindicated, the twins started cleaning up the mess.

"Well, the RCMP never did nothin' when we were kids so they can help us now," Dennis said.

He gently touched his bruised eye, and David could see the punch brought back unpleasant memories for his brother. He wondered out loud how they were going to face the Oslins at work the next morning. They decided that avoiding them would be the wisest thing to do.

A few evenings later, Norman and Sharon drove up to the twins' shack. The car was filled with their belongings, minus the butchered pig they'd eaten long ago. The twins could tell by Norman's expression that he was angry.

They stood on the doorstep as Norman got out of the car. He shook his head.

"You stupid asses," he said. "What the hell were you thinking?"

The twins shrugged.

"What happened here anyway?" Norman demanded.

The twins explained that the Oslins had smashed in the front door and were threatening them.

"Why did you report it to the RCMP?" Norman demanded.

"'Cause they shmashed Dennis," David said defensively. "An' they wrr-recked our p-pplace."

"Yeah, but you also told the mounties that those bastards stole the dynamite you had under your bed," Norman said.

"They was g-ggonna blow us up," David explained.

"Too bad they didn't," Norman growled. "I got fired because of this."

"How come?"

"How come?" he retorted. "How come? Because you told the cops the dynamite belonged to your brother and the name of the mine was stamped on the box, that's how come."

The twins looked at each other, then at their shoes.

"S-sorry, we d-didn't know," David apologized. "W-we didn't think of that."

"Couldn't you have lied or something?" Norman asked.

"We d-ddon't lie so g-good."

"I see that," Norman said. "Now I've got no job and we have to go home."

David looked past his brother to the car where Sharon was sitting. She didn't look too upset about the turn of events. He'd heard she was homesick.

"W-when are you g-ggoin'?" he asked.

"When do you think?" Norman yelled. "Now! You idiot."

The twins stood for a few minutes longer, trying to patch up the relationship with their brother.

"But don't tell Sharon—she doesn't know I got fired," Norman said, tone softening.

"Don't worry, we won't," David exclaimed.

Norman stared at him.

"God, that was stupid," he said, staring off down the road. "I never should have taken it . . ."

David felt sorry for his brother.

"Sorry Norman," he apologized again.

"Ah, that's okay," he said, waving it off. He shrugged as he walked to the car. Sharon waved cheerfully to the twins as Norman opened his door and got inside. He gave a small wave then drove off.

Not long after there was another knock on the twins' door. They opened it to find their brother Stephen standing there. Surprised, they invited him inside.

David hadn't seen Stephen since their argument on the outskirts of 100 Mile House the year before, but it turned out that Stephen was working and living nearby. They caught up on family news and he teased them about getting Norman in trouble.

He also told them that he planned to attend Eunice's wedding, scheduled for the end of March. The twins said they wanted to go to the wedding too, and it was decided they'd all travel together. David and Dennis obtained a leave of absence from work, for a promise they'd return in a few weeks.

Unfortunately, reporting the Oslins to the police caused them more trouble than they bargained for. The twins received a mailed summons ordering them to appear in court—something they hadn't expected. They didn't realize they would have to testify, thinking the police would take care of it for them. The court date would delay their trip home and might cost them a ride with their brother. They begged him to wait, not wanting to take the train again. He agreed.

The three left as soon as the twins emerged from the court house.

"So what happened?" Stephen asked as the twins dug sandwiches out of a bag they'd packed. "Did they get off?"

"No, they have to p-ppay a f-ffine," David said, biting into a sandwich. "An' fix the door they broke."

"What about you guys?"

"We gotta stay away from them," David snorted. "And they tole us to stay outta trouble."

Chapter 12

"**HAVE YOU EVER BEEN TREATED** by a psychologist or psychiatrist?" McMillan asked.

"Do you mean like counseling?"

"Yes."

"No, I never have."

"Have you ever been a patient in a mental hospital?"

"Yes, I went to see Domko," he said. "I took Mom there a few times."

"But you've never actually been admitted to a mental hospital?"

"Me? No!" he said, chuckling. "I'm not the crazy one, he was. People said we was the ones who drove him crazy, but not even us guys can do that good a job, you know what I mean, eh?"

McMillan laughed.

The family converged again—this time to celebrate Eunice and Mel's wedding. It was at the Canadian Forces Base in Gypsumville.

David approached family events with a mixture of excitement and caution. While he enjoyed seeing familiar faces, memories of their childhood together were thrust to the forefront.

He was disappointed to hear that their mother was back on the farm with Domko. It seemed that while the two couldn't live together they also couldn't stand to be apart. Rosie looked solemn and three year-old Markie chased seven year old Raymond playfully around the room.

It hadn't been that long since David had moved away from the farm, but it was enough time for him to gain some perspective on what his life had been—and what it could be.

"Well, look at Dennis and David," someone said as the twins joined the reception. "You guys think you're cowboys or what?"

David smiled, sensing the comment wasn't necessarily a compliment. They'd bought all new western wear in B.C., saving their best clothes for the wedding. He and Dennis had discovered they were teased less by strangers when they dressed well. However, people around home seemed to like it better when they looked "down-and-out." He sensed some jealousy from both family and friends, but pushed thoughts of this aside.

"Nn-nice d-duds," Walter said, smiling as he playfully punched David in the shoulder. "How's work goin'?"

"Good, r-real good," David smiled. "W-we got some time off for the weddin' but then we're goin' back." David knew he could always trust Walter to treat him with kindness and respect.

"How 'bout with you?" he asked. "You s-still at the plant?"

"Yep," Walter answered, "but I'm gonna hafta quit soon though."

David looked at him, puzzled.

"He keeps showin' up to borrow money," Walter joked, nodding in Domko's direction. "It's the only way I'll be able to get away from him."

"Does he ever pay you back?" David asked.

"Are you kiddin'?" Walter laughed. "And I'm trying to s-save up enough money to buy a farm—I can't keep his afloat, too."

David winced. "Why would you wanna buy a farm?"

Walter's eyes widened. "Why?" he smiled dreamily. "'Cause there's no life like it. You'll know ww-what I mean in a few years after you've worked for some joker who don't know half as much as you. Farmin' starts to look pretty g-ggood then."

David smiled. "I ain't shovellin' no more shit."

Walter chuckled as he shook his head. "Shovellin' your own shit ain't so bad as shovellin' someone else's," he said, again pointing at Domko. "Not everybody's as mean as that ol' bugger."

"Lots are," David stated.

They stood quietly together for a moment.

"I learned long ago that you gotta ignore what they say about you," Walter said as they shared a knowing look. "Prove yourself to the bastards. Show 'em what you're made of."

Within days, the twins were ready to return to British Columbia. Longer days and warm spring sunshine made David yearn for summer. Before heading west for the winter, he'd bought himself a motorcycle and was anxious to get it out of storage. He missed the freedom of the open road.

He and Dennis were friends with a teenager named Ken Price who lived with his mother and stepfather in Moosehorn. The young men had worked together on the floodway and spent most of their free time together. Their common bond was a love of motorcycles. David's 1955 Harley Davidson was stored alongside Ken's 1949 Harley in the Price garage.

The day after Eunice and Mel's wedding, David visited his friend and the two decided it was time to bring out the bikes. It was a splendid morning. They felt the sun on their backs as they opened the garage doors, letting in streams of sunlight and fresh air. Pushing the bikes outside they spent the day cleaning and tuning the machines while they made plans to travel together to B.C. David was certain there would be no trouble finding Ken a job at the sawmill.

Within days, their loaded bikes were on the highway to the West Coast. Dennis decided to ride back with Stephen. Rather than stopping in 100 Mile House, the brothers continued to Prince George, B.C.

David was rehired back on at the sawmill and Ken took Dennis's job. The pair rented one of the small shacks where the twins had lived before. David and Ken put in long hours, made a good wage and were pleased when Dennis arrived a month later. For the first time in his life, David started enjoying himself.

Ken brought an element of excitement to the twins' world. He was a handsome teen with black hair and bright blue eyes, attracting girls wherever he went. The boys tried to impress teenage girls they met and there was plenty of showing off and hanging out at night spots and restaurants. The young men joked and teased each other constantly.

Their antics and sense of adventure traveled with them from B.C. back to Manitoba early that summer. They were hired again by Ramsey-Bird Construction to finish building the floodway. They worked all summer, spending their evenings cruising the area around Birds Hill on their motorcycles and stopping at the Dairy Queen where Jack's daughter Gloria gave them free ice cream.

◆ ◆ ◆ ◆ ◆

In early September Sharon gave birth to a baby boy. They named him Lee. A week later she and Norman brought the child home from the hospital. As a new mother, Sharon was nervous. She'd had little experience with babies and was glad that Norman would be around to help on her first day home.

She fed and burped Lee and it wasn't long before he needed a diaper change. Not entirely sure what to do, she took him to the crib and removed his gown. As she slipped off the rubber pants, a strong smell rose from the baby.

"Whew!" she murmured, then paused.

"Wait here," she whispered to Lee as she hurried to find a damp cloth. When she returned, Norman was standing by the crib.

"He pooped," she said, sounding worried.

She gently opened the safety pin and slipped it off. She pulled back the diaper and was surprised by the mess the little baby had made. She hesitated. The cool air chilled Lee and he began to cry. This flustered Sharon.

"I don't know what to do," she said, feeling clumsy.

"Here, let me," Norman said. Taking the cloth from her, Norman gently wiped the baby, then slipped the dirty diaper out of the crib. She handed him a diaper which he refolded.

"It's better for boys this way," he said.

Grasping Lee's feet with one big hand he gently slipped the diaper underneath. He wrapped the cloth around the tiny body and fastened the pin, careful not to poke Lee's skin. He then took his warm hands and gently held onto the boy—transferring his own warmth to his son. The baby stopped crying and Norman stood silently gazing at the baby.

"There," he whispered. "Nothing to it."

Freeze-up came in early November and the construction crew received lay-off notices shortly afterwards. A month earlier, David had traded his convertible for a red 1957 Chevrolet. On the way back to the trailer from the dealership, the frame broke and the engine had fallen out on the ground. Too afraid to complain to the salesman where he'd bought the car, David got it fixed on his own. It had taken all his extra money plus he had to borrow from Dennis so that he could afford to get it fixed. He had just gotten it back from the mechanic when it came time for the twins to pack their few belongings and move back to Moosehorn for the winter.

They were a half hour into the long drive home when the car suddenly stalled. David managed to guide it to the shoulder before it came to a complete stop.

"What's wrong?" Dennis asked.

"I dunno," David said, starting to get angry. "This car's been nothin' but a problem." He sat for a moment, then turned the ignition. The engine turned over but it wouldn't start.

"What the hell?" he muttered, trying again. Soon gas fumes filled the car and he knew the engine was flooded.

"Now what are we gonna do?" Dennis asked.

"I dunno," David said as he shut off the heater and lights to preserve the battery. He stared out the window into the dark, windy night. November was a particularly bleak month in Manitoba with mostly overcast skies and temperatures that hovered around 25 degrees Fahrenheit.

He watched the traffic speed past in both directions. This highway was busy—especially on Friday night. The headlights of oncoming cars cast enough illumination that he could see a light dusting of snow blowing across the highway. He was in no mood to get out and flag down a stranger for help. He didn't know what good it would do either. They were too far from Moosehorn to hitchhike home because he'd have to come back the next day for the car. And they were too far from the city to have it towed back—that would cost too much money. Sensing what David was thinking, Dennis looked at his brother and scowled.

"I don't wanna sleep in the car," Dennis said.

"Me neither!" David yelled back.

They sat quietly for a few minutes.

"I never shoulda traded in the other car," David lamented. "Why did I do that, anyway? It was stupid. One of the stupidest things I ever done."

Dennis shrugged as he climbed into the back seat. He pushed everything they'd brought onto the floor. Muttering to himself, he began rummaging for blankets. Soon the pair were arguing. They bickered about who was at fault for their predicament. They discussed the purchase of the car and then argued whether they should have left at night or waited until the next morning. They finally turned away from one another, pulled the blankets over their heads and fell asleep.

They shivered all night, waking the next morning before dawn. Forgetting about the argument the night before, the brothers started joking. On an impulse, David turned the ignition key. Surprisingly, the car started right away. The twins looked at one another in amazement. The engine sounded perfect! Dennis climbed back into the front as David let the car warm up before slowly putting it into drive. He pulled back onto the deserted highway.

"Well, I'll be darned . . ." David said.

Dennis reached over to turn on the heater. Within seconds, the engine started to sputter.

"Oh no, it's doing it again," David moaned. "What's wrong?" He reached over and shut off the heater so he could hear the engine, which hesitated, then surged again. They drove for a few more minutes before turning the heater on again. The car jolted as the engine sputtered.

"It's the heater," David said. He quickly shut off the fan. "We gotta drive with no heat."

By the time they reached Moosehorn, they were chilled but relieved they had made it home. Since realizing the car would run with the heater turned off, they felt foolish for sleeping on the side of the highway. They decided to go to Norman's house to see if he could figure out what was wrong with the car. They stopped in the driveway of the small house that Norman and Sharon were renting and David tentatively shut off the engine.

"I hope it starts again," Dennis said.

"Well if it don't, Norman will have to help us, 'cause we got his car blocked in," David giggled.

The twins gave a brief knock, then stepped into the warm house. David was surprised to find their mother and half-siblings were visiting. Sharon and Norman were sitting with Caroline drinking coffee at the kitchen table. David knew that Domko was not there by the relaxed atmosphere.

In an animated way the twins relayed the story about spending the night in the car. They blamed each other loudly for the predicament. Everyone chuckled at the story, amused by the way it was told. When they finished, the twins sat at the table. Then David noticed his mother was holding a baby. David glanced at the floor where 15 month-old Jennie played happily with a toy, while the older children buzzed around her. Then he looked back at the newborn.

Oh no, he thought. *Not another one!*

He quickly realized with some relief that the child was Sharon and Norman's.

"Cc-congratulations," David said, pointing to the baby. He hoped that he sounded sincere.

To David, babies were a burden and he wondered what kind of life this child would have. Seeing his brother with new family responsibilities made David shudder. And while Norman and Sharon looked tired, David had to admit to himself they also appeared happy. Norman had a job driving for his father-in-law whose trucking business was growing and with only a few more flying hours to log, Norman would soon have his pilot's licence.

"So Ma," David said. "how are you?"

Caroline explained that she and the children were staying with Norman and Sharon for a few days—a needed respite from Domko. She seemed embarrassed and Norman got up from the table. David pressed for details, noticing that family members were reluctant to openly discuss the abuse they suffered.

"He's really bad right now," Caroline said quietly to nobody in particular. "He ran out of pills and I can't make him go for his check-ups."

She talked about their financial problems and difficulties because of a lack of farm labourers. As well, Domko had recently threatened Eunice and Mel with a gun because Caroline had given them a sealer of cream.

David didn't know what to say. He always felt pressure to "fix" his mother's life, but knew there wasn't much he could do. He wanted to ask her why she didn't leave Domko permanently, but didn't want to get into an argument. He could feel his confusion and anger mount as questions formed in his mind. Mostly he could push bad memories away, but contact with his family always brought back the recollections.

When something bothered David, he would withdraw and be unable to talk about anything else until he'd spoken at length about what was festering inside. He usually discussed what was troubling him with his twin who also dealt with unresolved issues the same way.

Fortunately, it was Dennis who broke the uncomfortable silence by quizzing Norman about the car and what might be wrong with it. They were immersed in conversation as David watched his mother coo and fuss over her first grandchild.

Sharon got up and made more coffee and toast for everyone. David watched Lee and wondered what Domko thought of the baby—a child that was half-Pischke and half-Russell. He felt both anger and resentment as he stared at the little child. He wondered if his mother had once cuddled him that way. He tried to remember the last time she'd given him a kiss but memories of poverty, hard work and turmoil on the farm were all that came back.

He told his mother about his job, how much money he made and the different things he planned to do. He bragged about how valuable he and Dennis were to Ramsey-Bird and about his new car. As Norman and Dennis teased him good-naturedly about the "lemon" sitting in the driveway, David began to feel like a failure. Caroline, caught up in her own thoughts and a fascination with her first grandchild, didn't seem to notice him at all.

"You're not going to believe it," Norman said, pulling himself from under the dashboard of the car.

The twins stood leaning on the open door. "What?" they asked together.

"Some idiot hooked the heater to the choke cable," he said, wiping dust from his hands. "So when you turn on the heater, it chokes out and stalls the car."

David shook his head. "That's it?"

"That's it," Norman said, grabbing a handful of tools from the seat as he slid back underneath. He mumbled and grunted as his big hands broke apart the misdirected connections and wired them properly.

"So I guess my c-ccar's not a l-llemon after all." David said, relieved that the repair wasn't going to cost him any more money.

"So where are you guys going to live?" Norman asked, changing the subject. He tossed a pair of pliers into the open tool box sitting on the driveway.

"Dunno," David answered. "You know of any p-pplace?"

"Les Plomp needs some work done and I heard he has a trailer for rent. Give him a call."

The next day the twins went to see Les Plomp and asked if he needed any help. They explained who they were and that they needed a place to live.

"Well, it just so happens I do have about a week's worth of construction work for you to do," Les said. "Meet me at 7 p.m. at my old caboose beside the Baptist church in Moosehorn and we can talk."

David and Dennis arrived there on schedule. Les drove in behind them, got out of his truck and motioned for them to follow him. He unlocked the door of the old caboose and led them inside.

"It's nothing fancy, but you are welcome to stay here," he said.

"Thanks," David said, glancing around the partially furnished room. "How much rent do you w-want?"

The older man looked the twins over and smiled.

"I won't charge you boys anything," he said. "You can stay here as long as you want."

"Th-thanks," David said.

The twins transferred their belongings from David's car into the old trailer. The next day they bought a few groceries, gathered wood and settled in for the long winter ahead.

Early one bitter January morning, there was a knock on the trailer door. David opened it to find Norman standing in the swirling snow.

"What took you so long?" Norman joked as he shook snow off his boots. "I thought maybe you guys had a couple of girls in here."

The twins giggled and their faces turned red.

Norman could see he embarrassed them and while it was good-natured fun with other men around, he felt like he was being nasty when the twins were alone. He shook off the feeling and changed the subject.

"Hey Dave, want to come to the city with me today?" he asked. "I've got to take a load of cattle in and pick up some freight."

David was flattered that his brother wanted him along. He began running his hands through his hair, then examined his clothes to see if they were suitable for a trip to Winnipeg.

"That way if I get stuck, I have someone to help shovel," Norman added with a snicker.

The brothers knew there was some truth to the statement, but David didn't care. He'd been feeling restless lately and was eager to go. He pulled on his boots and coat. Within a few minutes he and Norman were on their way south.

Because of the storm, they arrived in Winnipeg later than planned. The truck crawled along the snow-packed streets toward downtown. The city was at a near standstill because of the weather, but it didn't bother Norman. He drove first to the stockyards where the cattle were unloaded, then to a warehouse a few blocks away. He backed the truck up to the rear shipping door.

"I'll be back in a minute," he said.

David watched through a side mirror as Norman went up the stairs and through the employee entrance. A few moments later the large overhead door opened.

As soon as he saw Norman begin loading, David got out to help. Together they filled the truck amid jokes and chatter from the warehouse employees. They all seemed to like Norman and as usual, David was proud to be his brother.

A man carrying a ring of smoked garlic sausage came into the loading area through a door marked "employees only." He smiled, shook Norman's hand and then handed him the sausage. Norman grinned and then threw the sausage high in the air as everyone watched. Jockeying for position underneath, Norman looked like an entertainer as he grasped his hands behind his back and caught the coil of sausage in his bright, strong teeth. Everyone watching cheered and clapped.

Norman took a big bite then flashed them his irresistible smile. Waving, he made his way to the open loading dock door with David on his heels. The brothers jumped down into the snow, got into the truck and started for home.

Twisting the sausage between both hands, Norman handed David a chunk.

"That's your pay for coming with me," the older brother said, taking another bite. "Best damn garlic sausage in the city."

David nodded. He didn't care about getting paid as long as he was with Norman—and being fed.

Soon the truck was crawling toward the outskirts of the city. The Perimeter Highway had the reputation of being slippery and dangerous in bad weather. Norman checked his side mirror and wiped the windshield with a cloth. He slowed when he saw a car ahead of them slide into the ditch.

"Uh-oh," he said, tossing the remainder of the sausage on the seat. He drove slowly past the stuck car, then pulled over and stopped as near to the ditch as he dared. He jumped out of the truck, returning a few minutes later.

"I'm going to pull the guy out," he said, pushing the driver's seat forward and pulling out a logging chain from behind the seat.

David got out of the truck and bowed his head as he turned into the wind. His skin tingled from the furiously whipping snow. He stomped his way through the drifts to the back of the truck.

Norman handed him one end of the chain and pointed towards the back of his truck. He took the other end and began digging out the front of the snowbound car whose owner stood apologetically nearby waiting for the signal to get back in and steer.

Norman motioned that he was ready, then he hurried back to the truck. David's job was to signal to both drivers when to accelerate and brake. Slowly Norman inched forward until the chain was taut. With a jolt, he loosened the car from the snow. Within seconds, the car was back on the shoulder. David hurried to unhook the chain as Norman accepted thanks—and $5—from the motorist.

"Whew!" Norman chuckled as they got back in the truck. He slammed the door and shook the snow out of his hair. "See that Davey? I made five bucks."

"*You* made five bucks?" David challenged.

Norman scoffed. "*We* made five bucks, then." Glancing in his mirror, he pulled back onto the road and started north again. They'd traveled less than 500 yards when they saw another stranded car, this time a big Buick. The brothers looked at one another and raised their eyebrows.

"Some people see snow, I see money," Norman said cheerfully, as he pulled over again. "Are you in a hurry to get home? I think we should spend the day pulling people out. We'll make big bucks!"

David shrugged, put his gloves back on and stepped back into the wind. Norman approached the car and indicated to the elderly driver that they'd pull him out. Norman took the heavy chain and again handed one end to David who attached it to the axle under the truck. He crawled through the snow and began digging out the car, confirming that it would be easier to pull out backwards.

The elderly man behind the steering wheel eyed the pair suspiciously. He refused to get out of the car and when David motioned for the man to roll down his window, he did so grudgingly. Then he shouted obscenities at the teen for taking too long. Surprised by the comments, David backed away. Soon he motioned for both the man and Norman to start their motors.

It didn't take long before the car was back on the road. David crawled under the truck to unhook the chain while Norman knelt behind the car preparing to retrieve the other end. Suddenly, the man put his car in gear and began driving away.

"Hey!" Norman yelled, grabbing onto the chain. "You got our chain!"

The driver didn't look back as he pulled onto the highway, dragging Norman on the ground behind him. Norman let go after about 50 yards then he rolled over and jumped up.

"You old bugger!" he yelled shaking his fist in the air. He turned and began running toward David who was standing dumbfounded behind the truck.

"C'mon, let's catch him," Norman said.

David ran and jumped into the truck's passenger side.

"Can you s-still see h-him?" he asked as Norman pulled his door shut. Norman rolled down his window, put the truck in gear and stuck his head out. The car had all but disappeared in the opposite direction. Cars were crawling along the road and it didn't take long for Norman to realize that he'd never be able to turn the truck around and pass the slow-moving cars in time to catch the Buick.

"Ah, shit!" he said banging the steering wheel with his palm. "The ol' bastard got away on us."

David sat quietly as Norman muttered to himself. He drove slowly back onto the road and once again they were traveling north. They passed by a few more stranded motorists but were unable to do anything without the chain.

"Well, at least we still got the $5," David said cheerfully.

"Yeah, but we lost a $20 chain!" Norman growled. "How am I going to explain that to Hugo?"

David shrugged. They drove the remainder of the way home through heavy snow while Norman continued cursing old men in Buicks.

By late January, David had traded the troublesome Chev for a cream-coloured half-ton truck. As a birthday celebration, he and Dennis decided to have a meal at the Moosehorn coffee shop and afterwards visit their mother at the farm. As they sat in the restaurant chatting, David's attention was suddenly diverted to the table behind them where a group of men were talking about Domko. They were discussing how run-down the farm had become and how they'd soon be able to buy it "pretty cheap." David felt his cheeks warm as he listened to the men callously discussing his family and what was left of his dad's farm.

Standing up to leave, he faced the men at the table. He was surprised to see a man there who was considered a good friend by Domko. Their eyes met and the man turned away. Arriving after the twins, the men obviously hadn't known they were close by. Humiliated, David felt the heat of everyone's gaze as he turned and pulled out his wallet to pay for supper.

Stepping outside into the cold was a welcome relief for his hot, shaking body. As he and Dennis climbed into the truck, David was still angry about the men's callousness. In one way, he was surprised by their selfish attitudes, but he felt oddly gratified at the same time. His mother had always felt that there were people in the area who delighted in her hardships and failures. This corroborated how she'd been feeling.

There were only a few families whose actions and words had been consistently kind. As David put the truck in gear, he thought about one family in particular.

The Harwarts. Gus and Emma were now retired from the farm and living in Moosehorn. Their daughter, the children's faithful friend Marjorie, was living in Winnipeg. The same age as Norman, "Marjie" had liked them all, in spite of their embarrassing stutters, dirty appearances and bragging.

David smiled to himself as he remembered the times that he and his siblings would boast—telling Marjie and the other children at school that they had things when they did not. They tried to cover up their poverty by pretending that they were well-off, something they'd seen Domko do many times.

David could now see how transparent this behaviour was. He said a silent thank you to Marjorie for never teasing them or catching them in their lies. His appreciation of the young woman had increased ten-fold over the years as he gradually came to understand the meaning of true friendship.

When David turned off the highway onto the dirt road toward home, he smiled.

"Happy Birthday to us," he said cheerfully. "We made it Denny, we're 18 today."

"Yeah," Dennis said as he looked solemnly out the window. "Remember how we never thought we'd make it out of the bush?"

David shook his head in amazement. "There were lots of times we almost didn't."

The sun was setting on a beautiful day, sending pastel streams of colour across the sky. For David, the past few years had turned from a nightmare into a dream. They'd traveled to the farm periodically, without much thought of the past, but on this particular day, both he and Dennis were feeling reflective—and thankful.

"I couldn't go back to the old days again," David said, enjoying the beautiful sky. "I think it would kill me."

"Me too," Dennis said. "We've got it so good, I sometimes have to think hard to be sure it's real. We lived through hell, and I know it was hell 'cause the Devil was standin' there the whole time."

David laughed. "You've got that right."

The boys reminisced about the many incidents that had happened to them on the farm. Dennis looked instinctively to his right when they came to the small bluff of trees that shielded the east side of Jim's house. David slowed and looked as well.

"How's Jim doin'?" Dennis asked.

"Good, I think."

"Jim was the bravest guy I ever saw," Dennis said. "And he tells it like it is."

"That's for sure. Everyone else just kisses the ol' bastard's ass or they stay the hell away from him," David said. "Except for Gus too—he fought with Domko more than anybody."

The boys drove slowly and leisurely on the slippery road past the abandoned Harwart homestead. A warm feeling washed over Dennis as he looked at the old log house.

"I never told nobody but I used to wish that Emma an' Gus were my parents," he said, his voice cracking.

David looked at him and smiled sympathetically. "I know."

They drove in silence for a moment. Dennis shivered when he

looked toward the thick bush, then reached for the heater knob.

"Turn it up high," David said, laughing. "We got lots of heat now!"

The bush had an ominous look that made both boys quake a little inside. They had no fond memories of their childhood and only feelings of foreboding for the place they once called home. Instinctively, they knew what the other was thinking.

"I couldn't sleep in the bush again," Dennis said sadly. "Davey, how did we survive?"

"I don't know," David said, forcing a smile. "I think we had some of Dad's tough German blood. That's what made the ol' bastard hate us so much."

The church sat, as it always had, calm and unwavering in the cold wind.

"Do you ever talk to other people about what happened to us?" Dennis asked as he stared at the imposing structure.

"Sometimes I do, but mostly I just try to forget," David said as he slowly drove into the church's driveway. Looking to his left, he could see his mother's house through the bare trees. A flood of bad memories returned and he had to look away.

He put the truck in reverse and backed out of the driveway so that they would face away from the farm and yet Caroline could see their truck from the house. The sun had completely set now and he wondered how long it would be before his mother would be able to sneak out.

"Was the church good or bad?" Dennis asked.

"That church?" David said pointing with his thumb over his shoulder.

Dennis nodded.

"It was a good place," David said. "I figure the church and the Harwarts are what saved us from freezing to death."

They sat remembering for a moment, then Dennis broke the silence.

"How do you think Rosie is?"

A pang of guilt stabbed David and he winced.

"She's not good," he said. "We gotta get her out of there."

"How come the social workers don't take her away?" Dennis asked.

David shrugged. "Same reason they never came to get us, I guess. They're probably scared of him."

"Maybe Rosie can come live with us?" Dennis suggested. "We'll have to sneak her out so he don't know."

Eunice and the twins

Bob Domko

Domko, Caroline, Walter and Lorie
and Lorie's parents Goldie and Alvin Kirkland

View of the house from the bu
where the children

The barn

Norman Pischke in his early 20s

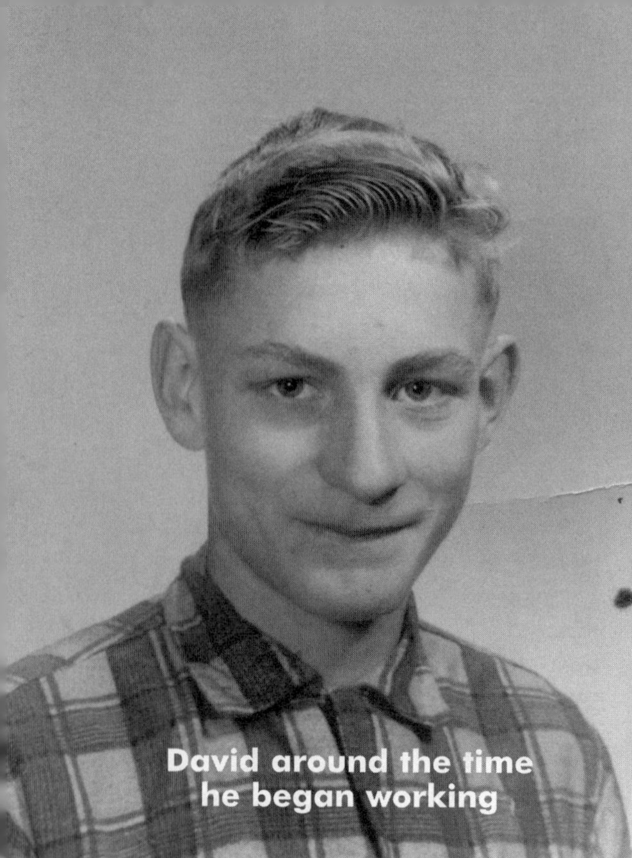
David around the time he began working

Dennis had grown in a handsome young man by his mid 20

Ken Price and Dennis

David, left, and Ken on their way to British Columbia

Norman and Sharon on their wedding day

Lloyd Rapke, Ken and Dennis in *Moosehorn, Manitoba*

Sharon and Norman with son Lee

George Klingbell

View of the Spearhill quarry taken from the top of a kiln

Staff at Canada Cement. Mike Kalanza, circled

Norman and Sharon with sons Trevor and L

Dale, David and Ian

Raymond and his girlfriend shortly before his accident

Norman with Trevor and Lee

Lorie, Bonnie, Caroline, Sharon and Robynne

Norman's plane in the mountains near Challis, Idaho

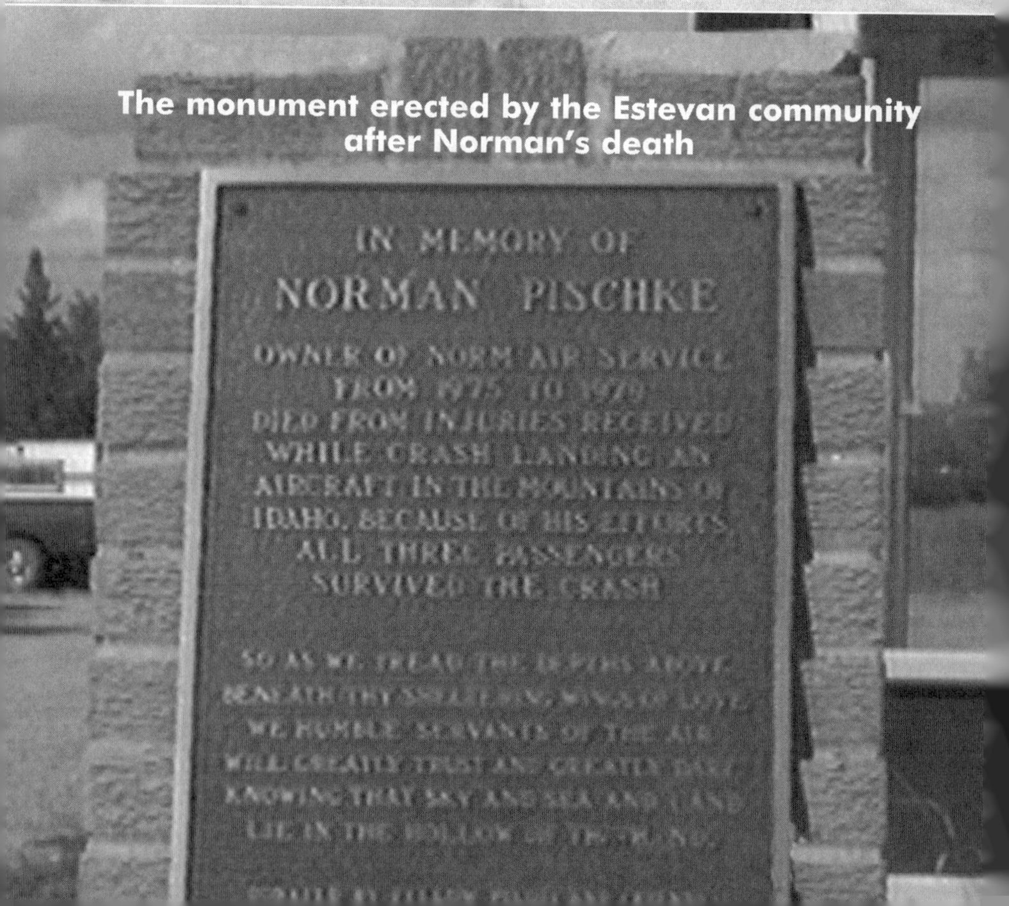

The monument erected by the Estevan community after Norman's death

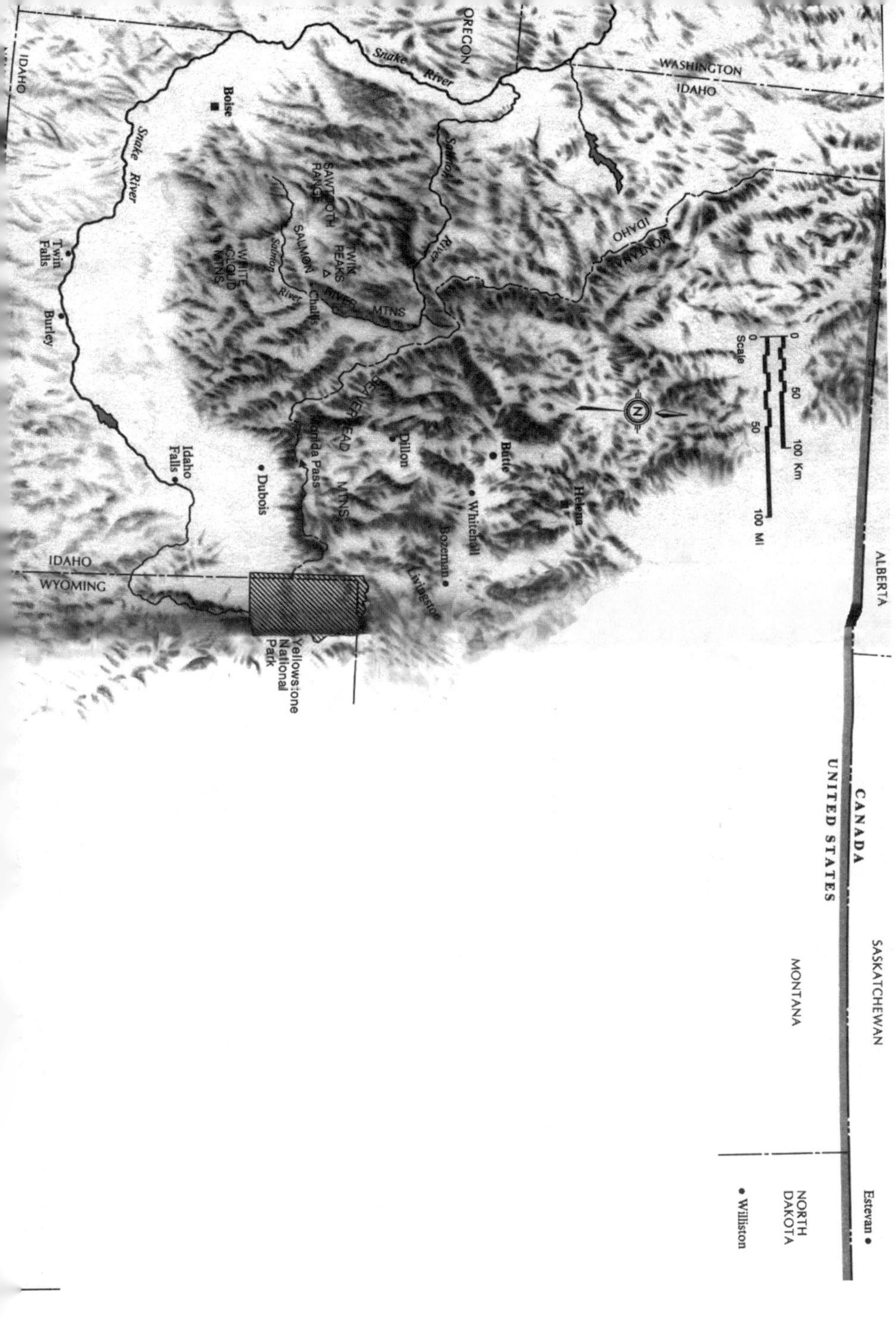

A map of the mountains where Norman's plane disappeared

The grave marker in Estevan, Saskatchewan

Caroline and Walter

Mike Kalanza at his niece's wedding in 1978

Members of the Kolansky family: Front, left to right: Mik Kalanza, Charles Wood, Nick Kolansky. Back, left to righ Doris, Ruby, Mary Chapman, Linda Wood and Ann Gilbau

Walls of the original Kolansky homestead in the bush at Elm Point. Taken in 2000

Mike Kalanza's house in Steep Rock

Jack Ramsey and his wife along with their daughter Gloria, Ken, Dennis and David, kneeling in front

George and Phyllis Rentz

David and Lynne

Lynne's daughter Sherry and husband Clayton Duncan

Dale and wife Kim

David with grandson Jake

Dale and David visiting Raymond in B.C., shortly before his death

Lynne's son David and wife Sandra Jensen

David and Sandra's sc Niall and Conor

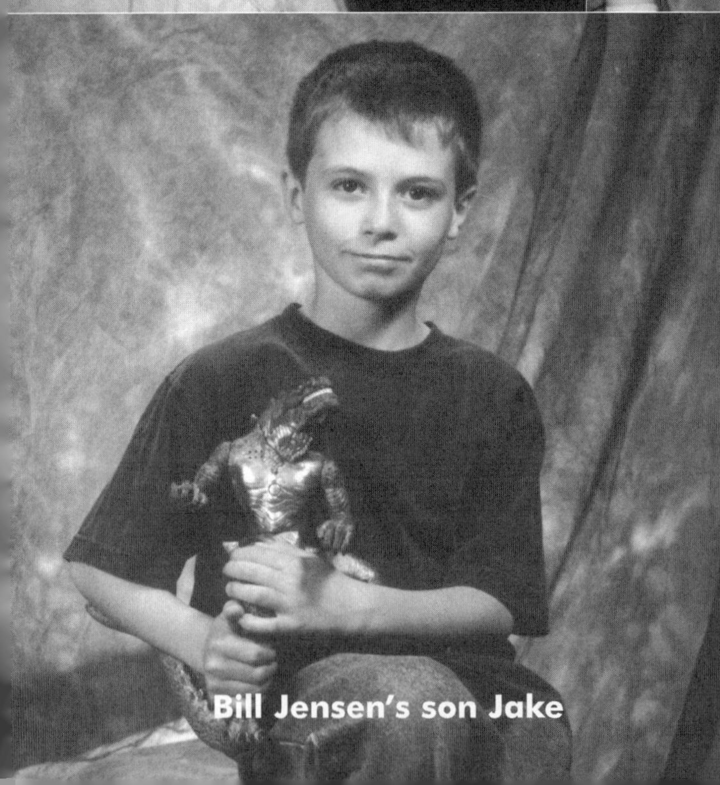

Bill Jensen's son Jake

Lynne's son Bill Jensen

David with his mother

Lorie, Walter and their granddaughter, Ayla

David enjoying a good meal

Eunice Bullerwell

David and Ken
on Halloween

Herb Robinson

Ken, David and Dennis after Herb Robinson's funeral

Sharon, left, with Kathy, center, at an educational display in Ashern, Manitoba
Taken early 1990s

The Makowski homestead where Mike was living when he disappeared. The house sat in the circle and was bulldozed around the same time the land was sold

David in the Kolodka barn where the family lived temporarily. Here, he's holding the mattress he and Dennis carried to the barn

The site where Mike Kalanza's body was found

chool teacher Alan Thomson

David and Lynne

Sergeant Robert McMill

Karen, Dennis and David at a
booksigning in Brandon, Manitob

David walking out of Lumsden, Saskatchewan. His stop in this town brought back a lot of pleasant memories

Dave with work supervisor, Dave Grant, at the walk kick-off in Banff, Alberta

David telling his story on Edmonton radio

David serving hot dogs to a Lumsden ball team

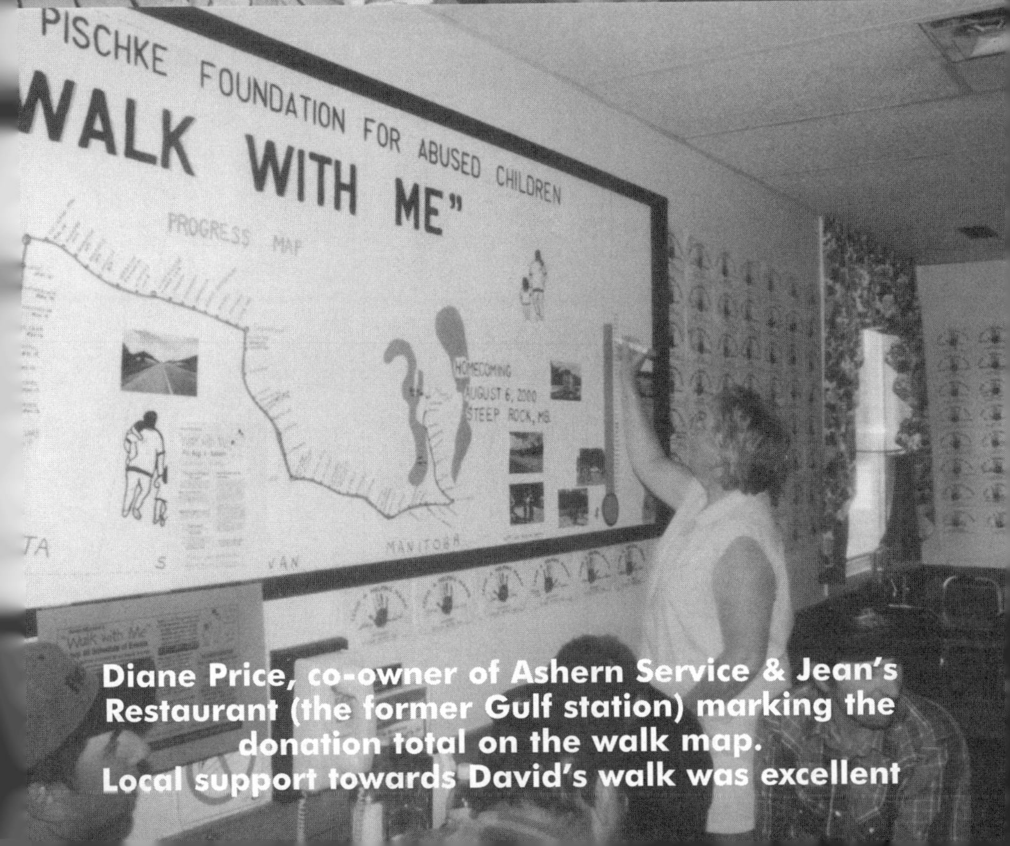

Diane Price, co-owner of Ashern Service & Jean's Restaurant (the former Gulf station) marking the donation total on the walk map. Local support towards David's walk was excellent

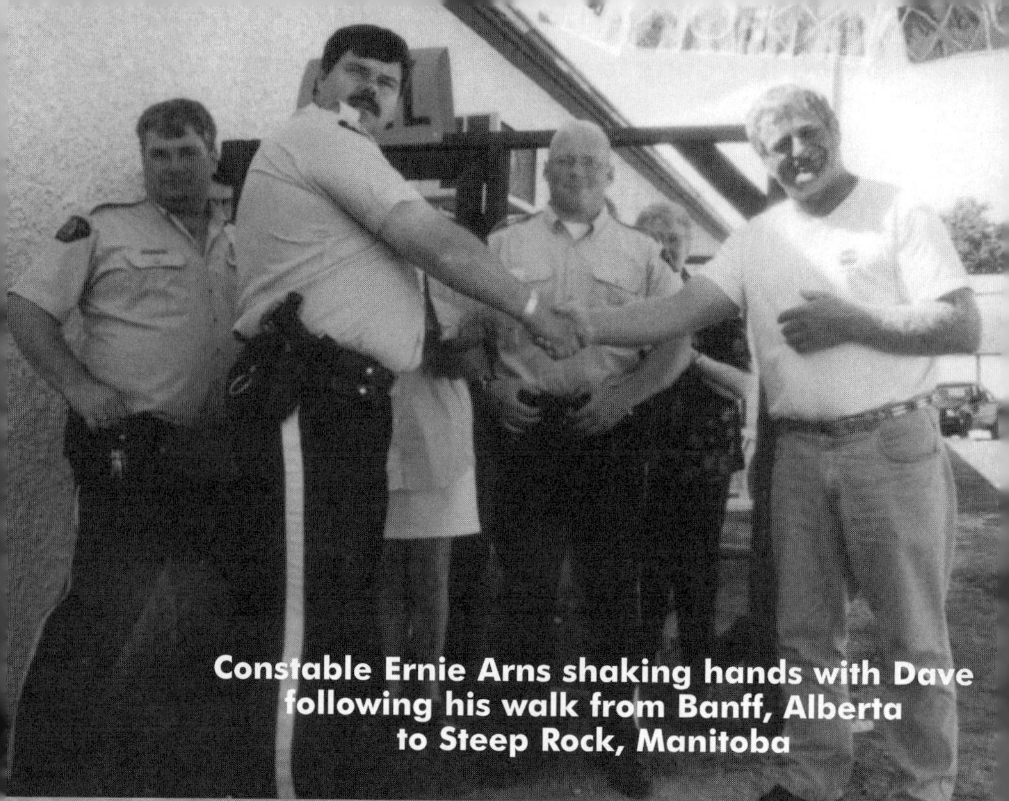

Constable Ernie Arns shaking hands with Dave following his walk from Banff, Alberta to Steep Rock, Manitoba

Lorne Park 'behind bars' in Ashern

David and a handful of youngsters cross the 'finish line'

Attendance at the Homecoming was outstanding

Friends who knew David as a shy teenager marvelled at his ability to speak in front of a crowd

David was full of appreciation towards the hundreds of people who supported the Homecoming and who donated to the walk

People walking with Dave into Steep Rock

A float in the Homecoming parade

Childhood friend Marjorie Harwart

David's final night on the road, spent with people from all over the province, who came to wish him well and take part in a tour of the old farm site

The motorhome used during Dave's walk, parked for the night just a few hundred yards from the church where he slept as a child

David glanced in his rearview mirror and saw his mother approaching the back of the truck.

"Mom's comin'," he said.

Opening his door, he stepped out and remembering what the men in the café had said, he felt the urge to return to the farm to help her out. Then as quickly as it came, he pushed the thought away.

"How are you doin' Mom?" he asked in a quiet voice.

"About the same," she said weakly. "I don't know what I'm gonna do."

Eight-year-old Raymond was tagging along behind his mother. David reached down and lifted the boy into the truck, then helped his mother inside. He slid in beside her and shut the door. Dennis reached over and turned up the heat another notch.

"What's he doin' now?" David asked.

"He thinks I'm trying to kill him," she sighed.

David snorted and Dennis shook his head in disgust.

"You're trying to kill *him?*" David asked. "How?"

"Poison," she said. "He won't eat anything I cook. He figures I killed Bill and that I'm trying to kill him too."

David started to laugh, but his amusement quickly turned to sorrow. He had to hide his tears by looking out the window. It was then he saw a man's reflection in the side mirror. He stiffened.

Dennis also sensed the imminent danger. They shot a quick glance at each other and then swinging around in the crowded cab, the teenagers saw a dark figure running awkwardly toward the truck.

It was Domko shaking one fist in the air while clutching a rifle in the other. All their familiar childhood feelings came flooding to the surface. It was as if the boys had been propelled back to the days when they were helpless children.

"It's that crazy bastard!" David yelled as he yanked the truck into gear, and slammed the gas pedal to the floor. The tires spun trying to grip the slick, snow-packed road. Staring intently into the rearview mirror, David could see Domko stop in the centre of the road and raise his rifle to eye level.

"He's gonna shoot!" David yelled, "Everybody down!"

Instinctively Dennis's arms shielded his head as he slid low on the seat. Caroline pulled Raymond down and covered him with her body.

Got to get out of here, David thought to himself, clenching his jaw tight. His heart raced as adrenaline surged in his bloodstream. *We don't deserve to die like this, not after what we've been through. If only I can get out of range . . .*

Moments seemed forever as the truck slipped sideways down the centre of the road, the back wheels sliding to the left. Suddenly one wheel caught on a bare piece of road, straightening the truck and propelling it forward. David pushed the gas pedal hard, the truck jolted, and they were speeding toward town. He glanced in the mirror and could see Domko still standing on the road, now just a speck in the distance.

"We m-mmade it!" David gasped, as he struggled to catch his breath. He hadn't felt fear like that in a long time.

Dennis and Caroline, shaking from the ordeal, complimented David's driving then sighed in relief.

"You gotta do somethin' Ma," David whispered. "You gotta do somethin' before the farm turns into nothin' an' you don't get a thing for it. It's still worth somethin'—how are you gonna survive? You gotta sell out now."

Caroline thought for a few minutes. The twins knew enough to keep quiet and let her think.

"Can you take me to the police?" she asked, her voice suddenly angry. She too had worked hard on the farm and could sense what people were saying about her and Domko. "We gotta send him back to Selkirk, but this time for good. I'm not putting up with this no more."

The twins looked at her. It appeared she meant what she was saying.

"I'm going to leave him and get a legal separation," she continued. "We just can't live like this."

The boys didn't ask further questions as they drove to Ashern. Each silently wished that their mother had done this much sooner, but that was not her way. It took her a long time to make up her mind, but once she did, she never changed it.

It was the first time since they were youngsters that the twins had been at the Ashern RCMP office. They rang the bell then stepped inside.

The officer who came to the front seemed much friendlier than the ones they remembered.

"Can I help you?" he asked.

They stood quietly for a moment, then David looked at his mother. She nodded.

"Y-yes, you can," David began. "We want to report that our stepfather just tried to shoot us. We were talking with our m-mother out by the farm, and he snuck up behind our truck and pointed his rifle at us. If I hadn't noticed him, w-we'd all be d-dead right now."

The officer looked stunned.

"Who's your stepfather?" he asked.

"Bob Domko," David said without hesitation.

It was then he realized how odd those words sounded coming from his mouth. Never once had he consciously uttered the man's name, not in anger and certainly not in fondness. This man had been nothing but his tormenter—and he'd always addressed him in that fashion.

"Domko? He should have been locked up a long time ago," the officer said. "It's a miracle he hasn't killed somebody. He never should have been released from Selkirk."

The twins looked at each other in amazement. Where was this man when they'd sought refuge as children?

"H-he tried to kill us many times and more than once he almost did," Dennis said firmly. "We were beaten and starved for t-twelve years and n-nnobody did nothing about it. We want you to do something about it NOW."

The officer called another constable and soon they were on their way to the farm. Caroline and Raymond sat in the back seat as the cruiser sped along the highway. The twins followed in the truck.

"'Member how we would ride like that?" David said, pointing at his mother's silhouette.

"And he'd beat the hell out of us when we got home," Dennis added. "But this time, they're taking him away."

"Do you think he's gone for good?" David asked.

"I don't know, but if he comes back, we'll just keep callin' the police," Dennis said without hesitation. "Is Mom gonna kick him out this time?"

David thought for a moment then nodded. "I think she means what she said. You know Mom when she makes up her mind."

Dennis leaned his head against the window and sighed.

"Do you think that Dad knows we made it?" he asked.

David looked at his twin and felt a warm strength flood through his body.

"I know he does."

Happy birthday, David thought as he turned off the highway into Moosehorn.

Chapter 13

"WHAT ABOUT YOUR HEARING?" Sergeant McMillan asked. "Have you had it tested recently?" "Pardon?" David asked.

"How is your hearing?"

"No damn g-good," David said. "I'm goin' deaf."

"Is that why you talk so loud?"

"That's what my w-wife says," he answered.

"What time did you go to bed last night?"

"About 10:30."

"What time did you get up?"

"6:30."

"How did you sleep?"

"Like a r-rock," David said.

"Do you always sleep well?"

"M-most of the time," he said.

"Do you have any fears or phobias?" he asked.

"Well, when I was younger I was scared of girls," he laughed. "Just ter-rified."

"What about now?"

"I can't stand the s-sight of blood, an' I don't like s-snakes," David answered.

Within a few days, Rosie left the farm and moved into the trailer with the twins. Domko was admitted February 23, 1966 to the Selkirk Mental Institution for the second time. Caroline and the younger children arrived at the trailer for a visit the following day.

"Come back to the farm and help me," she begged the twins. "Domko's gone now and he won't be coming back."

The brothers had been expecting the visit and weren't surprised by the request.

"H-hhow do we know he's g-gone for s-ssure?" David asked "He's left before, an' you've left, but then you g-guys always end up together again."

"I need help," she cried. "I can't run the farm alone."

After hearing the men in the coffee shop, David was convinced that selling out was her only choice, and he told her this.

"But I can't do that," she said, bristling at the suggestion. "How will I live?"

"You gotta do s-s-somethin' 'cause we're not goin' back," David said. "Not now, not ever."

They sat for hours and discussed her options. Having no understanding of the legalities of the situation, most of their dialogue was based on emotion and not fact. By the time Caroline was ready to go home, they'd argued, fought, hurled accusations and even laughed at the absurdity of it all. When the discussion was over, Caroline still felt trapped and the twins were still unwilling to commit themselves to the farm.

"We can't, ma," David said softly. "We'll be g-goin' back to W-wwinnipeg soon to work. You g-ggotta sell."

Caroline shrugged as she pulled on her coat and boots while Rosie gathered up the children.

"I'll think about selling," Caroline said. "But I don't know how we'd live."

"L-like the rest of us," David said, holding back the thought: *like human beings.*

By early April, the twins were again working on the floodway. Each time they returned to work for Jack, he gave them jobs with increasing responsibility. Now, at only 18, the twins were responsible for training new operators for the heavy equipment. Jack had little patience for incompetence, so they found themselves training a lot of new men.

Reminiscent of the time the RCMP arrived at the Canim Lake bush camp, a cruiser pulled up to the Ramsey-Bird Construction office looking for the Pischke twins. This time David or Dennis—the officer wasn't sure which one—had been seen shooting fish with a rifle in the ditch near Moosehorn. The incident had occurred on a weekend when they'd been logging overtime hours on the floodway. As usual, someone had blamed the twins for someone else's wrongdoing.

Their friend Ken came to the city one mid-June afternoon to try to convince the twins to go to Saskatchewan with him. The partners in Ramsey-Bird Construction had split the company in two. Their foreman George had followed one owner to Saskatchewan where the company had a contract for highway repairs. Ken wanted to work there and asked the twins to go along. David and Dennis weren't sure they wanted to move and told Ken they'd think about it.

That afternoon when they arrived back at the floodway office, they discovered that Jack had fired two more men—guys that the twins thought were good workers. That evening when they climbed into Dennis' recently bought car, they began discussing what would happen if they lost their jobs.

"What if we make a mistake an' get fired?" David asked his brother.

"He won't fire us," Dennis answered. "We're good workers."

"I don't know," David said. "Jack looked at me funny yesterday. I can't take no chances 'cause I got a car payment."

Dennis thought for a moment.

"Yeah . . . Mom would really be after us then to go back to the farm," he said.

David cringed. "I ain't goin' back there."

"Me neither," Dennis agreed. "But if we get fired, we don't have no excuse."

Dennis drove to the house they were renting—a two-storey, insulbrick home not far from where they worked. Because he'd just bought himself the car, the brothers took turns driving their vehicles to and from the work site.

"Look," Dennis said as they turned into the yard, "the kids are here."

Raymond and Mark were playing with a toy on the lawn.

"Oh no, it's Ma," David sighed.

Dennis parked his car beside David's 1959 brown Chevrolet. He'd traded the truck for it a few weeks earlier.

The twins walked to the house, wary of their mother and wondering about the reason for her visit. As they opened the door and stepped inside, they were greeted by an enthusiastic Kathy who had heard their approaching voices.

"Hi, David, hi Dennis," she called as she felt her way along the wall.

"Hi, Kathy," David said quietly. "What are you guys doing here?"

"We're here to visit," she chirped. "Ma said we should come see you in your new place." She grabbed his arm and placed her other hand on his chest. "We miss you."

David felt his resolve weaken as he and Kathy walked into the kitchen where their mother sat with Jennie on her lap. Rosie, who'd gone back to the farm when the twins moved to Birds Hill, was sharing a pot of tea with Caroline.

The door opened behind them and Mark and Raymond ran boisterously into the kitchen.

Caroline's and David's eyes met.

"Hi boys," she said in a feeble voice. "We came for a visit."

"H-hhow'd you get here?" David asked.

"The door was unlocked," she said.

"No, I mean how'd you get to the city?" he asked.

"We took the bus," she said.

"Shouldn't the kids be in s-sschool?" he quizzed her. "How 'bout you, Rosie? What g-ggrade you in?"

"I quit," she said.

"Quit? How come?" he asked.

"You know why," she said awkwardly. "I had to go home to work."

"What g-ggrade did you finish?"

"Seven."

"Did not," Kathy interjected. "You finished grade six and quit in grade seven."

David's expression showed his disappointment.

"I didn't see you helpin' none," Rosie said, turning away from him.

David sighed, looking at Caroline. "An' what about R-rraymie?"

"He's in grade two," she said. "Why do you care anyway?"

David was annoyed but knew it was time to stop pressing her for answers.

"I'm gonna take a shower," he said, dropping his lunch pail on the counter before going upstairs.

"Don't use all the hot water," Dennis yelled after him. "I wanna take one too."

When David returned 20 minutes later, he could smell supper cooking. Food always tempered his anger and as they sat down to the meal, Caroline explained why she was really there.

Domko had returned to the farm after being discharged from Selkirk June 6. He was agitated when he got off the bus so Caroline refused to take him to buy another gun. His other firearms had been confiscated by police when they arrested him after the incident in

February. This, of course, made him suspicious. During the next few days, he somehow acquired a gun and began threatening everyone again.

When Domko was napping, Caroline had called a neighbour, Arnold Gall, asking him to pick them up and take them to the bus depot. They had slipped out while Domko was asleep.

"So when he woke up you guys were gone?" David laughed.

Caroline nodded.

"Why didn't you just k-kkick him out?" he asked.

"It's not that easy," she said. "He owns some of the equipment and the cattle. He even owns some of the land. I can't keep him from coming back."

"Yeah, but you own the farm," David argued, "an' the house."

"Yes, but we're still married," she sighed.

David didn't understand legal matters. It made no sense to him. Caroline had obtained a legal separation from Domko, but couldn't keep him away.

As if she could read his mind, Caroline admonished him with a stern look. "I'm doing the best I can," she sighed.

The twins were anxious to talk more about moving to Saskatchewan. They could barely wait until everyone else was asleep. They lay awake staring at the ceiling of their room while they discussed their options. After a long talk, they decided to go with Ken to Saskatchewan. They missed George who'd been like a father to them and also feared Jack might fire them. As well, they didn't know how long their mother would be staying with them at Birds Hill. They weren't accustomed to the commotion of small children and the idea of living by themselves again was appealing.

The next morning they went to work and gave notice of their departure to Jack. By the end of the week, they had packed their bags and were on their way. Caroline and the children stayed in the house and David left his new car there for safekeeping.

Unfortunately, the jobs didn't pan out and three weeks later the twins and Ken were back in Manitoba. They returned to Birds Hill on a weekend to find that their mother, the children and David's car were gone.

"Where'd they go?" David asked angrily as he surveyed the empty house.

"Prob'ly back to the farm," Dennis said.

Ken drove them to a pay phone. David dialed the number at the farm and wasn't surprised when Caroline answered. He asked why she had returned home.

"I called Domko to see how things were going," she explained. "There was no answer. So I had Arnold check on him. Domko was nowhere around and his car was gone. It turns out he readmitted himself to Selkirk."

"What?" David asked. "He went back on his own?"

"I guess so," she sighed. "Only problem is, he left me with all this work to do."

"You didn't have to go back," David said lamely.

"What? And let the animals starve?" she said. "That's not right."

"You let us s-sstarve . . ."

There was a long pause at the other end of the line.

"I ran out of money," she said, refusing to be drawn into an argument. "What was I supposed to do? I couldn't even buy groceries."

"Why didn't you just steal vegetables from neighbours?" he said sarcastically. "That's what we had to do."

Caroline paused again.

"Well, it's only June so there are no vegetables ready to steal," she said sarcastically. "And besides, I'm not going to go crawling around the neighbours' yards."

"Make Raymie do it," David laughed. He realized how ridiculous he sounded but couldn't resist picking a fight with her.

"David!" she admonished, "be serious a minute. You know darn well the spot I'm in."

"Okay, Ma, I'm sorry," he said. "Did you get the m-mmoney I sent?"

"Yes, but I used it to pay the hydro bill and a man came around looking for rent," she said, still annoyed with him. "I'm not going to stay in the city and pay rent when I have a perfectly good house here."

"When did you leave?" he asked.

"A few days ago," she replied.

"Ma, where's my car?" he asked. "You didn't d-ddrive it, did you?"

"No," she said. "I can't drive in the city."

David was relieved.

"Then how did you get home?"

She hesitated. "I had Arnold come to pick us up and we used your car."

David winced. Arnold was a big, stolid man with rough mannerisms. He was not someone that David would want in his new car.

"Where is it now?" he asked.

"It's . . here," she said.

The hesitation in her tone told him something was wrong.

"What happened?" he demanded.

"Nothing . . ." she said.

"What, Ma? I can tell somethin's wrong."

"Well, we got a flat tire," she explained. "But we were almost home when it happened so the car's just over there."

"Over where? Is it still sitting on the r-rroad?" he asked.

"Right in front of the church," she said.

"Did he shmash it?"

"No, just a flat," she said. "But there was something wrong with your tire iron because he couldn't change the tire."

"But the car's okay?" he asked.

"Yes, it's right here."

David told her they were on their way to Moosehorn and he'd come by to pick up the car. He explained that the jobs in Saskatchewan hadn't worked out and that they would be applying at Ramsey-Bird on Monday. He hung up, puzzled by his mother's last comment about the wheel wrench.

As they drove home, the twins discussed with amazement the news that Domko had admitted himself to hospital.

"Too much work to do," David said. "He don't got us to do all the work, so he'd rather sit around the hospital."

They arrived at the farm just after noon. David was relieved to see the car on the road, but dismayed that one wheel was sitting on the hub, with the tire lying on the ground nearby.

He got out to see what was wrong and discovered that the studs on the wheel had been broken right off. He guessed that when Arnold had tried to change the flat tire, he'd turned the bolts the wrong direction and stripped the studs right off. David shook his head as he tried to think of a way to get the car fixed. He looked to Ken for advice and by nightfall the pair had fixed the car. David vowed to never leave it in his mother's care again.

That weekend the twins wondered aloud many times if Jack would hire them back after they had quit so abruptly.

"Jack said to come back if it don't work out in Saskatchewan," Dennis reminded his twin.

David remembered the boss had said this, but also knew that people say a lot of things they don't mean. He wouldn't believe it until they were back driving the heavy equipment and collecting a paycheque.

Fortunately, Jack was pleased to see the twins again and hired them immediately. They stayed all season, putting the finishing touches on the floodway. When the job was over, there was tremendous satisfaction for the twins and all the workers who'd been on the project from the beginning. As other men were given lay-off notices, Jack moved the twins from one clean-up job to another until there was nothing left to do.

One afternoon in early fall, he shook their hands and told them to phone back in the spring. The company was bidding on a few large construction jobs in Saskatchewan and might need their help in April. The twins said they would, packed their belongings and once again moved back to Moosehorn.

◆ ◆ ◆ ◆ ◆

He could feel the ground pounding under his feet as he raced toward the bush. The outline of the trees was faint but he ran all out knowing that Domko was right behind him. He could see the trees, but couldn't reach them. His heart pounded as his legs turned to rubber. He glanced back, and while he couldn't see the hammer in Domko's hand, he knew it was there.

He could sense that his faithful horse, Dolly, was waiting for him at the edge of the bush. She had uncanny perception, that horse, like she knew instinctively how the children had suffered. She'd wait and they'd climb on her back and Dolly would take off in a run, her long swift legs thwarting Domko's attempt to punish them. Many times she'd helped David and his siblings escape Domko's grasp.

Wait! David called out. *Wait for me Dolly, I'm coming!*

The horse turned to look at him and then instantly David was on her back. He felt her coarse mane in his hands and the sweat of her body on his bare arms as he leaned towards the horse's head. Glancing over his shoulder, he could see the snake that followed them, its long body slicing through the grass, its eyes blood red slits above a smiling mouth and twitching tongue.

Run, Dolly, run! he silently implored. Sensing his thoughts, the horse's legs pounded faster. But abruptly they crashed to the earth and he found himself standing on the ground looking down at her.

Exhausted, Dolly lay with mouth wide open, tongue lolling as she fought to catch her breath. She panted and struggled to stand but couldn't. Her eyes rolled in their sockets as the gaping wound in her head gushed blood. When David moved closer, the blood was inexplicably on his hands. He could feel the horse's pain as she drew her last frantic breath. She'd tried to escape, but her loyalty to the children had been punished by death.

David screamed as he jolted awake and sat up in bed. His body was drenched in sweat. At first he thought he was back at the farm, sleeping in the attic bedroom. But as his eyes focused on the room around him, he realized he was in his mother's new house in Moosehorn. Dennis stirred beside him, turning away and pulling a blanket high over his shoulder.

David panted, his body still in the throes of the nightmare. The disturbing dreams that had haunted his sleep in childhood were coming back. Guilt and horror surrounding the nature of Dolly's death were something he didn't want to think about when he was awake, much less have the vivid uncensored details enter his sleep. As he lay on the bed staring at the ceiling, he recalled the events of the week before.

It had taken all summer but he had finally persuaded his mother to sell the cattle and equipment. Norman had supported the idea and they already had someone eager to rent the land in the spring—Hugo.

While helping move Caroline's belongings from the farm house to a rented home beside the Russells in Moosehorn, David had casually asked her what had happened to Dolly—the children's favourite horse.

The horse had always avoided Domko and once they'd left the farm, Domko had found it impossible for a long while to catch her. Caroline told David that changed one hot summer afternoon when Domko became frustrated with Dolly, but was able to trap the horse in a small fenced area beside the yard. He chased her with a tractor until she collapsed from exhaustion. Then, while she was on the ground, he smashed in her skull with a sledgehammer.

Thinking that the animal had been sold, David hadn't been prepared for these grisly details. The story had sent him outside where he heaved his lunch onto the ground. He realized then that he'd softened in the few years he'd been away. He was no longer desensitized to daily violence. In the days that followed, he was overrun with guilt for failing to remove the horse from the farm. He could have stolen her to save her life, but he'd been so busy worrying about himself that he'd forgotten the helpless animal who had been so faithful to him. The shame was astounding—and now Dolly haunted his dreams.

Unable to fall back to asleep, David got up and went to the kitchen. He stood and looked out the window, marveling at the stillness and peace of the morning. His senses were still heightened from the nightmare and his thinking was surprisingly clear for such an early hour. He suddenly understood some of what was going on around him.

Domko's friends blamed the twins for the dispersal of the farm animals and equipment. David had suspected that people were blaming him and Dennis, but it still came as a tremendous blow when he realized that people were serious and not just gossiping. They actually blamed him for Domko's problems. He wondered how people could be oblivious to the way they'd lived.

Their ignorance explained the behaviour of the Gulf gas station owner. When he and Dennis had arrived in Ashern a week earlier and asked him to cash their paycheques, the man had tossed them back.

"I'm not cashing those!" he'd said.

"Why not?" David had asked. "They're c-company cheques—they're g-good."

The man had scoffed and then gone upstairs to his office, leaving the twins standing red-faced at the counter.

But now David understood. Rumours were circulating that he hadn't earned the money he used to buy his nice car and motorcycle. People in the area couldn't believe—or didn't want to accept—that the Pischke children could make an honest living.

David shook his head. He'd hoped that with the farm gone and Domko in the mental hospital, the family could begin to live a "normal" life. He'd naively hoped that the end of the farm would also mean the end of their struggles.

David made himself some toast. When he was finished eating he quietly pulled on his boots and leather jacket. He opened the door and stepped out into the fresh morning air.

Everything was quiet around him except for the calls from a flock of Canada geese flying low overhead in search of a grain field. In the distance, another flock heading south flew high to speed their journey to a warm winter home. Like the geese, David felt an urgent need to be somewhere else.

Rounding the back of the house, he pulled the plastic cover off his Harley which sat against the rear wall. He pushed the motorcycle to the driveway and slipping a leg over the seat, started the engine. The throaty noise penetrated the morning silence. A part of him wanted to hurry to avoid disturbing sleeping neighbours. But instead of skulking away, he revved the engine a few times.

To hell with them, he thought as he rolled down the driveway, shifted gears and rumbled down the street.

David spent that day in Winnipeg looking for work. He approached Moosehorn late in the afternoon, just as the skies clouded over and it began to rain. He slowly turned off the highway into town. Clothing soaked from the ice-cold drops, he suddenly had a strange feeling that he was being watched. In his rearview mirror he could see a dark car accelerating toward him. Glancing over his shoulder, he noticed it looked familiar, but the rain made it difficult to see.

He wiped his eyes with the back of his hand. David accelerated down the street, keeping the car in his mirror as it sped towards him. Panicking, because it appeared the driver was intent on running him down, he made an abrupt turn at an intersection and lost control of the motorcycle. As he slid across the slick road, David held onto the bike. The motorcycle came to a stop and in a daze, David scrambled from under it onto the shoulder in time to see Domko fly by. His car wheels were only a few feet from the bike.

Stunned and soaking wet, David stood for a moment in disbelief at what had just happened. He thought Domko was in Selkirk! Things like this always happened when he let his guard down.

It took a few minutes for the shock to subside and then David became angry. He stood his bike upright and checked it for damage. A few things were bent, but nothing that couldn't be straightened. His leg throbbed, but he pushed away the discomfort. Feeling self-conscious about having fallen, he looked around to see if anyone had witnessed the accident.

No one was out this cold evening and in a way David was thankful. He swung his leg over the wet seat and started the bike. He rumbled towards his mother's house, but stopped short when he saw Domko's car parked in the driveway. He accelerated past and went to Ken's house instead. He couldn't believe that she would allow Domko into the house. Not after everything he'd put the family through.

She should just kick him out, David thought. But after some consideration admitted that he couldn't stand up to the man either.

How did he gain so much control over us? he wondered.

The next morning David returned home to discover that his mother had made Domko leave after all. She'd let him in out of politeness because he wanted to visit his children. She had phoned the police as soon as he became belligerent. They came immediately. A social worker was called and Domko was returned to Selkirk.

Because of Caroline's situation, she was deemed eligible for provincial welfare payments and was no longer dependent upon Domko for her livelihood. She was becoming less tolerant of his outbursts and their roles were beginning to reverse. The medication kept him sedated enough that she could coerce him into doing what she wanted. Kathy and Raymond had witnessed enough violence that they were guarded in his presence; the younger two, Mark and Jennie, barely knew who he was. The combination of all these factors was making it difficult for Domko to impose his will and complicate their lives.

"What was he d-ddoin' out in the first p-pplace?" David demanded.

Caroline gave him a stern look.

"I don't know. I didn't let him out," she said.

"I know . . ." David stammered, this time less angry. "He almost r-ran me over."

"What?" she said.

"He t-ttried to r-rrun me over."

Caroline thought for a moment. "He'd mentioned something about punks on motorcycles, but I had no idea he was talking about you."

"Punks?" David scoffed. "That b-bbastard."

Caroline raised her eyebrows. No words were needed in reprimand as David knew she did not approve of swearing. Ashamed, he looked away then mumbled an apology.

"He told me that he'd been let out on a work program," she explained. "He was working for a farmer in Petersfield, but I guess things didn't work out so he came here. He's got no other place to go."

David scoffed. Then for a brief second, he felt bad. He understood how it felt to be displaced, but quickly shook off the feeling. He reminded himself that they were discussing Domko—a man who, in his opinion, deserved no pity.

"How are the kids doin'?" he asked, changing the subject.

"What kids?" she asked.

"You know, Kathy an' Raymie an' Markie," he said, opening the cupboard and taking down a glass. He poured himself some water. "Do you think they like it here?"

"Uh, yeah," she hesitated. "I'm surprised because you don't ask about them much."

David shrugged. "Just w-wonderin'."

"Kathy will like being in town, I think, because we're not working outside and leaving her alone," Caroline continued. "Markie starts school next fall an' Raymie, well, he's not doin' too good at school."

"Why?" David asked.

"Well, I don't know. The teacher suggested we get his eyes tested, so we did, but it's not that. She said he's really good at writing stories and art, but he's not too good at other subjects."

David was surprised. "He's good at art? Like me an' Dennis?"

Caroline nodded.

They sat for a few moments. David felt a twinge of jealousy that he and his half-sibling shared the same talent.

"I got a job," he announced.

"Well, that's good. Where?" Caroline asked.

David told her that the following Monday morning he would start work at a loading dock in Winnipeg. He planned to stay with friends.

"I'm gonna buy a b-bbeater to drive around W-wwinnipeg," he said. "Is it okay if I leave my n-nice car h-hhere?"

Caroline said she didn't mind.

"But nobody's g-ggonna d-ddrive it, right?" he said.

Caroline laughed. "Who's going to drive it? Markie?"

David thought about Arnold, but decided not to mention that incident. The two smiled and for the first time in ages he felt warm feelings for his mother.

David worked in Winnipeg for the next few months, visiting Moosehorn on weekends. He and Ken made plans for the spring to work and live wherever Ramsey-Bird sent them. They speculated where they might go, what jobs they'd do and naturally how much money they'd make. On weekends, they usually shared a few beers and caught up on the local gossip.

One weekend David came home to find that his nice car was not where he left it in the driveway. He knocked on his mother's door, then let himself in. The moment Caroline saw him, she turned away and started to cry.

"Ma, what's wrong?" he asked. "Where's my car?"

Caroline broke down while telling him the story. Rosie and her boyfriend had gotten into trouble and they'd come to Caroline for help. They needed to leave and she'd loaned them David's car, hoping that they'd come back right away. It had been two weeks and she'd only heard from them a few times. They'd gone somewhere west.

At first David didn't know what to say. Then he got angry.

"They left in my car?" he hollered. "Ma, I told you not to let anyone drive it!"

"What was I supposed to do?" she wept. "I thought they'd come back right away."

David sat down at the kitchen table and held his head in despair. He knew most of Caroline's misdeeds were accidental, but it dismayed him that he and Dennis suffered so often from her poor judgment. Why now, after all his hard work, was his life still in turmoil?

He couldn't find words to express himself and felt his anger begin to boil. He stood up and stomped through the house, ranting and raving. Caroline cried—even apologized. When David's anger was finally spent, he sat down and cried too. Then he made Caroline promise to let him know the minute Rosie called. She vowed that she would.

Soon David gave up all hope of ever seeing the car again and began looking around for another nice vehicle. A few weeks later, Rosie and her boyfriend returned on the bus. They told David that they'd needed money and had sold the car. They apologized profusely and promised they'd pay him back.

Meanwhile, David, Dennis and Ken had been hired by Ramsey-Bird to work on a highway repair crew near Lumsden, Saskatchewan It would keep the young men busy until fall. They piled into Ken's car and left on another work adventure.

Chapter 14

"**I ASKED YOU EARLIER WHO** you respected the most," McMillan said. "Now, I want to know who you disrespect the most?"

"Well . . .," David said, "the same way I re-spect guys who gave us a chance, I disrespect all those who never did. An' you know there's one guy who has hated us right from the s-start and he's the reason why I'm here today."

"Who's that?" McMillan asked.

"Gusti."

McMillan raised his eyebrows.

"You know, you interviewed him for the polygraph too," he said. "Gus Breitkreitz from Moosehorn."

"Why do you feel he's responsible for you being here?"

"Because he hates us with a passion," David said. "He's the one who c-called Crimestoppers about us guys c-commitin' the murder."

"How do you know that?" McMillan asked.

"Because there aren't too many guys who'd do it, an' he said he'd always get even with us. So I guess that was his way," he said.

"Well, you're just making assumptions," McMillan said.

David nodded. "I know, but he's been sayin' stuff about us for years," he said.

David took an instant liking to Lumsden, a picturesque town, nestled in a rolling valley in south-central Saskatchewan. He was also glad to be working for George again and didn't feel as nervous about meeting new people as in years earlier. It helped that both he and Dennis kept their hair cut fashionably and that they showered regularly. Their new clothes helped them blend in with men their age and the leather jackets and boots gave them a "tough" appearance.

David knew that when starting with a new crew, it was best for them to keep their mouths shut. So for the first while, they just smiled and let Ken do all the talking.

"Which one of you lads will be the first to find a girl?" George kidded one afternoon as the work crew filed into a café, taking all the tables. He sat down beside David and turned over a coffee cup. "Lots of nice farm girls around here."

The twins blushed and tried to hide behind their menus.

"What about these two studs here?" another man laughed, nudging Dennis. "You've been here two weeks already and no girlfriends yet?"

Just then a young waitress approached the table. The men hushed and gave the twins a glance but the boys pretended they didn't notice. All David could think about was placing his order without making a fool of himself. He hoped that the guy before him ordered something he liked.

"The Special," George said to the waitress.

The woman smiled as she wrote it on her pad. Then she looked at David.

"S-same," he said.

She nodded and turned to Dennis.

"S-same," he said.

The waitress looked from brother to brother, eyebrows raised. She said nothing, but the men all laughed.

"Yeah, we can't keep 'em straight either," one fellow said. "Waitresses usually like it when they order the same thing."

The twins blushed as she wrote down the order and disappeared into the kitchen. She returned and filled their coffee cups. While the other men were talking to each other she spoke quietly to David.

"Do you have a girlfriend?" she asked.

"No," he flushed.

"Well, see that girl over there?" she said, pointing to the far end of the café.

David turned and looked over his shoulder at a small, dark haired girl sitting by herself.

"Yeah?" he said.

"She thinks you're cute. Her name's Brenda," she explained. "She's a friend of mine and asked me to talk to you."

One of the men heard what was being said and began teasing David the moment the waitress left. Just then Brenda looked over and smiled at him.

Throughout the meal they could barely keep their eyes off one another. By the time he'd ordered dessert, David was wondering how he'd get the courage to ask her out. Brenda got up to leave and gave him one more quick glance.

"D-ddid you s-ssee her eyes?" David gushed to Dennis as the door closed behind her. "She's got the m-mmost b-bbeautiful eyes I ever seen."

The men laughed.

"Davey's in love," Dennis teased.

"Her eyes?" the man beside Dennis exclaimed. "Turn around next time, boy, and take a look at her ass."

For the next few days, David tried to work up the courage to ask "love eyes" out for a date. It didn't take long for word to spread amongst the men that he had a crush on her. They teased him constantly, calling her "love ass" to rile him.

One rainy day, when David knew they'd be finishing early, he decided to ask her out. Nervous all morning, he could barely look at Brenda as she sat two tables away facing him. He purposely left his jacket at the table when it came time to leave.

"I forgot my coat," he said to Dennis, as he turned to go back inside. "You wait here."

Dennis shrugged and got into the car.

David ran back to the café.

Do you want to go for a drive? he thought.

All little words, not hard to say.

Do you want to go for a drive?

Do you want to go for a drive?

He opened the door and went inside. *Do you want to go for a drive?*

He slowed his pace, trying to look casual as he stepped back into the restaurant. Brenda was reading at the table as he approached.

He pointed to his coat.

She nodded and smiled.

"M-mmy name's David," he said.

"I'm Brenda," she said.

He hesitated beside her table for a few minutes, gathering courage.

"D-ddo you w-wwant to g-ggo f-for a d-drive?" he asked stuffing his hands in his pockets.

Brenda smiled back at him sweetly. "Sure, when?"

He hadn't thought that far.

"Uh, w-wwhen do you w-wwant?"

"I don't know, when do you want to go?" she asked.

Please stop making me talk, he thought.

"W-wwhen-ever you w-wwant," he answered. "Today?"

"Today?" she asked. "After school?"

"Uh, yeah," he smiled, motioning to the window. She seemed to understand. He'd learned to be quite expressive and most people knew what he was talking about without having to say a lot of words.

"You're off early because it's raining?" she asked.

He nodded.

"Okay, I get off at 3:30," she said. "You're going to pick me up then?"

He nodded again.

"Here?" she asked.

"Okay," he said.

"Okay, see you then."

"S-sssee you then."

Unlike his first date, his courtship of Brenda went surprisingly well. For the rest of the summer David and Brenda spent every free moment they had together. Once the initial ribbing wore off and the men realized that David was serious about her, the teasing stopped. They spent their evenings driving around Lumsden, going for ice cream and talking. As David became comfortable with her, he was able to chat without embarrassment, and she always waited patiently for him to finish. He told her about his job—and how he drove the huge pieces of heavy equipment that smoothed out the slopes and ditches alongside the road.

Having a female friend to talk to was something new for him and David discovered he wasn't as dependent upon Dennis when he had a woman in his life. He enjoyed the "softness" of her company. He found that men never talked about things. They just grunted and changed the subject whenever the discussion wasn't about beer, women or work. A woman, he found, could be patient and kind—lending an ear to all his hopes and dreams. He discovered that Brenda was attracted to his friendly, outgoing nature. This made him feel good about himself and for the first time ever, David was in love.

One afternoon he saw something odd when he was working on the highway. He was busy smoothing the slope on the new road when he noticed a commotion ahead. A car had careened off the road into the ditch where it jolted to a stop. David saw the door fly open and a woman jump out. She began running away from the car. The driver put the vehicle in gear and chased her. She ran towards a clump of trees along the road allowance.

Instinctively, David turned his machine in the direction of the pursuit. Shifting gears, he accelerated toward the car. He watched as the woman dodged in and out of the gaps between parked equipment. The driver, obviously frustrated, spun in soft dirt as he tried to catch her.

David hoped to get to the woman before the car did. But while watching the unfolding scene ahead, he hit a deep ditch too fast, ramming the machine against an approach. The shock of the impact knocked David's head against the roof of his cab and his knees slammed against the steering column. The force of the blow was so painful that it took him a few moments to regain his composure.

By then, the driver had coerced the woman back into the car and seeing David approach, had sped off in the distance. For the next week, David expected to hear that a woman's body had been discovered somewhere along the highway. He memorized the description of the car—just in case. It made him wonder about women and why they stayed with men they feared.

When the road was finished and the time came for the crew to return to Manitoba, David left Lumsden with mixed feelings. Part of him wanted to go home, but he didn't want to leave Brenda behind. Too young for a commitment, he promised to visit her regularly and she vowed to write. They corresponded for a while and he visited once. Unfortunately, the relationship couldn't withstand the seven hour drive and the two grew apart.

While David's romance with Brenda had been short-lived, it gave him confidence that nobody had seen in him before. Dating her had helped him mature and now it was much easier for him to relate to women. He realized that they were less likely to tease him about his speech than male friends. So he began gravitating towards females—juggling girlfriends between the country and the city. At the time he had a job in Winnipeg strapping and loading farm equipment for transport by truck to dealerships.

The money he earned helped him pay for a new car. It was very important to David to always have an eye-catching vehicle. It made him feel secure—and a flashy car attracted friends, both male and female. He moved around a bit, living by himself or with friends, and sometimes slept in his car in a girlfriend's driveway.

One weekend late that fall, David was in Moosehorn and while out walking was stopped on the road by a local farmer. The man was someone David liked and respected. They stood and talked for a while, then the man told him that a local farmer named Gus Breitkreitz, whose house had burned down a few weeks before, had moved into the old Pischke house at the farm. The man said that normally he wouldn't interfere, but he'd seen a horse being dragged down the road to the farm and felt the Pischkes should be told.

David thanked him and went to find Dennis. After determining that Caroline knew little about this, the two drove out to the farm at dusk to investigate. While they were curious what Gus would say, they also feared a confrontation. Neither twin liked the man, and they made no secret of it. Gus had been good friends with Domko and he openly gossiped about the family, spreading rumours about the twins, blaming them when Domko "ended up in Selkirk."

With their mother still owning the land, the twins reasoned that "technically" they could be considered Gus' landlord. They liked the feeling of authority this gave them.

They drove to the farm, parking the car in the driveway before cautiously approaching the house. They knocked on the door but there was no answer. David tried to look in a ground-level window, but it was covered from the inside.

They walked around the farmyard and David noted that it seemed smaller to him since he'd grown up. The church was actually much closer than he remembered, and the chicken house was tiny. Because of his past, the barn had an ominous and dangerous look that still made him wary. His eyes fixed on the spot at the front of the barn where he'd nearly been stabbed with a pitchfork.

"Let's see if he's in there," he suggested to Dennis.

The twins walked tentatively toward the barnyard, slowing as they neared the open doors. David had to convince himself that there was no longer anything to fear inside. His heart thumped regardless.

It took a few seconds for their eyes to adjust to the dimly lit building. They could see a form near the back lying on the cold, dirt floor. As they got closer, the sound of their footsteps caused the animal to stir. The twins were sickened by the sight of a young, injured horse. Its coat had been rubbed raw on one side. The animal whinnied in pain.

They turned and ran out of the barn.

"Oh no, did you see that?" Dennis exclaimed. "What do we do now?"

"I don't know, let me think," David said as he collected himself. He knew the horse was suffering and it made him think about Dolly. "Cruel bastards!"

The animal needed to be put down but David knew that even if he had a gun he'd never be able to stomach the ordeal. He looked at Dennis who appeared as if he might faint.

David shook off the image of the dying horse and strode to the house. He knocked loudly. This time when Gus didn't answer, he tried the knob, but the door was locked. He remembered that he still had the house key from the time he helped his mother move. He retrieved the key from the car and went back to the house where Dennis stood waiting. He inserted the key in the lock and pushed the door open.

"Somethin's in the way," he said as he stuck his head inside. The obstacle was an old pair of boots and work clothes that littered the floor behind the door. Numerous strings of commercial fishing nets were hanging from nails in the hall.

Joined by Dennis, they cautiously stepped into the kitchen which was barely recognizable now. There was a faint smell throughout of garbage mixed with rotting fish. The kitchen was being used as a workshop and there were tractor parts and tools strewn all over. In places, the floor was damaged where Gus had been cutting wood.

The house had never been well maintained, but the twins knew their mother would never approve of it being willfully damaged.

"Ma's not gonna like this," Dennis said.

"Yeah," David agreed. He was looking forward to getting Gus into trouble with Caroline. "We better go tell her."

They closed the door and drove straight to their mother's house.

As the twins expected, Caroline was angry about the reported condition of her farmhouse. She told the twins to go back and kick Gus out. Since it was already dark, they decided to wait until morning.

That night they visited Norman and Sharon, telling them what they'd seen at the farm. David considered asking to borrow Norman's gun—but decided against it. He was afraid he'd "chicken out" and didn't want to be teased.

Norman gave the twins a padlock and the next morning they drove back to the farm. David knocked forcefully on the door, but again there was no answer. The twins glanced at the barn and then at each other.

"Sh-should we go look?" Dennis asked.

David nodded. Slowly, they approached the barn, whose doors were now closed.

"Gus . . ." David yelled, as he slid open the door. "You in there?"

No answer came.

"Hey, Gus," he called again as he pushed opened the door all the way, "are you in h-hhere?"

The morning sun filled the barn with light. The brothers looked at the spot where the horse had been the night before and were relieved to see it was gone. Then they noticed the animal hanging from the rafters—it had been skinned and quartered.

"Blech!" Dennis said.

David stared at the bloody meat which was nearly frozen.

"What's he gonna do?" David asked. "Eat it?"

Dennis shuddered. "I s'pose." Horse meat was eaten by some people in the area, but few would admit it.

"C'mon, let's go," David said, shutting the door behind them. "Let's get his stuff out before he gets back."

The twins busied themselves piling Gus's belongings outside the house. It took a few hours and as time went by, they began working faster. They'd come this far without having to face Gus and the harder they worked, the less angry they were. They now wanted to avoid a confrontation.

"Ma will have to deal with him now," David said as he screwed the padlock in place. "At least we know he don't got no bolt cutters."

They got in the car and drove back to town. David dropped Dennis off at Caroline's.

"See you next weekend," he waved as he continued to Winnipeg.

Walter phoned one evening soon after that and asked David to pick him up after work. David arrived just after 5 p.m. to find his usually jovial brother preoccupied. David asked what was wrong.

Walter explained that he'd bought a used car from a Main Street dealership. The vehicle hadn't started properly from the moment he'd got it home. He'd called back to complain, but the salesman refused to talk to him.

Frustrated, Walter had made up his mind to go to the dealership to get a new starter for his car. David was expecting a showdown and wasn't looking forward to it. They stopped in front of the dealership and casually got out of David's car. They went onto the lot and began looking at used vehicles.

Both were pleased that the lone salesman was occupied with another customer. Walter waved David toward the back of the lot after spotting a car which resembled the one he'd bought. He told David to look casual, like he was interested in buying the car, then he dropped to the ground.

"What are ya doin'?" David asked.

"I'm gettin' a new starter," Walter whispered back. "Tell me if anybody comes."

Pulling tools out of his coat pocket, Walter slipped under the car. David stood there, trying to look like he was browsing. He could hear Walter banging underneath the vehicle. David looked towards the sales office in time to see two men walking across the lot toward him. He inched his way back to where Walter was hidden.

"Walter!" he whispered. "Somebody's comin',"

Walter didn't hear him and kept banging.

"Walter!" he said louder as the two men approached. One wore a hat that read "Security" across the front.

"I almost got it," Walter called out.

"Shhh!" David whispered, trying to block the sight of his brother's boots. The two men stopped in front of David.

"Can I help you with something?" the security guard asked.

"Um, yeah, I'm l-llookin' at c-ccars," David said lamely.

"Who's down there?" the salesman asked, pointing at Walter's legs.

"M-mmy br-rrrother," he said.

"What's he doing?"

"Ch-checkin' the engine."

Just then, Walter stopped banging. A few moments later, he slid out from under the car. David was relieved to see that he didn't have a car starter in his hands.

"What are you doing?" the man asked again. They stood with their arms crossed, waiting for an explanation.

"Oh, us?" Walter stalled while he thought of a lie. "We're lookin' at this here cc-car because we got one just like it at hh-home, and I'm hh-havin' trouble with the ss-starter."

"Yeah, an' we got it apart, an' got a new starter, but c-ccan't figure out how to get it b-back together," David added.

"And it's tricky on this here mm-model, you see, 'cause the starter's up behind—do you know anything about engines, maybe you can help us," Walter continued.

The salesman and security guard said they didn't know a thing about mechanics.

"Gg-good," Walter said, no longer worried how credible their story sounded. "L-llike I said, it's reeeeeally tricky on this here model."

"That's f-fffor sure," David added.

The men stood and listened, obviously baffled by the brothers and their elaborate story on how difficult it was to replace a car's starter.

"An' we really dd-don't want to take the engine out," Walter said.

"No t-ttime for that," David said, "gotta take the car to w-wwork in the mornin'."

The brothers smiled at the confused employees.

"Bb-but n-now I think I got it figured out," Walter said, tucking his wrench in his pocket. He started walking away, signaling David to follow. "Thanks so much for your hh-help. We really ap-pppreciate it."

"No problem," the salesman said as he waved good-bye. "Anything else we can do, just stop in."

Walter waved and nodded as they climbed into David's car. They kept straight faces until they were out of sight.

"Talked ourselves outta that one," Walter said proudly.

He still didn't have a working starter, but wasn't too disappointed. He'd never been much of a thief. What the experience did give him, though, was a new story to tell.

"Norman would sure be proud of us," David laughed.

Walter agreed. "Yep, Norman would be proud."

Rose married a man named Al Gardner and they were expecting their first child in June. In their honour, Caroline organized a family gathering at her house around the same time. David and Walter drove out from Winnipeg together, arriving after everyone else. They waved to Dennis who had just pulled into the driveway. As Walter parked his car, David noticed Gus drive by, stop and then back up. Gus got out of his car and strode toward Dennis' car.

In his early 50s, Gus was a tall, lanky man with big hands and a homely face. Everyone called him "Gusti," a moniker he hated. He often reminded people that he wasn't Icelandic—but Russian—and that his name was, in fact, Gustav. People ignored this and called him Gusti anyway.

He was from a hard-working, well-respected family of immigrants who'd farmed in the area since the early 1900s. Gus was a self-proclaimed loner who was always looking for ways to make a fast dollar. He bought and sold machinery, raised livestock and even ran the Moosehorn trucking business before selling it to Hugo in the early 1950s. Not an educated man, he was nevertheless intelligent. But he was also a known gossip, getting caught up in the everyday goings-on around town.

Gus wasn't approachable or someone instantly well-liked but had many good points. He was kind and generous to his family and was helpful and good company when he was with people he liked. Gus always had a humorous story to tell, but when he encountered people he didn't like his words could be thoughtless and even cruel.

He'd never liked the Pischke twins, having heard numerous stories about their bad behaviour from Domko. Since they'd moved him out of the farmhouse, he despised the pair even more.

Dennis stared at Gus who was now beside his car. He motioned for Dennis to roll down the window, which he did. David and Walter came around from behind the car just as Gus reached in, grabbed Dennis by the front of the shirt and punched him in the head with his other fist.

"Hey!" Walter yelled as he pulled Gus away from Dennis. The yelling escalated and the two men began fighting in the yard. It took the remaining Pischke brothers and a neighbour to break up the fight.

"I'll get you little bastards!" Gus fumed as the neighbour led him back to his vehicle. The brothers stood on the lawn until Gus was out of sight.

"What was that all about?" someone asked.

They filed into the house and the twins explained what had happened a few months before. When Gus had confronted Caroline shortly after he discovered his belongings outside on the ground, she'd been unable to admit she had asked the twins to evict him.

"Well, Walter," Norman teased as they sat down to have a drink, "I didn't know you had it in you."

"Me neither," David added.

"Or me," said Dennis. "You really gave it to him."

Walter joined in the banter about the fight, and they snickered about it for a while. But when the conversation switched to other topics, Walter was silent. Looking into his older brother's eyes, David could see that the scuffle with Gus had meant more to Walter than anyone else had realized. David had come to know his 27-year-old brother better over the past few years, and respected his kind and generous ways. Their eyes met and while no words were exchanged, David knew that Walter's days of watching his siblings take a beating were long over.

"Are you one of the Pischke boys?" an RCMP officer called out.

David was walking from the store to his car parked on Main Street in Moosehorn. He stopped to look at the officer who was leaning out of a patrol car window.

"Y-yeah," he said.

"Can I talk to you for a minute?" the officer asked.

"S-ssure," David said, walking towards the cruiser.

The Mountie got out of the car.

"What are the names of some of the kids who live out near

Bayton?" he asked.

David shrugged. "There's some Metners an' some Meisners . . . Bittners, why?"

The officer hesitated. "Well, we've had a complaint about broken windows at your farmhouse and I was wondering who lives out there."

"Oh," David said, "when did they get b-bbroke?"

"We're not sure," the officer replied. "Where were you this week?"

"Me? I was in t-ttown last w-wweekend, an' in the c-ccity all week," David said.

The officer took out his notepad and began writing.

"So you weren't out at the farm then?"

"No," David said. "Why?"

"You don't know anything about broken windows?" he quizzed.

"N-nnothing," David said, stunned. "Why are you askin' me for?"

"When the vandalism was reported, we were told that you and your twin may have done it."

"What? That's r-rridiculous. Why would I shmash our own windows?"

"I don't know," the officer said. "I'll look into all of this. Where is your brother staying in case I have to talk to him?"

"You can call Mom's—she'll know where he is," David said, giving the man his mother's phone number.

"Good," the Mountie said, getting back into the car. "Thanks for the help."

David walked slowly to his car and got in.

Why would I break windows at the farm? he thought to himself.

It took a few minutes for the ludicrous accusation to sink in, and then he became angry. He wondered who might have pointed the finger at him, then decided to drive to the farm to check the damage himself.

As he stopped the car in front of the house and got out, he looked up at the window that he and Dennis would jump out of at night. It was still intact.

That's a long ways down, he thought as he rounded the house. Two windows at ground level were broken, but the other upstairs window was fine.

Two broken windows, he thought. *Who'd do such a thing?*

And then he noticed a tractor parked in the yard not too far away. He stared at it for a few minutes and then slowly turning, looked back at the house. There, in the upstairs window, stood Domko leaning against the sill as he glared out at David. Their eyes locked and the young man instantly felt like a boy again.

This is a dream, he thought. *Like the dream about Dolly. Wake up, wake up!*

But this time it wasn't a dream, it was real.

He didn't want to run, not this time. He thought about staying there to fight like Norman or Walter would do. They didn't run from anyone and it was about time he stopped running too. Both men sensed that neighbour George Kiesman's prediction was on its way to becoming true. George had once told him that he'd be sorry for being so short-sighted and hard on the children. "Those boys are going to grow up one day Domko, and they may make you sorry then for beating them."

David felt his jaw tighten as he stood fast and stared back up at Domko whose expression was also rigid as he slowly moved away from the window.

David wanted to run, but he forced his legs to walk slowly toward the car, his muscles tense and ready for confrontation. He opened the door, got in and slowly drove away. It had been a remarkable outward display of bravery on his part, but inside he was trembling with fear.

Chapter 15

"WHERE DO YOU WORK NOW?" McMillan asked. "I work at Steep Rock," David said, "for Continental Lime. I've been there for, let me see . . . it'll be 30 years this fall."

"That's a long time," he said. "What is your occupation?"

"I'm a crusher," he said.

McMillan laughed. "No offense, that's just an interesting job title."

"I operate the big crushing machine," David said.

"What does it do?" he asked.

"It crushes the stone and then it gets burned into lime," he said. "Then we ship it to W-winnipeg."

"What do you think of your job?" he asked.

"It's real good," David said. "I'm one of the top guys there now, I got lots of seniority an' they always call me when they need emergency repairs done."

"That's good, so it sounds like you really enjoy your work?" he said.

"Very much so," David said.

"And what do you think of your co-workers?" he asked.

"Real good, m-most of the guys are r-real g-good. There's a few, but there's always a few at any job that you don't get along with too good, but mostly I get along with them all r-really good."

"So you've made some friends there, then?"

"Oh yes, yes," he said. "An' I hafta tell you that a great guy once told me to keep that job and it would be good to me for the rest of my life. An' he was right. He's gone now, but I made him a promise that

I'd watch out for his wife. So every fall I go down to her place and cover up the septic line with s-straw and go back, usually me an' Dennis, and we uncover it in the s-springtime. It's our way of helpin' people who've helped us."

David continued working in the city for a paving crew building the Lagimodiere overpass in southeast Winnipeg. He came home weekends to see family and friends. One afternoon he arrived for a visit at his mother's house. David told his mother that he'd seen Domko at the farm. She explained to him that Domko had been working since mid-May for a farmer named Bernie Gmitzyk who lived near Faulkner. The Gmitzyk's had decided to give him a job, but had taken him back to the mental institution when he became despondent at the end of June—just days after David saw him at the farm.

She also told him that some neighbours were angry with David—and she wondered why. David concluded that when he told the RCMP officer the names of neighbouring children, it appeared that he was blaming them for breaking the windows. Outwardly, David laughed it off, but it bothered him that he'd inadvertently offended these people.

They chatted for awhile, then Caroline made a suggestion.

"Why don't you put in an application at the quarry?" she said as they sat around the table. "I heard they need help."

Now that the farm was gone, she gave more objective advice to her children. David liked the thought of getting a job at the nearby limestone processing plant. It was a good idea, especially since he'd be laid-off as soon as the overpass was complete.

"John Brown is the supervisor there," Caroline said, knowing how shy David could be. "He's a nice man. You should go talk to him. I think the quarry is open on Saturdays."

Lacking a reasonable excuse not to go, David got into his car and drove six miles to the village of Spearhill, on a back road northeast of Moosehorn. The quarry, sitting on the edge of the village, was owned by Winnipeg Supply and Fuel—one of the largest employers in the area.

David turned off the road and followed a dusty gravel lane to the employee parking area. As he got out of his car, the sound of heavy equipment moving stone vibrated off the quarry walls. A truck drove by slowly, and a man gave him a nod and a wave. Huge kilns with giant smoke stacks loomed overhead as David walked to the building that he thought might be the company office.

He stepped inside and closed the door behind him, shutting out most of the noise. A man looked up from his desk. David recognized him as John Brown, a relative by marriage on his father's side of the family.

"Can I help you?" the supervisor asked.

David stood with his shoulders slumped, eyes to the floor. He had been practising what he'd say, but the words were now caught in this throat.

"I-I-I'm l-lllookin' for a job," he said quietly.

The man stared back. "You're one of the Pischke twins, right?"

David nodded and their eyes met.

"David?" John asked.

"Y-yes."

"Pleased to meet you, Dave," John said, coming out from behind his desk and extending his hand. "Actually, your timing is excellent. Do you have a résumé with you?"

David shook his head "no."

"What kind of job are you looking for?" he asked.

"Aaa-nything," he stammered. "I can d-ddrive trr-rucks. I'm working for a road building company in W-wwinnipeg."

The supervisor had heard how reliable and hardworking David's older brothers were. He knew that if he could harness this young man's potential, he'd have a diligent, loyal employee.

"We've got lots that needs to be done and if you want a job, you can start Monday," John said.

"M-mmonday? This c-ccomin' M-monday?" David asked. "I can't 'cause I gotta give notice in W-wwinnipeg."

"Sure," John smiled, handing David a hard hat. "You just get in here as soon as you can. C'mon, I'll take you for a tour before the boys shut down."

David put on the hard hat and followed John out the door. Once again he was hit by a wall of noise.

"Not so bad when you're inside," John yelled as if reading David's thoughts. "Over there is the pit and this here is the kiln. We're going to be re-doing the kilns and that's the first job I'd like to put you on."

They continued through the quarry as the supervisor explained how they excavated rock, loaded it onto trucks and took it to be crushed and burned.

"The end product is lime, which is loaded onto boxcars and trucks over there for freighting to Winnipeg," he said.

David listened as they turned and began walking back toward his car.

"You come back next week and we'll get you started," John said, extending his hand again.

David took the man's hand for the second time, noticing the strength of John's handshake. He firmed his own grip and tried to look his new boss in the eye.

"That's better," John smiled. "See you then."

He nodded and left.

David gave a few days notice at the Winnipeg company, then moved his belongings to Moosehorn for what would become a permanent stay. He arrived at the quarry early the following day and found John in his office.

"Where shall I s-start?" he asked.

John said that because the company was switching from wood to coal as a fuel source, a different type of brick would be used inside the 100-foot-tall kilns. David would be working on relining the five kilns with brick. He'd receive on-the-job training from a man named Gene Bauch.

Gene was from Moosehorn and had been working for the company for a few years. He was a husky man in his early 40s with a ready smile and kindly disposition. He enjoyed training the younger men and immediately took to David who felt fortunate to be working with the jovial, quick-witted man. Gene, and loader operator Eddie Kiesman, made David's early days at his new job enjoyable.

Gene and David began relining the inside of each kiln by first knocking out the old brick and then mortaring new brick in its place. With an old winch, David and Gene were lowered inside the kiln cylinders to stand on a platform where they worked.

"Close your eyes, and don't look down," Gene would advise David as he slowly lowered the young man inside. Often the old winch would slip, dropping a few feet before catching again. David would let out a scream, thinking he was going to drop to his death. He'd recover his footing, and take off the straps when he reached the platform. A few moments later, Gene would appear at the top and be lowered down beside him. As they spoke, their voices echoed off the kiln walls.

"So, David," Gene said one afternoon, "got yourself a girlfriend?"

David blushed. He'd been working with Gene for just over a month and knew how he liked teasing the other young men about their relationships. So far he'd been able to avoid discussing his love life by changing the subject when his co-workers asked. But Gene pressed further.

"C'mon," he said, "a young fella like you must have a girl somewhere."

David smiled. He did have a girlfriend, but it was much more than just a passing attraction. He'd managed to keep the relationship secret until now, but soon everyone would know how he felt about Bonnie Shiells.

He'd met the attractive and exuberant young woman at a dance that summer. He'd been dating a few other girls off and on, but as soon as Bonnie expressed an interest in him, David broke off the other relationships and began dating her exclusively. He'd fallen deeply in love with the vivacious young woman and now that he had a steady job he was thinking about getting married.

This was more information than he wanted to share with Gene, however, so David simply said he did have a girlfriend and her name was Bonnie. The teasing started that day. A regular target in the past for bullies and nasty comments, David could easily tell when he was the butt of a joke or being included in the fun. Gene was always kind in his teasing and was an expert at keeping a straight face. David often wondered if Gene was serious or not.

"What are you waiting for?" Gene said one afternoon. "A beautiful girl like that—if you wait too long, some other guy is gonna snap her up."

David would just smile and make playful excuses. David's naive nature and Gene's dry wit made a comedic combination. Gene would work quietly alone while thinking up ways to tease David. Then in an unsuspecting moment, he'd catch the teenager off guard. David learned to playfully joke back and soon the two were entertaining the men at work with their banter.

They worked on the kilns all that fall and through the winter. David lived with Eunice and Mel at Spearhill until spring when he moved back in with his mother. Dennis also began working at the Spearhill quarry so the twins were together once again.

David and Bonnie were spending every free moment together and decided to get married. They were planning a summer wedding so Bonnie, who had been working in Winnipeg, quit her job and moved back to Moosehorn.

David and Bonnie were married June 21, 1969, in the United Church at Steep Rock. A reception and dance followed across the street in the community hall. Norman was best man. Dennis, Glen Clearwater and Bonnie's brother Brett were groomsmen.

Norman was in his element as he stood before the crowd and welcomed Bonnie to the family. Everyone knew the young man's comments were sincere as he and Bonnie got along well.

"And you all know that June 21 is the the longest day and shortest night of the year," Norman teased, citing David's shyness and lack of experience with women. "That's why David picked today to get married."

The hall erupted in laughter.

He continued telling stories about David and finished off by warning Bonnie that, "David can eat his weight."

Feeling quite grown up, David was pleased that his mother had respected his wishes and didn't include Domko in the festivities. He was also glad to see that his siblings seemed happy. Norman and Sharon were expecting their second child in December. Walter and Lorie were unable to attend, but sent their best wishes. After a brief honeymoon, David and Bonnie returned to discover that cupid's arrow had struck during their wedding reception. Dennis had been introduced to Bonnie's cousin Robynne Shiells, and a romance was beginning to blossom there.

David and Bonnie rented a tiny house in Steep Rock for a few months, then moved to an old log house David's company owned in Spearhill. The house was small and a bit rundown, but David did some repairs and Bonnie cleaned and decorated. Soon it was a comfortable home. Bonnie was a pleasant young woman to live with—good natured, an excellent housekeeper and a fantastic cook.

By fall of that year, David and Gene had finished relining the five kilns. David was moved to a new job—blasting rock at the quarry. Gene was pleased that his workmate was doing well and had joined the ranks of married men. He started asking David when he was going to begin a family. Very proud of his own wife and children, Gene believed a happy home was the key to a satisfying life.

"C'mon Dave," he said, "you gotta start having kids. You know where they come from right? A little practice beforehand doesn't hurt—gotta make sure you get it right."

David would just smile and prepare himself for the next round of teasing.

Frequently, Gene would catch him off guard.

"Did you practise last night, like I told you?" Gene would yell across the crowded yard. "You know what they say—practice makes perfect!"

Late that fall, David returned after a day of gathering wood. Wood was an inexpensive way to heat a home and he knew it was going to take more than a few cords to keep their poorly insulated house cozy that winter. He cut and hauled all day and when he arrived home just after dark, Bonnie had a wonderful meal waiting for him. They sat down to supper and she seemed particularly happy. That night they shared a special dessert.

"I have some good news for you," she said excitedly, waiting until she had his full attention. "I'm pregnant. I just found out."

David was shocked. At first he didn't know what to say. It was obvious that she was pleased—her moist eyes danced in the light and her expression was tentative as she waited for his reaction.

"When?" he asked.

"You mean, when am I due?" she asked.

"Yeah," he choked.

"Summertime—probably July," she smiled.

Inside, he was a jumble of mixed feelings. He knew that to have the "normal" life he so desperately craved, he'd have to have children just like everyone else. But he'd barely recovered from his own childhood and was ambiguous about impending fatherhood. His emotions volleyed back and forth as he told himself that his child's life wouldn't be like his own. But thoughts of Domko persisted in his mind.

What if I die? Just like my Dad? Who would care for my kids? Would Bonnie be just like Mom and marry another Domko?

He looked with great affection at his wife's hopeful face. Smiling, he told her how happy he was. He decided it would be best to keep his fears to himself.

That winter and spring, the couple spent a lot of their spare time at Bonnie's parents' house. Margaret and Herb Shiells lived at the south end of Steep Rock right beside Mike Kalanza. One afternoon they were sitting around the kitchen table visiting with friends when everyone started talking about Mike.

"Has he retired yet?" one person asked. "I heard that he's 65."

"You'd think that he'd have enough money now that he doesn't have to work so hard . . . yeah, but you know old Mike, he can't resist making a dollar . . . he's worked for Canada Cement for years . . . and he's so stingy he doesn't spend a cent of it . . . he'll never stop working . . . I heard he bought both parts of Elm Point—the piece that his father owned and the other half that used to belong to his brother Alex. Both went up for tax sale and he got them by paying the back-taxes . . . you're kidding? What a steal! . . . he's drilling wells and clearing land . . . and I heard that after working all day at the plant he's been seen at home cutting hay by lantern at night . . . Does he ever sleep? . . . I heard he drilled a well for Fred Cook and didn't charge him anything for it . . . Mike, not charge? Not a chance . . . No, it's true . . . And what about the old Makowski place? I heard he's renting that land too . . . Is he still the caretaker at the rink here? . . . Holy shit, how's he gonna get all the work done? . . . Like I said, he doesn't sleep much."

David got up to get a drink of water. As he stood looking out the kitchen window, he could see Mike working outside in his yard. He watched the man putter around the various pieces of equipment he had scattered across the lawn.

David wondered where Mike's sons were living. Now in their mid-20s, Nick and Ted had moved away. David had seen them occasionally, but hadn't spoken to them since they were children.

He remembered that when Norman was just a teenager he had gone to work drilling wells for Mike. He hadn't lasted much more than a week, unexpectedly hitchhiking back to Moosehorn one afternoon. Norman had told David that while he was working with one of Mike's sons, something on the drilling rig had broken. Mike had flown into a rage, blamed the teenagers for it and smashed his son over the head. Norman left that day and never went back.

"I saw enough of that shit at home," Norman explained to his brother. "I'm not going to work for someone like that."

"Dave!" Bonnie called out. She stood in the back doorway with one hand in the air, the other resting on her pregnant stomach.

David looked up from what he was doing in the yard to see his young wife waving him inside. As he walked towards the door, he marveled at how beautiful she looked in the warm July sun. As he got closer, though, he could see she was troubled. She went back into the house and he followed.

"What is it?" he asked.

"I'm not feeling so good," she complained. "I don't know . . . I've got pains, I think maybe I'm going into labour."

David froze. He stared at Bonnie who was looking back at him expectantly.

"What should we do?" she asked, bending slightly.

"Sit down," he said, taking her arm and leading her to the chesterfield.

"Maybe we better go to the hospital," David added nervously.

Bonnie grimaced. "I don't want to go too soon. What if it's just false labour?"

"Then we'll come home," he said.

"Yeah, but I'll be so embarrassed."

David nodded. He hated hospitals and wasn't all that eager to go himself.

They stayed home for a while longer, but when the pains began coming at regular intervals, they decided to make the drive to Ashern.

David's mind whirled as he helped his wife into the car and drove along the dirt road toward the highway. Within 25 minutes, they were in Ashern. David helped Bonnie out of the car and into the emergency room. The nursing staff took over at that point, and Dr. Gordon Steenson appeared from inside one of the rooms. Dr. Steenson had tended to David a few times when he was a child. Steenson was a round, soft-bodied man with wispy hair and thick-rimmed glasses.

"Hello David," the doctor said calmly, "how are you doing?"

"F-fine," he said.

"A bit nervous, I take it?"

David nodded.

"Don't worry, we'll take good care of her," he said. "And how's your neck?"

"F-fine," he stammered again. The memory of the time he'd fallen off a hay wagon and fractured his neck was suddenly fresh in his mind.

"That lump back there, does it bother you?" Steenson asked as he wrote something in another patient's file. He had the uncanny ability to do three things at once.

"N-not m-much," David said, reaching to touch the hard knot on the back of his neck. He didn't realize it was that noticeable.

"A lot of scar tissue there," Steenson murmured. "It might bother you when you're older."

The nurse interrupted with questions about Bonnie as the doctor slipped away to tend to another patient. David followed as his groaning wife was taken to a room down the hall. He stayed with her until the labour pains became intense. Seeing her in pain was more than he could stand.

"I gotta go," he whispered, feeling sick.

Bonnie was too preoccupied to offer her thoughts either way.

David waved and slipped out of the room. He hurried down the hall and out the door after leaving a phone number where he could be reached. Overwhelmed, he got in the car and drove back to Moosehorn to visit Ken who had married a striking young woman named Jane. He and his friend sat at a table and had a few drinks in an effort to calm David's nerves. It wasn't long before the phone rang.

It was someone from the hospital looking for David.

Still unable to talk to strangers on the phone, David asked to have the message relayed to him. The baby had been born; Bonnie had had a difficult time—he needed to get there right away.

David hurried from the house and got in his car. He sped down the highway, parked in front of the hospital and ran inside. No one was there to meet him, so he went down the hallway to the room where he'd last seen Bonnie. Totally unprepared, he opened the door to find the delivery room empty. It hadn't yet been cleaned and he was horrified to see a bloodied hospital gown and towels. The afterbirth sat in a metal basin nearby. He turned and ran from the hospital. Thinking that Bonnie had surely died, he didn't know what else to do. He drove home and waited for a phone call. He paced the floor all evening, wondering if his wife was alive. He hoped the baby had survived the birth, but had no idea how he'd care for it if Bonnie had bled to death.

He'd come to expect the worst in situations like this. He was so nervous he knew he'd never be able to use the phone. He stayed there and waited.

Later that night, the call came.

He tentatively picked up the phone and was both relieved and overjoyed to hear Bonnie's voice at the other end. She was back on the ward and had called to find out where he was. He explained as best as he could what had happened, and how he'd been overcome by the amount of fluid and blood that was left in the room after the delivery.

By this time, it was too late for him to visit. They decided it would be best if he waited until morning. He fell into a fitful sleep only to be awakened by another nightmare. He dozed again and was grateful in the morning when he stepped outside and the world seemed normal again.

He drove to the hospital and waited for a nurse to take him to his wife. He went into the room where he found Bonnie holding the baby. He was overjoyed by the sight. He moved a little closer and his heart swelled with pride as he looked down at the tiny bundle in Bonnie's arms—a son they named Dale.

In late November that year, Dennis and Robynne were married. Eunice and Mel were adjusting to life as parents, having adopted a baby boy they named Marlo. Sharon gave birth to a son, Trevor. Walter and Lorie were kept busy with their children—Kim, Rhonda and Gene. Rose and Al were living near Moosehorn with daughter Theresa.

A year later, Eunice gave birth to a beautiful girl they named

Melissa. Then in mid-December, Robynne gave birth to twin daughters she and Dennis named Deanna and Dawn. The little girls were exquisitely fine featured with their father's fair colouring and their mother's striking good looks.

Now Caroline had five grandsons and six granddaughters. She gave them equal love and attention and they loved her in return.

❖

Chapter 16

"HAVE YOU EVER BEEN ARRESTED or charged with a crime?" McMillan asked.

David looked stunned. "Me? I already told you that," he said. "No, we've never been arrested or charged with nothin'."

"So you haven't spent any time in jail," he asked again.

"No!" he exclaimed. "We never did a thing wrong. Not even a parking ticket!"

"You keep saying 'we,'" McMillan noted. "Who else are you talking about?"

"Me an' Dennis," he said.

"Come see what I bought!" Norman exclaimed as he knocked once on the door and burst into David and Bonnie's house.

"Hey, you don't live here no more," David joked to his brother who'd owned the house before him.

"I'm on my way out to the farm with a bunch of guys, do you want to come?" Norman asked.

David looked at Bonnie. She was busy with Dale who'd just turned two and baby Ian who'd been born a few months earlier.

"Go ahead," she waved, "I'll meet you later at Mom's."

David nodded and followed his brother out the door. They climbed into Norman's car which sat idling in the driveway. After selling their house in Moosehorn to David and Bonnie, Norman and Sharon had moved into a trailer in the old farmyard. They planned to fix up the aging house and eventually move in.

"Hey, did you ever s-sort out that deal with Hugo an' the gas?" David asked.

Norman thought for a moment.

"Oh that . . . yeah, I talked to him about it a long time ago."

"You sure?" David asked, somewhat annoyed. "'Cause me an Denny got blamed for takin' that barrel of gas—he thought we was stealin' it, you know. He gave us hell an' we couldn't 'fend ourselves 'cause you weren't there."

"I know, I heard," Norman said.

"But did you tell him that we paid you an' that you said we could take it?" he pressed.

"Yeah, yeah, I told him," Norman said firmly.

"'Cause Hugo still looks at me kinda funny an' I don't want him thinkin' we s-stole," David said.

Norman shrugged. "Hugo's runnin' a big business now, he doesn't have time to be thinking about you."

"Yeah, I guess," David said. "How is it goin'? You like dri-vin' for him?"

"Yeah, it's great," Norman smiled. "He's made me a supervisor."

"A s-ssupervisor? R-really?" David said. "So you boss guys around?"

Norman laughed. "Not really."

"Well, I dunno," David laughed. "D-do we hafta start callin' you s-sir?"

"Damn well should!" Norman laughed as he turned onto the road leading to the farm. He drove a little farther, then slowed.

"Well, Davey boy, I think you're gonna be impressed," Norman chuckled.

As he passed the church, he pointed to the bush between it and the farm house. "Look through there."

"I don't see n-nothin'," David said.

"Just wait, you'll see her in a minute," Norman grinned as he turned into the driveway. He drove past the house and stopped the car. There in the pasture was a Super Cub, two-seater airplane on the other side of the fence.

David gasped. He'd heard that Norman was going to use money from the house sale to buy a plane, but didn't think he'd do it.

"You b-bought a plane?" David exclaimed. "Well, look at that."

Norman laughed as he got out of the car.

"Want to go for a ride?" he asked in an eager tone.

"Sure," David said. "When you g-gonna teach me to drive?"

"Not drive," Norman corrected, "fly." His tongue gently massaged the word, the way people do when they talk about things they love.

David smiled as they strolled toward the plane. Norman opened the door and the two looked inside. David ran a hand along the smooth exterior of the plane's fuselage. He felt very proud of his brother and told him so.

"Big shot," David joked. "First a supervisor, now this. You won't w-anna be 'sociated with us guys no m-more."

Norman laughed off the suggestion. Just then a caravan of cars pulled into the driveway. It was a group of Norman's friends who had come to see the plane. One of them was Mel Kiesman—a tall, thin young man with a fun-loving personality and goofy smile. Mel was always into some kind of mischief and his happy-go-lucky attitude attracted many friends.

He was as wild and charming as Norman, with a voice that could crank out a tune just like country and western singer Hank Williams Sr. Everyone wanted to be in the company of Norman and Mel—knowing it was a guaranteed good time.

David's heart felt bigger when he was around Mel, remembering he was one of the few older kids who stuck up for the Pischke youngsters when they were being teased by other children at school.

Mel had spent a lot of time with Walter, Stephen and Norman. He had even accompanied them on visits back to the farm when they needed to retrieve something or give money to their mother.

"You want me to kick his ass for you?" Mel would say with eyebrows raised high. "I'll do it—I'm not scared of the old bastard."

Peace-loving Walter would just shrug and laugh. "Nah, we'll leave him alone this time. But you'll be the first to know if I need some ass kickin' done."

Mel was one of those people who could see the good inside the Pischke kids—past the stuttering and struggles they faced as adults.

Loren Dewar and Anita Russell were the next to drive into the yard. Loren had a lot in common with Norman as both loved planes and the Russell girls. The young men had become close friends while they talked about flying and worked on their vehicles together.

Loren flashed his lights at the others just before he got out of his car. Everyone chuckled. He'd bolted a pair of airplane landing lights on the front of the car near the headlights. When nobody else was around, he'd turn them on at night while driving on the highway lighting up the road for more than a mile. Quiet, bright, athletic and well-liked, he played forward for the Ashern Hornets hockey team.

Another friend, Lorne Park, was behind Loren. He parked beside the other cars. Lorne was a newcomer to the area. He also played for the hockey team and had become good friends with Mel and Loren. Intrigued by the idea of flying, Lorne was building himself an ultra-light plane. He had come to the Interlake as a school teacher, spending a year in Lundar before moving onto a job with Manitoba Hydro.

Lorne was similar to Loren in height, but the physical resemblance ended there. Lorne had black, curly hair and a dark complexion—genetics he'd inherited from his native grandmother. From a large family at Poplar Point near Portage la Prairie, Lorne was intelligent and quick and his green eyes danced when he told a joke. His acerbic wit sometimes left dullards wondering if they'd just been insulted.

"Well look at that!" Mel hollered as Loren and Lorne fell in behind him. The trio strode across the yard toward Norman's new plane. Mel let out a long, slow, whistle. "She's a beaut!"

Norman laughed and offered rides, in turn, to David and each of his friends. Within minutes, the Super Cub was soaring overhead.

By this time, David had been working at Winnipeg Supply and Fuel for two years. He was beginning to feel confident about his abilities and had even earned a promotion to crusher operator which was a huge boost to his morale. He started working as a machine operator around the time that he and Bonnie had bought Norman's house. Initially David had been nervous about taking the job. He was replacing a longtime employee, Herb Robinson, who was away on sick leave. Herb came to the plant one day and talked to David about the unfortunate turn of events that had forced him to leave.

"That's okay, Dave," Herb said, "I can't do the job any more. The dust is too much for me. I'm still taking cancer treatments but they said when I'm feeling good, I can come back and work as the janitor. It's not glamorous, but it's work I can do."

David nodded.

"You stick with the job, David, and it will be good to you," Herb said. "You'll do well if you stay with the company—they'll treat you good."

The two men shook hands. At that moment David vowed he would always respect Herb for having confidence in him and for making it easier to take this important step in his life. He and Herb were also neighbours in Moosehorn and David started helping the older man around his home whenever he needed assistance.

◆ ◆ ◆ ◆ ◆

David gave a quick rap on his mother's door then let himself in. He could hear laughter coming from the kitchen where family members were visiting. Dennis, Robynne, Eunice, Mel, Rose and Al were there.

"Hi Ma," David said, waving to everyone around the table. Looking past into the living room, he could see Kathy and Jennie playing on the floor. Sitting on a chair nearby was Domko. He just sat there, watching television as if he'd never left.

David cornered his mother by the counter.

"What's he doin' here," he whispered.

Caroline shrugged.

"Ma, what's goin' on?" he implored. "He's not back, is he?"

Caroline looked tired. She quietly explained that a social worker had called on Domko's behalf. He'd been begging to go back to Moosehorn to live with her. He agreed to keep taking his pills and said he would contribute his share of household expenses. He'd asked for one more chance and she had agreed.

"How long's he been here?"

"A week," she said. "He's been good and the kids are happy to have him here."

David thought that "happy" might be a bit of an overstatement. What Domko's children looked forward to was their father bringing them treats, which seemed to make up for his frightening, erratic behaviour.

David shook his head, deciding not to comment. It didn't seem right to him that his stepfather could just come back into their lives and sit there as if nothing had happened. David was expected to be polite but that was ludicrous. Everyone seemed to be going along with it, so David tried to relax.

As he pulled another chair up to the table, David started to wonder if maybe *he* was the odd one. Was he making too much of this? So what if Domko was there watching television? As long as he wasn't hurting anyone, what difference did it make?

He found it hard to accept Domko's presence but what else could he do? Since the family never discussed the abuse it was difficult to raise the issue.

Maybe we were bad kids, David thought, trying to make sense of the "adults" acting as if nothing was wrong.

Soon David was drawn into the conversation.

"Okay, so this German is walking down the street and he sees this Polish guy with a very long pole and a yardstick," Al told the group. "He's standing the pole on its end and trying to reach the top with his yardstick. Seeing how stupid the Polack is, the German grabs the pole, lays it on the ground and measures it with the yardstick. 'There,' he says, '11 feet long.' The Polack grabs the yardstick and shouts, 'You idiot, I don't care how long it is! I want to know how high it is!'"

The group burst into laughter.

Even Caroline giggled as she saw the humour of the joke.

Seconds later, there was movement in the dark living room. Domko flew into the kitchen with a letter opener raised over his head. David and his siblings were sitting facing the living room, but it hadn't occurred to either Mel or Al not to turn their backs on Domko. The pair swiveled, just as Domko lunged at Al with the letter opener. Shocked, he dodged to one side and grabbed Domko's wrist.

All the Pischke siblings jumped up from the table. Instantly enraged by the attack, Al leaped to his feet and knocked Domko against the wall. Stunned, the Pischkes watched as Al punched Domko, this time hard enough to knock him to the floor.

"David, do something!" Caroline called out as she stepped between her husband and son-in-law.

Al gave Domko a kick in the legs as the older man lay on the ground.

"You ever try that again you sonofabitch, and I'll give you some of what you used to give my wife," Al seethed.

"David!" Caroline called again. "Come and get him out of here."

Obediently, David went to his mother's side. Caroline gave Al an embarrassed look then helped Domko up from the floor. He still clutched the letter opener in one hand.

"Take him to Henry Harliss's house," Caroline instructed.

David nodded.

"Give it to me," he said firmly pointing to the letter opener.

Domko looked at him and grunted. Slowly he extended his hand and gave the weapon to David.

David hadn't been this close to Domko in more than five years. As the man stood, he realized for the first time how short his stepfather really was—only five foot, three. David was a full eight inches taller, and yet he'd always felt small in this man's shadow.

Careful not to touch the muttering man, David walked with him to the side door. He kept a full three feet between them as they walked down the driveway to David's car. They drove in silence to Grahamdale. David got out of the car and waited as his stepfather followed him to Henry's door. He was relieved when his mother's friend answered.

"M-mma asked if he c-cccould cc-come here," David said.

"I know," Henry said. "She just phoned."

David nodded. He returned to the car as Domko disappeared inside.

A few days later, Domko was returned to the Selkirk hospital. David wished that the man's friends, Gus and Hugo, had seen first hand how volatile he really was. David couldn't help but think that Domko should go live with both of them for a while.

"Did you hear what happened?" David said as family members sat around Caroline's kitchen table a few weeks later.

"Norman crashed his plane," he said.

"What?" Caroline gasped. "When?"

"Yesterday," David replied.

"Is he all right?"

"Yeah, he's fine," David answered. "He was tryin' to take off, but I guess there was s-snow on the wings an' he stalled it. Wasn't too far from the gr-ound. Good thing, 'cause he crashed. Nobody got hurt though."

"But he's only had that plane for a few months," Caroline said. "Is it insured?"

"I don't know," David said.

"He could have been killed," she replied, shaking her head. She suddenly looked very tired. "I never did like the idea of him flying."

"Ah," David scoffed, "you know Norman. Not scared of n-nothin'."

They sat and talked for a little longer while all the grandchildren played together.

"I've decided that I'm going to move," Caroline announced without warning.

Thinking his mother was eying another house in town, David asked where she would like to live.

"B.C.," she said.

"B.C.?" David asked. "Where? Why B.C.?"

"Well, I've got to get away from here," she said.

David wondered why, then realized that he and his siblings hadn't been getting along all that well. Domko's visits and phone calls were becoming quite regular, too. David guessed that his mother wanted to get away from the stress and pressure of trying to keep the family together and on civil terms. She still had three young children to raise along with Kathy to support. Listening to everyone's day-to-day problems and grievances was simply too much for her.

"Do you know what Domko tells the doctors at Selkirk?" she said to David.

"What?" he asked.

"That it's all my fault," she added, starting to sound angry. "He says he gets along with you kids just fine and the only time he gets angry with you is when you listen to me. When I get involved, he thinks we're plotting against him."

David scoffed. "That's r-ridiculous."

"Yes, well it seems that things are going that way nowadays," she said, abruptly changing the subject. "Did you hear what happened the other night at the Grahamdale bar?"

"No, what?" he asked.

"Well, some punks were giving Mike Kalanza a hard time, threatening him, and he pulled a knife on them," she said. "He told us himself after church."

"What?" one of David's siblings said. "That old bugger. What's he doin' in the bar anyway?"

Caroline scoffed. "He's not that old—67 isn't too old to go to the bar."

"Yeah, but I heard he doesn't even drink," David said. "Why would he go there?"

"I don't know," she replied. "I didn't ask him that. He likes to socialize. I think that's the only reason he's a Witness. It sure isn't because he takes his studies very seriously."

"So what does he carry in that briefcase anyway?" a voice asked from the living room. "Watchtowers?"

"I heard he keeps all his money in there," someone else said to a chorus of laughter.

Caroline laughed too. "I don't think so."

"Yeah, well he must be loaded because I heard he just bought the Makowski place and paid cash for it . . . I heard that he doesn't even do his banking around here, that he goes to Portage la Prairie where his brother lives and keeps all his money there . . . How much money do you s'pose he's got?"

"There's a man for Caroline," someone joked.

"Don't talk like that!" she scolded. "I'm not interested in Mike. I don't want any man actually. I've had enough of that nonsense. Besides I'm still married."

"That don't matter," David piped up.

Caroline gently cuffed him in the head as she walked by and everyone snickered, including David.

"I'm quite satisfied with my life the way it is," she responded. "But like I said, the world is getting worse."

David got up and tuned out Eunice, Dennis and Caroline as they discussed the Jehovah's Witness interpretation of world events.

"When are you l-leavin' for B.C.?" David asked, changing the subject.

"As soon as Al can take us," she said.

David was relieved that she wouldn't be asking him to drive her west.

"Where are you going to l-live?" he inquired.

"Well, Stephen is still there, so we'll probably stay with him until we find a place. Probably either 100 Mile House or Williams Lake."

"It's n-nice there," David said.

She had been receiving provincial welfare for the past few years and before that he and his siblings had been helping her financially. He wondered how she planned to support herself.

Within a week, Caroline and the children were gone. In some ways it was a relief to David who now had less to worry about, but knew he'd miss his mother regardless.

David and Bonnie enjoyed socializing and now that they lived in Moosehorn, friends and family began dropping by regularly. One evening they sat around the kitchen table with a group of friends. Being married was helping his speech as he had someone to talk with daily. He also found socializing helped. After a few drinks, he was able to relax and his natural storytelling abilities began to surface.

"So Dave, we all see that you're starting to put on a little weight," a friend joked. "Bonnie must be a good cook."

"She's a damned good cook," David replied.

"But he's still awfully skinny," someone said.

"Yeah, but you didn't know him before," someone else mocked. "You should have seen him and Dennis—skiiiinneee!"

"Skinny?" David chortled. "Skinny? You think we're skinny now, you shoulda seen us! We was so skinny that if we turned sideways we disappeared."

The group broke into a chorus of laughter encouraging David on.

"Yeah, that black, ugly bastard never gave us n-nothin' to eat," he said. "We'd be sittin' there watchin' as he would be eatin' . . ."

"Who'd be eating?" someone asked.

"Who's be?" David exaggerated. "He's be! Who's be yittink? Fraa!" David said thrusting his arm in the air and drawing more laughter with his imitation of Domko.

"An' here me and Denny are just starvin' to death, so of course as soon as we got the hell outta there . . ."

"Domko is his stepfather," someone whispered to a confused newcomer.

"Well, then we started eatin' good," David continued. "We'd go into the café at Birds Hill an' charge up our meals an' we ate twice as much as them other guys."

Everyone laughed.

"Sometimes our food bill was more than our paycheques!" he added. "Yeah, and Kenny, 'member when I first got my Harley, I wasn't even heavy enough to start it! I was almost six feet tall an' 130 lbs. I'd stand up on the kick-starter and rrr-rrrum, nothin' would happen, re-member? I had to get you to start it for me."

Ken nodded in agreement while the friends giggled.

"An' bushed! You shoulda seen, the other day I was watchin' the Beverly Hillbillies on T.V., well crrrist, that was us! I 'member me an' Denny movin' Mom an' the Domkos to Winnipeg when I had my truck. I was driving an' Mom, Dennis an' Rosie was in the front an' we had the seat pulled up as far as it would go so Kathy, Jennie, Raymie an' Markie could sit behind the seat."

A chorus of laughter erupted again.

"Can you believe it? An' so there I am drivin' along an' we gets to the city an' of course we got a whole pile of junk piled in the back of the truck. I slow down and turns a corner an' have to stop. And there's this really cute girl standin' there an' she looks at us—oh my god, this goddamned bushed outfit. You never seen nothin' like it before in your life, and I'm so embarrassed. Right, Dennis? Just like the Beverly Hillbillies."

"Yeah," Dennis snorted, "I just hid my face"

"But you know, Dennis, we wasn't *exactly* like the Beverly Hillbillies," David corrected, taking another sip of his drink. "No, we didn't have no ceeement pond."

"Or no oil patch, neither," Dennis added.

By now their friends were nearly hysterical from the interplay between the brothers. It was at times like this that David was at his hilarious best. His naive, awkward and helpful nature attracted people to him and he made friends easily. Everyone enjoyed being around the twins who were quickly becoming "the life of the party."

By the next year, David and Bonnie were spending more and more time with her parents and brother in Steep Rock. While David got along well with the three of them individually, he didn't like being with them as a group. Sometimes they'd invite other people over and, depending on who it was, David felt left out or ostracized.

His stories didn't create a bridge for him with Bonnie's family, like they did with other people—but rather seemed to give them ammunition against him. Bonnie was too busy with Dale and Ian to notice. Not wanting to sound like a whiner, David pushed his concerns aside.

When nobody seemed to notice, he'd slip outside and go for a walk.

One afternoon he was on his way back to the house when he heard somebody call his name. He looked up to see Mike standing in the front yard.

"Hey, Dave, c'mere for a minute," Mike shouted.

David hesitated. Rumours were circulating that Mike had been somehow involved in a recent murder in the area. The whole town was gossiping about two versions of the story. The first rumour was that a man had been murdered by two men in Grahamdale. The perpetrators supposedly put the body in the trunk of a car and then went to the Grahamdale bar. While there, they started bragging that they'd killed a man. As they became even more intoxicated, they opened the trunk to show off the dead body to onlookers. Somebody called the police and the suspects were arrested.

The other account was that three men were visiting Mike in his second house at Faulkner—the old Makowski homestead. They'd been sitting around the table talking. Mike drank some tea, suddenly felt sleepy and took a nap. He awoke a few hours later to find a dead man on the floor of his house and one of his own guns lying beside the corpse. Mike called the RCMP, explained what had happened and the police later arrested the suspected killers who were found drinking in the Grahamdale bar. This was the version that Mike was repeating.

David was curious what the older man wanted. He didn't have the nerve to turn away and ended up following Mike into his backyard.

"You're Bonnie's husband, right?" Mike asked.

David nodded.

"Thought so. One of the twins. I remember you. You're a nice strong fellow, gimme some help over here," he said.

Mike was exactly as David remembered him. The older man's eyes were clear and bright and his smile showed a set of straight but stained teeth. His skin was tanned dark from many hours spent in the sunshine. His movements were swift and strong, and David had to remind himself this man was nearly 70 years old. Most men his age, and some a lot younger, spent their spare time sitting on easy chairs in front of the television. But not Mike.

David followed the older man through a mountainous pile of scrap iron towards the back of the lot.

"They're telling me that I need to get all my machinery out of town," Mike said. "That's why I bought the Makowski place. It's somewhere I can store my stuff without being harassed."

David was expecting Mike to talk like Domko and was surprised that he didn't have an accent. He did have an odd voice, though—

squeaky and halting.

"Help me, will you, I need to get this stuff on the trailer," he said.

David bent over and grasping one end of a heavy piece of metal helped Mike lift it onto the trailer. He was surprised by Mike's strength as the old man easily lifted his end.

They chatted as they worked. Mike told him how much he had left to do that season. He knocked down bush with his bulldozer for local farmers and drilled wells. He'd retired from the cement plant in town and was receiving three pensions—Canada Pension, Old Age Security and one from Canada Cement. He also bragged that he owned company bonds.

Mike briefly discussed the murder, saying that he expected to be called as a witness. He seemed excited by the prospect.

David stayed outside and worked for a few hours. The longer David talked with him, the less eccentric Mike seemed. When David went into the house in the early evening, Bonnie's family wanted to know what they'd talked about.

David shrugged. He relayed some of what Mike had said, but not much of it was interesting to the family. He joined the gossiping, but felt bad about it later. Was Mike an eccentric, miserly old man who was beginning to lose his mind from spending too much time alone? Or was he just a fiercely independent workaholic in need of some friendly company?

No one seemed to know for sure.

Subsequently—on January 28, 1974—Thomas Goodall was convicted of murder and sentenced to 15 years in prison. Mike was called as a witness but did not have to testify. Rumours spread rapidly that Goodall had threatened to some day get even with Mike for his involvement with the police investigation.

Chapter 17

"**HAVE YOU EVER BEEN TREATED** by a doctor for a nervous condition?" he asked.

"No," David laughed sarcastically, "but this here is e-nough to make me want to go to Selkirk!"

McMillan smiled. "So you have no problem with your nerves?"

"No, 'cept my family gets on my nerves sometimes, does that count?" he laughed.

"Everybody's family gets on their nerves, right?" McMillan echoed.

"Yeah, I guess . . . but you don't got a family like mine," he said. "It's sur-prising that we all aren't in Selkirk after the horrors we lived through an' then it didn't stop there. First I had about 12 years of hell on the farm an' then I had another 12 years after that."

"What do you mean?" McMillan asked.

"My family's so goddamned misfunctional it isn't even funny. Everyone alone is good, but together—oh my God."

The lights of oncoming traffic shone brightly in David's eyes as he stood on the highway waiting for the semitrailer to arrive. It was a cool evening and the last traces of daylight were now gone.

Stars shone brightly and he stared at the moon, distracted only by the occasional car or truck. He'd listen to the sound of each oncoming vehicle and try to guess whether or not it was the semitrailer he was expecting.

Soon he heard a rumble far off as the truck began to gear down. The semi pulled off the highway and stopped, giving David enough time to climb into the cab.

"How are you tonight, David?" the trucker asked. He replied that he was fine and the pair traveled down the dusty dirt road to the quarry.

David had been called to the office a few months earlier by the boss who'd asked him if he'd be interested in working extra hours in the evening. The boss said there were a number of trucks on back haul that couldn't get to Moosehorn until evening. David's job would be to load the trucks with lime, let himself into the office, weigh the load and fill out the weigh bill. Then he'd ride back to the highway with the truck. This would be a great help to both the company and the truckers, and it was an easy way for David to make extra cash.

David accepted and one evening after a trucker dropped him off, he waved good-bye and decided to go to the Moosehorn Hotel for a drink instead of walking the short distance home. Since it was a Friday night, he wasn't surprised to see the bar full of people. A number of his friends were sitting around a table. They waved him over and it wasn't long before he'd had a few drinks. Everyone was joking and laughing and then David started telling stories.

"Did you hear what happened to Norman a while ago?" he asked. "Well you know Norman's workin' for Hugo, an' since he got his new plane, he's been crop sprayin' for guys all over so he's been workin' around the clock . . ."

"He got another plane?" someone asked.

"Oh yes," David said. "You know Norman, he can't be without his plane. The other one got shmashed up an' was a write-off. Anyway, he's drivin' back home from up north an' he's on a back road, bumpin' along in that red dump truck he drives, an' it's late afternoon," David said, stretching out his arms and pretending to drive.

"All of a sudden, boom! He hits somethin', so he gets out an' looks and he's run over this black bear. So it's layin' there dead on the road an' he wonders what's he gonna do? So he drags the bear to the back of the truck and lifts it into the truck box! He decides he's gonna take it home an' show the kids—maybe get it stuffed later or somethin', I don't know."

"He lifted it into the truck by himself?" someone asked.

"Crrrist yes!" David exclaimed. "You know Norman, he's strong as a goddamned ox, anyways he drives first to show Mom and pulls into the driveway. He goes inside to get everyone an' when they come out to look . . . the bear's gone!"

David paused, waiting for everyone to get up to speed on the story before he delivered the punch line.

"He'd only knocked the bear out . . . it wasn't dead. So when he stopped in Moosehorn, the bear woke up an' climbed out of the truck!"

Everyone laughed as David took a sip of his drink.

"This stunned bear coulda woke up anytime an' killed him," he said feigning seriousness. "But that's Norman for you, it don't matter to him, just lift a bear an' load him in the truck."

"And so did they ever find the bear?" someone asked.

"Noooo," David said seriously. "He's roamin' 'round Moosehorn somewhere, wonderin' how the hell he got here."

As usual, David had the entire group convulsed with laughter.

"That Norman, I tell ya, he's always doin' somethin," David smiled as he took another sip.

Everyone agreed, and before long others were telling "Norman" stories. The two men at the next table were listening and threw in the odd comment too. Soon David began to notice that they didn't find the stories humorous.

"That's bullshit," one man said trying to intimidate David. "That Pischke is a lazy sonofabitch. The only reason he's got the job with Russell is that he's married to Hugo's daughter."

David was shocked by the derogatory remark. Norman had been in a car accident when he was a teenager and it had been his fault. Some labeled him as careless after that, but lazy? Never.

"Yeah, old Russell is an asshole too," the other man said.

David listened in shock while the men talked among themselves. They started to get louder as their conversation continued and an uneasy silence fell over the nearby tables as everyone focused on these men criticizing Norman and Hugo.

Red with embarrassment and nervous about possible confrontation, David got up and left. He hurried home and immediately phoned Norman.

"They're sayin' some pretty terrrrrible things 'bout you an' Hugo," David said, describing the men at the hotel.

"How do you know they were serious?" Norman asked.

"'Cause they didn't laugh in the right places," David said.

"Okay, thanks," Norman said abruptly hanging up the phone.

Less than 30 minutes later, there was a knock at David's door and Norman strolled in. He'd been to the bar to question the two men whose insults David had heard. It turned out they were Hugo's employees working under Norman's direction.

"What did you do?" David asked.

"I grabbed them and hauled them out of the bar. I told them if I ever heard them talking about me or Hugo again, I'd kick their asses," Norman said.

David laughed. He wished he could be as straightforward as his brother, but at the same time was worried he'd made two more enemies in town.

While David was outside cleaning his car one summer evening, Norman drove into the driveway. He shut off his car and got out.

"We're in shit again," he said as David stopped what he was doing.

"Wadda ya' mean?" David asked.

"Well, actually not me . . . you," Norman said, moving closer and lowering his voice. "I don't want you to turn around, but in the back lane about five doors down, a cop is parked behind the garage."

David turned to look.

"I said don't look!" Norman instructed. "Come on let's go in the house and I'll explain."

The brothers turned and David walked stiffly through the back door with Norman directly behind him. When they got inside, Norman shut the door and the brothers went into the kitchen. David peered out the window toward the lane.

"What the hell?" he said in astonishment.

"You heard there's been some cattle rustling going on?" Norman said.

"Yeah, so what?"

"So the RCMP have been camped out in the back lane watching you. They think you've been stealing cattle."

"Me?"

"Yeah," Norman said lighting a Colt.

"How? Why me?" David complained. "I w-wouldn't even know w-what to do with a bunch of cattle if I got 'em."

"Yeah, but they don't know that," Norman answered.

"What am I doin' with them? Where have I got 'em hid, anyways? Crrrist, I don't even got a truck. How am I haulin' them away?"

Norman nodded in agreement after all the questions. "I know, but they've been seeing you go out at night and getting into a truck and someone called police to report it as suspicious activity."

"Sus-picious! I've been w-workin'," David yelled, looking out the window again. He could see the headlights and front bumper of a police cruiser hidden behind a neighbour's garage.

"Actually rumour has it that you and Dennis are working together. Someone reported you," Norman said. "I think they're from the church."

"The church?" David asked. "That lousy outfit. It's probably one of them!"

"Well, I don't know, but I thought I should tell you," Norman said as he turned to go.

David shut the door behind his brother, relieved that he didn't have to load a truck that night.

During the next few weeks, David brooded that someone would mistakenly think he and Dennis were thieves. He couldn't remember stealing anything, apart from items that Domko had forced them to take, or food when they were children. Even that hadn't happened often.

Now a man, he realized the importance of a good reputation. He reflected on the past, remembering times when people had made odd comments or digs about him or Dennis. He'd laughed it off, thinking they were joking.

Sometimes people had even become angry. Like the time he was in the Ashern gas station he always patronized and the owner had confronted him at the counter. He'd accused David of stealing the garage's jack. David had flatly denied the accusation. He knew nothing about the disappearance of this piece of equipment and was confident that Dennis didn't know anything about it either. At the time, it hadn't bothered him much, but now he couldn't get it out of his mind.

I gotta stop buyin' gas there, he muttered to himself.

David fell into a mild depression. He avoided going outdoors and tried to keep his family out of sight. He discussed the false cattle theft story at length with Bonnie and his friends, but became angry when someone suggested he confront the officer watching him. He distrusted the RCMP and even resented them. With stubbornness being one of David's stronger traits, he absolutely refused to go to the police to establish his innocence.

The cattle thieves were eventually caught, but by that time, David's reputation had been badly damaged. Most people in the area had heard the name "Pischke" associated with thievery and David could say nothing in his own defence—because all the comments made were behind his back.

◆ ◆ ◆ ◆ ◆

In the spring of 1975, Norman and Sharon packed their belongings and moved to Estevan, Saskatchewan, a good-sized town southeast of Regina. They'd gone there the fall before to inquire about buying Estevan Air, which flew from an airstrip near the Canada-U.S. border.

By then Norman had his commercial pilot's licence and experience crop spraying. He'd built up a good clientele but needed facilities for his operation. He hoped it would grow into a full-time business for him. He was also in the process of obtaining his flight instructor's licence so he could teach would-be pilots to fly. He renamed the business Norm Air and spent most of his time in the skies.

The following year, Winnipeg Supply and Fuel moved its operations to Faulkner from Spearhill. David was sent ahead to begin blasting a quarry at the new site. Gradually, the Spearhill kilns and buildings were demolished and everything was rebuilt at Faulkner, a few miles southeast of Steep Rock.

When all the equipment had been moved, David resumed his position as crusher. Dennis also moved with the company and he and Robynne purchased a piece of nearby land and began building a house. Walter left his job as production foreman in the Union Carbide Winnipeg press room after purchasing a farm near Amaranth, Manitoba. Norman continued to fly between Estevan and Moosehorn as a number of his spraying customers were located on Manitoba's Hwy. 6.

◆ ◆ ◆ ◆ ◆

A crowd gathered one summer afternoon along the highway near Ashern's main street. Lorne Park had finished building his ultralight plane and was planning to take it for its first flight. Mel and Loren and a few other friends were among those curious to see the homemade plane in the sky. They gathered to watch as Lorne towed it onto the field. Mel cleared as many stones as he could from the proposed runway while Lorne checked the plane over to make sure it was ready to go.

"Where did all these people come from?" Lorne muttered under his breath as he climbed into the plane. He felt a bit self-conscious making his first flight in front of so many spectators.

"Ah, don't worry about them," Mel laughed. "Just fly right over 'em."

As they talked, they heard a plane in the distance. While Lorne reviewed a mental checklist, the whine of the plane's engine grew louder. Everyone looked up and saw Norman flying overhead. Recognizing his plane, they all waved and shouted. He then disappeared behind a row of trees.

The crowd watched excitedly as Lorne started the ultralight and began accelerating down the makeshift runway. He steadily gathered momentum but just as the plane reached take-off speed, one wheel hit a large rock. The impact crushed the nose into the ground and flipped up the back end of the plane, catapulting Lorne out of his seat through the air. He landed on the ground and opened his eyes after the initial shock wore off. His first thoughts were of how he looked to all the people watching him. They were now running across the field toward him. Lorne didn't move until he regained his bearings. He wasn't in a lot of pain and was glad that he hadn't broken any bones. As he stared at the sky, he heard the roar of Norman's plane once again. Rolling over on one side, he got up just as Mel and the others reached him.

"Are you all right?" Mel laughed, relieved that his friend was conscious.

"I don't care about me," Lorne said, brushing himself off. "How's the plane?"

"Ah, you smashed her pretty good," Mel said, his voice muffled by the sound of Norman's approach. This time as he flew by, Norman swooped down low over the crowd. When he saw that Lorne was looking, he tipped his wings in greeting.

"Nice try" he was saying as he circled once more. Turning in the direction of the crowd, he prepared to land. It took a few moments for the spectators to realize they were standing where Norman planned to touch down. Everyone scattered as the plane roared in and the wheels made contact with the bumpy ground. After landing, Norman turned the plane and taxied back to where the group was standing.

"I'll be back in a little while," Lorne said as he began walking across the field. People gathered around Norman who climbed out of his plane to survey the damage to Lorne's ultralight.

Lorne returned a short time later, after collecting himself.

"How does she look?" he called out as he approached. Norman was crouched examining the plane's engine.

"Nothing that can't be fixed," he smiled as he stood up and wiped his greasy hands on his pants.

Lorne reached into his pocket and pulled out a wad of cash.

"Here," he said, handing it to Norman. "I want you to teach me to fly."

Norman threw back his head and let out a belly laugh. Reaching out he took the money and put it in his pocket.

"How much did you give me?" he asked, chewing the end of his smoke.

"$1,600," Lorne replied.

"Sounds good. When do you want to get started?"

"Right now."

"You sound like my kinda student," Norman smiled and waved towards his plane. "Let's go."

The pair climbed into the plane and took off. Once they reached a healthy height the lesson began.

"So how much do you know about flying?" Norman asked.

"A little bit," Lorne said, surveying the controls. "I've been interested for a while, so I've read a lot."

"Good," Norman said, smiling. "Reading is good, but you'll really learn by flying."

The twice-weekly lessons continued for a few months while Norman signed up other students and traveled between Manitoba and Saskatchewan. As Lorne's piloting skills developed, so did a strong friendship between teacher and student. Norman liked Lorne's quick wit and the two shared a similar sense of humour.

One afternoon they were flying with Lorne at the controls.

"How do we flip this thing?" he asked. "I know that there is only one way to turn it so the engine doesn't stall, but is it against the spin of the prop or with it?"

Norman chuckled. "What do you think?"

Lorne was a quick-study—one of the most adept students he'd ever trained.

Lorne thought for a moment. "Which way is the prop going?"

"I don't know," Norman joked. "From here I can't tell, I'd have to get out in front to start it."

Lorne thought about it for a moment.

"What the hell, just try it," Norman coaxed. "If you go the wrong way, it won't kill us."

Lorne shrugged and turning sharply to his right, flipped the plane. The ashtray emptied in their faces and then the motor quit. Lorne had to think quickly about what he'd been taught. Pointing the nose of the plane down, he turned the other way, keeping in mind that everything is backwards when the aircraft is upside down. The plane turned upright, the motor gave a puff and then a bang, before starting again.

Norman brushed ashes from his face and chest, then grinned at Lorne.

"Well, I guess that was the wrong way," he chuckled.

◆ ◆ ◆ ◆ ◆

By spring of 1976, Norman's Estevan employees included both his brother Raymond and his friend and brother-in-law Loren who had since married Anita. Loren obtained his pilot's license and was working on earning his instructor's rating as well.

Raymond, who'd lived in B.C. with his mother for a short time, had become a fixture in Norman and Sharon's household and now that they owned their own business, he'd followed them to Estevan. Eighteen years old, he also enjoyed flying and was a full-time employee—quite satisfied to help Norman with whatever needed doing around the airstrip.

Life was going well for David and Bonnie. In her spare time Bonnie liked to curl and play baseball. She enjoyed spending time in Steep Rock with family and friends. David had never participated in sports and filled his spare time by working on vehicles, hauling wood and learning how to do all his own carpentry. They had planted a garden with help from Bonnie's dad who enjoyed weeding and harvesting. Bonnie did some freezing and canning.

People often commented about the size of the small family's grocery bill—David had an inordinate fear of running out of food and started insisting on full cupboards all the time. Because he couldn't stand to be cold in the winter, he had amassed a huge wood pile and even thought about putting in another stove.

David always owned two vehicles—an old clunker he drove to work and a beautiful car that he kept spotless for times he and Bonnie went out.

And while Bonnie was an excellent housekeeper, David began putting pressure on her to keep the house immaculate. He feared that visitors would see dirt on the floor and place him in the same category as his stepfather. David began showering at least once, sometimes twice—occasionally three—times a day.

He also believed that because he worked hard that his children should have whatever they needed and wanted. While many other area families shopped at secondhand stores, David refused to allow his children to be dressed in hand-me-downs. And because Christmas was something he'd never celebrated as a child, it became a huge event with plenty of food and gifts for everyone, even though they couldn't really afford it.

In the back of David's mind, he wondered if he was a good father. He'd had no example to follow and wasn't sure how to raise his sons to be hardworking, responsible adults. He put most of the childrearing responsibilities on Bonnie's shoulders.

Then one evening, the phone rang. Bonnie answered.

"Could I speak to David?" the voice on the other end asked.

Bonnie covered the receiver and whispered, "It's your mother."

David cringed. A call from Caroline usually meant something was wrong.

"Hello, hello," he said cheerfully. He'd learned that saying the word twice seemed to fix his stutter.

"David," she said, her voice breaking. "I've got some bad news. I got a call today from the hospital in Selkirk. They said Domko has suffered a stroke."

"A s-sst-troke?" he queried.

"Yes. They're not sure how paralyzed he's going to be or if he'll even make it."

David didn't know what more to say. He'd matured enough to know that "hooray" wasn't the appropriate response at a time like this. He didn't want to hurt or anger his mother, but at the same time he wasn't sure what she expected him to do.

"I think I'd better come see him," Caroline said, pausing while he heard her blow her nose on a tissue. "And I want to bring the kids . . . in case he dies. They'll get to see him one last time."

"So when do you want to come?" he asked.

"Just as soon as I can," she said. "I have enough train fare for us to come, but not enough to get back. Will you help?"

"S-sure, Ma," he said. "H-how much do you n-nneed?"

David had just enough money to pay his own bills, but didn't want to tell his mother that. He knew how people gossiped and didn't want anyone saying that he couldn't earn enough money to comfortably support his family.

Caroline and the children arrived a few days later. David and Dennis picked her and the children up from the train station. They drove to Selkirk to visit Domko. Caroline went ahead and when it was all right for the family to go inside, the twins herded the children into their father's room. David and Dennis lingered outside the door.

"Should we go in?" David asked his brother.

Dennis shrugged.

Curious, David poked his head inside the door. His mother looked at him, and the softness in her eyes coaxed him into the room. Quietly, David made his way toward the bed.

Domko was sitting propped up in bed with pillows. He was wearing blue and white striped pyjamas. A sheet and blanket were pulled up to his chest, folded neatly and tucked between the two mattresses. His face was clean-shaven and his skin looked freshly washed. His hair was combed neatly and for a moment David didn't recognize him. Domko turned to stare at him and David noticed that the man's eyes still flashed in the same unnerving way they always had. The difference now was that the malevolence David saw stemmed from fear instead of hatred.

David said hello but Domko turned away. Now confined to a bed, he was paralyzed on his right side. He tried to speak, but words came out in a jumble. It was impossible for anyone to understand what he was saying, even Caroline. She strained patiently to listen, but couldn't make out the strange string of words.

The visit didn't last long as it was obvious the commotion was too much for Domko. He showed no reaction as Caroline gathered up the children and left.

The family filed down the hallway and out the front door of the hospital. David was relieved to step out of the stale, restrictive atmosphere into the fresh afternoon air. He felt free and somewhat satisfied that the stroke had taken away Domko's ability to yell and lash out. Domko was now in a "living hell," and the thought crossed David's mind that maybe he'd been there all along.

Word about Domko's condition spread through the family. Everyone, including Stephen, gathered at David and Bonnie's house the day after Caroline arrived. Norman and Sharon flew in for the weekend, landing in a field on the outskirts of town. Both Norman and his wife loved Caroline dearly and didn't want to miss seeing her.

The family shared stories, took a few pictures and ate a large meal. With the exception of the last few days, Caroline was living a happy, contented life in B.C. She seemed relaxed and looked better than she ever had and was pleased to see everyone together.

For the most part, they all got along well, though, as with most families, there was some tension over unresolved issues from earlier times. It was obvious that everyone was thinking about Domko and the profound affect he'd had on each of their lives. David and Dennis weren't getting along well and hadn't for years. Their constant arguing had reached the point where nobody took their bickering seriously any more. They still spent a great deal of spare time together, even though their religious differences caused constant tension.

The family seemed preoccupied and on edge as day wore into evening. Fortunately, Norman was there to entertain everyone with his stories. Listening to him was a welcome distraction. He talked about his business and latest exploits. Everyone knew that Norman didn't get caught up in family politics and wasn't interested in petty complaints. He only got involved when he had something to gain or lose. He didn't fight for the sake of it.

Walter felt the same way as Norman. He was busy trying to expand his farm and increase the size of his cattle herd. Pettiness was the furthest thing from his mind.

That night the men stayed up late socializing. After Raymond had a few drinks, he started making sarcastic comments to David. At first David thought his half-brother was joking. But as Raymond drank more, the comments turned nasty. It was obvious to David that his half-brother wasn't trying to be funny.

"My Dad was right," Raymond slurred. "You are useless. You didn't amount to nothin'."

David was both stunned and hurt by the remark. Since they'd grown up, he'd started to accept Raymond as his sibling and thought they were getting along well. He was surprised that Raymond would think hc wasn't successful.

He kept his thoughts to himself until Raymond left.

"Well, what does he expect I'd be doin' right now?" David asked his brothers.

Walter laughed it off. "Ah, don't worry about him, he had too much to drink."

But David was angry anyway.

"Well, he must r-really hate me, whether he's drunk or not. He's a Domko, that's for s-sure. Can't s-stand to see a Pischke doin' good, that's all."

"He doesn't have a problem with me," Norman piped up.

"Yeah, well I hope n-not," David said. "You're signin' his paycheque."

"Yeah," Norman laughed. "If he talked to me like that, I'd kick his ass."

Everyone laughed.

"Well he sure don't like me," David brooded. "What did I ever do to him?"

"You teased the shit out of him," someone said.

"Did not!" David said.

"Did so! And you teased Markie too," he added.

"When?" David asked.

"When you used to catch him in the blanket," one of his brother's argued. "Remember, you'd wrap him up tight and he'd turn all hot?"

David laughed. "We was just playin'!"

"Yeah, well, that kind of playing isn't funny if it goes on for too long."

"Well, we was just playin' with him an' if he didn't like it, how come he'd bait us into doin' it by whipping his blanket at us an' runnin' by?" David countered. "If he didn't like it, he shoulda just stayed away."

"He was a kid, that's why," the brother argued.

"We was kids too," David said. "Nobody ever played with us. All we ever got was the hell knocked outta us. We never did that to him, that's for sure."

The brothers sat quiet for a moment.

"Raymond was just getting you back for all the times you teased him," Norman said.

"Well, a bit of teasin' ain't n-nothin' like callin' somebody useless," David added defiantly. "Raymond's not a kid no more."

"He was just kiddin'" Walter said.

David raised his glass and laughed. "Didn't sound like it to me."

The following afternoon there was a sharp knock on David's door. He opened it to find his mother standing there crying.

"Ma, what's wrong," he said stepping back to let her in.

Caroline wiped her eyes and then walked passed him to the kitchen where she sat at the table.

"What's the matter?" he asked again.

"It's the kids," she said.

"What kids?"

"Your sister and brother."

"What about them?"

"They're blaming me for everything."

David pulled out a chair and sat at the table.

"What do you mean?"

"You know," she sniffed, "for everything that happened at the farm."

Still feeling the sting from Raymond's comments the night before, David stiffened.

It didn't surprise him that his siblings might confront their mother. The thought had crossed his mind too, but he'd decided it would be best to just let it go. Whenever the past was raised, Caroline always started to cry. It was almost as if she was still trying to come to terms with it all herself.

What David wanted to say was this: *Mom, we don't understand. How come you couldn't protect us from him? Why didn't you talk about Dad—to keep his memory alive for us. Why weren't you stronger? How come in the end you appeared to side with Domko?*

Why do you still visit him and treat him with respect when he treated us all so badly?

But he couldn't say any of this.

And he wasn't angry with his siblings who were searching for the same answers.

He couldn't understand why his mother would never discuss her life or the reasons for her past behaviour. She didn't realize how badly her grown children needed to hear, firsthand, the realities of the situation she'd faced as an adult.

"You can stay here," David said to Caroline, pushing his own annoyances aside.

He understood what was happening in the family, but was powerless to explain it to her. Over the year, he'd noticed that as long as Domko wasn't being discussed, family members seemed able to cope with the past. But with Caroline back visiting, it was making the children question again whether they deserved the childhood they'd endured. It seemed like they all were seeking both answers and someone to blame.

David couldn't verbalize this, though, so he just smiled at his mother and made small talk about other, less important, matters.

◆ ◆ ◆ ◆ ◆

"Let's move," Bonnie said one evening as she joined David in the back yard. "I'm tired of living around here."

She'd recently been the target of family pettiness and felt drained.

They sat for a few moments on the stoop. "We can't," David said. "Where would I work?"

"I don't know," she said. "You'd find a job."

"But I got a good job here," he said.

"You can get on somewhere else," she coaxed. "You're such a good worker."

"Nowhere that pays this good," he argued. "Nobody else will hire me for what I get paid here."

David was right. Times were changing and employers were now looking for staff with a good education. David noticed that more young people were obtaining their high school diplomas. He couldn't remember for sure, but thought the last level he'd passed was only grade five.

"Wouldn't it be nice to leave here and get a fresh start," she said softly, "like Norman and Sharon?"

While the thought of abandoning his past and moving away from both their families appealed to David, he hesitated about giving up the best job he'd ever had. It seemed that his employers appreciated and respected him. This was one of the few places where he'd felt instantly comfortable and competent.

"No, we can't move," he said. "We'll just have to ignore everything that's going on."

Bonnie sat quietly for a few minutes, then got up and went into the house.

In the spring of 1977, Loren Dewar and another pilot were flying near Redvers, Saskatchewan. Loren was showing the other employee how to check an oil line that Norm Air had the contract to patrol. The plane crashed and Loren was killed in the accident. The other pilot escaped with serious, but non-life-threatening injuries.

The accident devastated Norman. He felt like a part of the business died when his close friend perished. But true to Norman's unshakable spirit, he rallied everyone in the family after a few weeks of mourning.

"Life has to go on," he said in a matter-of-fact tone. "We have to keep going and do things as we always have. Loren would want it that way."

This became Norman's mantra. The rest of his employees, members of the community, his wife and sister-in-law all leaned on him and relied on his unwavering strength.

❖

Chapter 18

"SO DAVID," MCMILLAN SAID, shifting his weight in his chair, "what would you say is your ambition in life?"

"My ambition?" David repeated.

"Yes—what do you want to do with the rest of your life?"

"Well, first off, I w-wanna pass this lousy test."

McMillan smiled. "Then what?"

"Hmm," David thought. "Well, I'd kinda like to help people, you know k-kids. Kids who are in the same boat as us guys."

"How are you planning to do that?"

"Well, I can't do nothin' if I end up in jail," he chided. He could sense the comment didn't amuse the officer. "Okay, well, I dunno. Maybe I'll go on a w-walk or s-something."

McMillan looked puzzled.

"You know, to raise money," David said in clarification, "so that kids can have opportunities that I never got."

The officer nodded.

The whirr of a lawn mower awoke David early the next morning. He recognized immediately that it came from his neighbour's yard. Herb rose early each day to start doing outside chores. It wasn't a problem on weekdays as everyone in the neighbourhood was up and getting ready to go to work. But on weekends, it was annoying. David liked to sleep in—at least past 7 a.m.—especially after a night of socializing.

"Herbie's at it again," he said to Bonnie as he slid out of bed.

"Someone should go over there and hide his lawn mower."

The following weekend, David and Bonnie hosted a barbeque in their backyard.

"Norman is the best pilot there ever was," David stated that evening as they sat in the dark by lantern light. He'd been drinking whiskey and was feeling in a story-telling mood.

Norman was gaining renown for his ability as a bush pilot and David was proud of him. He bragged that his brother had as much moxy as any bush pilot around. Norman flew supplies into northern bush camps and the men considered him a godsend.

"Did you guys hear w-what he did?" David asked, not waiting for a reply. "Somebody at Estevan dared him to land on top of his hangar."

"On top?" a friend asked.

"Yes!" David answered, "Oh yes, *on top.*"

"What's a hangar?" another fellow asked.

"The hangar is the building where Norman s-stores his planes," David explained. "It's like a big g-garage—oh, about 100 feet long."

"And he landed on top of it?" the man asked.

"Yessss," David said. "S-somebody dared him, saying, 'you know Norman, I bet you can't land your airplane on top of that hangar.' And so Norman says, 'I bet you I can.' And the other guys standin' around, they all laugh of course. So Norman says, 'I'll land the plane on the hangar, but you guys have to promise me that when I do, you'll climb up and hold it down for me so I can take off again.'

"Of course, nobody thinks he can land on top, so they agree, thinkin' he's just gonna fly right off the end an' shmash the plane."

Everyone laughed. These were the stories that they'd waited all evening to hear.

"An' you know Norman," David continued, "he's one helluva pilot, let me tell you. He goes an' gets into the plane, takes off, circles around an' as he starts to slow down, pretty soon he chokes out and boom! He lands on the top of the hangar!"

By now, David is standing up, acting out the story.

"Of course that's not the scarrry part," he emphasized. "Now these guys have to climb on top of the hangar an' hold the plane down while Norman takes off."

"Why did they have to do that?" someone interrupted.

"Be-cause," David explained, "in order for him to get up enough speed to take off again, he's gotta rev the engine as if he's going down a runway."

Everyone nodded.

"So, they climb up there, an' of course Norman's laughing. They have to do this because he won the bet," David chuckled. "But then he turns serious, cause he doesn't want to fly off the end of the hangar and just shmash on the ground.

"So he gets in and starts revving the engine, an' he yells out, 'Don't let her go until I say so.' Naturally all these guys are scared . . . an' I mean they shoulda known better than to bet Norman! They're holdin' the plane down an' then all of a sudden he yells, 'okay!' an' the guys let go, and there she goes, Norman takes off."

Everyone roared as David sat down. More than half the humour in the story was watching David tell it.

"Yep, that Norman," his brother said shaking his head. "They shoulda known better than to make a bet with him."

The socializing continued until 1 a.m.

"We gotta go home now, Dave," one friend said, as the last of the visitors got up to leave. "We've got to get up early."

David chuckled. "I'll be up early too, but not because I want to. Old Herbie will be out there first thing mowin' his lawn."

The men nodded. They'd heard David tell good-natured stories about Herb cutting his grass early on Sundays, and how David had hinted many times to his neighbour to wait until afternoon. Herb was so anxious to do some work, he just couldn't wait that long.

David sat for a moment and then a bright, mischievous look came over his face.

"I got an idea," he said, jumping up. He started walking towards Herb's house.

"Where are you going?" someone called after him.

"Shhhh!" he giggled, raising his finger to his lips. "Come with me."

The friends followed as David slipped quietly across the lawn. He opened Herb's garage door and went inside. He emerged a couple of minutes later, pushing the lawn mower. He guided it over the gravel road and onto the grass.

"What are you doing?" a friend whispered.

"I'm gonna take the blade off," David chortled. "Go get me a wrench."

The friend laughed and disappeared into David's shed. He emerged carrying a small tool box.

David flipped the lawn mower over and loosened the bolt that held the blade in place. He put the bolt in his pocket, then slipped off the blade. He stood up, chuckling while he hid it in the shed.

"That should do 'er," he whispered as he pushed the lawn mower back into Herb's garage.

"I'm gonna sleep good in the morning," he giggled.

The next morning, David awoke to the sound of Herb's lawn mower.

Opening one eye, he lifted his head slightly and glanced at the clock beside the bed.

"What the hell . . ." he muttered. He remembered that he'd disabled the lawn mower the night before. He staggered out of bed and went to the window, craning his neck to see into Herb's yard.

Soon Herb came into sight, pushing the lawn mower across the grass, oblivious that the machine had no blade. The man cut his grass so often it hardly had time to grow enough for him to notice it wasn't being cut!

David burst into laughter. He got dressed then went into the kitchen for breakfast. As he made himself something to eat, his conscience started to get the better of him. By noon, he was quite ashamed of himself for playing the trick on his friend. When the older couple went out that afternoon, David snuck back into the garage and replaced the blade. He decided not to tell his neighbour about the prank.

One morning the following spring, David and Bonnie went to Steep Rock for a visit. David sat and watched his wife as she helped her mother make lunch. His heart swelled with emotion as he stared at her. They'd been arguing more than usual lately, and she'd withdrawn from him. David wasn't sure why. All he knew was that she was wonderful.

Bonnie's the type of woman that when I go to work in the morning, I look forward to comin' home to at night, he thought. The problem was, he was never able to put his thoughts into words. His daydreaming was suddenly interrupted by the roar of an engine coming from the neighbour's yard.

"What's that?" he asked his mother-in-law as he got up from the table. Glancing out the window, he could see thick smoke coming from Mike Kalanza's yard.

"Oh that's Mike again," she said. "I wish he'd get that equipment out of town."

David pulled on his shoes and stepped outside. He'd noticed a huge machine in Mike's yard when they drove in and now he'd get the chance to find out what it was. The noise was deafening. David went into the yard and saw the older man standing beside the largest Caterpillar bulldozer David had ever seen. It was a C12—two diesel engines mounted side by side with a cab in the middle. Mike stood with his back to David, dwarfed by the big machine.

"Hey Mike," David called out, but the man didn't hear him over the noise of the engines.

David walked up behind Mike and tapped him on the shoulder. The older man turned around, visibly startled.

"Oh, it's you David," he said, relieved. "Came over to see my new Cat, did ya?"

David nodded. "We can h-hear it all the way in the h-house," he yelled.

"Yeah, by golly," Mike smiled, "she's powerful all right."

"What are you doin'?" David said as he covered one ear with his hand and leaned closer to Mike.

"Just checkin' it out," Mike said. "They've been vandalizing my place you know. Somebody put water in the gas tank of my combine. And someone took the transmission out of my other Cat—the D7. I just wanted to make sure they didn't do nothing to this one."

"Someone took out the tr-ransmission?" David asked.

"Yeah, when I was away at my niece's wedding," Mike said. "So, what do you think of her?"

"Your niece?" David asked.

"No!" Mike laughed, pointing to the Cat. "This here machine."

David smiled. "She looks good."

"Yeah, I'm gonna make lots of money with her, lots of money," Mike said. "I'm gonna make a big drain from Lake Manitoba to Lake Winnipeg and when it's all drained out, I'm gonna sell the land."

David stood for a moment unsure what to say. He turned his good ear towards Mike.

"W-what's that again?" he asked.

"I said, I'm gonna do some drainage work," Mike replied. "You wanna drive the Cat for me?"

David shook his head no.

"Why not?" Mike asked.

"I'm w-working," David replied.

"Where are you working now?" Mike asked. "I saw you driving south."

"I'm still w-working at the plant, but right now me an' Dennis are building up the banks around the S-spearhill quarry," David said. "The company wants to close off the roads in there since they're not using the quarry anymore. So they got me an' Dennis down there closing it all up so guys don't go in there."

Mike nodded. Turning back to the bulldozer, he said, "So, what do you think? Think I can do it?"

David shrugged. That wasn't a good enough answer for Mike who stood there staring intently at him.

"Yeah, I guess so," he answered.

Mike nodded as he turned and motioned for David to follow. He climbed up on the machine to shut it off. As he hoisted himself up, David noticed something protruding from the bottom of one leg of his pants. It looked like a stick of some kind. Mike saw him staring at it.

"That's to keep my heel from hurting," he said, pulling up his pant leg to reveal a stick taped securely to his leg with black electrical tape. "I can hardly stand on it anymore, so I taped this here broken hockey stick to my leg."

The stick stuck an inch into Mike's shoe and absorbed the impact of his stride, taking pressure off his heel.

David laughed at the ingenuity. "That's g-gonna hurt like hell when you pull it off," he said, pointing to the tape.

Mike shrugged. "Not as much as my heel."

David laughed and shook his head at the man's logic.

The two worked outside for a little while longer then David waved good-bye and went in for lunch. After the meal, a handful of people came over to visit. David began telling a story but half way through one of the visitors started making fun of his stutter. It took the humour out of the story and embarrassed David—especially when Bonnie and her family members laughed. David refused to say anything else for the rest of the afternoon.

When it came time to leave, he went outside to wait in the car for Bonnie. He could hear Mike still banging around in his yard.

The young couple got into an argument on the way home and weren't speaking to one another by the time they opened the house door. The phone was ringing. Bonnie answered then quickly handed it to David.

It was Caroline. She'd come home for a week-long visit and was staying at Rose and Al's house.

"David, I need you to take me to the hospital," she gasped. "Raymond's been in an accident."

"W-what h-happened?" he asked.

"I don't know for sure, he rolled his truck," she cried. "Hurry, David."

He hung up the phone and bolted out the door. Raymond had also been visiting friends in the area. Within a minute David was at Rose's house. Caroline was waiting for him on the street.

"W-what h-happened?" he asked again as she climbed into the car.

"I'm not sure, we just got the call from Al," she sobbed. "He told me that Raymond was brought into the emergency room—he was in an accident and it doesn't look good."

David turned south on the highway towards Ashern. It was dusk. He wondered out loud where the accident had taken place. Then, as the car mounted the small hill separating the two towns, David saw flashing lights ahead. A tow truck was backing into an approach. A few other vehicles had stopped and onlookers were at the side of the road looking at Raymond's truck lying on its roof in the ditch 100 feet from the highway.

David's heart ached for his mother who stared out the window in shock. Once he was past the truck, he sped up again until he rounded the last curve on the highway and pulled into the emergency entrance parking lot. The ambulance was parked by the door with its lights flashing. They hurried inside.

The nurses recognized who they were and gave David and Caroline a sympathetic look. Dr. Steenson stepped out of an examination room. David's stomach lurched at the sight of fresh blood stains on the doctor's overcoat. He averted his eyes until the man was close enough that he could look directly at his face.

"Caroline . . . David," Steenson said, "we're stabilizing Raymond in preparation for the trip to Winnipeg. David, will you be able to take your mother into the city?"

"S-sure," he said.

"Caroline, could I speak with you alone for a moment please?"

Caroline nodded and followed the doctor into the empty waiting room. David stood awkwardly by the nurses' desk. He noticed that the emergency room was busy that night. Two other families stood nearby and he could hear teenage voices coming from another examination room.

Caroline and the doctor returned five minutes later.

"All right, David, you take care of your mother, you know what I mean," Steenson said softly. "I'll finish stitching Raymond now."

"Can I see him?" Caroline asked.

"No, not yet," the doctor said. "He is sedated and won't recognize you. It's best you wait."

Silently they turned and stepped back outside. The ambulance driver was leaning against the back of the ambulance waiting. He nodded at them.

"I'll need to get a few things from home," Caroline rambled. "And what about the kids? Who will take care of them?"

"Don't worry, Ma," David whispered. "we'll take care of everything."

Caroline nodded. "You don't mind taking me in?"

"Course not," he said as they climbed into his car. It was a few moments before they spoke again.

"So what did S-steenson say about R-raymond?" David asked.

Caroline sat quietly for a moment.

"He said that he's got some cuts, a few bad ones, but he's . . . okay," she paused. Reaching a shaky hand into her purse, she pulled out a tissue. ". . . but he broke his neck."

"Oh," David said.

"Yeah," she murmured. "He said that Raymond will never walk again."

"Oh my God," David whispered. "You're k-kidding?"

"No," she cried. "That's what he said.

"Oh no," he whispered.

"Maybe Steenson's wrong," she said hopefully. "He's just a country doctor, maybe when Raymond gets to the city they'll know better."

David agreed.

Both sat quietly as they again approached the accident scene, this time from the south end. There was broken glass at the intersection and skid marks that David hadn't noticed before. By this time, the tow truck had hauled away Raymond's pickup.

"It's okay, Ma," David said, "he's gonna be okay."

Caroline quickly packed her things while David fueled the car. Within 20 minutes, they were on their way south again. By now it was dark. As David drove through Ashern, he could see the hospital from the highway—and slowed. When he saw that the ambulance was gone, he rushed his mother to the city.

They arrived at the Winnipeg Health Sciences Centre just after midnight. They had to wait in the emergency room lobby for hours before the doctor came out. He spoke to them just before sunrise. He said Raymond had been operated on and was in the intensive care unit. In order to stabilize the young man's head, burr holes were drilled in his skull and a metal halo had been attached to his forehead. He'd be in traction for a while—at least until the bones healed.

This was all so foreign to Caroline and David that all they could do was listen and nod. The doctor explained that Dr. Steenson had been right. Raymond was likely going to be a quadriplegic and would need an operation later that day—a colostomy and a catheter had to be inserted to help drain his bladder. They were overwhelmed by all the information.

Caroline was allowed into the intensive care unit for a short visit.

David waited in the hallway. Heavily sedated, Raymond didn't recognize her. Since there would be a wait for the second operation, they decided to drive back to Moosehorn. Caroline would ride back later that day with someone else.

During the next few days, David was able to piece together what had happened. Raymond was going to meet his girlfriend at the beach when the accident occurred. He'd been driving too fast on the highway—racing with another car. By the time he realized that the car ahead, containing his girlfriend and her friends, was braking to turn, it was too late. He skidded, clipped the back end of the car and rolled the truck end over end. It came to rest in the ditch on its roof. Fortunately, the passenger in Raymond's truck and the girls in the car escaped serious injury.

Norman and Sharon flew in to Winnipeg and Caroline returned to the city where she stayed for a week. When it was time for her to return to 100 Mile House, David drove his mother to the train station. He went back later to visit Raymond. He walked into the hospital room not sure what to expect. Raymond, wearing a hospital gown, was lying suspended in bed. His skin was pale and his limbs lifeless.

But what shocked David the most was the apparatus that circled his head holding it completely still.

Raymond mumbled a quiet "hello" as David stood beside the bed.

"Hi guy," David said, not sure how he sounded. "How are ya doin'?"

Raymond stared but said nothing. Then he started to cry.

David felt helpless watching the tears stream down Raymond's face as he lay suspended above the bed. David pulled a few tissues from a nearby box and gently wiped away his brother's tears.

"I'm gonna be like this for the rest of my life," Raymond whispered. "I'm only 20. How am I gonna live like this?"

David didn't know what to say, so he just stood there listening.

"I sure made a mess of my life this time," Raymond lamented.

David tried to console him but the words sounded empty. When he left the hospital, he felt that he hadn't been much help at all.

During the drive home, he said a silent thank you to God or whomever was watching over him the day he'd fractured his neck as a youngster.

That could have been me, he thought.

Raymond stayed on a ward at the Health Sciences Centre for the rest of the year. The halo was eventually removed and he was able to sit in a wheelchair. The family visited him regularly—especially Rose who'd always gotten along well with her younger brother. Raymond regained a small amount of movement in his arms during the next few months but had limited feeling in his upper body. He had no sensation whatsoever in his legs.

Chapter 19

"DO YOU NEED A BREAK?" the officer asked.

David shook his head no—he was fine.

"Well let's keep going then," McMillan said, scrutinizing the sheet of paper on his desk. He scanned the page as if looking for an appropriate question.

David fidgeted while he waited.

"So what's been the worst day of your life?" McMillan asked, looking up.

David was surprised by the question.

"The w-worst day?" he asked. "C-can I say my entire ch-ildhood?"

McMillan chuckled. "No, just one event that sticks in your mind."

"Jeez," David said, raising his hands to his face and covering his eyes, "There's been so many. How am I gonna pick?"

"There must be one thing worse than the others," McMillan said. "Something that changed your life."

"Yeah," David said quietly, letting his hands drop to his lap. "It was back in the late 70s."

"What happened?"

"It would hafta be the day Norman died," he said.

David first heard that Norman's plane was missing the morning of May 6, 1979.

Norman had been hired May 5 to fly a private charter from Estevan to Boise, Idaho. When Norman didn't call home that night Sharon began to worry. He always let her know when he'd arrived safely.

Suspecting something was wrong, she began phoning around. By early the next morning she had determined that the plane had failed to reach its destination.

By that afternoon, David and Dennis had already consulted with Walter. They had decided to join the search and rescue team assembling in Bozeman, Montana. They were told to wait a day or so because it was still storming in the mountains where it was suspected the plane went down.

Two days later, David, Dennis, Walter and Hugo Russell were on their way to Estevan in David's car. They had been briefed before they left.

Apparently, Norman had started out the morning of May 5 in his Cessna 172 Skyhawk with three passengers—Don Johnson, his 17-year-old daughter Donna Johnson, and 25-year-old Brent Dyer. Brent was married to Don's eldest daughter Cindy. The passengers were planning to go to Boise on an overnight trip. This was also an opportunity for Brent, one of Norman's flight students, to log flying hours. They'd made a stop to refuel at Livingston, Montana, and were scheduled to arrive at their destination, Boise, before 8 p.m.

"Does Norman have an ELT?" David asked his brothers as they started driving to Estevan along the same highway they'd traveled in Norman's car to B.C. David giggled at the memory as they passed Marquette but then his eyes filled with tears.

"He put ELTs in all his planes," Walter said quietly. "But the government changed the regulations and he had to take them out because the lithium batteries sometimes explode. I know he's still got the ELTs, but I don't know if he changed batteries and put them back in or not."

"What does ELT stand for anyway?"

"Emergency location transmitter," Walter said. "It sends out a signal that alerts rescuers when planes go down."

The brothers sat in silence as they turned onto the Trans-Canada Highway.

They arrived in Estevan late in the day. They stayed in Norman and Sharon's trailer overnight, then rose early the next morning and made the final leg of the trip to Bozeman. Steven was there talking with search organizers when they arrived. He waved, then made his way over to his brothers.

"S-sso what do you think?" David asked.

Steven shrugged.

"No ELT," he said. "I really don't know."

The brothers stood somberly in a room at the Bozeman Airport watching search organizers scan maps in an effort to determine Norman's flight path. Norman had discussed his proposed route with a man at the flight service office in Livingston. When he left, airport personnel thought he was going to fly from Livingston to Bozeman and then to Whitehall—a sickle-shaped route following a canyon to Dillon, before turning south to Idaho Falls. From there, he would continue to Boise. By following that route, he would avoid the storm that was brewing.

The airport staff had noticed him sitting for a few minutes at the end of the runway and wondered if he'd decided at the last minute to take a different route—perhaps to do some sightseeing over Yellowstone National Park.

Walter joined the organizers and inspected the map.

"If he sat at the end of the runway like you guys said, then he went directly over the mountains to Dillon," Walter told the searchers. "He was probably studying the maps so that he'd know exactly where to go."

Walter was not only the missing pilot's older brother, he also had some flight training. If anyone could predict where Norman might go, he was the one. He shared his feelings with the organizers who appeared to listen but nevertheless sent the group of assembled volunteers to search the area around Yellowstone National Park.

Walter shook his head. "I don't think this is right. Maybe Norman went this way, but I don't think so. Norman wouldn't have wanted to add extra hours to a trip. He would have flown the most direct route—over the mountains."

The brothers all agreed. But they were forced to follow the instructions they had been given for the search. Walter and Stephen went up in separate planes to act as spotters while David and Dennis stayed behind to follow up leads in the ground search.

"Mostly what you have to look for is a place where the tops of the trees look to be sheared off," the search pilot explained.

Walter nodded as he stared out into the vast park. Whenever they saw something unusual, he'd signal and the pilot would circle around for another look.

David and Dennis drove into Yellowstone National Park and investigated a number of sightings which led nowhere.

The four brothers assisted for nearly a week, but after days of searching the park area, both on land and by air, decided it was time to go home. They broke the news to a disappointed Hugo.

"Don't go yet," Hugo had insisted. "We have to keep looking."

"It doesn't look good," Walter said taking the older man aside.

"But we can't stop now," an exhausted Hugo begged. His eyes were rimmed with tears at the thought of losing the young man who had become like a son to him over the years.

"If he's alive, then he would have walked out by now," Walter explained.

"Maybe he is alive, but can't walk out because his leg is broken," Hugo said. "We can't just leave Norm out there to die."

Walter's gut wrenched at the thought.

"It's been over a week Hugo. You know Norman, if he was alive, he would have got out of there by now. Or signaled us, or something."

Weary from the long hours and stress of the past week, Hugo collapsed in a chair in the search headquarters office. He put his head in his hands and wept. He waved the brothers away and they quietly left the office.

Walter returned a few minutes later to find that Hugo had regained his composure. He agreed to leave Bozeman, but asked to be dropped off in Estevan so he could support Sharon and the boys.

On May 24, twenty days days after the plane disappeared, two of the three passengers, Brent Dyer and Donna Johnson, walked out of the mountains into a farmyard near Challis, Idaho. They told searchers where the plane could be found. The body of Don Johnson was removed from the wreckage May 25 and airlifted out of the mountains.

The search for Norman intensified. His body was discovered the next day, approximately a half mile from the crash site. He was sitting in the snow, leaning up against a rock. His body was airlifted out May 27.

The survivors confirmed that Walter's assessment of Norman's route had been correct. When they'd started out that fateful morning from Estevan, the weather had been favourable—Brent piloted the plane, landing first in Williston, North Dakota, where Norman bought a few maps and checked the weather forecast. Next, they'd stopped in Livingston, Montana where they went into the airport office. Norman reviewed the maps and spoke with a man at the flight service station. There were reports of dangerous weather ahead. Norman and the man worked out a route so that the plane could avoid the worst of the storm.

Norman had stopped at the end of the Livingston runway to further examine the maps and get a mental picture of what he was flying into.

He let Brent take off and fly for a while, until they hit a cold front and Norman took over the controls. Rain pelted the plane and turned to ice, covering the wings and body and reducing the plane's ability to maintain altitude. To thaw out the aircraft, he was forced to fly lower where the air was warmer. He navigated through several canyons, but then ran into trouble near the top of the next canyon. To keep the plane in the air, he'd been flying at full throttle. Because of this, the ice-laden plane, which could normally climb to 14,000 feet and above at 770 feet a minute, was unable to reach the altitude necessary to clear the canyon top.

Knowing he was going to crash, Norman reduced his speed and chose a landing spot between the trees. To lessen the impact he reduced the speed of the plane and deliberately ran the wings into the tree tops while keeping the nose as high as he could. The plane did a belly flop on the mountainside and came to rest in the snow.

Bleeding from the head, Norman had suffered a severe brain injury which surprisingly did not impair his ability to comprehend, although his speech had become garbled. All four aboard survived the crash, but Don Johnson was seriously injured. That night he had heroically covered his daughter with his coat. By the next morning he was dead.

That morning Norman was able to gather wood for his injured passengers, build a fire and even help them move around inside the plane. Physically, he appeared strong. When he was confident that they were comfortable, he disappeared down the mountainside.

Walter was right. Norman had attempted to walk out of the mountains for help. He survived for more than 24 hours after the crash, before dying from his injuries.

The gathering before Norman's funeral was somber with only close family members present. Jalmar Erickson drove to Estevan to officiate at the burial. David felt instantly relieved when he saw the heavy-set man get out of his big car and stride confidently toward the family.

"How are you all doing?" he smiled in a peaceful way. Taking David's hand firmly in his own, he said "And how are you, Mr. Pischke?"

This felt so familiar it brought tears to David's eyes.

"F-ff-fine," he stammered.

"That's good," Jalmar said warmly, shaking hands as he moved through the crowd. "So we have Norman's family all together. Beautiful people, all of you. Thanks so much for inviting me. I think we should say a prayer."

Jalmar's service offered some comfort to the family. Sharon's sister Anita, barely over the grief of losing her husband less than two years before, summoned the courage to deliver the eulogy.

Because Norman had been missing for nearly three weeks, most of the family had recovered from the initial shock and had done most of their grieving over losing him. Sharon had struggled—performing her day-to-day tasks and caring for their boys, now 13 and nine—in a state of shock. She showed little emotion during the ceremony as she fought to hide her wounded spirit.

Sharon had experienced an odd sensation, a premonition of sorts, when Norman had taken off that fateful day. It was an eerie feeling that she'd never see her husband alive again. It was something that she'd pushed aside. But now she had to cope with the reality of life without Norman. In spite of rumoured marriage difficulties, the couple had shared a special bond understood by everyone who knew them well.

Norman had been an excellent father. He spent a lot of time with his sons and when he wasn't working, could be found hunting, fishing or horsing around with the boys. The children had loved him dearly and tried to put on a brave face, especially 13-year-old Lee, who was mature beyond his years. History was repeating itself as another generation of Pischke boys were now destined to grow up without their natural father.

This was a sad time for everyone involved. The outpouring of support from the community of Estevan helped ease some of the pain they were feeling.

Caroline took Norman's death hard. Her third-born son had always been a pillar of strength to her, both physically and emotionally. She was barely recovered from the difficulties and stresses associated with Domko's stroke and Raymond's accident and now the loss of a son took a heavy toll.

She sat with David following the funeral and recalled how Norman had phoned her before taking off for Boise. He'd chatted casually as he always did, then said he'd see her soon. Caroline cried while she told David that she'd always worried that Norman would someday be killed in a plane crash. She'd scolded him each time she heard about a 'close call.' He'd laughed it off and assured her that he'd be fine. And until now, he always had been.

Got to find Norman, David's mind raced, as he trudged through the thick bush near the fields where he thought his brother had crashed.

Got to find him.

Suddenly he came to a clearing where a light shone down from the sky on a rock where Norman sat. His brother was smiling his usual smile, waving at him, encouraging him to come closer.

Norman! David silently yelled. *It's you! You're alive!*

David ran towards his brother and then all of a sudden Domko was there too. He was standing by Norman and it was like his older brother was a boy again. He still had the same defiant look as he stared back at the man. David stopped. He wanted to help his brother, but was too frightened to move. Suddenly the snow deepened and David sank up to his knees. As he looked down, he saw that the snow had turned to a pool of blood that swirled around his legs. He sensed this was Norman's blood. He tried to scream but no words came out. He was trapped by a huge gray wolf with yellow eyes standing in front of him. Blood dripped from the animal's jowls as it moved closer. David tried to run, but his legs were stuck and the harder he tried to move, the more frightened he became. He tried to scream again. As quickly as it had appeared, the wolf was gone and Domko was standing in its place. His eyes flashed and he smiled an evil grin as he raised a sickle high above his head . . .

David awoke with a jolt. His body was drenched in sweat and he fought to catch his breath. His body shook from the thumping of his heart.

Bonnie stirred next to him. "What?" she asked sleepily.

"Oh n-nothin'," David whispered, out of breath, "just another n-nightmare. Go back to sleep."

She sighed and turned away.

David stared at the outline of everything in the bedroom. He listened, his muscles tensing at every small noise. These nightmares were now happening on a regular basis, and the wolf was back. It had visited him on many occasions when he was a boy sleeping in the attic at the farm.

In this period of grief, Bonnie and the boys began spending more time in Steep Rock with her family. Norman had been one member of David's family who Bonnie got along with very well. His death was a terrible blow to her.

David spent less time with her and the boys as he began working longer hours to earn extra money. This also helped occupy his mind. For David, Norman's death was another dreadful incident in a family that had been struck by tragedy and misfortune for as long as he could remember. He missed his brother terribly. The times that he and

Norman shared private jokes and their hours together were etched permanently in his mind.

A book about the crash entitled *The Sacrament* by Peter Gzowski, was released in 1980 by McLelland and Stewart Ltd. It was written in cooperation with the crash survivors, but met mixed reaction from the Pischke family. Sharon had declined to participate in the interviews process and nobody else from the family had been asked.

One afternoon while friends sat around discussing the book, David pointed out what he thought the crash survivors had overlooked about his brother.

"Maybe they figured that Norman was careless, you know, because of his easygoing attitude," David explained. "But what it was with Norman, he was just very confident. Not scared of n-nothin'—I mean after what us guys lived through! You think Norman's gonna be scared? Not on your life."

"An' Norman was very responsible, that's for sure. He wasn't much for rules and regulations, but he was a helluva pilot. He just had that way about him that you felt very safe. A worse pilot woulda crashed an' they woulda all been killed."

"But why do you think he flew through the storm?" someone asked.

David thought for a moment. "Because Norman said he was going to take them, so he did. It wasn't really stormin' when he left an' he probably thought it wasn't that bad. He flew in lotsa storms before. He musta logged 5,000 hours in that plane. An' you know, those Skyhawks are so damn safe. Pilots get overconfident flyin' 'em.

"If they wanted to go and were excited about going, well Norman's not gonna suggest they wait out the weather. He's not scared, see? It's fear that makes guys cautious," David explained. "It was the mountains that done him in. Inexperience in the mountains and the bad weather. Norman didn't figure on the mountains bein' as tough to get through as they were.

"I only wish we could have looked in the right spot," he said. "But how were we g-gonna know? There was some sidekicks there, tellin' the searchers where to look, but they weren't right either."

Brows furrowed at the last comment.

"He means 'psychics,'" someone whispered.

There were a few giggles, then a hush fell over the group as everyone became lost in thought.

"Norman was a great guy, that's for sure," David said, words thick with emotion. "I remember when he was a kid, Mom givin' him a spanking once for swearing at an Indian. You know Ma, she's like that. She had no tolerance for us guys bein' rude. I remember Norman tellin' us the story about how he used to write his own notes for missing school, an' the teachers knew it was him, 'cause his handwriting' was so poor an' the spelling was all wrong. Harmless stuff, really. He would have done anything to save those people—anything."

"It's too bad he's gone," someone said.

"That's for sure," a friend added.

"Did you notice in the book they say it was a bird—a whiskey-jack that led them guys out of the mountains?" David asked softly. "They thought it was some kinda angel or spirit sent down to save their lives, right?"

The group sitting around the table nodded. A few chuckled at the idea.

"How come it wasn't a coyote or a deer or a bear?" David asked.

"Because the bear would have ate them?" someone quipped. Everyone laughed except David. Then the mood turned serious again.

"Why do you s'pose it was a bird? I mean, if it was some kinda guide from heaven why do you suppose it was a bird, of all things?"

Everyone nodded somberly as the usual jovial David continued with his serious thought. "What do birds do?" he whispered. "They fly."

Chapter 20

"YOU'VE TOLD ME THAT YOU respect people who are kind and generous," McMillan said. "Name a person you know who's like that."

"Dead or alive?" David asked.

"Either," he said casually.

"Well, that would have to be a man who used to take us in when we were kids. He was a neighbour, a fan-tastic man, Jim Deighton," David said. "He died this March. He was livin' in the senior citizens home in Moosehorn. Just a fan-tastic man."

"Why did you respect him so much?" he asked.

"Because, he wasn't afraid of Domko," David explained. "No sir, an' he didn't care that we was dirty. He never turned his back on us. He did get mad a few times at us kids—because Domko was tryin' to turn him against us, but Domko's strategy never really worked. Yep, poor ol' Jim. Just a fan-tastic man."

Caroline traveled from B.C. to Winnipeg a few times during the next year to visit Raymond during his rehabilitation. By the summer of 1979, the doctors had concluded that not much more could be done for the 21 year old. Equipped with a special chair he began to slowly adjust to the realities of living with a severe disability.

Caroline phoned David from B.C. to ask him if he would take Domko to see Raymond in Winnipeg. This would be the first time that Domko had seen his son since the accident. Caroline felt it was important for them to see each other one last time. Raymond would be flying to a new home at the end of the week in Vancouver. The hospital staff had recommended a residence for Raymond that was designed especially for disabled young adults. He would not likely ever return to Manitoba.

Reluctantly, David agreed. Caroline thanked him, then called the hospital so that Domko would be prepared to make a trip to the city.

When David arrived in Selkirk, he was surprised to see that Domko was sitting in a chair waiting for him. Most of his right side was still paralyzed, but with the help of a walker, Domko could get around.

A nurse was there to accompany them to the car. Slowly, and without a word, they made their way outside. The nurse helped Domko into the car—much to David's relief. On the way to Winnipeg, Domko tried to say something, but David was unable to understand.

When they arrived at the hospital, David dropped off Domko at the entrance before parking the car. Domko shuffled inside and waited for David to lead him to Raymond's room. As they rode up the elevator, David couldn't believe the twists their lives had taken. It hadn't been that long ago that Raymond had called him "useless" and while he'd long ago forgiven the young man for the inconsiderate comment, he'd never forgiven Domko for placing the thought in the boy's head in the first place.

David felt an overwhelming sense of vindication—not against Raymond but toward Domko who'd always bragged that his offspring were so much better than the Pischke children. To know that Raymond had been injured through his own foolish, indulgent behaviour was meaningful to David. The Pischke children—all working and doing their best to raise respectable families—weren't so bad after all.

They walked wordlessly to Raymond's room. A nurse, who was leaving when they approached the door, gave David a shy smile, then disappeared down the corridor. David let Domko go in first while he stood just out of sight. He watched as Domko pushed his walker toward the chair beside Raymond's bed.

Raymond sat propped up in the bed, staring at his father. Domko sat down and the pair stared at each other for a few minutes before the older man took his son's hand in his, laid his head on the bed and began to sob.

The following year, Caroline and Kathy moved back to Moosehorn. Mark had returned when he was in Grade 10, so it made sense to her to live in the same place as the majority of her children.

Jennie, nearly 16, stayed in 100 Mile House. Caroline, now 58, moved into the senior citizens home while she decided where she wanted to live permanently.

By this time, Stephen was married and had three children. Dennis and Robynne had a son named Ryan; Eunice and Mel adopted a daughter named Dreena. Rose had given birth to two more daughters—Tiffany and Vanessa.

Sharon tied up loose ends in Estevan, shut down the business and with David's help, moved back to Moosehorn with her sons. She rented a house in town while she too decided where she wanted to live.

"Did you hear they buried Gus Harwart today?" someone mentioned at work when David was in the lunch room.

"What?" David asked.

"Yeah, he died a few days ago."

David had been meaning to pay a visit to the old man, but preoccupied with his own thoughts and problems had never gotten around to doing it. He fought back tears as he got up from the table and quickly went outside. He spent the remainder of the day thinking about the kindly man who'd never turned his back on the Pischke children. Thoughts of Gus made David wonder about Jim. He decided to pay the older man a visit the next day.

He arrived at Jim's place to find the 71 year old working outside. He still lived in the same house he always had. In David's recollections not much had changed.

"Still chopping wood?" David hollered as he strode across the yard.

Jim stopped to look at the visitor. It took him a few moments to recognize who had arrived.

"David!" he said, as he put out his hand in greeting. "Good to see you again, my boy."

"G-good to s-see you too, Jim," David said. He was pleased to find that his old friend still looked healthy and fit. He was thinner than he'd ever been—which accentuated his somewhat homely, gaunt features. But he was as mentally aware as ever.

"C'mon inside, I got some fish I'm going to fry for lunch," Jim said. "You'll stay, won't you?"

"Ever known me to c-come across the yard an' pass up a meal?" David joked.

"Can't say that I have," Jim laughed.

He opened the door and motioned for David to follow him inside. The familiar smells and decor filled David's mind with memories and all the old childhood feelings came flooding back.

"Jim," he said softly as he looked around in amazement, "nothin's changed! Not a thing."

"Yep, I know," Jim laughed. "Never had no need to buy anything new. Everything I have works just fine. Only difference is Ruby ain't here. You remember Ruby, don't you Dave?"

"Remember her!" David exclaimed. "How could I forget her. She was a *beauteeful* woman . . ."

Then he stopped. When Jim and Ruby had divorced, the parting of the ways had broken Jim's heart. David tried to think of something to say to interrupt the uncomfortable silence.

"Hey Jim, you 'member how me an' Dennis used to come here, all banged up an' you'd threaten to kick Domko's ass?" he said cheerfully.

Jim brightened. "I sure do. How could I forget that?"

He put two plates on the table and slipped a cast-iron frying pan from one side of the old cook stove to the other. He opened the fire box and added a piece of wood. Within a few minutes, the pan was smoking. As Jim talked, he added butter to the pan and then the filleted fish. The smell brought back happy times to David.

Jim made a pot of tea and they spent the afternoon laughing, joking and reminiscing about the past. Near the end of the visit, Jim's eyes filled with tears as he recalled his more painful memories of David's childhood.

"These are terrible things to remember," Jim said, shaking his head. "I don't know why the bugger was allowed to get away with it for so long."

David smiled. "I know. It's too b-bad."

David reflected on how wonderful it was to be visiting Jim, eating fish from the same old pan, and knowing that when it was time to leave, he would go to a warm, safe home.

It was the best feeling in the world.

◆ ◆ ◆ ◆ ◆

"Get him off of there!" Mike yelled one afternoon late that fall. David had just come out of his in-law's house to find his six-year-old son Ian sitting on a piece of Mike's machinery.

"He might break something," Mike complained.

David waved amicably as he went to the tractor and lifted his son down.

"Keepin' busy?" David asked Mike as the older man approached.

"Well, yeah," Mike exclaimed. "I got three places you know. I've got to keep checkin' all the time to make sure nobody's stealin' from me."

"Oh?" David said, "three?"

"Yeah," Mike said. "I got this here place, my place at Elm Point and the farm in Faulkner."

David laughed. "Mike, that's a lot of work, when are you g-gonna retire?"

"Retire?" Mike quipped. "I am retired! I get three pension cheques now."

"I know," David said slowly, "I mean when are you g-gonna stop workin' so hard?"

"I don't work hard," Mike scoffed. "I've been thinkin' about sellin' Elm Point— what do you think?" He stared intently at David, waiting for an answer.

"I don't know," David said. "It would cut down on your work if you didn't have that place to look after too."

Mike nodded. "I got some people interested, by golly. I think they're gonna buy it too."

"Good, good" David said.

Later that afternoon, David and Bonnie were sitting in her parents' living room when they heard a loud knock on the door.

"Oh no," David cringed, "that's prob'ly ol' Mike looking' for me. Tell him I'm not here."

Bonnie laughed.

"Dave, Mike's here to see you," his mother-in-law Margaret called from the kitchen.

David got up from the chair and went to greet him.

"Hey Dave, can you come give me a hand?" the older man asked. "I need a little help."

"Sure," David said. "Whatcha doin'?"

"I'm fixin' the track on my Cat and I can't do it by myself," he said.

"Okay," David said, pulling on his boots, jacket and mitts. He followed Mike outside into the cool wind and noticed how oddly dressed the older man was. Rather than buying himself a warm winter coat, Mike was wearing layers of old clothes.

David could see that he had on at least two pair of pants, numerous shirts and an old jacket. His tattered gloves were stained with oil and grease.

He led David to where he was fixing his machine and they made small talk while they worked.

"Ever been to Portage, Dave?" Mike asked.

"Yeah, I been there a f-few times," David answered.

"Well, when you're there, where do you eat?" he asked.

"I can't remember, why?"

"Well, my brother Nick, he's got this restaurant called Nick's Café and it's the best place to eat in Portage," Mike said. "And it's cheap too, real cheap."

David smiled. "Yeah, but is the food any good?"

"Oh yeah! It's the best food in Portage. All the workers eat lunch there. He's puttin' the other restaurants out of business, my brother is."

David nodded. He couldn't imagine what Mike's brother would be like. He thought that if he was anything like Mike, he wouldn't want Nick touching his food.

"A real good businessman, Nick," Mike said, as if reading David's thoughts. "You should meet him sometime."

David smiled. "You n-never know Mike, I just m-might."

The men worked for a few more minutes, then Mike explained what else needed to be done.

"Okay, Dave, now we gotta get this pin out," he said. "I've done it before. First we gotta heat it up real good and then pound it out."

David watched as Mike lit a tiger torch and held the flame to the pin. The wind kept blowing the flame, directing the heat away from the pin. David went to get a canvas tarp and wrapped it around Mike's work area to keep the gusts out.

"How's that?" he hollered over the strong wind.

"Good, I think I almost got it," Mike called back.

David stuck his head inside and watched for a few more minutes.

"You know Mike, I think it's hot enough—should we try?" he asked.

Mike nodded.

"Who's g-gonna hold the punch and who's gonna hammer?" David asked. Mike looked up at David.

"Well, I'll hold the punch and you hammer," Mike decided. "You're younger, stronger and probably steadier than I am."

David was relieved by the man's suggestion. Mike readied the punch as David pulled back the tarp and picked up a sledgehammer.

"Are you ready?" Mike asked. "We better hurry before it cools."

"S-sure," David nodded.

"Okay, I'm gonna turn off the torch." Mike shut off the flame, picked up the punch and held it to the hot end of the pin.

"Ready!" he hollered, looking up at David.

Positioning himself in front of Mike, David swung the hammer but the pin didn't budge. He swung again, this time a little harder. Still no movement. He swung again. Nothing. Frustrated, he swung a fourth time, putting even more "ooomph" into it. Mike's head snapped back.

"Aaahhh!" he screamed as he let go of the punch. A piece of metal had broken off the punch and hit him in the face. Reaching up with one hand, he felt until his hand came to a metal shard stuck in his forehead.

"David!" he hollered as he looked up. "Pull it out! Pull it out!"

The sight of the metal sticking out of Mike's head made David queasy. He turned away, while edging closer, and then without looking, reached out to feel Mike's face.

"Hurry!" Mike demanded. "Pull it out!"

David pinched the metal between two fingers and gave a little tug. Nothing happened. *Oh my God, it's stuck right in his skull!* he thought.

Gripping tighter, he pulled again. This time the metal popped out in a stream of blood.

"Aaaahhh!" David yelled as he jumped back. He ran towards Margaret's house. By the time he'd opened the door, his legs had turned to rubber and he tumbled inside. His stomach heaved as he fought to keep his lunch down.

"What's wrong?" Bonnie asked as he staggered inside.

"It's Mike," he gasped. "He's bleedin'."

"Is he all right?" she asked, hurrying to the window and looking outside.

"I th-ink so," he groaned.

"Are *you* all right?" she asked.

David nodded that he was. "Just gotta lie down for a bit."

He fought to erase the image of Mike's injury from his mind, but like a stuck record, it kept playing back over and over again. He gave his head a shake.

He went to the bedroom and lay on the bed. Just as he was starting to feel better, there was another rap on the front door. He sat up and peeked out at Bonnie answering the knock.

Mike stepped inside. "Where's Dave?" he asked. He'd taken part of an old bed sheet and wrapped it around his head like a turban.

"I'll get him," Bonnie giggled. "He can't stand the sight of blood, you know."

"I got it covered up now," Mike called after her. "Think he can come back out and give me a hand?"

David got up and met a smiling Bonnie at the door.

"How's your head, Mike," he asked. He was still feeling woozy but was amused by the sight of Mike's turban at the same time.

"Good," Mike said. "Let's go get that thing finished."

With his nausea gone, David was able to resume work and within the hour the pair had the track fixed and back on the bulldozer.

The following spring, Sharon moved into the old Pischke farm house. She and Norman had done the bulk of renovating before they'd moved to Estevan. Because she'd always loved that house, she decided it was time to move back to where she'd spent many happy years. She hired a few students to help her paint and did some minor renovating and redecorating herself. Soon she bought the quarter section from Caroline.

A year later, Sharon married Louis Coté—a kind, intelligent man who was a well-respected teacher at Ashern School. He was a wonderful role model for the boys. Trevor, still reeling over the loss of his father and the changes in his life, wasn't sure how to feel about the new living arrangements. A few months after Sharon and Louis' wedding, he spoke to his grandmother about the situation.

"Is anyone chasing you with a pitchfork," Caroline had asked gently.

"No!" Trevor replied. He was surprised that she'd suggest such a thing.

"Well, then it's not so bad, is it?"

After making the land deal Caroline gathered all the Pischke children and gave each of them a share of what had been their father's farm.

Initially David had been surprised by his mother's generosity, especially since she'd been poor her entire life and still had barely enough money to meet her needs. After giving it more thought, though, he realized that Caroline had always been a kind, generous and forgiving person.

Having lived away from Domko for a while, she seemed more interested in what her children were doing. She lavished her grandchildren with love and attention. The animosity that had existed between her and her children had subsided. And while David was still troubled by the events of his childhood, he was beginning to appreciate his mother for the woman she'd become.

David and Bonnie took the money she gave them, approximately $3,000, and bought themselves a trailer. It was a nice unit that they took to Steep Rock beach on weekend camping trips.

Chapter 21

"OKAY DAVID," MCMILLAN BEGAN, "we've finished with the background portion of the questioning. Now I have to ask you a few questions we call safety-valve questions."

"All right," David said. "What kinda questions are they?"

"Well," McMillan explained, "if there is anything in your background you're feeling guilty about, then I need to know before you take the polygraph."

"Why?"

"Well, it helps to clear your mind so that there's no doubt what question you're answering."

"Like what do you mean?"

"For instance, let's say that you stole something at one point—let's say you were helping a friend and you took home a hammer and never returned it. Didn't forget about it, just never bothered to return it. It's in the back of your mind that you still have that hammer. If I ask you on the polygraph if you've ever stolen anything, and you say no, it will register that you're lying because in your subconscious you're thinking about that hammer."

David looked puzzled.

"What are you thinking?" the police officer asked.

"I don't know," David said. "You tell me. I'm thinkin' that I don't know if that machine is gonna be able to tell if I'm lyin' or not."

"Okay, let me explain another way," McMillan said. "Let's say we're interviewing a man who is currently in jail for murder and we suspect he may be a serial killer. We can't just ask him if he committed a murder, because we know he has killed victim number one, right?

David nodded.

"But what we want to know is whether he killed victim number two as well. So we discuss the murder of victim number one, get that cleared away, then ask him about victim number two. Understand?"

David nodded.

"What I'm saying is, we have to be very specific in our questioning to get a true picture of what happened. We need to know what questions are going to trigger an ambiguous response."

"So what would you ask then?" David said.

"We'd maybe phrase the question like this: 'Other than the murder of victim number one, have you ever killed another person?' Do you understand?"

"I see."

"All right, I'm going to ask you a series of questions relating to the crime we're investigating."

"Okay," he said.

"Outside of this case, have you ever hurt anyone either intentionally or unintentionally?" McMillan asked.

"Hurt anyone?"

"Yes, you know either with words or by physically hitting them?"

David grimaced. He held his breath for a moment then exhaled slowly as he stared at his hands.

"Everybody has hurt people by saying things when they're mad," he said. "Does that count?"

"Keep going," the officer said. "This will help me properly formulate the questions when you're on the polygraph."

"Okay, so I've done that," David said.

"Unintentionally?"

"Yes, f-for sure."

"How about intentionally? Have you ever said anything with the intention of hurting someone's feelings?"

"Everyone has, haven't they?"

"Yes, but I'm asking you."

"I s'pose," David answered.

"So the answer is yes then?"

"Yes."

"All right, how about physically. Have you ever hurt anyone unintentionally?"

"Well prob'ly," he said cautiously.

"Good," McMillan said.

"How about intentionally?" he asked. "Have you ever hurt anyone intentionally?"

David's face flushed and he looked at the floor.

"Like what do you mean?" he asked.

"Well, have you ever been in a fist fight?" McMillan queried.

"N-no, never," David said quickly. "I never been in a fight. My friends an' me, we always just had fun—none of us are bad guys. Harmless, really."

"All right, any other fights, like have you ever hit your wife?"

"Which one?" David asked.

"How many do you have?" McMillan chortled.

"Well, I only got one now. But I was married before. To Bonnie."

"Did you ever hit Bonnie?"

"Yes," he said.

"How about your current wife," he added softly. "Have you ever hit her?"

"No. N-not once."

"Okay," McMillan said. "How about your kids?"

"N-never like Domko!" David said defensively. "I gave them each a spankin' a few times when they did somethin' really bad, but I never beat them, just a smack on the ass—an' only a few times, that's all. Does it count?"

"What do you think?"

"Yes, I s'pose."

David drove his old car to the Moosehorn school, parked in the front lot and locked the car tight. He hoped it wouldn't be too badly vandalized while he was inside. It was Hallowe'en night and he'd been hired by the principal to guard the school. There had been quite a bit of vandalism the year before and they wanted someone trustworthy to stand guard.

The caretaker let David in and showed him how to lock the door when he left. David turned out all the lights and walked from room to room. He watched out the windows for suspicious activity as he went on his tour. An overhead light out front illuminated most of the parking lot and since it was dark, David could see everything that was going on, but nobody could see him inside.

A carload of teenagers drove into the lot, stopped, noticed David's car and sped away. A few times he had to step outside to scare away pranksters but it was a quiet night, short of one incident.

While he was pacing up and down the hallway, he noticed car lights slowly enter the front lot. He hurried to the door in time to see the car pull onto the grass and disappear around the side of the school. David darted down the hallway toward a back classroom. He slipped inside and crept to the window. He watched as the car drove slowly behind the school then into the playground. It stopped. The lights stayed on for a few minutes, then were shut off. Nobody got out of the car and he wondered what was going on.

Maybe they are just teenagers in a romantic mood, he chuckled.

He wasn't sure what to do. As long as they didn't vandalize anything, he saw no harm in the car sitting behind the school. After about 10 minutes, the car was started again, the lights came on and it slowly drove back in the direction it came. David hurried back through the hallway to the front door. He saw the car pull out and speed down the street.

Huh? he thought. *That was strange.*

The remainder of the evening was uneventful. By 1:30 a.m. he decided it would be safe to lock up and go home. He stepped outside, pulled the door shut and began walking to his car. Something didn't look right and when he got closer he realized that the car was sitting on blocks and the tires were gone.

They got me! he thought. He walked around the car, but the tires were nowhere to be found. He suddenly felt very conspicuous as if he were the one being watched.

Shaking his head, he began walking down the street toward home, wondering who could have played the prank on him.

Kenny, he thought. *I betcha it was Kenny.*

As he walked, he could see lights approaching. The car slowed and a friend everyone called "Tobe" stuck his head out the window.

"Hey Pischke, what are you doing?" Tobe asked.

"I'm w-walkin' home," David said. "S-somebody took my wheels."

"Somebody stole your car?"

"No, I mean they just took the wheels."

"Oh!" Tobe snickered. "What happened?"

"I was babysittin' the school an' got tricked," David said.

"Oh . . . need a ride?" Tobe offered.

"Sure," David said as he climbed into the passenger's side.

Once David was in the car, Tobe looked at him and grinned.

"First," he said with a wide smile, "I need you to give me a hand."

Tobe was a hulk of a man with blonde hair and fair skin. He had a ready smile and enjoyed joking around. He was also fastidious—always neat, clean and well-dressed. He socialized with the same people as David, a group of a half-dozen fun-loving couples in their early

30s, all of whom lived in the Moosehorn area. They were always playing tricks on each other and Hallowe'en was a night in the year when no one could be trusted. David looked at Tobe. He wondered if he was being set up.

"I gotta get even with Price," Tobe said. "You have to help me."

David thought for a moment. Michael Price was owner of the local body shop and gas station on the highway. He was a well-known prankster who had played a trick on Tobe the Hallowe'en before.

Tobe and his girlfriend had been out for the evening and arrived home late. Michael and his wife Diane watched from a friend's house across the street as Tobe pulled into his driveway in his Lincoln Continental. The big man got out, walked to the house, unlocked the door and went inside. One by one, the lights in the house came on as Tobe checked each room.

Mike and Diane had let themselves into Tobe's house earlier that evening and had mixed up all the furniture so that nothing was in the right room. Suddenly the door flew open and Tobe ran outside, jumped in his car and sped north to the Price home, suspecting Mike and Diane were the guilty parties. By the time the Prices caught him in their house, he'd already moved two pieces of furniture into the basement. His plan to move everything downstairs had been thwarted.

Now it was time for him to get even.

"What are you g-gonna do?" David asked.

"I'm gonna knock over his outhouse at the gas station," Tobe said.

"You gonna shmash it?"

"I don't know," Tobe laughed. "I don't care. I gotta do something to get even with him."

"I know what you mean," David said. "That Michael! He was prob'ly the one who took my tires."

"Yeah, the bastard!" Tobe laughed. "You'll go into the shop tomorrow and the tires will be stacked there with a big 'For Sale' sign on them."

David laughed. "Yeah, someone will point, 'Hey aren't those Pischke's tires?'"

Both men laughed.

"I'll help you, but we can't shmash it. Michael needs it for his customers."

"Okay," Tobe said as he drove across the highway and pulled into the service station parking lot. They sat for a moment in the car to make sure nobody was in the vicinity of the two-door outhouse at the south end of the lot.

"The coast is clear," Tobe whispered.

They got out of the car and walked towards the plywood building.

"H-how are we gonna d-do this?" David asked.

"We'll just knock it over," Tobe said enthusiastically.

"No, wait," David said. "You go behind an' push an' I'll stand in front to make sure it doesn't shmash."

Tobe hurried around to the back of the outhouse.

"Ready?" he yelled.

"R-ready," David said. He stood between the two doors marked ladies and gents. With his hands outstretched, he braced himself to break the fall of the outhouse. He could hear Tobe grunting from behind but the outhouse only moved a tiny bit.

"Pischke!" Tobe hollered. "Are you holding it?"

"Yeah, but give it a push," David yelled back.

"I am!"

"Push harder!"

Tobe grunted as he tried to lift the building enough so that it would topple over.

"Man, this bastard is heavy!" Tobe shouted. "Heaviest shithouse ever made."

David speculated that his friend had likely had a few drinks and perhaps was a little more relaxed than he should be for the job.

"Okay," David said. "Stop, stop! You come around and hold it an' I'll push."

"All right," Tobe said, appearing from behind the outhouse.

"But d-don't let go," David warned. He made Tobe promise that he wouldn't let the building crash to the ground.

Making his way around the back, David stood back for a moment to survey the rectangular-shaped building. It sat at the edge of the grass on the gravel. Bending over, he could see parts of it were frozen to the ground.

"I see what's wrong," he called out. Bending his knees, David slipped his strong fingers under the plywood at the base. He lifted first with his shoulders and arms until he felt the building give.

"Okay, I got it," he yelled. "You r-ready?"

"Ready!" Tobe called out.

"Here she comes," David grunted as he slowly stood up, lifting the outhouse with him.

"I got it! I got it!" Tobe laughed bracing the outhouse as he slowly backed up.

Suddenly, David heard a loud thunk, followed by a sloosh and then a wail as the outhouse crashed to the ground. The five-gallon pail had been placed on the roof. When it fell, it dumped all its contents on

Tobe's head. Looking like a giant top hat the pail's journey ended when the rim of the pail jammed over Tobe's shoulders. That was the thunk. Knees bent, Tobe stumbled backwards, then fell forward as he reached up to lift the pail off his head. When the suction broke and the pail loosened, there came a sloosh when two weeks worth of human waste cascaded down his shoulders. The wail started once Tobe recovered from the initial shock and realized what had happened.

"Aaaaaah!" he screamed, as he bent over and began vomiting. "Pischke, help me!" He vomited again.

When he'd heard the thunk and the outhouse crashed to the ground, David had run around to check on his friend. He arrived just as the pail hit splattering him on the arm. He immediately began to gag and throw up.

"I can't see!" Tobe yelled. "Pischke, do something!"

David stood there unsure what to do. The closer he got, the more he gagged. He plugged his nose.

"Tobe," he said through pinched nostril. "Comeb hereb."

"Where? I can't see a goddamned thing!" Tobe wailed.

"Ober hereb," David said. He reached out and gently took the back of Tobe's pants. It was the only spot on his friend that hadn't been covered with slop. Leading Tobe across the parking lot, David found a frozen puddle and broke it with his shoe. He forced Tobe to bend over the puddle and scooped water into his friend's eyes. He did this until there was nothing left in the puddle.

"How's that?" David asked.

"No damn good!" Tobe screeched.

"Okay, come over here," David said gagging and throwing up again.

"What the hell are you pukin' for?" Tobe yelled. "I'm the one who's covered in shit!"

Tobe staggered from puddle to puddle while David tried to help him wash his face. When they'd got most of the muck off, Tobe's disgust turned to anger. Michael had got him again.

"That sonofabitch!" Tobe hollered. Enraged, he picked up a huge tow chain and threw it against the gas station. David stood back and watched. Within a few minutes, Tobe's anger dissipated and his shoulders slumped.

They stood beside the toppled outhouse and stared.

"And the goddamned thing didn't even break!" Tobe said with disgust. "At least it could have smashed a little."

The whole scene started to look humorous to David, but he didn't dare laugh. He stared seriously at his friend, hoping Tobe couldn't see his mouth twitching.

"You promised me you weren't gonna let it fall," David said, pretending to be serious.

"You!" Tobe screeched, a sudden look of comprehension coming over his dirty face. "You did this. You were *holding* the outhouse. . ."

David held up his hands and shook his head as he took a step backwards.

"No! Tobe! It wasn't me, really," he said innocently. "Honest, I had nooo idea."

Tobe scowled and stared at him for a few moments before his expression softened. He looked down at his arms, chest and legs.

"Look at me," he said. "How am I gonna get home?"

"I don't know," David said. "But I know one thing f-for sure—you can't get in the car like that."

Within a few minutes, David was driving slowly down the street with Tobe sitting on the hood of the car. He straddled the antenna, one big hand holding the aerial and the other a windshield wiper.

"I hate that sonofabitch," Tobe muttered, "I swear to god, he's my best friend and I hate his guts."

"Whooa!" he squealed, as he fought to keep from sliding off the hood. "Slow down Pischke, you goddamned maniac!"

David touched the brakes and Tobe slid across the hood.

"Aaaah!" he begged. "Slow down!"

David turned into his friend's driveway and parked. He stepped out of the car as Tobe slid off the hood. He grimaced as he stood stiffly under the yard light.

"I'll walk home from here," David said.

"Now what am I supposed to do?" Tobe asked.

"Well, you can't go in like that," David smirked. "You are covvverred in shit!"

"To hell with you!" his friend yelled.

"No, Tobe—seriously, just wait," David said as he looked around for a moment. He went to the edge of the driveway and returned.

"Hold still," David said.

Standing a few feet from his friend, David reached out with a stick and gingerly flicked a grubby wad from Tobe's shoulder.

"Thanks," Tobe said sheepishly.

David turned to leave.

"Hey, Pischke," Tobe yelled after him.

David stopped and turned around.

"You tell that bastard it was me and I'll kill you," he said, almost in tears. "I'll fuckin' kill you."

The next morning the phone rang at David's house. He was dreading the call.

"Hello?" he said sheepishly.

"How could you?" Tobe asked.

David cringed.

"Pischke, I thought you were my friend," he lamented. "How could you tell him on me?"

"I didn't," David pleaded. "He came here first thing in the mornin' an' he stared at me—you know Michael—and he said, 'Which one you guys got it, you or Tobe? Come here and let me smell you.' Course what was I gonna do?"

"You told him?" Tobe hollered. "Couldn't you have lied?"

"No . . . not 'xactly," David hesitated. "He stared at me an' I, well . . . laughed."

"You laughed?" Tobe yelled. "Now I hate you both."

One afternoon the following spring, David was working on a contract job repairing the fire hall in town. He was working with a few other men and while they worked, he began telling "Domko" stories. He told then in such a way that they made fun of his stepfather—strongly emphasizing his odd way of speaking.

"I'm s-still scared of him!" David laughed. "I have these goddamned dreams an' the bastard is chasin' me. For-tunately, I wake up before he catches me. But w-when I was a kid, there was no w-wakin' up from his black, ugly face. An' the smell! I'm tellin' you—we could smell him down wind . . . and up!"

The group laughed as David thought of more to say.

"I'm still scared of him. He don't smell so bad now, but he's still got that mean, ugly, ugly look," he said.

He was interrupted by another man.

"What? You're afraid of that little guy?" the man said. "How could a big guy like you be afraid of that little shit?"

David didn't know what to say.

"Well, we weren't al-ways this big," he stammered.

"Ah, you were bigger than him by the time you were 12," the man laughed. "Domko was all talk, no action."

"No he w-wasn't," David said. "He was a real jack o hyde, I tell you. You didn't know him l-like we did."

The man scowled as he tried to understand the malapropism.

"He means 'Dr. Jekyll and Mr. Hyde,'" one of David's friends whispered. "He does it all the time. You'll get used to it."

"He was so scary, we just ran," David said. "We all ran. Even Norman! An' did you ever know Norman to run from anything?"

The workers agreed that Norman had been fearless.

"See?" he said to the man. "I told you."

"Yeah, well you turned out all right," replied the worker. "It couldn't have been that bad."

David was speechless. He was so shocked he couldn't even begin an explanation of how bad it had really been.

"You brothers are all successful and hard workers," the man continued. "Domko made good men out of you. You should thank him for it."

That night, and for weeks later, David tossed and turned as he tried to make sense of the discussion of that afternoon. He'd struggled with himself for years, trying to make sense of the past. Hearing that some people believed Domko had made him into a "good man" was difficult to bear. The same words had been said about Domko when he was brought to the farm nearly 30 years before.

Life just wasn't making sense anymore.

Organized religion, which he'd rejected long ago, had taught him that bad events in life were a punishment for earlier sins. As children they'd been told that evil people were sent to live with the Devil. So what did that say about them?

When David became a parent, he understood the frustration adults sometimes feel when dealing with their children. He compared his own behaviour to Domko's and saw a huge difference between himself and his stepfather. He didn't want his children to fear him, but he wanted their respect. He also wanted them to respect his possessions and other people's property.

Sometimes he'd explode in a fit of anger and frustration, and the intensity of it would shock his wife and children. Talking to others and watching his friends raise their children, he discovered that he wasn't the only parent who yelled.

It had taken a great amount of self-control to keep himself from lashing out like the example he'd seen from his stepfather. He could only remember spanking his boys on a few occasions after they'd done something deliberately careless or destructive. Sometimes he'd been criticized for being too lenient with his boys. Where was the balance? He'd spoiled them with gifts and by letting them off scheduled chores. He hadn't been a perfect father and he knew it. But he loved his boys dearly. And he loved Bonnie too.

But he didn't get along with his mother-in-law. Relationships were too complicated for him and his comments were sometimes crass. He often blurted things out without thinking first.

No woman likes to be called "fat ass" but that's what he called Bonnie sometimes. She was so slim and beautiful it was obvious to *him* that it was a joke but Bonnie took insults seriously. She began returning the verbal attacks and the communication in their marriage started to break down.

They argued about money. She said she didn't feel loved. He wasn't romantic or affectionate, believing that providing well for his family was the best way to show them how deeply he cared. She said he didn't talk enough.

So instead of taking her in his arms and telling her what every woman needs to hear, he covered up his feelings of love and replied with sarcasm and jokes.

Shortly before their marriage completely broke down, they'd been arguing and he called her a name that had caused her to slap him across the face. Instinctively, he had reached out and slapped her back. The slap had done huge damage to their relationship which, by now, was hanging by a few fragile threads.

Bonnie left for an entire weekend and was intoxicated when she returned home. Angry at her for being gone so long and having heard rumours that she was seeing another man, David gave her a kick in the backside and told her to get into the house.

Shortly after that, they sold the house in Moosehorn as part of a plan to buy a home in Steep Rock. They moved into the trailer at the beach while they looked for a new home. Barely speaking to one another, Bonnie gathered up her things on July 10, 1983, and walked out the door. The last three years had been tumultuous in their 14-year marriage.

When Bonnie left, she took Dale with her. David and Ian stayed in the trailer for the rest of the summer. David spent many lonely nights trying to sort out what had happened to his life.

At first, he blamed Bonnie for the marriage breakdown. Confused, angry and hurt, he found himself in a deep depression. Friends began to worry that he might hurt himself in his despair.

Soon he admitted that he was at least half-way to blame for their problems. He wished now that he'd moved away with Bonnie and the children when she'd asked. He reasoned that without the influence of her family and the constant reminder of his dysfunctional upbringing, maybe—just maybe—they would have relied on each other more and listened to others less. His childhood misery had been kept hidden, even from Bonnie, with jokes and storytelling. Now though, the memories were beginning to affect his everyday life.

To make him feel better, Dennis and Ken suggested they go visit their old boss Jack McGuiness in Regina. The men made the trip and spent the weekend reminiscing about old times. Jack had been happy to see them and it helped David to temporarily forget his troubles.

Lorne Park was in a reflective mood as he drove into Ashern. He enjoyed going for coffee and sitting with whomever was there at either the Texaco coffee shop or the Gulf restaurant. He drove into the Texaco lot and found a parking spot. It was the weekend and he was feeling restless.

Lorne had married Linda Yanke in 1972 and after renting a house for a few years, the couple had decided to settle in the area. They bought an acreage five miles northeast of Ashern where they were raising their two children, Crystal, 10 and Jim, 7.

Lorne had stopped drinking years earlier and had a good job with Manitoba Hydro in the collections department. He'd moved from player to coach of the Ashern Hornets senior hockey team. Recently he'd been elected Reeve of Siglunes municipality. Lorne had political aspirations, but the soft-spoken man didn't like public speaking.

He had achieved quite a bit in 10 years yet he put on no airs or pretenses. He was as comfortable in a makeshift shack in the bush as he was in a board room in Winnipeg. He liked nothing better than to shock a government official meeting him for the first time. Always clean and tidy, Lorne knew the stir he made dressed in casual clothing and sporting a long, salt and pepper-coloured beard. He wore rubber boots year round, with the tops turned down for comfort. He taught many an unsuspecting soul a lesson about the shortsightedness of judging a man's intellect by his appearance.

Lorne waved to an acquaintance as he got out of his truck and walked toward the gas bar. He passed by the Arnason Funeral Home's hearse parked close to the building. As he pulled open the gas station door and stepped inside, he felt immediately comfortable. The business was bustling with customers paying for gas and convenience items.

Lorne pulled out a cigarette and walked toward the coffee shop. He noticed Jalmar standing by a pot of freshly brewed coffee on a warmer.

"Mr. Park!" Jalmar called out. "Come have coffee with us."

Lorne waved and nodded.

"I can't stay long," Jalmar said as Lorne entered the coffee shop. "I'm on my way to a funeral."

Cigarette smoke lingered overhead as people talked quietly and offered polite smiles and waves to passers-by. Jalmar finished refilling everyone's cups, then sat down at a table with two other men. Lorne took the seat beside him.

"Lorne, you know Mike, don't you?" he said pointing across the table.

Lorne nodded.

"How are you doing, Mike?" Lorne asked.

Mike stared at him for a moment. "You're the hydro man, aren't you?" he asked.

Lorne nodded. "I'm one of them."

"I think there's something wrong with my meter," he said. "You're charging me too much. I don't use that much hydro."

Lorne thought for a moment.

"Come into the office on Monday, bring your bill and I'll take a look," he offered.

"I'm not going to make an extra trip to town," Mike argued. "Can't you come see me in Steep Rock? That's where the meter is."

Lorne smiled. "Okay Mike, I'll come out as soon as I get the chance."

He shared a look with Jalmar. Both men were well-known for their patience with the more eccentric people in town. While most others would get angry, both Jalmar and Lorne ignored people's eccentricities.

"Well, I've got to go," Jalmar said, glancing at the clock as he stood up. "Been nice talking to you."

An attractive woman in her late 50s came into the gas bar.

"Mike, now there's a woman for you," said a man at the next table, nodding in the direction of the newcomer. "And she's the same religion and everything."

Mike glanced back over his shoulder. "That old bitch?" he exclaimed.

The comment surprised Lorne and he raised his eyebrows. "I don't know Mike, she's at least 20 years younger than you."

"Too old," he said.

"Okay, then how about her daughter, is she more to your liking?" Lorne asked.

Mike shook his head no.

"The granddaughter, now that's more like it," he said.

Lorne cringed. The girl he'd referred to was only about 12 years old.

"Mike, you dirty old man!" he said.

Mike laughed. "I like to get them young and train 'em right."

Lorne shuddered as he thought about his own young daughter. This was a stark reminder to him that there were men who harboured perverse thoughts. He wondered what would possess a man to think like this. He hoped that Mike was harmless.

"So whatever happened to Mel Kiesman's boat?" someone asked, changing the subject.

Lorne was jolted back to the present.

"It was grounded that day on the beach at Silver Bay, close to Jalmar's Bible camp, and it hasn't been moved since," he said. "Too many bad memories, I guess."

"Has it been a year yet since Mel died?" someone asked.

"Two," Lorne said quickly, butting out his cigarette and taking another sip of coffee. "To the day."

It was the anniversary of his closest friend's death which had put him in a reflective mood.

The tragedy two years before had struck Lorne hard. For weeks afterward, everyone had talked about how "it was just like Mel" to give his own life to save a friend. At Mel's funeral, Lorne realized that of the four "flying" buddies, he was the only one still alive.

Mel had bought a paddle wheel-style cruise boat and had been taking a group of friends for an afternoon ride on Lake Manitoba. One man fell off the boat. When the group realized that the calls for help were serious, Mel had jumped in to the water in an attempt to save his friend. Both men had drowned in the incident. Lorne hadn't been on the boat that day but thoughts of what had happened still haunted him.

He stood up, grabbed the coffee pot and refilled their cups. They discussed the numerous fatal accidents that had happened over the years and soon were talking about Norman's plane crash and the book written about it.

"I read that book and was quite offended by it," Lorne said dryly. "I read in there that Norman had told one of the survivors that 'he was the best young pilot he'd ever trained.' I was quite hurt. Norman had told me that I was the best young pilot he'd ever trained."

Everyone laughed.

"But I suppose he told that to everyone," Lorne smiled.

The men made small talk for a little while longer, then Mike got up to leave.

"Hey, Mike," one man said. "pay for our coffee, will you?"

Mike scoffed. "Get your own coffees!"

Everyone laughed.

"Well, I should get going too," Lorne said.

He talked for a few more minutes then went to the cash register and stood in line. One clerk was working the cash register while the other was talking to Mike. As the line dwindled, Lorne passed Mike and overheard him arguing with the clerk. She was trying to explain to him the playing rules on the scratch-and-win lottery ticket he'd bought. Looking at it once again, he was convinced that he had a winning ticket.

"No," she explained again. "That's not right. If it had been like this . . ." she said pointing again at the ticket, " . . . then you would have won."

Mike stared at her angrily. "You're tryin' to cheat me."

"No, I'm not, really," she said, trying to explain it to him once again.

He waved off her explanation with a grunt, then shuffled toward the door. He gave her one more look over his shoulder. "I won the lottery," he said defiantly, then continued out the door. "They're cheatin' me. I won, but they won't give me the money."

A few days later, Lorne decided to go out to read Mike's meter. He mentioned to another hydro employee that he planned to go and was surprised by the warning he received.

"Well, I'd call first," the man said. "Mike's been known to point a gun at guys who show up unexpected."

Lorne raised his eyebrows. "You're kidding?"

"No, I'm not. Poor old Mike is turning kinda paranoid. Everyone says he's starting to lose it."

Lorne got into the hydro truck after lunch and drove to Steep Rock. Mike met him in the driveway, holding his hydro bill. He immediately started to explain to Lorne that he couldn't possibly have used so much hydro. Following Mike to the meter mounted on the house Lorne examined it and made a few notes.

"How much is your bill?" he asked.

Mike handed him the bill and pointed to the total at the bottom.

"What?" Lorne asked. "This says you owe us $12."

"I know," Mike said. "That's too much."

Lorne stared at him. "The base rate is about $8," he explained. "So less the tax, that means you used less than $3 in hydro last month.

"But I didn't."

"Yes, you did."

"No I didn't."

"Do you live in this house?"

"Sometimes," Mike answered.

"Where do you live when you're not here?" Lorne asked.

"At the farm," Mike said. "And I stay at Elm Point. Why do you want to know?"

Lorne could see the man was becoming suspicious.

"No reason, other than I'm just trying to find out if this is your principal residence. If it is and you stay here all the time, you can expect to have a hydro bill of a lot more than this. The fact is, you don't use much hydro at all."

Mike stared at him.

"Compared to most people, this bill is very low," Lorne said. "So low in fact that I think your meter is broken—it's not charging enough."

"Not enough?" Mike hollered, grabbing the invoice. "It's too much! I'm not paying it."

Lorne shrugged. "Well Mike, you have to pay it. If you don't, then we'll have to disconnect you. It's not too bad right now in summer but winter will become pretty unpleasant without hydro."

"You can't cut me off in winter, it's the rules," Mike stated.

Lorne smiled. "Yes, but if I cut you off now, I don't have to hook you back up for winter. You'd have to go find someplace warm to live. Maybe you'd have to move in with one of the ladies from the church."

Mike laughed at Lorne's wit.

"It hardly seems worth it for $12," Lorne cajoled.

Mike insisted that he hadn't used that much hydro. Lorne did all he could to placate the man but suddenly Mike's attention turned elsewhere.

"Last night I shot someone," he said.

Lorne stood for a moment wondering if he'd heard right. "Pardon me?"

"They were trying to steal a part of my Cat over there," Mike said excitedly. "So I took my gun and shot them. I think I hit one too—he hasn't come out from under the tarp yet. Gonna start to smell soon."

Lorne looked again at the covered machine. Both he and Mike took a few steps closer. He could see bullet holes in the canvas.

"Go check for me to see if he's dead," Mike said.

Lorne looked at him. "I don't think it's legal to fire a gun in town."

Mike shrugged. "Don't matter. Just a bunch of dirty rotten thieves anyway. Who cares?"

Lorne was convinced that nobody was lying under the canvas. He also thought that the noise Mike had heard the night before was nothing but the tarp blowing in the wind. He saw this as a frightening example of Mike's paranoid behaviour that people were now talking about regularly. He waved good bye to Mike, got into his truck and drove back to Ashern.

"I noticed that you've been advertising Elm Point for sale," Dwight Cook said to Mike one afternoon when he saw him parked by the road. "Do you still want to sell it?"

Dwight was known through the region as a successful cattleman who was both shrewd and fair. He'd known Mike most of his life. As a young boy, he remembered Mike arriving at his father's house for evening visits. Mike would always bring his View-Master and reels—which in the days before television and hydro were a huge event for Dwight and his siblings. Mike also brought treats he shared with everyone. He was always clean, polite and thankful for a home-cooked meal.

In subsequent years, the Cook family had a handful of dealings with Mike and always found him to be honest, fair and straightforward.

The Cooks owned homes and land just south of Steep Rock near Elm Point. They also leased ranch land on Peonan Point, a peninsula of land that jutted into the northern end of Lake Manitoba. The family—which included Dwight's sister Delight and her husband Dave Knapp—made frequent trips to Peonan Point. Taking the road north was time consuming, but the seven-mile ride across by boat could be accomplished in under half an hour. The ranchers owned a good, fast boat but had no place to dock it. Elm Point was on the lake directly across from the Point. That's why they wanted the land—so they could build a marina. But first they needed to make a deal with Mike.

Dwight had heard rumours that his elderly friend was on the verge of senility, but saw no evidence of this one evening when they met to seriously discuss the prospect of the Cook/Knapp partners buying Elm Point.

Mike was attentive and in full command of the situation as they agreed upon a price of $40,000—at the time the going rate for 237 acres of land in the area. Dwight saw no gun or briefcase and there was no talk about Mike trying to shoot anyone. He was basically the same man Dwight had remembered, except he was nearly 78 years old. By the sound of it, he still worked as hard as the average 40-year-old man.

Dwight met Mike in Ashern to sign a deal at the lawyer's office. To celebrate the sale, Mike offered to take Dwight to lunch. They went to the Wagon Wheel restaurant on Railway Avenue and ate soup and sandwiches followed by a bowl of ice cream for dessert. Mike picked up the tab, shook his friend's hand and the two went their separate ways.

❖

Chapter 22

"AREN'T YOU GONNA ASK ME?" David said to the officer.

"Ask you what?" McMillan replied.

"About Bonnie," David hedged. "About me h-hittin' her."

The officer sat back in his chair.

"'Cause it only happened twice," David explained. "An' I know it was wrong, I'm not makin' no excuses for myself."

"All right," McMillan said. "What's important is that you tell me about these incidents so that it doesn't cause you to react during the test. Understand?"

David nodded.

"All right," he said. "Not connected with this case, have you ever done anything illegal or immoral?"

David looked surprised. "What do you m-mean?"

"Well, illegal would be something you could be arrested for."

David raised his eyebrows. "I dunno, maybe. When I was younger I would drive after h-havin' a few drinks. If I'd got caught, would they have arrested me?"

"Is drinking and driving illegal?" McMillan asked.

"I guess," David said.

"What else?" the officer asked.

David thought for a moment.

"Well, I set a fish net outta season with a friend once. I fell out of the boat an' almost drowned."

McMillan laughed.

"How about anything immoral?" he asked.

"What counts as im-moral?"

"Well, let's say—cheating on your wife. Have you ever cheated on your wife?"

"Which one? No just kidding," David chuckled. "No, ac-tually I can say honestly that I never cheated on my wife. Not Bonnie or Lynne."

"That's good," McMillan said. "Not many guys can get past that one."

"So, I guess I'm not all bad," David said sarcastically. "I mean, I lie an' I steal an' I'm a wife beater, but I'm no cheater. What does that say?"

"I don't know, what does that say?" the officer asked.

"It means that this whole thing is bullshit," David said, "and all you're doin' here is makin' me feel low."

"Well that's not the purpose of it. It's not to make you feel bad, just to get the air cleared."

"Clear, my ass. You're just lookin' for somethin' you can nail me with."

McMillan shook his head. He really didn't want to have this conversation again. But David persisted and by the time he finished ranting, he was as angry as he'd been when he came in the door.

One spring afternoon Mike drove from Moosehorn to the Steep Rock General Store. He got out, locked his car and went inside. The owner was standing behind the counter.

"Good morning, Mike," she said. "How are you?"

He nodded and stared at her for a moment.

"Any mail for me?" he asked.

"We'll have to check," she said. She rounded the end of the counter. "You haven't been in for a few days so there might be something there."

"Hmmm," he said, "probably just bills anyway."

As she came closer to him she recognized a familiar odour. At first she thought that a skunk must be outside, but then she realized it was Mike.

"Mike," she said, "have you got skunks out at your place?"

Mike grinned. "Well, you know how there are always guys coming and stealing from me, well I figured out a way to fix 'em good."

"How's that?" she asked.

"Well, I caught a skunk and I've got it tied up in the yard," he explained. "That way, by golly, they'll get the surprise of their lives when they come in the night."

She stared at him and then laughed.

"But Mike, what about you?" she asked. "The skunk—does it spray you too?"

He shrugged.

"Well, I haven't quite got him trained not to spray me," Mike said. "But I'm feeding him a bit—that should help him get used to me."

She laughed as she reached into Mike's mail slot. She handed him a few flyers, a newspaper and an envelope.

"That damn hydro," he muttered, studying the front of the envelope. "I got another hydro bill!"

She smiled. "We all get hydro bills, Mike. Have you got a problem with yours?"

"They're chargin' me too much," he exclaimed. "I just shouldn't pay it."

"Well, have you had your meter checked?" she asked.

"Don't matter," he said, "they keep chargin' me anyways."

The woman didn't know what else to say. By this time, the whole store smelled of skunk.

Mike picked out a few items and complained about the prices before pulling out a wad of cash and peeling off enough bills to pay for his groceries. He carefully counted the change she gave him, then stared at her intently. He grunted, turned, and left the store.

By this time, "Mike" stories were circulating regularly throughout the community. He was threatening to shoot people—and had pulled a gun on a few individuals. Mike and Gus Breitkreitz were often seen traveling to Jehovah's Witness meetings together. People also joked about seeing the pair scouring dumps for junk which they'd load into the backs of their trucks and haul home. Because they lived similar lives it wasn't surprising that they got along as well as they did.

Nobody knew whether the rumours about Mike were truth, exaggeration, speculation or pure fiction. But one thing was certain, he liked to flaunt his money and give the illusion that he was rich. He always carried a big wad of cash in his pocket and would flash it when he pulled it out to pay for something. It was behaviour he couldn't resist, but at the same time he feared being robbed. Rather than putting most of his money in a safe place, he began carrying a handgun instead.

The fall after Bonnie and David's marriage broke down, David needed to see the dentist. He stopped one afternoon to make the appointment at the receptionist's home in Ashern.

Lynne Jensen was working in her backyard when David drove up on his motorcycle.

"David," she said, surprised to see him. "How are you?"

"F-fine," he said. "Well, no not really, I got a tooth that's bothering me, I need to see the dentist."

"Okay," she said. "Come in tomorrow and we'll see if we can fit you in. If I remember right, there is an appointment open near the end of the day."

"All right," he said. He looked like he wanted to say something else, but instead got back on his motorcycle and drove off.

The next day Lynne went to work and wrote his name in the appointment book.

"Hi, David," she said when he walked in, "so how are you today?"

"Not too d-damn good since I have to see the dentist," he chuckled. "I hate the dentist."

"That's okay," she laughed. "I won't tell him you said that."

"No," he joked. "You know, it's just the ne-edle part I hate. The rest don't bother me."

They chatted for a few minutes while he waited for his appointment. When she asked him what was new, she was surprised by his answer.

"You heard that me an' Bonnie split up," he said casually.

Lynne was shocked.

"No, I hadn't heard," she said. "When did that happen?"

"This lousy summer," he said.

"Oh . . . that's too bad," she said.

Lynne remembered that she and her ex-husband had spent some time with David and Bonnie at social events when both couples were still together. She'd always thought David and Bonnie were happily married and was quite surprised by his news that they were divorcing.

"It was comin' f-for a long time—I just didn't know it," David joked self-consciously.

"Oh, just a minute," she said as a patient emerged from the dentist's office. Lynne disappeared for a moment then returned.

"Okay David, it's your turn," she said.

He rolled his eyes, then clasped his jaw pretending he was going to faint.

"If I don't come out in about an hour, come lookin' for me," he said, exaggerating how frightened he was. "You can just call my M-Mom to retrieve the body."

She chuckled at his sense of humour. When he emerged from the dentist's chair an hour later, they chatted for a few minutes.

"I need another appointment," he said. "R-root canal."

"Ouch," Lynne said. "Nobody likes those things."

She made another appointment for him and he left. He returned a few days later and again they chatted while he waited. Afterwards, he seemed reluctant to leave the office. David seemed at loose ends.

"If you ever feel like talking, come by the house," Lynne said.

Catching the hint, David nodded and left. A few days later, Lynne returned home from work to discover that David had been by to see her.

It struck her then that the man might be interested in developing the friendship further. A few days later she wasn't surprised when he again showed up on her doorstep.

Lynne invited him in for coffee and they talked for hours. He poured out his heart to her, explaining everything that had gone wrong in his marriage and the current divorce proceedings. There was sadness and confusion in his eyes. She understood because her own separation had not been easy—after 21 years and three children, her marriage breakup had been a severe strain as well.

Lynne and her friends were planning a trip to Winnipeg that coming weekend. Sensing that David was lonely, she invited him to come along. He said he would, but needed to take his mother to Selkirk and would join the women in the city afterward.

To Lynne, David was a fun-loving man with a wonderful sense of humour and a warm personality. She enjoyed spending time with him. She was intrigued by the strapping fellow whom she'd never viewed as anything more than a friend until now.

When people started noticing the bond they shared, they asked Lynne about the future of the relationship. She told them that she and David were just friends—after all, he was eight years younger than she was. She didn't expect it to go any further than that.

David, on the other hand, had other plans. He'd always thought Lynne was nice and now found himself attracted to her. She was a lovely woman—with light brown hair, green eyes and soft features. She was lots of fun and a tremendous listener. Lynne loved to talk too—and so did David.

Their blossoming romance caused a few tongues to wag, but the two were smitten with one another. Soon they spent all their free time together and for both, it felt like they were getting a second chance at love.

◆ ◆ ◆ ◆ ◆

When it became too cold to stay in the trailer, David and Ian moved to a rented house in Moosehorn. One evening in late November, Lynne returned home from work to find David's car parked in the driveway. He paced as he waited for her outside.

"Hi," she said. "How are you today?"

He shrugged and looked past her. She could tell something was bothering him.

"What is it?" she asked. "You seem troubled."

He shrugged but said nothing as he took grocery bags from her and followed her inside.

Once they were in the kitchen, she looked at him again.

"What is it?" she asked softly. "Is there something wrong."

He poured himself a soft drink and sat down.

"I gotta go to Mom's," he said.

"Oh, what's the matter?" she asked.

He paused as if trying to summon strength.

"I hafta go help her," he began. "She called me to say that old Domko died and she has to make arrangements and wants us there."

"Oh, I'm sorry," Lynne said, struggling to remember, "Domko—he's your stepfather right? Her husband? He's been in Selkirk for a while, hasn't he?"

David stared at his glass. He couldn't look her in the eyes, but she could tell he was near tears.

"What happened?" she asked.

"S-stroke . . . it finally killed him," he said, voice breaking.

"Oh, I'm sorry David, I didn't realize you and he were close," she said, reaching out and touching his hand.

"Close?" he rasped. "Close? Not on your life."

His deep blue eyes bore into her and for a moment, she felt alarmed by the intensity in his voice. "That ol' bastard shoulda died long ago."

Lynne didn't know what to say. With the exception of discussing his divorce, she'd never seen him upset before. David took another sip and then rubbed his eyes and sniffled.

"Nope, it's just as well the sonofabitch is dead," he said. "He n-never did nothin' but tor-ture us."

She tried to understand what he was talking about, but was having a difficult time. He obviously loathed the man but seemed truly upset.

"Because," he said, "because of Mom."

"Oh . . ." she nodded.

Lynne had met Caroline while visiting Sharon's house a few weeks earlier. David's mother had appeared to be a kind, quiet, content woman.

"Yep, be-cause of Mom, I know how hard this is gonna be for her," David said sucking in his breath, "An' be-cause now I'm gonna have to face all them JWs."

"That's right, your mother is a Jehovah's Witness, isn't she?"

"Oh yes. She sure is."

"Well, don't worry, I'm sure it will all be fine. They're not going to try to convert you."

He chuckled. "I'm n-not worried about that."

"Then tell me David, what is it?" Lynn asked.

"When things like this happen, it brings it all back," he whispered. "You know, you go along thinkin' everything is fine and then boom, it hits you!"

"What hits you?" she asked.

"The memories . . . an' the beatings," he said, his voice trailing off.

She sat quietly, unsure what to say next. Lynne's own childhood had been unorthodox—her parents divorced when she was a little girl and after the split, she stayed with her father. Unfortunately, he was an alcoholic who'd been unable to care for her. She lived with her grandparents who raised her. It hadn't been a difficult upbringing, but different than most children's because she didn't have a mother and father around.

"Well, some men are abusive," Lynne said. "He had a steel plate in his head, didn't he?"

"Steel plate, my ass. He was the goddamned Devil!" David exclaimed. "But not so bad that he couldn't tell the Pischkes from the Domkos. Oh no, he treated his own kids good, but he treated us worse than animals. So what kinda crazy is that?"

He glanced at his watch, then back at Lynne.

"I gotta go," he said as he stood to leave.

"All right, well I'll see you later then?" she asked.

David nodded, pulled on his jacket and went out the door.

The days preceding Domko's funeral were a blur to David.

Caroline leaned heavily on him and Dennis during this time. Arrangements were made by a funeral home in Selkirk for the service to be performed at the Kingdom Hall.

David had to put aside his feelings about the Witnesses and pretend that he wasn't bothered by the hypocrisy of the situation. He and Dennis spoke about it, but even that was difficult since Dennis was a practising Jehovah's Witness.

Had Domko been baptized by this religious organization?

Nobody in David's family seemed to know.

David arrived at the funeral home for the viewing shortly before the service. He stood quietly by the door as people came and went. Timidly, he glanced toward the front of the room. He could see the casket with a spray of flowers on a table. The top was open and people were filing past. Everything was serene as they spoke in hushed tones.

The room had a faint odour that reminded David of the hospital—but it was a bit different. He took a few steps closer to the casket then looked away again, offering polite smiles as visitors passed. There weren't many people there. Walter had opted not to attend. He'd told David on the phone that he wasn't going to be a hypocrite and show up at the funeral of a man who'd treated them all so badly. Stephen, Raymond and Jennie were all living in B.C. and none of them came. Eunice was not there and neither was Rose. Maybe they'd arrive soon? David didn't know. Kathy was sitting at the front with her mother but nobody knew where Mark was. Dennis was there. And so were Caroline's brothers.

As he moved closer, David heard someone whisper, "He looks so peaceful."

David stared at the ground and felt his anger start to build. He glanced up and saw Domko lying stiffly on the soft cushions, the creamy satin lining in sharp contrast to his dark, rough appearance. When David was as close as he dared, he studied his stepfather's face. He half-expected the old man to jump up and yell at him. He stared at Domko and the stillness for a long time and soon the reality of it all began to sink in.

Domko was dead. For real.

David couldn't help but notice that even in death the man had the same rigid expression.

They couldn't get that mean look off his face, David thought. It figures. An' it's good. Because it's only right that he looks the same when he's dead as he did when he was alive.

Domko's body was sent to the crematorium and the funeral service began shortly afterwards. This left just a few wreaths at the front of the hall. A Brother from the church delivered the service and David tried not to listen as the man eulogized Domko. Sitting at the front with his mother, David glanced behind to see Caroline's brothers listening solemnly. He wanted to grab them and shake them for helping perpetuate the abuse that had been in his mother's family for years.

There were so many things he wanted to say—to the Jehovah's Witnesses, the Kolodkas, and everyone else who had turned a blind eye to their suffering. But David knew that this was not the time nor the place.

He glanced at his mother and saw her wiping her eyes with a tissue.

It angered him that she was crying. All he could do was hope that the tears were of relief—finally to be finished with that chapter in her life.

Mom deserved better than him, but she never believed it, David thought. *Too bad we all had to suffer.*

Later someone asked, "If you hated him so much, then why did you go to his funeral?"

"I had to go to see if the Devil could really die," he answered.

Chapter 23

"I HAVE ONE MORE QUESTION for you David, and then if you're ready, I'd like to hook you up to the polygraph machine," McMillan said. "How does that sound? Then you can get out of here, which I'm sure you're looking forward to."

David laughed. "That is if I don't fail the test an' you lock me up."

"You've said nothing here so far that makes me want to arrest you. Unless you plan on confessing to the murder or another serious crime, I doubt very much that you'll be arrested tonight."

David smirked.

"Are you ready to continue?" the officer asked.

David nodded.

"All right, have you ever wanted to kill anyone?"

The question hit David like a hammer.

"Are you g-gonna ask that w-when I'm on the polygraph?" he stammered.

"Why, do you have a problem with that question?"

"No . . ." David said.

"Then why do you ask?"

"Well, it's just that from wh-en I was a kid," David said, "the ol' bastard . . . how's the machine g-gonna know the difference?"

"Well, there is a big difference between wanting to kill someone and actually killing them, don't you agree?" McMillan said, studying David closely. "You know the difference, right?"

David stared at him, then nodded.

"Not associated with this case, have you ever wanted to kill anyone?" McMillan asked again.

David hesitated.

"Well?" McMillan asked, waiting.

David took another deep breath.

"Yes," he whispered.

The following spring, Domko's ashes were shipped by bus to Moosehorn. Rose picked up the package which she delivered to Caroline. After some discussion about what to do with all that remained of Domko, Caroline decided that he would want to have his ashes buried or spread at the old farm.

Caroline and Eunice drove out there one afternoon to perform the task. They pulled into the driveway and got out of the car. Sharon and Louis had decided to live in his house a few miles away, so the old farm house was empty again. Caroline and Eunice walked around for a few minutes before deciding it would be simplest to dispose of the remains by burying them in an existing hole. Eunice found a loose post in the fence near the church. She lifted it up while Caroline opened the package and dumped the ashes into the hole. Eunice said her good-bye to Domko as she replaced the post.

When Domko's estate was settled, Caroline received approximately $40,000. It was the most money she'd ever had at one time and was thrilled that she would be able to buy a house. After looking around for a while, she settled on a quaint, three bedroom bungalow in Ashern for her and Kathy.

David and Lynne were growing closer. He was planning for the future and thought it was time to find a practical, affordable place to live.

He decided to build a house and bought a lot on the northeast side of Moosehorn. He discussed his plans with Lynne who encouraged him to continue renting in town while he built the house himself. It might take a year, but he'd save on labour costs by doing it mostly on his own. Together, they began looking at house plans. They ultimately picked a log home which would reflect his down-to-earth nature. They'd construct it with a hip roof—barn style, with an open ground level and an upstairs loft with three bedrooms. He wanted two bathrooms—one upstairs near the bedroom and the other near the front entrance. He planned to someday add an attached garage, plus a closed-in porch that would run along one side of the house and across the front. Of course, the house would be heated with a wood furnace and they'd have a fireplace too. David had big plans and enough youthful enthusiasm to follow through.

David and Ian moved into Lynne's house that spring. It took some adjustment. Lynne smoked while David did not. She liked the house cool but he kept it hot and was obsessively neat. And while she knew he had a voracious appetite, she'd never fed him regularly before. The grocery bill skyrocketed. Although the love they shared felt as powerful as a first-time romance, they still had adult responsibilities.

At 12, Ian was a handful and Lynne's three children—in their late teens and early 20s— still needed parental guidance. They came to Lynne and David with their problems. Fortunately everyone got along well. Ian accepted Lynne. He was initially jealous of the attention his father gave her, but soon grew to appreciate her motherly ways. Lynne's children—David, Sherry and Bill—were instantly attracted to David's outgoing, helpful personality and a strong bond formed among them all.

For the most part, Lynne was accepted into David's circle of friends and he mingled well with her crowd. Some friendships were lost—a common occurrence following divorce. But they became acquainted with couples neither had associated with before. Soon strong friendships were forged.

"Hey Dave!" Mike called one Saturday afternoon as he walked along the sidewalk in Moosehorn. "Come here." Mike had bought groceries and appeared to be on his way home.

David walked across to where the old man was standing.

"What's up, Mike?" he asked.

"I need some help. Those bitches have got me kicked out of town, so I gotta move all my equipment to the farm," Mike said. "Will you give me a hand? I need a hand."

"Sure," David said promptly. "I think Ian would prob-ably like to help too. He can drive tractors and he's always lo-oking for odd jobs."

"Good," Mike said smiling. "I'll pay him. Can you come tomorrow?"

"Sure," David said. "We'll be out first th-ing in the m-morning."

Mike nodded and waved as he climbed into his old car.

The next morning David and Ian arrived at Mike's house in Steep Rock. David was relieved to see that a good portion of Mike's junk had either been disposed of or moved. He noticed the tarp was off the Caterpillar.

"What happened to your Cat?" he said, curious to know how the older fellow would answer. He noticed gunshot marks on the chassis and had heard rumours that Mike was shooting in his yard at night.

"I shot a guy who was trying to steal parts off it," Mike said, scanning the machine. "I don't know where he went though—I can't find him. He must have crawled away."

David frowned. He'd heard this same story from Mike a few years ago. He wondered if Mike was talking about a new incident or dwelling on the past.

David and Ian spent the day helping the old man move his belongings. When they were finished, David waited in the car while Mike went to get money to pay Ian a day's wages. When the boy climbed in beside his dad, he looked like he was going to cry.

"All he gave me was a dollar," Ian sniffled.

David stifled a giggle.

"A dollar? That's it?" the father asked. "Well, you know Ian, Mike's a pretty old guy an' he's tight—you know what I mean, eh?"

Ian nodded.

"Ac-tually," David said thinking quickly, "you weren't really helpin' him today, you were helpin' me. He asked me to give him a hand, an' I brought you along. So I guess it's me who owes you money."

Ian brightened. "How much you gonna give me?"

"Well, I don't know, how much do you think you're worth?" David said nudging his son. The two negotiated a satisfactory amount during the drive home.

One day, David invited the whole family to a party. He had something up his sleeve—exciting news he wanted to share with everyone. It was a lovely summer afternoon as family members gathered at the house. Part way through the evening, he handed Lynne a rock with a ribbon tied around it. Surprised, she looked at it.

"What's this?" she asked.

He smiled. "You need a rock."

Puzzled, she looked at it again. Then he reached into his pocket and brought out a ring box. In an embarrassed, awkward way, he handed it to her.

"David!" she exclaimed. Opening it, she found an engagement ring.

The whole family smiled at her.

"Well?" someone asked.

She looked at the room full of people and chuckled self-consciously.

"Well, what do you expect me to say?" she laughed. "I can't say 'no' with you all looking at me, now can I?"

That evening the family celebrated David and Lynne's engagement. A wedding date would be set once Lynne's divorce was final.

David was pleased to see that everyone in the family seemed to be settled in their lives. In spite of petty disagreements from time to time they all appeared to be doing well.

By this time, most of Caroline's grandchildren were nearly grown—Lee, Norman and Sharon's eldest son was 19 and the youngest grandchild, Rose's daughter Vanessa, would soon be starting school. The grandchildren knew that their grandmother was always there with a nonjudgmental ear to listen to their problems.

Caroline seemed especially content. She liked all her daughters-in-law and still kept in close contact with Sharon. She was also fond of Lynne.

"He was quite smitten by you," Caroline said to Lynne when they had a quiet moment together. She went on to explain that before asking Lynne for a date, David had gone to Caroline for advice. He wasn't sure how to go about approaching Lynne. Caroline had suggested he stop by to ask about his troublesome tooth.

"So you were responsible for that visit to my house!" Lynne exclaimed. "I wondered what that was about."

Caroline giggled.

The family sat chatting and gossiping into the night.

"So did you hear the latest about Mike Kalanza?" someone asked. "He tried to shoot somebody."

"What? Again?"

"Yeah, one night he was scared so he hid in the outhouse all night. A guy showed up early in the morning to do some work for him and he began shooting at him from the outhouse."

"He slept in the outhouse all night?" a voice piped up.

"I doubt that he got much sleep," David quipped.

Everyone laughed.

"So, what's his problem? . . . Paranoid . . . I think maybe he's going a little senile . . . Well what do you expect? He's lived alone for . . . how many years? . . . Since his boys left and that's been about 25 years now. . . How old is Mike, anyway? . . . 75? . . . No, he's older than that, I'd say he's pushin' 80 . . . Somebody had a flat tire near his place and . . . He shot them? . . . No, but he shot at them. I guess the person drove off on the flat . . . I would too! . . . He was shooting at people in town? . . . No, this was out at his place in Faulkner . . . Dumb ass, anyway . . . I heard he has dynamite and has said he'll blow people up . . . how'd he get that? . . . his well drilling business . . . He's probably worried somebody's gonna grab his briefcase . . . Yeah, well if they did, they'd get old Mike along with it. I heard he has it handcuffed to himself . . . What does he carry in that briefcase anyway? . . . All his money—everybody knows that . . . He'd better be careful or someone's gonna clunk him over the head and take it . . . Why would he carry his money around like that? . . ..You know those old misers. Don't trust the banks . . . I don't trust 'em either! . . . What? You don't have any money, what are you worried about? . . . That's why! The bank took it all!"

Everyone laughed.

"So how much money do you suppose he's got anyway? . . . I heard he's got millions . . . I doubt it . . . Why? . . .I don't know, maybe a hundred thousand . . . Well, I heard he won the lottery . . . with Mike, who knows?"

"You got that right," David added. "Well, Ma, we said you shoulda hooked up with Mike when you had the chance."

"Yeah, but then she'd have to have Mike too," someone laughed.

Caroline chuckled. "All right, enough of this nonsense about Mike. He's just an eccentric old man and we shouldn't be gossiping about him."

Everyone giggled as the subject changed to something else.

Shortly after the announcement of David and Lynne's engagement Lynne was taken aside by an acquaintance and warned about David. He told her that David was a violent man and she ought to be careful.

Lynne was shocked. She'd never seen any indication of violence in her fiancé. He'd become angry and bordered on the irrational at times when he discussed his divorce settlement, but Lynne knew that anger was a natural reaction during the emotional turmoil of divorce. She'd seen him lose his temper and holler, but he'd never lashed out in a physical way—not at her or anyone else.

Lynne put the accusation about David being violent in the back of her mind. She started examining David's behaviour a little closer though—just in case. Then one night she was frightened awake by David who was thrashing on the bed, caught in a terrifying nightmare. It took a few moments before he was conscious enough to speak coherently.

"What's wrong?" she asked.

"N-nnightmare," he gasped. His body was covered in sweat and he trembled as he sat up. Lynne switched on the bedside lamp.

"Are you okay?" she asked softly. She'd had nightmares before and her ex-husband had them occasionally, but she'd never seen anyone so affected by a dream.

He nodded that he was fine.

She reached out and put a hand on his back.

"What was it about?" she asked.

He shook his head "no"—he didn't want to talk about it.

". . . glass of water," he rasped, as he got up and left the bedroom. He returned a few minutes later with a cup in his hand. When their eyes met, he immediately diverted his to the floor. He climbed back in bed and lay stiffly on his back. Lynne turned off the light and all was quiet in the dark. But she could feel the bed vibrating to the beat of his heart.

"I'm taking a run out to Mike Kalanza's place," Constable Bob McAfee said as he slipped on his jacket. "If I'm not back in a couple hours, send someone out looking for me," he joked.

He'd received a call from Mike's sister who lived in Winnipeg. She was concerned because she hadn't heard from Mike in a month. Usually he called her more frequently and she was starting to worry about him.

A stocky, boisterous officer with a confident voice and hearty laugh, McAfee was a 14-year veteran with the RCMP. His remark about "coming to look for him" wasn't entirely a joke. The police mostly considered Mike a harmless eccentric, but they'd heard lots of stories about the old man shooting at strangers and the constable didn't want to find himself on the wrong end of a stray bullet.

McAfee stepped out the door of the small detachment and drove his cruiser north. Mike's sister had said that her brother now spent most of his time at the Faulkner house, and that's likely where he would be found.

It took 30 minutes and a few wrong turns before the constable arrived at Mike's isolated farm. He sounded the siren a few times before cautiously pulling into the driveway. He scanned the yard, but there was no sign of the old man.

There were piles of junk throughout the yard as well as equipment in varying stages of repair. An old outhouse sat at the edge of the bush north of the house. McAfee wondered if it was still being used. Spotting a handful of little shacks in the yard, McAfee also made a mental note that Mike's car was sitting beside the house.

He opened the cruiser door and stepped out while looking around cautiously.

"Mike!" he called out. "Mike . . . you around anywhere?"

He waited for a few moments, then made his way carefully to the door of the house, glancing into Mike's older model Pontiac as he passed. He knocked on the front door and waited, but there was no answer.

He scanned the yard before walking back toward the cruiser. Noticing drag marks on the driveway he decided to follow the marks to the road where it was clear that a vehicle had pulled something out of the driveway, heading south.

He got back into his cruiser and followed the trail which led him to a dump site near Faulkner. When he got there, he noticed an old, dark green truck parked close to where Mike was rummaging through the mountainous pile of scrap. McAfee pulled the cruiser behind the truck and got out. He saw immediately that the truck didn't have a licence plate.

"Mike!" he called out.

The old man turned. He stared at the officer for a moment before turning back to his scavenging.

"Mike," McAfee said as he walked towards the older man. "Your sister called. She asked me to come out and check on you. You haven't called her in a few days."

Mike grumbled as he pulled something he wanted from the pile.

"I've been busy," he said. "I don't have time. I've lots to get done before winter."

McAfee nodded. "Yeah, I know what you mean, but you know Mike . . . that truck there isn't licensed."

Mike turned toward him and smiled. "I know. What are you going to do about it?"

"Well," McAfee said, "I'll drive you back to the house and you can make arrangements to get a licence for it."

"How am I gonna do that?" Mike asked.

"You could go to town and buy plates for it.

"I don't want to buy plates for it, because if I wait a few more days, then my insurance will be cheaper, so I want to wait."

McAfee nodded.

"Well then leave it here and come back for it when you have plates."

"I can't do that!" Mike hollered. "Someone will steal it."

"All right, then have it towed home," McAfee said.

"No," Mike protested. "If I have it towed home, that will cost too much money. Besides, how will I get home?"

"I'll drive you back."

Mike stared at him for a few minutes. "I don't want you to drive me back, I'll drive myself. I got the truck, I can drive."

"Well, I can't let you do that," McAfee said, annoyed. "It's an unlicensed vehicle and if you get into an accident, you'll be in big trouble."

"What are you going to do if I drive it?" Mike challenged.

"I'd have to charge you," the officer said.

"Okay then, charge me," Mike said.

Exasperated, McAfee returned to his car, wrote out a ticket then went back and handed it to Mike. The constable was surprised that although Mike was oddly dressed in unmatched, old clothing, he was clean and freshly shaven. He had no noticeable body odour—odd for a hermit.

Mike took the paper and shoved it into his pocket.

"You got nothin' better to do than drive around giving tickets to farmers," he grumbled. "No harm in me driving this truck to the dump. No harm at all. And you let guys get away with stealing from me."

McAfee sighed.

Mike had complained to him earlier about a clutch being stolen from one of his machines. McAfee had interviewed the man Mike had accused. He discovered that the "theft" had taken place 15 years ago and that as far as everyone was concerned, the issue had been resolved.

For everyone except Mike.

"You know we checked into that Mike and it's old news," McAfee said. "Besides, didn't we determine that old Cat of yours doesn't even need a clutch?"

"Then how come it doesn't run?"

"Well, I don't know," said the exasperated officer. "We can't keep looking into these old complaints. You bring us something new and we'll take a look at it."

Mike glared at him.

"Oh yeah," McAfee said as he turned to go, "phone your sister. She's worried about you."

Mike nodded and went back to picking through the dump.

A few weeks later, Mike walked into the detachment office wanting to speak to an officer. Constable Helmut Neufeld was on duty that day and sat down with the old man.

"What's the problem, Mike?" Helmut asked.

Helmut was an intense, by-the-book officer who took every complaint and crime seriously. He was wiry, quick and alert. He was known for pursuing suspected criminals with dogged determination that left people either chuckling or admiring his resourcefulness. He'd taken complaints from Mike before and was familiar with the man's history.

"There are guys stealing from me," Mike said, "and I want you to catch them."

"Well, do you know who they are?" Helmut asked.

Mike said he wasn't sure. He raised the issue of the missing clutch again. Helmut had already heard this story a few times. He needed Mike to tell him something new if he was to take the complaint seriously.

"And there are guys out to get me," Mike complained. "You know I had to shoot at them."

"Who is out to get you?" Helmut asked.

Mike stared back at him. "It's all right to shoot at somebody if they trespass, right?"

"Well, actually no, Mike," Helmut said. "You shouldn't be shooting at anybody."

"But what if they are threatening me?" Mike asked.

"Then you come in and file a complaint and we'll take care of it," Helmut explained.

Mike scoffed. "That's what I'm doing right now."

"Yes, but you haven't told me who's threatening you."

"Well, I just want to make sure that if I shoot someone who's after me, I won't get into trouble."

"Mike, I can't tell you it's okay to shoot at people," Helmut stressed. "You can't be doing that. Tell me—who are you complaining about?"

Mike stared at him intently.

"And somebody stole my chainsaw," he said. "It was a good one too, a real good one."

"Do you have any idea who took it?" the officer asked.

"Them guys who've been stealing from me!"

Helmut sighed. "Well if you aren't going to tell me who, how can I help?"

Mike shrugged as he got up to leave. Helmut walked him to the door and was surprised to see that Mike's vehicle wasn't sitting on the street.

"Hey Mike, where's your car?" he asked.

Mike smiled. "I don't park right here," he explained. "I don't want them to know I'm coming to the police station."

Helmut shook his head and watched as Mike, glancing over his shoulder a few times, walked around the building and disappeared.

"Who wants to go out and check on old Mike Kalanza?" Sergeant Dave Asmundson called from his office.

A chorus of groans rose from the main area where on-duty officers were completing paperwork related to their investigations.

A few moments later Helmut stuck his head inside the sergeant's office.

"What now?" he asked.

Dave Asmundson looked up from his desk. A laconic man, Dave had been with the RCMP for 19 years, the sergeant in Ashern for the past three of them. His straightforward way of doing business left no question who was in charge.

"We just got a call from one of Mike's neighbours who said that they haven't seen any activity around his place for a few days," Asmundson explained. "They think he might have died."

"Oh," Helmut said. "They didn't check on him?"

"No. They want us to do it."

Helmut glanced at his watch. "I'll take a run out there."

Asmundson nodded.

"Put your siren on before you drive in," someone called from the main office.

Helmut nodded as he pulled on his jacket and gloves, then left the detachment.

Not exactly sure about the location of Mike's farm, the constable drove to Faulkner then pulled over to the side of the road. He stepped out of the cruiser when he saw a tractor approaching. It was late November and the temperate fall days of October were long past. A cold wind whipped his face as he stared up the road. He stood waiting until the tractor came to a full stop beside him. The farmer, dressed in a snowmobile suit, was hauling hay from a field to his nearby farm. He shut off the tractor's engine.

"Hi Helmut, how are you?" he asked as the officer approached.

"Fine," Helmut said as he glanced up and down the road. "Can you give me directions to Mike Kalanza's farm?"

"What did Mike do now?" the farmer asked.

"Nobody's seen him for a few days so we're checking on him," the officer explained.

The farmer pointed Helmut in the right direction—he was close, only one road back and a few miles to travel before he'd be there.

"Not familiar with this back country," Helmut laughed. "You farmers are pretty honest—no need to visit here very often."

The farmer laughed. "Either that or we just never get caught!"

Helmut chuckled.

"I'd be careful though if you're going to Mike's," the farmer said. "People are saying that he's been acting pretty crazy, shooting at anyone who drives by."

"Think it's true?" Helmut asked.

"I don't know, that's just what I heard," the man said. "You know how people talk."

"Yeah, but by the sounds of it Mike shoots first and asks questions later," Helmut said.

The farmer nodded. "In that case, you can't be too careful."

The men waved to each other as the farmer restarted his tractor. Helmut got back into the cruiser, doubled back and was soon on the road to Mike's farm.

Helmut turned on the siren as he drove into the yard. There was a two-inch thick blanket of snow on the ground. Cautiously, he got out of his car and noted there were no tire tracks in the driveway. He glanced up. There was no smoke coming from the chimney either.

As he approached the house, he saw no footprints around either it or the car parked nearby.

"What the heck . . ," he said as he knocked on the door. Nobody answered. He knocked again, this time harder. Still no answer. He turned the doorknob and wasn't surprised to discover the door was locked. He moved away from it and scanned the yard. He noticed Mike's old truck parked beside a huge piece of equipment partially covered by a tarp. The truck had two inches of snow on its roof as well.

He's either gone somewhere and not told anyone, the officer thought, *or else he's dead inside.*

Helmut started walking around the house, careful not to catch his boots in the pieces of scrap iron sitting beside the foundation. It occurred to him that the junk could have been piled there to deny burglars access to the windows.

"Why doesn't he just get a dog?" Helmut mused as he peered in a window. He couldn't see anything through the small crack in an old curtain hanging the full length of the window.

"Okay, I'll try the next one," he muttered to himself as he clambered out of the pile and walked to another window.

Stepping on what looked like a rusted bed frame, he cupped his hands as he peered in. This time he could see inside, but his view was limited by thick plastic stapled inside to keep cold air from seeping through the poorly insulated frame. Inside, the house appeared to be in shambles. He wasn't sure which room he was looking into, but there were piles of junk all over the floor, tables and chairs. Through a doorway, he could see more piles in the next room as well.

Helmut looked at the window frame which was worn and unpainted except for a few peeled splinters of white—or was it light green?

He climbed down and circled the house, looking for another window. An old fridge was lying beside Mike's woodpile near the house to stabilize the pile. Neatly cut and split, three-foot lengths were piled chest high. The tidy pile was in stark contrast to everything else in the yard.

Helmut shook his head. He wasn't surprised that the old man was a bachelor. He thought of his own wife, Rosana—organized and fastidious. She and any woman remotely like her would never tolerate a mess like this.

He pulled a few pieces of wood from the pile and stacked them under the window.

Helmut was already thinking out the procedure he'd have to follow next. If he suspected that Mike had died in the house, he'd have to go back to Ashern for another officer and a warrant. He wouldn't want to go inside without someone present. He'd heard rumours that Mike had money stashed in his house. The last thing he needed was a story going around that he'd helped himself to some of Mike's cash.

He stepped carefully on top of the wood and when he had his balance, cupped his hands to the sides of his head and pressed his face against the window glass.

"Aaaah!" Helmut screamed as he jolted back from the window, slipping off the wood. Someone on the other side was staring right back at him. He looked up to see Mike standing there grinning.

Bent over, hands on his knees, Helmut turned away as he tried to catch his breath.

"For Pete's sake, Mike!" he yelled. "What are you tryin' to do to me anyway?"

Not long afterwards Helmut heard the front door open. By then, he'd regained his composure and walked around to the door.

Mike was standing there smiling.

"How come you didn't answer the door?" Helmut demanded.

"Because I didn't want to," Mike said. "There's no law that says I have to open my door—not to you, not to anyone."

Helmut groaned. "Maybe not, but I was sent out here to check on you because nobody's seen you around. The least you could do is not lead me on like that."

Mike laughed.

"How long you been holed up in there, anyway?" Helmut asked.

Mike shrugged. "I don't know. Does it matter?"

"No," the constable said, "but how are you keeping warm?"

"My stove. I got a wood stove."

"How come it's not going?" Helmut asked, pointing to the roof. "No smoke."

"Oh, well it takes a lot of wood, so I only fire it up when it gets really cold."

"It's pretty cold, I'd say."

"Yeah, well that's my business."

Helmut nodded. "I guess it is."

"So have you caught those guys who've been stealing from me?" Mike asked. "See that Cat over there? Somebody stole the transmission out of it, so now it doesn't run. How am I gonna make any money if it doesn't run?"

Helmut waved him off as he started back toward his car.

"See you later Mike," he said, obviously annoyed at the old man. "Glad to see you're still with us."

Mike stared at him as Helmut backed out the driveway.

Chapter 24

"ARE YOU READY NOW?" McMillan asked. "We've gone through your background and I'm confident that you're both physically and mentally capable of taking this test. We went through all the trigger questions and we've reviewed what I'll be asking you during the test."

David nodded.

"Are you comfortable with all the questions I'm going to ask you?"

David thought for a moment, then nodded.

"Come with me then," the officer said as he got up from the table.

David followed him into an adjoining room. It was a converted cell, painted off-white. There was a table with a small computer on top and two chairs sitting on either side of the table.

"It looks like a goddamned execution room," David muttered.

"I apologize for the decor," McMillan said. "Unfortunately, it's a small detachment and this is the only available room."

David snorted.

"This is the polygraph machine here," the officer said, pointing at the apparatus on the table.

"That's a computer."

"Yes, everything is computerized now."

"I wasn't ex-pecting a computer. I thought it would be like a big box with a paper runnin' down one side."

"That's what everybody thinks," McMillan said. "Actually, these machines have come a long way since they were first invented."

"Well, I heard they aren't too ac-curate," David chided.

"The testing is 95 percent accurate," he said. "Polygraphs got a bad rap in the U.S. during the 1970s and misconceptions about these machines have been perpetuated in movies. We've come a long way since then. It's quite a precise machine and the staff who operate it are all uniformly trained. Our performance as testers is monitored as well."

They stood looking at the computer for a moment. It was connected by cable to a metal box sitting on the table. A number of wires were attached to the box.

"You can sit down over there," McMillan said, pointing to one of the chairs beside the table.

"What about the other five percent?" David asked as he carefully sat on the chair.

"Pardon?"

"You said it's 95 percent ac-curate. What about the other five percent?"

"That percent represents the tests scored 'inconclusive.'"

"Incon-clusive?" David stammered.

"Yes," McMillan said. "Those are the tests that come back inconclusive if we can't call them either way. It only happens five percent of the time."

"What causes that?" David asked.

"Well, if the question formulation isn't clear enough, or if a person is ill or physiologically out of whack. That way we don't call innocent people guilty or the other way around."

David sat quietly for a moment, not sure how this might affect him.

McMillan could sense his apprehension.

"In other words, we have to be sure," he said.

David nodded.

"What are the chances I'm g-gonna leave here and people will say I beat the polygraph because I'm such a good liar?" David demanded.

"People may say that," McMillan said, "but they won't be right."

"What about people who fool the machine?" David asked.

"David, very few people, and I mean very few, can do it," the officer said. "Can you control involuntary responses like your heart rate and blood pressure?"

David shook his head no.

"To do it a person would have to study and practise and have access to a machine—you don't have that do you?"

"No," David answered. "But what about guys who have no conscience?"

"Everyone asks that," McMillan smiled. "A person without a conscience isn't going to beat the polygraph either. They still know they committed the crime and while they may have no remorse, they are still worried about being caught."

David seemed to understand.

"The criminally insane . . . maybe," the officer said. "But I've already determined that you are perfectly sane.

David chuckled.

"Now, what I need to do is place this chain around your waist," McMillan said once all the explaining was finished. "Please hold your arms up."

David raised his arms while McMillan fastened the chain around his diaphragm.

"This one has to go across your chest just under your arms," the officer said. "Hold your arms straight out."

David complied. McMillan fastened the chain and then told him to relax his arms once again.

Lifting up two metal sensors, he slipped one over David's index finger and the other on the ring finger of his right hand.

"This monitors your galvanic skin response," he said.

"Like in the hospital," David offered.

"No that records your pulse. This monitors your sweat gland activity."

David felt his forehead prickle at the hairline. He was warm. What if he sweated during the test? What would happen then?

"Okay now, move your left arm out from your body," McMillan said as he lifted up a nylon cuff.

"I need to put this around your arm as if I was taking your blood pressure," he said. "But you need to hold it away from your chest."

David nodded.

McMillan slipped on the cuff and inflated it so that David could feel the pressure of his heart pumping blood through the veins in his arm.

McMillan sat down and began typing something into the computer.

"Are you comfortable?" the officer asked.

"Not really," David said. "This chair is too high."

McMillan apologized for the chair height but said there was nothing they could do about it.

"Are you ready?" he asked, keeping his eyes on the computer screen.

David nodded.

"All right then," he said, "let's get started."

David and Lynne were married May 30, 1985, in her living room. They'd said beforehand that they wanted a simple wedding and everyone seemed to understand their desire for a quiet ceremony. The only witnesses were attendants Ken Price and Lynne's daughter Sherry. Jalmar arrived at the house in the hearse to officiate at the marriage. They joked that he was going to either "marry or bury" them.

When the ceremony was over, David and Lynne drove to Caroline's house. She was thrilled by the news and welcomed her new daughter-in-law with a hug.

That summer they continued building the log house that David had started. They decided to put Lynne's house up for sale. When it sold, they rented an older house in Moosehorn, just a few blocks from where they were building. This created a short commute for Lynne to the dentist's office, but it made working on the house much more convenient for David. They bought building supplies with the small amount of equity Lynne had acquired in her house. David worked a lot of overtime at the plant for extra cash. They bought and built as they could afford.

Lynne never did see the supposed nasty side of David with the exception of yelling when he'd lose his temper. Sometimes he said things she knew he didn't mean. She blamed this on the difficulties he had expressing himself. He treated his sons well and her teenage children adored him. David was always ready to joke and fool around.

One afternoon late that summer, an elderly neighbour asked David if he would re-roof his house. The job would take a full week and while David knew he had other things to do, he agreed.

David came home and Lynne noticed right away that something was bothering him.

"What's wrong?" she asked.

"Well, I was asked to do a job in town."

"I hope you said no," she said.

"Not really," he hesitated. "I said I'd go."

Lynne sat quietly for a moment.

"David," she sighed, "how are we ever going to get the house finished if you use your holidays to help everyone else?"

"Don't worry, Lynne, we'll get it done," he said. "What was I gonna say?"

"How about 'no,'" she said.

"I can't do that," he said. "You know me."

"Yeah, I know you all right. I swear that you and your brother

Walter are the two most generous people I've ever met," she laughed. "You'll go work for others, usually for free, before you'll take care of yourself."

David laughed. His blue eyes danced as he looked at her.

"Us an' Dad. Everyone says he was the same way."

In the early morning hours of November 1, a vehicle with its lights off drove slowly up to the house David and Lynne were renting. When the engine was turned off three men quietly got out of the vehicle and gingerly closed the doors. They had worked out a plan beforehand and without a sound, crept into the yard.

When David and Lynne got up the next morning they looked out the window to find an outhouse in the back of David's truck. The pranksters had somehow loaded it from the site where David was building the new house into the truck box while David and Lynne slept.

"Well, Lynne, it's official," David laughed. "We're now full-fledged members of Moosehorn."

"Who did that?" she exclaimed.

"Probably Michael or Kenny," he said. "Or maybe both. But I know one thing for sure—it wasn't Tobe. He doesn't go near them things no more."

"Now what are we going to do?" she laughed. "How are we gonna get it off the truck?"

David laughed. "I guess that's our problem."

"We got another call to go check on Mike Kalanza," Sergeant Asmundson said as he stepped out of his office one late afternoon. "Who wants to go?"

"What's up now?" Helmut asked.

Asmundson looked at a sheet of paper he was holding. "A woman named . . . Margaret Shiells from Steep Rock called earlier. She said she's concerned about Mike because he was supposed to meet her Monday in Steep Rock. Apparently she's his neighbour in town and someone came out from the city to see Mike's house which is for sale. But he never showed up."

Helmut glanced at the calendar. It was Wednesday, November 13.

"Maybe he forgot," somebody suggested.

"Mike?" Helmut exclaimed. "Not a chance. The opportunity to sell something and forget? I don't think so."

Asmundson continued. "She sent her husband Herb down there to check on him and he came back saying there was nobody around.

Mike's car is parked by the house but everything is quiet."

"Probably locked himself in again," Helmut mused.

"I don't know," Asmundson said. "But we better check it out. I'll come with you."

"All right," Helmut said. "I'll go—but he'd better not freak me out again."

Everyone chuckled as the officers pulled on their jackets and left the office.

They drove to Faulkner and just like his last visit, Helmut turned on the siren before entering the driveway. Like the year before, there was a fresh blanket of snow covering the ground and everything in the yard. They noticed one set of tire tracks that went only half way in and then back out.

"Those must be Herb Shiells' tracks," Asmundson said.

They parked the car and got out. As before, there was no evidence of anyone around. The yard looked almost exactly the same as it had the fall before, except that the vehicles were sitting in slightly different spots. They went to the door and saw that this time it was padlocked.

"That's odd," the sergeant said. He tried the knob, then knocked.

"Mike, you in there?" he hollered. "It's Sergeant Asmundson."

There was no answer.

He glanced at Helmut.

"Mike!" he called again as he hammered on the door. "If you're in there, open up."

Still no answer.

"Hmmm," he said. The officers backed away from the door to survey the house.

"Over here," Helmut said as he rounded the corner so that he could look in the same window where Mike had stared back at him a year earlier. Half expecting the old man to be standing at the window grinning, Helmut was surprised when Mike's face did not appear. He approached the window and stood on something so that he could peer in, but saw nothing this time.

"Huh," he said. "No Mike."

Helmut went to the edge of the bush while Asmundson checked Mike's car. The 1976 Pontiac sat with the block heater plugged into an outdoor outlet. The trunk was open and something that looked like a stove pipe was sticking out. The keys were not in the ignition.

"Hmmm," Asmundson muttered, brow furrowed. He listened as Helmut called Mike's name over and over again into the dense outcroppings of bush that surrounded the property.

Helmut returned a few minutes later. "Nothing around any of the buildings," he reported. "No tracks, no sign of anything."

They walked around the house again and Helmet noticed the old fridge still sitting where it had been the year before. They looked at one another.

"You don't think?" Helmut said.

They moved closer and the constable reached out and slowly opened the door. There was movement inside—a dark brown mass was on top of something in the fridge. He lifted the lid higher and both men peered inside.

"Gees!" Helmut hollered as he jumped back letting go of the fridge door.

"Rats! Did you see that?" he exclaimed as his body shook. "I've never seen so many rats in all my life."

They opened the door again. They saw that the freezer had been a makeshift grain bin and that the rats had somehow gotten inside and eaten half the grain.

"I swear, Mike Kalanza's gonna be the death of me!" Helmut said.

Asmundson chuckled, then his mood turned serious.

"Well, what do you think?"

"I don't know," Helmut answered. "It'll be dark soon."

The sergeant nodded. "First we have to be sure that he isn't just visiting a relative. I put in a call to his sister before we left. Hopefully, the office will have heard from her by the time we get back."

"There's not much we can do alone," Helmut said, glancing at the bush. "Where would we start?"

"I know," Asmundson said thoughtfully as he stared at the sun which was low in the sky. A glance at his watch told him they had only an hour of daylight left. "There's not much more we can do right now."

They decided to return to the detachment office.

"Well, what do we know?" Helmut asked once they were driving south.

"We know that he isn't at either house," Asmundson said. "He could be visiting someone, but both vehicles are at Faulkner."

"Maybe a family member picked him up?" Helmut pondered. "But that would be a bit unusual for the old man. Mike's pretty independent."

The sergeant nodded. "And why would he go somewhere when he had an appointment that could have led to the sale of his old house?"

The men sat quietly for the rest of the drive to town.

The officers returned to the office and reported what they'd found—or rather didn't find—at the Kalanza farm.

A message to call Mike's sister was waiting for them. The sergeant emerged from his office a few minutes later saying that she didn't know where Mike was. A call was made to Mike's brother, but he hadn't heard from the missing man in weeks. A few neighbours were also contacted but nobody had seen him for days.

"Let's get a warrant," Asmundson said, turning back into his office.

"And we're going to need bolt cutters," Helmut added grimly.

The next morning the officers returned to the farm. Everything appeared as it was the evening before. When they got out of the police cruiser, the sergeant walked to the house while Helmut surveyed the yard and made notes as he went.

They cut the padlock and wiggled it off the rusted hinge. They glanced at one another as they pushed open the door. Instinctively, the first thing they did was sniff the air.

"Well that's a relief," one of them said and the other agreed.

The odour in Mike's house was from his ancient belongings—the musty smell of miscellaneous junk all cluttered in one place.

There was a faint smell of garbage in the messy porch, a combination of coffee grounds, orange peels and wet paper. What they'd anticipated was the smell of rotting flesh. Temperatures had been below zero for the past week, but they weren't sure whether it was cold enough to freeze a body to the point it wouldn't decompose. Fortunately, there was no such smell.

"Mike!" Asmundson called. "It's the RCMP."

They listened for a moment but received no reply.

They walked into the kitchen and were shocked by the amount of junk in Mike's house. They followed a narrow trail through it as they moved from room to room, encountering piles of odds and ends that established without doubt that Mike was a "pack rat."

"He's not here," Asmundson said, hands resting on his hips and looking around.

"Now what?" Helmut asked.

"Well," Asmundson said, distracted, "I can't believe all this stuff . . ."

Asmundson radioed the Ashern detachment, instructing the remaining on-duty officers to join the investigation. They arrived within an hour. Helmut worked with Asmundson who was searching the house for signs of foul play.

By mid-morning, Mike's youngest brother Nick Kolansky arrived at the farm. In his late 50s, Nick was the opposite of his brother in many ways. More than one eyebrow was raised as he stepped out of his newer-model car and introduced himself.

A successful businessman in Portage la Prairie, Nick was well-dressed and soft spoken. While both he and his brother were short, stocky and forthright, the similarities ended there. Mike could be brash and rude while Nick was well-spoken and diplomatic. Obviously concerned about his brother's whereabouts, Nick offered to help in whatever way he could. He was pointed in the direction of the house where the sergeant and Helmut were searching for clues.

"Hello," Nick called out as he stepped into the house. He glanced around and then went into the kitchen where the two officers were comparing notes.

"I'm Nick Kolansky—Mike's brother."

The officers shook hands with him.

"No sign of him yet?" Nick asked as he scanned the kitchen.

"No," Asmundson said.

"What can I do to help?" he asked.

"Well," Helmut said, "you can help us figure out if anything is out of place."

"I know," Nick said, obviously embarrassed, "Mike wasn't the neatest guy there ever was."

They looked around as if not sure where to start.

Nick stood for a few minutes surveying the kitchen.

"Well you know," he began, "the first thing I noticed when I came in is that the floor here looks tidier than usual."

The officers sighed. The house was so cramped, the only area where the floor was visible was the kitchen. It was obvious that Mike spent most of his time there.

"Anything else?" Asmundson asked.

Nick looked around. "I don't know," he said, walking toward the kitchen table. A grocery bag sat on top. Carefully, he opened it and looked in. It contained fruit and a few other items.

"Well, I'd guess that he came home recently and got into the house because it looks like he brought this in," Nick said.

"No grocery stores would have been open on Sunday," one of the officers said absentmindedly. "Would he shop at a convenience store?"

Nick nodded. "Maybe. If there was something he wanted he would. Mike has diabetes, you know, and he needs to eat certain foods to keep his blood sugar right."

"What about his health otherwise?" Asmundson asked.

"Fine, I think," Nick said, "but he has a clogged artery in his leg that is quite painful at times."

"Anything else we need to know about him?" the officer asked.

"Well, Mike was missing part of one finger," he said.

"Which one?"

"Let's see, the baby finger on his right hand, at the top joint," Nick said. "He lost it in an accident at work."

Just then another officer walked in to update Asmundson on what was happening outside. When the man left, they continued to search around the kitchen and discovered a continuous roll of towel of the type commonly found in restrooms. It had been discarded in an old pail.

"Does this mean anything?" Nick asked, pointing at the roll sitting in the half-full pail of water.

Helmut bent to examine it. "I don't know . . ."

They looked around the house a little longer.

"Mike was rumoured to have a lot of money," Asmundson said, trying to be tactful. "Do you know much about his finances?"

"Mike didn't have a lot of money," Nick stated.

"But a rumour went around that he won the lottery," Asmundson said.

"I never heard that, but I doubt it," Nick said. "Mike liked to flash his money, and he always carried up to $1,000 on him, but as for having a big stash somewhere, I really doubt it."

"If he did have any money, where would it be?" the sergeant said.

"In the bank," Nick said.

The officers stared at him.

"We were all under the impression that Mike doesn't like banks," Asmundson said.

Nick shook his head. "He complained and watched things carefully, but he operated pretty much like most of us. He deposited money in the bank and got loans just like everyone else."

The officers looked at one another.

"Like when he bought this place," Nick added. "He got a loan from the bank in Portage—I went with him."

"How much money do you think he had?" Asmundson asked.

"I don't know," Nick shrugged. "It's not something you ask your brother. I do know that he got $40,000 from the Cooks when they bought Elm Point from him. And he had savings bonds from Canada Cement."

"If he did have any cash, bonds or papers in the house, do you know where he would keep them?" Asmundson asked.

Nick thought for a moment. "Maybe downstairs?"

They searched the basement but found nothing.

"Oh yes, he did tell me once that he kept important things like that in the freezer," Nick recalled. "He did have some money in there, I'm sure of it, but how much I really don't know."

The men opened the freezer door and dug around inside. They found a plastic bag containing the Canada Cement bonds.

"That's it?" one of the officers asked.

"Looks like it," Nick said.

Helmut appeared from a bedroom carrying a gun in each hand.

"I've counted eight so far," he said. "At least that's all I've found."

The sergeant motioned for Helmut to put the weapons on the table. "Loaded?" Asmundson asked.

Helmut shook his head no.

Asmundson checked to see if either had been recently fired. As Helmut added more guns to the collection, the sergeant checked each one.

"Look at this," he said, turning over a .22 calibre rifle. An RCMP sticker indicated the gun had been a piece of evidence in an investigation.

"Oh yes," Nick said as the officers paused to look at the sticker. "That gun was used to kill a man."

"Pardon?" Asmundson queried.

"Back in 1973 I think it was," Nick explained. "A guy named . . . Goodall was the one who did it."

"I heard about that," Helmut piped up as he searched the living room.

Asmundson scowled. The story was beginning to sound familiar to him as well.

"Found another one," Helmut called out as he emerged from the living room.

"Where was that one?" Asmundson asked.

"Under the couch cushion," he replied.

The men chuckled.

The officers retrieved nine guns in total. The search continued into the late afternoon until the door opened and another officer came inside.

"No luck," he announced. "Nothing in the bush that we found."

Asmundson frowned then looked back at the guns on the table.

"All right, let's lock this place up and come back out tomorrow morning," he said.

That night when he returned to the office, Asmundson reviewed his notes. The only snow that came that fall arrived on November 11. Nearly two inches fell, covering any evidence that could have led them to Mike. What it did give police was a time frame. They knew that he had disappeared between the time he was last seen—the evening of November 10, after a Jehovah's Witness meeting—and the morning of November 11 before the snow arrived.

Temperatures that week hovered around minus six degrees Celsius during the day, and dipped to minus 15 at night. As tough as Mike pretended to be, everyone knew that the odds were slim of an elderly man surviving a week alone in the bush, especially if he were sick or injured.

Asmundson pulled a few files from his cabinet and made a phone call. He decided to check on the whereabouts of Thomas Goodall.

Word spread quickly through the community that old Mike was missing. Early the next morning the police, a tracking dog unit, and volunteers assembled at Mike's farm to conduct a mass search of the area.

David was at work on Friday when he heard the news that Mike had disappeared. Someone said that police were searching the area around Mike's farm with trained police dogs. Volunteers from Faulkner and Steep Rock were scouring the nearby bush.

"They think maybe he wandered off," a co-worker said.

David frowned. He didn't think it was likely that Mike had wandered anywhere. But he did believe it was entirely possible that the old man had gone hunting or accidentally shot himself with one of the handguns he liked to carry.

Maybe he was foraging around one of the dumps and was lying there injured after an accident. If that was the case, someone would find him soon.

David's mother had warned him as a child to stay out of the bog that separated the Kolodka and Makowski properties. David wondered if Mike was stuck in there. It also occurred to him that someone might have robbed and killed the old man. But he laughed off that idea—after all, things like that only happened in movies. Besides, who from the area would do such a thing?

Dwight Cook finished his morning chores and came into the house. He and his wife were planning to go to town. Their preparations were interrupted by a phone call from the police. Had he or his dad seen

Mike Kalanza lately? Dwight said that no, he hadn't, and was told that the old man was missing. The suspicions were that Mike might have wandered off, become disoriented, and possibly died from exposure.

Dwight hung up the phone. He didn't think so.

He glanced out the window.

When was the last time he'd seen or heard from Mike? He recalled seeing the man during the summer. They'd stopped to talk on the street and Mike had complained about the amount of income tax he had to pay that year.

He'd shown Dwight his bank book. There had been a deposit of \$40,000 and Dwight presumed it was the cheque Mike had received when Dwight purchased Elm Point from him the year before. There was also a withdrawal of approximately \$3,000 which Mike said was his tax bill for the year.

Mike had been annoyed that day about giving so much money to the government. But Dwight recalled him as being mentally fit—eccentric, but certainly not senile. Dwight couldn't imagine Mike wandering off. Getting lost? Possibly. But Mike had never had an aimless moment in his life.

No, the time he saw Mike in town wasn't the last he'd heard of their old friend, he thought.

In the early fall Mike had approached Dwight's father Fred and asked for help in harvesting his grain crop. Fred had agreed and the two older men spent the day working together in the field. It was a chance to partially repay Mike for his earlier generosity. Two decades before, Fred's house had burned down and Mike refused payment for drilling Fred a new well.

A hunting accident, Dwight thought to himself. *Or was he out in the bush and maybe had a heart attack or stroke.*

That night during the blessing of their evening meal, the Cook family said a special prayer for Mike—asking for his safe return home.

"You're kidding?" Lorne Park said as he drank his morning coffee in the Texaco coffee shop. "Mike's missing?"

"That's what we heard," another customer said.

"Are they sure?" Lorne asked. "You know Mike, maybe he's at his place in Steep Rock."

"Nope, they already checked there," said the customer.

"Hmmmm," Lorne said, taking another sip. "That's strange. I just saw him a few weeks ago. He was in complaining about his hydro bill again."

"Oh yeah?"

"Yeah. What do they think happened to him?" Lorne asked.

"That maybe he fell down an old well," the coffee drinker said.

"Not a chance," Lorne said, shaking his head. "He drilled all the wells in the area. Mike may have been odd, but he was no dummy. He'd never fall down a well that he'd dug."

His listener shrugged.

"Who's searching?" Lorne asked.

"Everybody," the man said. "A bunch of people from Faulkner and Steep Rock and the police. I heard his brother and sons are out there too."

"Do they need any more searchers?" Lorne asked.

"Maybe."

Lorne hurried from the coffee shop and went to the hydro office. He called a friend, a local pilot who owned his own plane. The friend was always quick to offer assistance in cases like this where an overhead view could throw a whole new perspective on a search. Lorne and his friend flew to the search area, spending most of the day scouring Mike's land and surrounding fields from the sky, but saw nothing. They had a helpless feeling, but at least they were doing something.

"So what do you think happened to him?" the pilot asked as he flew as low and slow as he dared.

"I don't know," Lorne frowned.

He'd heard all the rumours about Mike and wondered if anyone in the community was capable of robbing and killing him. He shook the thought away. It occurred to him that Mike might have told people he'd won the lottery after believing he'd been cheated at the Texaco station two years earlier. That sounded like something Mike would do. Maybe that's how the rumour started.

"Whatever happened, it doesn't look good," Lorne said.

A group of search and rescue specialists, 18 in all, were dispatched from CFB Gypsumville to conduct a three-day, shoulder-to-shoulder search of Mike's property and the surrounding area. RCMP officers returned to the Kalanza house each day for the next week. They continued to scour the premises for clues that could lead to Mike's whereabouts. After following numerous leads for two solid weeks, all which led nowhere, police announced that the formal search for Mike Kalanza had come to an end.

The RCMP had their suspicions of foul play but they kept their theory carefully hidden. With a lack of any physical evidence and no body, all the police had was a missing person.

Everyone who thought they knew Mike Kalanza had a theory about what might have happened to him. Some thought that Mike had died in the bush and the searchers had missed the body.

There was a possibility that he'd shot at someone and they'd fired back. Or maybe he'd gone out on the thin ice and fallen through. Some people suggested that he'd left on a trip—like his father Onufry had when he'd retired from Canada Cement. Perhaps Mike was sitting on a beach in Hawaii laughing at everyone.

People said that Thomas Goodall had vowed to get even with Mike after he assisted the police during the 1973-1974 murder trial. But Asmundson had checked that out and discovered that Goodall was in jail when Mike disappeared.

There were a few lingering thoughts that Mike may have become the victim of a self-fulfilling prophecy: afraid of being robbed but still spreading the belief that he was wealthy. People could think of no other motive for someone to kill Mike—if he'd been killed at all.

Within a few weeks, the furor and speculation over Mike's disappearance subsided and life returned to normal. To most people, Mike was an eccentric old hermit who was feared by some and avoided by many.

For members of the Kolansky family, however, Mike was their older brother who'd provided leadership and stability during difficult times. Understanding and accepting his idiosyncrasies they grieved over his disappearance.

People in the area liked to speculate about Mike's relationship with his sons, but both Nick and Ted showed genuine concern about the disappearance of their father. Both men were private individuals who spoke little about their childhoods. If there was any animosity between themselves and their father, it didn't show.

For the first few months, Mike's family members awoke each morning wondering if his body would be found that day. They doubted he'd be found alive, but hoped that his remains would be recovered so they could give him a decent burial. Mike had lived a somewhat colourful but honest life and they felt he deserved whatever respect could be salvaged from his equally colourful, albeit unsolved, death.

Then one day the phone rang at Mike's sister's house.

"Where's Mike?" a voice said.

At first she thought it was someone looking for her brother, someone who didn't know that he'd disappeared. Surprised, she didn't know what to say. Then the caller said it again. This time the question was accompanied by a teenage giggle before the caller hung up.

It took a few minutes before she realized the implications of the phone call and was gripped by fear. Her heart began to quicken and her hands started to shake. She wanted to call her brother Nick, but her mind went blank and she couldn't remember his number. She had to sit down.

Mike's sister stared at the floor and suddenly felt overwhelmed. She wanted to lock all the windows and doors, but sat there paralyzed instead.

Few people knew her maiden name.

She had an unlisted phone number.

But Mike had it written on a slip of paper in his wallet.

Chapter 25

"FIRST I'M GOING TO GO through a card test with you, and I want you to pick a card and memorize the number," McMillan said, holding out eight cards, face down.

David chose a card and looked at it.

"Put it under your hand, don't show me what it is."

David obeyed.

"Now, I want you to look at that dot on the wall," McMillan said, pointing to a speck on the white wall over his left shoulder. "Do you see it?"

David nodded that he did.

"When the questioning begins, I want you to close your eyes and keep them closed for the duration," the officer said. "Do you understand?"

"Y-yes."

"Okay, now I'm going to ask you some numbers and when I get to the number on the card you picked, I want you to lie," he said.

"You want me to lie?" David asked, shocked. "What the hell? I'm not g-gonna do that."

"But you have . . ." McMillan began.

David interrupted. "No g-goddamned way am I g-gonna lie. If I do, then you're g-gonna say I'm a liar, aren't you?"

By this time McMillan was exasperated. It had been a long, difficult evening and now it looked as if David was going to stop co-operating.

"I need to see your reaction when you lie on the computer screen," the officer explained. "Everyone is different. You have to lie so I can interpret your answers to the remainder of the questions properly.

David scowled at him.

It took the officer some time, but he finally convinced David to tell the lie.

"Okay," he said warily. "But re-member, you told me to."

"Don't worry. This is how we begin all tests."

David nodded.

"Are you ready?" McMillan asked.

David nodded that he was.

"Are you sure?" McMillan asked again.

"I'm s-sure." David could feel the heavy pounding of his heart in his chest. He was beginning to sweat and wondered if the machine would interpret this as a sign of dishonesty.

"David?" McMillan said.

"Yes?"

"Please look straight ahead at the dot then close your eyes. And try not to fidget."

David did as he was told. He stared at the dot then closed his eyes.

"Now I'm going to ask you the number questions, are you ready?"

"Y-yes."

"The card you picked, was it number 3?"

"No."

"Number 5?"

"No."

"Number 8?"

"No."

"Number 7?"

"No."

"Number 2?"

"No."

"Number 6?"

"No."

"Number 1?"

"No."

"Number 4?"

"No."

"All right, that's all," McMillan said. "You can open your eyes."

David did.

McMillan looked up from the screen.

"It was number 6, wasn't it?" he asked.

David was surprised. The machine was right.

"So are you comfortable beginning the test now?" McMillan asked.

David nodded. "Okay, let's go."

David tried to relax as McMillan studied the screen.

"Please close your eyes and we'll begin," McMillan instructed. "Here we go."

"Do you live in Canada?" he asked slowly and clearly.

"Yes."

"Are you presently in Manitoba?"

"Yes."

"Did you kill Mike Kalanza?"

David hesitated. The words were still shocking, and he tried not to react. His heart leapt the same way it had when he lied about number six. He thought about the question again.

Did I kill Mike Kalanza?

"No," he said firmly.

The crank calls to Mike's sister continued periodically for the next two years. Occasionally, Gus Breitkreitz would phone the Ashern detachment to check on the police investigation into his friend's disappearance. But other than that, everyone else seemed to forget about old Mike.

Constable McAfee left the Ashern detachment in 1987 and was replaced by Constable Ernie Arns. One of the first things Sergeant Asmundson did upon Arns' arrival, was update him about ongoing investigations. One afternoon the pair took a drive out to the Kalanza farm.

"How did he live in here?" Ernie asked as he stood in the doorway of the ramshackle house. The strapping young officer bent his six-foot, four-inch frame as he ducked through the doorway. The soft floor of the old house creaked under the officer's weight.

"It's quite the place," Asmundson replied.

Ernie made his way through the trails behind Asmundson.

"Well, if there was foul play and robbery was the motive, they left behind a lot of valuable stuff," Ernie said, making note of the numerous antiques and collectables scattered through the house.

Together they went through the house again, still searching for clues and hoping that a pair of fresh eyes might pick up something they'd previously missed.

Soon afterwards, a sale was held at the Faulkner farm and Mike's assets were auctioned off. The house in Steep Rock was also sold while the Faulkner house and land were bought in 1989 by a neighbouring farm family.

The house was bulldozed and the other buildings in the yard were either carted away or destroyed. All that was left standing was the outhouse. Proceeds from the sale of Mike's assets were to be held in trust until he was declared legally dead.

In the spring of 1987, David and Lynne were invited to a house party at Caroline's. Although she never celebrated birthdays because it was against the Jehovah's Witness' beliefs, she did acknowledge important milestones and found reasons to bring her family together. Caroline admitted she was looking forward to her 65th birthday in September and eagerly awaited her old age pension cheque.

That evening everyone had a really good time. Eunice and her mother had often been at odds with one another, but their arguments had decreased in intensity over the years. Rose and Caroline had always gotten along well. And while Rose had had a few difficult years after she left the farm, she seemed to be coping better now than she ever had before. This pleased Caroline who by this time had quietly told her children that it was up to them to come to terms with their pasts.

Caroline was in a particularly good mood, and on this evening she ate and drank whatever she wanted. The children chastised her a bit for indulging in food that she shouldn't eat. Her diabetes had been acting up a bit lately, but she brushed off their protests saying she was a big girl who could take care of herself.

The next morning, however, she called David to say she wasn't feeling well. David and Dennis both went to the house and took her to the hospital emergency room. She was examined by a physician who said she'd likely overdone it the night before. He advised a good rest.

The twins took her home and Caroline went straight to bed. Lynne stayed with her for a while and the brothers went home.

The following morning Lynne received a phone call at work from Rose. She said that she'd called Caroline's and Kathy had answered—saying her mother was still asleep.

Lynne glanced at her watch. It was 11 a.m. Caroline wasn't a person to sleep in. She immediately called Mel who was able to leave work and go check on his mother-in-law. He phoned Lynne back within the hour to say that Caroline was dead. The doctor concluded that she'd died in her sleep of a massive heart attack.

Word of her death sent David into an emotional tailspin. He remembered the look on her face when she'd stepped into his new house. She'd been proud that he'd built such a lovely home.

As critical as he'd been of her earlier failure to face family problems, he also deeply loved his mother. He drove from work to Ashern in a daze, not believing what he'd heard. He remembered his childhood days when his mother would lie in bed in a deep depression. He'd thought she might die then and the fear he'd felt as a child resurfaced. The forebodings of doom and failure all came rushing back. At 39, David had lost his mother.

What am I gonna do without Mom? he asked himself over and over again.

In the next few days, funeral arrangements were made from David's home. All the children gathered, including Stephen, Raymond and Jennie. Everyone was visibly shaken by her sudden passing. The grandchildren who were old enough to understand the finality of death were devastated.

Caroline's funeral was held at the Kingdom Hall in Ashern. Unlike Domko's funeral, the kind words about Caroline rang true. As David sat and listened to the eulogy, surrounded by all his siblings, he understood the reasons for his mother's behaviour.

Yes, Caroline had made some mistakes, but David concluded that his mother really had little choice. She hadn't been a bad person, but had been stuck in a quagmire of poverty and despair. She never explained to him why she had tolerated Domko's behaviour, leaving those questions unanswered. There was no closure to the memories that remained.

David's last memory of his mother was that she looked peaceful. He was relieved to see that she didn't have the same look in death as Domko had. Her cheeks were a dusty pink and the ends of her mouth turned up slightly. She looked like she was sleeping and experiencing a pleasant dream.

David and Lynne hosted the funeral lunch at their home. For some of the guests, it was the first time they'd been in the new house. David was surprised when old Gus Breitkreitz walked in. They nodded politely to one another. Gus was friendly and pleasant and it appeared old resentments were forgotten.

Caroline's estate was settled and her personal items were shared among family members. David took a pair of his mother's rubber boots—short, duckie-style lined boots she often wore. The family decided that Kathy would stay in the house to avoid disrupting her routine. This worked for a short time, but it became immediately apparent that home care visits did not provide enough supervision, so Kathy moved in with Rose and her family. The house was sold afterward and the estate split evenly among the children. Caroline's remains were interred later that summer in the Grahamdale cemetery—beside her mother Rosalia Kolodka.

David's good friend and former neighbour, Herb Robinson, died in February 1988. David was relieved to find that Jalmar was officiating at Herb's funeral. David, Dennis and Ken were pallbearers and they took Jalmar aside beforehand. They showed him three tiny bottles of alcohol, explaining that they'd each had a drink and wanted to place the little bottles in the casket after the funeral was over.

David explained that shortly before Herb had passed away, he made the three of them promise to "have a drink on him" at his funeral. The men had laughed it off, saying Herb would be around for many years. But the older man knew his health was failing.

"Promise me," Herb had insisted.

They had.

Would Jalmar mind if they did this?

Jalmar placed a comforting hand on David's shoulder.

"To grant a man his dying wish is a noble thing to do," he said with a wink, "even if it does involve a sip of alcohol."

That spring, David, Lynne and Dale went to visit Raymond in B.C. David and Raymond had a few long talks where they settled their differences. They discussed their childhoods and Raymond admitted that Domko had occasionally beaten him as well. For David, the revelation put a whole new perspective on his stepfather's motivation for abusing the children.

Raymond was never able to come to terms with his paralysis, but he did find a hobby that he loved—target shooting. Much to David's chagrin, he discovered that Raymond, like Domko, was an excellent marksman. The young man had a small social network that he'd developed and regularly rode the handi-transit to a nearby shooting range.

However, David was saddened to notice that after Caroline's death, Raymond seemed to lose his will to live. It came as no surprise when he received a call in early June that Raymond had died. Because they had developed a strong bond to Raymond, Eunice and Rose took the news much harder than David. He believed that his half-brother had been released from a living hell.

The harmless Hallowe'en pranks around Moosehorn continued until the fall of that year. A pall had been cast over the group when Dennis Bauch died in a house fire in July. It seemed to mature everyone as they mourned the death of their good friend.

Dennis Bauch's death particularly bothered David, as Dennis was Gene Bauch's eldest son. Gene, the man who'd trained him at the quarry, had died from cancer in 1982—in the prime of his life. This added yet another name to the growing list of losses David suffered during this period.

The sadness, plus the unresolved emotions from David's past, were beginning to influence his daily life. While his work habits seemed unaffected, his personal relationships were suffering. He seemed distracted most of the time as he fought to make sense of what was happening around him.

He continued telling stories and being the "life of the party," but his insides ached. He was questioning who he was and why his life had turned out this way. It was a mid-life crisis of sorts, complicated by a past he'd shared with no one.

In a quest to understand why his emotions were churning, David went with Lynne on a week-long road trip. They visited David's former supervisor George Rentz in Khedive, Saskatchewan, then traveled on to Estevan where they drove to the airstrip Norman once owned. It had been ten years since his brother's death and David was struggling to put into words how he was feeling.

He stepped out onto the tarmac and felt the wind blow through his hair. The breeze reminded him of the day that his brother had come to take him off the farm.

"Lynne, it's so strange," he said. "In some ways it's like forever since I saw him an' yet it seems just like yesterday he was right here."

As he looked around, he half expected Norman to step out of the hanger at any moment. Just then, the door opened and David's heart quickened. A man who David didn't recognize gave him a strange look. They stared at one another as the man slowly walked away.

David was pleased to see that a monument had been erected in Norman's honour. He stood and read the plaque, then pulled out his video camera to take a picture of it.

He went to the hangar and like the man outside, a few people paused to stare at him. It was then he realized how confusing it must have been for them to see him. As he had aged, he had grown to look more like Norman. He'd put on a pair of glasses exactly like Norman's at the Moosehorn bar recently, startling a few friends.

"Hi," he said to the strangers. "I'm David Pischke—Norman's brother. He used to own this p-place."

The airstrip employees responded warmly to his introduction. For David, it was nice to meet a few strangers who'd known his brother. He wished he'd visited there earlier when Norman was still alive. Later they visited the cemetery where his brother was buried.

The next day David and Lynne drove to Yellowstone National Park. David got out of the truck and gazed at the mountains where Norman had been lost. David then looked at the sky and silently posed the question everyone asks when they try to resolve the past.

Why? What was the purpose of it all?

Visiting the area close to where Norman had perished helped make his brother's death real in David's mind, but it did nothing to ease the unhappiness in his heart.

◆ ◆ ◆ ◆ ◆

In 1988, Helmut Neufeld was transferred from Ashern to the Morden detachment. That same year, Sergeant Dave Asmundson was transferred to the Selkirk highway patrol. It bothered both men to leave the Ashern area with Mike Kalanza's disappearance still unsolved. Asmundson was particularly troubled about leaving as by this time he was convinced that Mike had been murdered.

In mid-August of 1990, partial remains of a skeleton were discovered by a hired man putting up hay in a field approximately a half mile from where Mike had lived. Everyone speculated that the old man's body had finally been found.

However, the facts that emerged pointed to someone else. It was quickly determined that the skull belonged to a young Aboriginal woman.

After the discovery of the native woman's bones, an old rumour resurfaced. The story was that Mike had once gone to Winnipeg and brought back a prostitute whom he locked in an old granary at the farm. People speculated that maybe this was that woman.

This theory did not hold water as the prostitute story had first surfaced when Mike was in his mid-40s—and this young woman had been deceased only a short time. Now it looked as though the police had two murders to solve.

By the winter of 1991, the whole area was a-buzz about the death of another of the area's eccentric bachelors. Stewart Clancy had lived near the Spearhill quarry. Shortly before his death, Jalmar and a few other friends, including Lorne Park, had convinced Stewart that he shouldn't keep his money in his home. Three people were present when the money was counted. One of them was Jalmar. Approximately $250,000 was put in a hockey bag and deposited in the bank.

The next summer—on July 26, 1992—the entire region was thrust into mourning when Jalmar died of a massive heart attack. His death left a huge void in the community. He'd been an important part of so many lives. More than 800 people attended his funeral at the Ashern Centennial Hall. Lorne Park was a pallbearer.

One summer evening, David was telling stories around a campfire at the Steep Rock Beach park.

"And gawd we was bushed," David said. "Bushed! Right, Kenny, you re-member?"

Ken smiled. "Yeah, you were bushed all right."

"An' we couldn't talk, no sir," he said. "So, this one time I got the company truck an' I'm takin' it somewhere an' I got to get gas. Course I'm too scared to ask the boss for the money, so I just figure I'll pay outta my own pocket an' then collect later. So I pull up to the gas pumps an' right away I see the gas jockey, an' I don't know him. So I get scared right away. So what am I gonna do? I want ttt-tw-twenty dollars worth, but do you think I can say it? No sir! . . . So, I looks at him an' I'm gonna say ttt-tw-twenty, but instead I say, 'Fill 'er up.'"

Laughter pierced the warm, dark air as David's booming voice continued. "Fill 'er up. Can you believe it? I'm drivin' this huge truck an' I get in there to pay an' it took all my money! I only had about five bucks left for the rest of the week. Embarrrassssing! You've never been so embarrassed in all your life as we was on that farm. An' after we left, we didn't have a goddamned clue . . . an' what an ugly, ugly place it was."

Someone called out that he'd never go there in the dark. "That place is haunted," he said.

"You got that right!" David exclaimed.

And then someone told a story about people who'd seen a ghost at the farm.

"Well you know," David said, "the farm was cursed."

"What?" someone asked.

"Yes, oh yes, it was cursed," David said. "My grandpa got the farm at a tax sale an' old Gus Gall had owned it before that. He told my grandpa that the place was cursed an' that nobody would ever do good there."

"An' then look what happened. Dad died an' then the old bastard showed up and he ended up in Selkirk. I know people say we drove him crazy, but I don't think so. And then Norman and Sharon lived there before going to Estevan an' were staying there when he died. Sharon and the boys moved back there an' thank God she moved out. Hugo bought it and died soon afterward—it's an ugly, ugly place."

"Who owns it now?" someone asked.

"The Weigelts, but they don't actually live on the farm," David said. "Good thing! They're really nice people. Nicest people you ever wanna meet."

"Hugo didn't live there either," someone said.

David waved off the comment. "He's still dead, isn't he?"

"Ah, that's nonsense," a man piped up. "There's no such thing as ghosts and curses."

"All right, why don't you move there then?" someone challenged, jumping to David's defence.

"Not on your goddamned life!" the man retorted.

Everyone laughed.

"You know," David said, "I'm g-gonna tell you guys about somethin' I never told nobody before."

The crowd around the fire hushed as they settled in for another one of David's stories.

"Me an' the other kids was out hidin' in the bush—as usual," he began, tone serious. "I can't re-member what year it was, but we was out there by the beaver dam when we were maybe 12. Anyway, we all of a sudden saw this bright light. It wasn't the light from Koch's neither, it was bigger an' high up in the sky. An' we ran an' hid an' when we came out of the bush, we noticed lots of trees was snapped off at about, oh, ten feet high. I don't know what that was, but I'll never forget it."

Everyone was quiet for a minute.

"Yeah, but Dave, you and Dennis also thought that it was an alien invasion the first time you saw a snowmobile," one of the group chuckled.

David laughed. "Yeah, I know. Gawd, we was bushed!"

The group burst into laughter.

"There we were out by the beaver dam an' all of a sudden we see these guys comin' across the ice on machines. An' they got on these goddamned helmets and we figure they're spacemen like what we saw in a comic book."

David stood up and began acting out the scene, pausing for a moment to clarify his knowledge of comic books.

"Not that Domko never bought us no comic books, no sir, we saw one when we were at the Koch's place. So we saw these spacemen in a book, an' here we are lookin' out across the beaver dam an here they come! An' I yell, 'Oh no, Dennis, they're comin' to get us!' So we start runnin'."

"Meanwhile, it's just the neighbours looking for their calf, one that Domko stole and butchered an was eatin' the night before. So he's standin' there talkin' to them, and of course me an Dennis are hidin'. He looks so innocent—says, 'No, I's not be seeink but-a-some calf.' An' the bastard's got a piece of meat stuck right between his front teeth!"

By now, everyone was doubled up with laughter as they watched David act out the entire scene.

"Well, I'll tell you," one man piped up, "I agree with Dave. There's somethin' weird on that farm. One time me and a few guys were not far from there and all of a sudden there was this huge light and noise. Man, did it give us the creeps. We took off out of there fast, and let me tell you, I won't ever drive by at night."

Everyone sat quietly, nodding and looking at one another.

"Well, Dave," someone said, breaking the silence, "you've had quite a life. You should write a book."

David laughed.

"I know," he chuckled. "Let me see, we were on the farm for 12 years, that's 365 days to a year, times twelve, that's how many days?"

It was quiet for a moment, then someone called out, "4,380."

"Four thousand, three hundred and eighty . . . hear that, 4,380 days and I'm not 'xaggeratin' when I say I got a story for eeevvvvery day!"

The group roared.

"That's for sure, one for every day," David said thoughtfully. "That would be one damn thick book!"

A local RCMP officer visited David's home that winter to ask if he knew anything about fences being cut along a popular snowmobile trail. The officer was told to question the Pischke twins—they were always getting into trouble. David was surprised by the accusation. Yes, he had a snowmobile, but no he didn't cut a fence and neither did anyone he rode with. The things they did were limited to harmless pranks played on one another. As an adult he couldn't remember ever being involved in causing wilful damage to another person's property.

When the officer left, David began lamenting the number of times he'd been questioned over the years by the RCMP. Lynne was surprised at how much it bothered her husband. She tried to convince him to "just let it go."

"I'm trying to!" he hollered. "I'm trying to f-forget the past but the bastards won't let me."

"What past?" she asked. "Who won't let you?"

By now, Lynne had noticed that David would sometimes get "stuck" on a subject. He'd become angry to the point of appearing obsessive.

"Everybody!" he said. "You don't understand. It's bad enough tryin' to f-forget the old bastard . . . but when they keep bringin' s-stuff up—you don't know what it's like for us guys livin' around here."

Lynne shook her head. "You're right," she said. "I don't have a clue what you're talking about."

The path ahead was lined with poplar and spruce trees. The snow was deep as he hiked along, following his earlier tracks. They'd taken this route before—he paused to look around.

Where was Dennis? They were late to get to work and it was disconcerting. They couldn't be late otherwise they might lose their jobs. They'd been hired to do work—across the small lake that separated their farm from the rest of the world. It was a wonderful place, but they had to get through the trees first. David looked over his shoulder for his twin who was somewhere behind.

We have to hurry, we can't be late, he told himself as he trudged through the snowdrifts. *If we don't make it we'll freeze. The people will be gone and we'll never light a fire with these matches.*

He emerged from the trees into a clearing—and realized that he'd walked too far! Now he'd be late for sure. He couldn't miss work—he had to hurry back. He began running and soon he was in a meadow and little JeeJee was there. The girl took his hand and led him to where Caroline stood.

Ma, he thought, *it's you. You're not dead!* He felt tremendous relief. She looked as she did when David was a child. Her handsome features were framed in a soft light and she was young, beautiful and unburdened.

She beckoned to him and at once he was by her side. She walked with him pointing at their surroundings and he instantly knew she was telling him about the people in his life, telling him that everything was going to be all right.

She was gently encouraging him to be happy. He tried to explain that his life wasn't that simple—that things couldn't be explained away that easily. She smiled. And then she was gone. His heart ached—wanting to see her for another minute, to ask her questions. She seemed so wise and open, maybe now she'd be ready to talk with him about the past.

Suddenly Dennis was there and it was time to go. They started running. So late! Dennis wanted to take one path, David another. They separated but David could still sense his twin nearby. He ran but seemed to be going nowhere. A yellow-eyed wolf appeared in his path. It was a sickly looking animal that skulked ahead of him. He knew it was the same wolf he'd seen in his dreams before. He chased after the wolf and ran it down. As the animal snapped at him he fought with it. Suddenly it had Dennis! It grabbed him by the hands and his twin screamed for help. David scrambled around in the snow and then lifting a broken tree limb, he began smashing the wolf on the head. Each blow caused Dennis to scream louder, but David had no choice—he smashed in the wolf's skull and then Dennis was free.

They'd killed the wolf—it had been a terribly cruel thing to do—but there was no time for regret just now. David glanced at his watch but he couldn't read the face as it was shaded in black. He was frantic—and very, very late. The air was cold and he knew that if they didn't hurry, there would be nothing left for them to eat. He watched in horror as Dennis suddenly disappeared from sight

Dennis! he silently screamed. He dove toward the hole that his brother had fallen into and grabbed for his arm, but Dennis slipped from his grasp. Dennis was drowning in a pool, but David couldn't see him. He jumped into the swirling water and reached frantically for his brother who was sinking into the darkness. He could feel his own lungs filling with water. Dennis was pleading for his help, but he just couldn't see through the black wall . . .

David screamed and bolted upright in bed.

The only person who understood how he felt was Dennis. Unfortunately, David couldn't talk to his twin because their adult relationship was strained. What had begun as harmless quarrels when they were teenagers had escalated to full-blown grudge matches as adults. Unbelievably stubborn, neither brother would give in. Often this put family and friends in the difficult position of having to choose sides—straining friendships and creating hard feelings.

One day David climbed into his old truck and drove to pick up some lumber that he needed to finish a project. Both he and Dennis purchased wood from a member of the Jehovah's Witness congregation who operated a small milling business from his home.

David pulled into the driveway, parked the truck and got out. As he was walking to the man's house, the door opened and the older gentleman stepped out. He strode across the yard toward David.

"You!" he yelled. "You get away from here."

Shocked, David stopped. Before he could utter a word, the man lit into him.

"Somebody's been stealing lumber from me and I finally figured out who it was," he said. "It's was you, wasn't it? You were here the other day and helped yourself, didn't you?"

"N-n-no," David stammered. "It wasn't me."

"You're Dennis Pischke, aren't you?" he challenged.

"N-no, I'm David," he said.

Surprised, the man paused.

"Oh . . ." he said, "I was told it was Dennis—but it doesn't matter, neither one of you can buy wood here again."

"Wait a minute," David said. Initially, he'd been shocked, but now he was annoyed. "Steal wood? You think we've been s-stealing wood from you?"

"Yes," the man said. "I've been missing lumber and haven't been able to figure out who was taking it, but I finally did. They told me it was you Pischkes, or your brother Dennis—whoever."

"Who told you that?" David demanded.

"Never mind," the man said.

"What makes you think it was us," David asked. "I didn't do it, an' I know Dennis didn't do it neither. We don't s-steal."

The man chortled.

"Once a thief, always a thief," he said.

Chapter 26

"**ARE YOU AFRAID I'M GOING** to ask you a question we haven't reviewed?"

David wondered why this was important. He didn't know how to answer. Was this a trick?

"No," he said weakly.

"Are you going to tell the truth today?"

Another question David had been expecting. Of course he was going to tell the truth, that's why he was there.

Am I telling the truth?

"Yes," he said firmly.

"Do you know who killed Mike Kalanza?" McMillan asked.

David wondered if rumours counted. He'd heard names bandied about and wondered if the names stuck in his mind would count as "knowing" Mike's killer. He thought again.

Do I know who killed Mike Kalanza?

"No," he said.

"Were you present when Mike Kalanza was killed?"

"No," David said firmly.

"What's this?" Karen asked holding up a slip of paper.

"Oh, there was a man here to see you yesterday," answered a young woman from her desk in the newspaper office in Ashern where the two women worked. "I had a hard time understanding him. He seemed pretty angry and excited. He mentioned something about a cult, the Devil, child abuse—something about what happened when they were kids."

"Who is he?" Karen asked. As the local newspaper reporter, she was curious.

"I'm not sure . . . Pischke, Dennis Pischke," she said.

Karen nodded. Later that day she asked a few people if they knew the Pischkes. She was told to stay away from them because they were troublemakers. She phoned the number and arranged a meeting anyway. The telephone conversation seemed as crazy as the note, and she didn't think it would amount to much of a story. But she followed the directions to David Pischke's house in Moosehorn. She took along her notebook and a few cassette tapes—just in case.

Karen was surprised when Lynne Jensen answered the door.

"Lynne," she said. " I know *you.*"

"You look relieved," Lynne smiled. "But I'm not Lynne Jensen anymore—I married David Pischke."

Karen was introduced to the twins and Dennis' wife Robynne. David was busy in the kitchen setting up a video camera. They'd done some video taping out at a farm the evening before and wanted her to see it.

Karen was having difficulty understanding the brothers because they had an unusual way of speaking. Their speech problems seemed to get worse with excitement. She found it interesting how they spoke in tandem—one brother, she wasn't sure yet who was who—would start talking and the other would finish the sentence.

They sat at the kitchen table while David played back the amateur video. At first Karen couldn't grasp what they were talking about. Soon she understood that they were detailing the horribly abusive childhoods they'd survived. But one question lingered in her mind.

"Okay, I have to stop you guys for a minute," she said. "What has this got to do with stolen wood?"

The brothers were quiet for a moment. Then they explained that being accused of stealing wood from an elder in the local Jehovah's Witness congregation was the latest in a series of accusations against them. The wood incident had upset Dennis so much that he'd demanded an apology from members of the local congregation—and the organization as a whole—for turning a blind eye to them when they were children. To make matters worse, when the real wood thief was discovered, no apology had been offered to the Pischke twins.

"E-nough is e-nough," David chimed in.

Dennis' commitment to the Witness had wavered in recent years. A derogatory comment about his mother and sister by a church elder had given Dennis the impetus to quit the religion altogether.

"So who is this Domko," Karen asked.

"Okay, okay," David said. "He was our stepfather . . ."

"A real devil," Dennis added.

And they began telling Karen their story. Actually it was a series of stories that started when they were three and continued until Domko's death in the early-80s.

There was one story that stood out in her mind that night.

"We tried to shoot him but the gun jammed. We were about eight years old an' we overheard Walter an' Norman talkin' about one of the neighbours who had told them to 'shoot the bastard.' Walter an' Norman were sayin' how to do it and that it would be important to shoot him in the head, so that way he'd get killed an' not just injured, 'cause if we didn't kill him there would be hell to pay," David said.

"Hell to pay," Dennis repeated for emphasis.

"Anyway, so them guys decide not to do it. But me an Dennis and the girls were gettin' all beat up, you know what I mean, eh? So we decide that we gotta do it."

"How old were you?" Karen interrupted.

"Oh, I dunno, what do you think, eh Dennis—eight years-old?"

"Yeah, that's about right," Dennis said.

"So, we go into the granary and we get Dad's old gun . . ." David began.

"Wait," Karen said, "you were only *eight* years old?"

David didn't understand why she'd be shocked by this.

"Yeah," he said. "Anyways, so we got some bullets and one time when we were chasin' the cows out to the pasture, we hid the gun in a pile of rocks. A few days later we go out there, an' we get the gun an' hide in the bushes. We was watchin' and then all of a sudden, we seen him comin'. So I yells, 'Dennis, c'mon we gotta hide!' So we run an' hide behind these logs right near the edge of the bush. We crouch down an' of course I'm too chicken to do it, so I give the gun to Dennis."

Dennis laughs. "Yeah, he's going to make me do it!"

"So I says, 'Dennis, hold it up an' rest it on a log, an' be sure to aim for his head so that we kill him for sure."

" . . . An' I'm scared!" Dennis said, pretending to quiver. "I never shot nothin' before!"

"There we were hidin' behind the logs an' then all of a sudden we smell him comin', I mean you could *smell* him comin'. Have you ever smelled bear crap?" David asked.

"No," Karen answered, shocked.

"Well, he smelled like that," he chuckled, then became serious again.

"So we duck down an' then we see him walkin' through the bush lookin' for us. See, we didn't come back after chasin' the cows. So he wants to haul us home an' make us do more work, but of course we know one of us is gonna get a beatin', usually Dennis . . ."

David paused for a moment as his voice cracked with emotion.

"So I whisper, 'Okay, Dennis, now. Pull the trigger!' Dennis closes his eyes and squeezes . . . and click! N-nothin' happens! Domko hears it an' stops an' looks around an' I'm thinking, oh no, he's g-gonna find us but he looks away. So I said, 'Dennis, pull it again' and he closes his eyes and pulls the trigger again, and click! the gun jammed *again!"*

"It was full of chop dust from being in the granary," David explained. "By now, of course, Domko's just a little ways away so we don't move and it seemed like hours that we sat there before he turned and walked out of the bush. Well, let me tell you, we jumped up an' ran in the opposite direction as fast as we could. We got outta that bush and ran to a clearing. We stood in the middle and Dennis pointed the gun in the air and pulled the trigger, an' Boom! it went off."

Tears started to fill David's eyes as he struggled to finish the story.

"We looks at one another and I said, 'Oh no. He really is the Devil an' he's never gonna die.' We took that as a sign that we was doomed. An' we gave up an' never tried n-nothin' to fight back ever again."

The group sat in silence. Karen and the men's wives were stunned.

"Hmmm," David shrugged and then chuckled awkwardly. He raised a hand to wipe away a tear. It seemed that with the anger gone, it was time for David to come to terms with what they'd suffered.

Overwhelmed, he started to cry. The man who was known in the area as a wonderful storyteller, who would have friends and strangers convulsing with laughter within minutes—was unable to continue. He broke down completely.

For the first time in their marriage, Lynne had heard one of the "real" Domko stories. She got up from the table and in a state of shock wrapped her arms around David's thick shoulders. Dennis was crying too and Robynne consoled him in a warm embrace. The stories they'd told previously were always humorous.

Their stories, a combination of laughter and tears, continued all night. Overwhelmed with information, Karen told the group that she would have to meet them again for more interviewing. She wasn't sure how much she could do for them—after all, the newspaper she worked for was a community paper with a readership of only 13,000. But she said she'd try. She glanced at her watch. It was 2 a.m. She'd been there for seven hours.

It took four more long visits before the article about the twins' lives ran in the February 13 and February 20, 1995, issues of the Interlake Spectator. Following the publication of the story came an outpouring of sympathy and outrage that sent shock waves through the region.

The story was read by investigative journalist Peter Warren of CJOB radio in Winnipeg. He phoned the twins and asked them to appear as guests on his morning talk show. They agreed.

Following the 9 a.m. news, the twins were introduced and began telling their story. Midway through the morning, Warren cancelled what he had scheduled for the second half of the program. He and his listeners sat mesmerized by the stories the twins told between heartrending sobs.

The entire time the switchboard was lit up with callers wanting to express sympathy to the twins. Others phoned to thank the brothers for coming forward with their story—because they too had been abused. Some callers said they had been neighbours of the Pischkes and confirmed the truth of what they were saying.

Near the end of the program, David told Warren off the air that people had said the twins should write a book. When the program was live again, Warren broached the subject.

"So I hear there's a book in the works," the radio host said.

"Oh yes," David said. "An' I want to thank Karen Emilson for the super job she did . . ."

"Is she the one who's writing the book?" Warren asked.

"Oh yes, yes," David said, " . . . well, I haven't asked her yet."

Warren laughed. "Well, I guess you've asked her now!"

The phone began ringing at the Interlake Spectator's Ashern office and before the day was done, there were over 50 orders for a book that hadn't yet been written.

◆ ◆ ◆ ◆ ◆

In the months that followed, the twins continued to tell their story in excruciating detail. Karen made notes and arranged the events in chronological order. She interviewed many of the people the Pischkes talked about including Walter and Eunice, the Harwart sisters, the Koch family and Jim Deighton. While Karen and the twins were absorbed in the writing of the book, life in the area continued normally.

That summer a school teacher named Alan Thomson moved to Moosehorn. He was hired by Lakeshore School Division to teach science to grades nine through 12 students at Ashern Central School.

In his early 30s, Alan was an enthusiastic man who was well liked by most students. His wide smile and bright eyes gave him an approachability that the students liked. His exuberant nature worked well, particularly with the outgoing students who liked to play sports.

Alan worked in Ashern during the week, commuting on weekends to Elm Point, which he had purchased in the fall of 1994. He had big plans for the land which included upgrading the marina and developing a swimming area. He hoped to subdivide the beachfront area and sell cottage lots. Eventually he would build his own home there, but for now his first priority was making the place attractive for cottage owners.

Now that he owned 237 acres of land, Alan decided that he'd like to buy a horse. He'd had one as a teenager and enjoyed riding. He asked around Moosehorn to see if anyone knew of a horse for sale. He was directed to Gus Breitkreitz who lived at the south end of town. Alan arrived at Gus' house to find the older man outside puttering. He introduced himself.

"You're the guy who bought Elm Point, aren't you?" Gus inquired.

Alan nodded that he was.

"I used to know the man who owned that piece of land," Gus said. "Ever heard of Mike Kalanza?"

Alan said that he had, but admitted the name didn't mean much to him. "The reason I'm here is horses. I understand you might have a horse for sale," Alan said, changing the subject.

"Have you ridden before?" Gus asked.

"When I was younger," Alan said. "Have you got one?"

"I have a well-broke mare over there," Gus said pointing to the field at the south end of his house. "She's got a bit of a nasty attitude, but like I said, she's well broke."

"Okay, I'll take a look," Alan said.

The two men walked over to the fence, then slipped through.

A dark-coloured horse stood in the distance eating grass.

"Go catch her," Gus said.

Alan started toward the horse. The mare looked up and when he got within 10 feet, she trotted away. Alan looked back at Gus.

"Keep going," he said, waving him on.

Alan followed the horse who stood watching him. Again, when she was just within arm's reach, she'd bolt.

"Gus!" he called back. "What good is a horse if I can't catch her?"

Gus laughed. "Don't worry, once you catch her she's a good horse."

Alan followed the animal around the pasture for at least 20 minutes before he finally got close enough to grab the rope tied around her neck. He assumed that Gus hadn't been able to catch her to bring her over himself.

"Good!" Gus yelled. "Now get on her back!"

Alan stared at the horse then looked back at Gus.

"But she only has a rope around her neck!" he hollered back.

"Yeah, well that's how well broke she is!" Gus laughed.

Alan looked back at the horse who eyed him suspiciously.

"Yeah, right," he said under his breath.

He grabbed the loop around her neck and preparing himself to be bucked off, hopped up and swung a leg over the horse's back. It took him a few moments to wiggle on, but he was surprised to find that the horse didn't move at all while he was struggling.

This is a good horse—very well trained, he thought as he nudged her back toward Gus.

"How much do you want for her?" Alan asked.

"How much you got?" Gus replied.

The deal was struck and Alan now owned a horse. During the next few months, he visited Gus occasionally and even bought a few pieces of equipment from the older man. The pair were becoming friends.

One evening Alan was visiting with Gus. Suddenly the old man got up and went to another room. He returned with a statuette of a man riding a horse. Embedded in its centre was a clock.

"Here," Gus said handing it to Alan.

"Oh, that's pretty nice," Alan said.

"You can have it," Gus said warmly. "Give it to your son."

Alan was touched by the man's generosity. "Thanks Gus," he said, turning it over. "Are you sure you want to give this to me? It looks like it might be an antique."

Gus scoffed. "You take it. I got no use for it."

Alan thanked him and placed it on the table.

"Do you want me to go outside to get some wood?" Alan offered. The room was starting to get cool. Gus hadn't added anything to the woodstove since Alan arrived. All that sat on the floor were a few large logs.

"Hell no," Gus said. "What do you think chainsaws are for?"

He picked up his chainsaw, started it and cut the wood into three-foot lengths right there on the living room floor.

On November 28, 1995, Karen received a phone call at the newspaper office.

The man identified himself as Gus Breitkreitz whom Karen had never met or heard anything about. He placed the call in response to a request Karen had made in the local newsletter. She was looking for information about missing school records—research material she needed for the book she was writing about the Pischkes.

"You shouldn't be writing a story about those twins," Gus said.

Karen was surprised. "Why not?" she asked.

"Because they're just trying to make themselves look good," he said. "They're just trying to make everyone think they're nice guys."

"Well, they are," Karen said.

Gus laughed. "No, they're not. They are the ones who killed Mike Kalanza."

Karen was shocked.

"Pardon me?" she said.

"I'm saying they killed Mike Kalanza," Gus repeated.

"But Mike's body has never been found, how do you know he was murdered?"

"Well, what happened to him then?" Gus asked.

"I don't know," she replied, "but what makes you think the twins killed him?"

"Well, how do you think they got all that stuff they have?" he asked. "They've each got big, beautiful homes—how do you think they got the money?"

"Well, Gus," Karen reasoned, "they're almost fifty years old and they've been working steadily since they were teenagers. Anyone who has worked his whole life has stuff—I mean their homes are nice, but they're nothing more than what most of us have."

Gus laughed as he insisted that she didn't know the twins like he did. He also went on to say that he had been friends with Mike—that they'd gone to Jehovah's Witness meetings together. In fact, he'd been one of the last people to see Mike before he disappeared.

Gus made a few other statements and when the conversation ended, Karen sat in disbelief. She often used a recorder during an interview so that she could listen to conversations again when she was writing the story. She made a few notes in her research journal then popped the tape with Gus' conversation out of the recorder and placed it in her pocket.

Puzzled by the murder accusation she discussed the conversation with her husband and a friend. They concluded the comments were nothing but a rant by a small-minded individual with too much time on his hands. Karen filed the tape away, deciding not to tell the twins about the accusation. By now she understood how sensitive they were about such comments and didn't want to upset them further.

Over the next year, whenever Mike Kalanza's name was mentioned, Karen watched the twins reaction and paid close attention to the things they said about him. She also listened carefully when the twins related their past encounters with Gus. Because the book was only going to cover a 12-year period when they were children, many of the stories the twins told about their adult lives would not be included.

Their stories did, however, give her an understanding of how profoundly affected they'd been by the abuse they'd suffered. Gus' phone call proved what the twins were saying—there was still a contemptuous dislike for them in the community among Domko's former friends.

Just months before the book was released, Karen heard the accusation about the twins again. This time it came from a man who the twins worked with. While he did not say it in a straightforward way, he indicated that he had been talking to Gus and the two of them knew who killed Mike Kalanza. Karen asked if he meant David and Dennis Pischke. He'd smiled and said, "I know what they're capable of."

Karen decided to tell the brothers about both conversations. As it turned out, they'd heard the accusation before. Outwardly they brushed it off, but soon it became apparent that they were bothered by the allegation.

The process of writing the book was an enlightening experience for everyone involved.

The twins had never been aware of Domko's official medical diagnosis. Records obtained from the Selkirk mental institution showed that he'd been diagnosed as a paranoid schizophrenic with violent tendencies. The records also contained interviews with Domko that gave them an insight into his state of mind. As well, the medical records indicated that he was likely an abused child himself as notes in his file said he had an "intense fear" of his own father.

By the fall of 1996, the book titled *Where Children Run* was released. The twins and Karen appeared once again on the Peter Warren show. Because of the publicity, the book's initial print run sold out within a month and an additional print run was ordered. It became a Canadian bestseller within six months of its release. Each twin received a royalty from the book sales.

There was a disconcerting moment when a staff person at CJOB phoned Karen to tell her that the radio station had been contacted by a listener who said the Pischke twins had killed someone. Believing that the caller had been Gus Breitkreitz, Karen explained the 1995 phone call she'd received from Gus. The matter was soon forgotten.

The twins were thrust into the spotlight. They were both shocked and pleased by the positive response to their story. They attended book signings and soon were receiving a stream of phone calls from strangers who admired their courage in telling the story.

Heartbreaking letters arrived from people who gave detailed descriptions of their own abuse. People began recognizing the twins in public places and asking for their autographs. The brothers were overwhelmed because initially they had just wanted to tell their story. They had no idea how well-received it would be. With the exception of a few naysayers, the twins were believed and esteemed for sharing their plight with everyone.

To some extent the twins had worked their way through the bad memories by putting them in print. It was validation that what they were saying was true.

Working together on the book helped heal old wounds between the brothers and solidified their relationship. People who knew them said that both David and Dennis had never been more content.

Finally, it seemed the twins had overcome the stigma of their childhoods.

Then, on June 10, 1997, Mike Kalanza's body was found.

Chapter 27

"HAVE YOU EVER TOLD A LIE?"

"Yes."

"Have you ever hit anyone in anger?"

"Yes."

"Have you ever stolen anything?"

"Yes."

McMillan sat quietly for a moment as David fought the urge to squirm in his chair.

"Okay David," McMillan said, "you can open your eyes now."

Relieved, David opened his eyes. He looked at the officer who continued to study the computer screen.

"You seem to be having a problem with one of these questions," he said. "What are you afraid of?"

David blanched. "What do you mean?" he rasped.

McMillan stared at the screen. "Is there something you haven't told me?" he asked.

The weather on the day Mike's body was found was the opposite of the night he'd disappeared.

It was a warm, sunny afternoon in June. A group of grade nine Ashern science students climbed into a school bus for a field trip to the Spearhill quarry. They were accompanied by their teacher Alan Thomson. He'd decided to take the class on a fossil hunt. He originally had planned to take them to Steep Rock but changed his mind a few days earlier because Spearhill was closer. The shorter bus ride meant more time for the students outdoors.

When they arrived at the quarry, the class was split into a handful of groups. They quickly spread over a half-mile area in the quarry. One group of students came across an old shoe as they searched for fossils at the base of a rocky cliff. The shoe seemed attached to something and on closer inspection, the boys realized the cloth above the shoe was a pant leg. In a state of disbelief, they continued to excavate further. When they realized it was a body, they yelled for their teacher and classmates.

As the groups of teens emerged from behind bush and small outcrops of rock, a few of the boys who'd made the discovery began clearing the area around the shoe. They finally came to a piece of carpeting that covered the torso of a man.

By the time the teacher arrived at the scene, the body was mostly uncovered. Within minutes fascination turned to shock. Some students backed away, struck hard by the reality of what they'd discovered. The students who found the body were questioned by Alan, who sought information he thought the police would need.

Alan and the students finished uncovering the body. When the remains were completely exposed he and the students saw they'd found the body of a man dressed for cooler temperatures in layers of clothing. The outer layer was a dark brown suit. He appeared five foot, six inches tall and was lying face down. Scarves were wrapped around his head blindfolding him, but the students could see hair sticking out above and below the scarves. His hands were behind his back. There was an obvious bullet hole in the back of the bound head.

Alan sent a student back to the bus to alert the driver. When he emerged from over the hill the bus driver peered down and called out, "That's Mike Kalanza. That's how he used to dress."

Alan told the students not to touch anything while he went to the bus with the driver to radio the RCMP.

"This is Alan Thomson calling and I'd like someone to come out to the Spearhill quarry," he said identifying himself as a teacher at the Ashern school.

"What is this regarding?" the officer asked.

"I don't want to discuss it with you on the open air waves," Alan said. "It's quite important."

"Well, we have to have a really good reason before we send a patrol car out," the officer replied.

"Well okay then," he said, hesitating. "My class has found somebody who's been murdered."

There was a pause on the other end.

"We'll be right there," the officer said.

Alan called his wife and asked her to bring his camera and video camera. He gave her directions to the site. When he returned to the scene, the body looked as it had when he left.

When the initial shock of the discovery wore off, the students all reacted differently. A handful of girls asked to go swimming while some boys and girls backed away completely from the grisly scene. Others, fascinated by the skeleton, stayed to observe with their teacher until the RCMP arrived.

"This guy was shot," one of the boys said, pointing at the hole in the back of the head.

"Yes, you're probably right," Alan said.

As a science buff, he found the scene fascinating. He had earned a degree in molecular genetics and after obtaining his Master's he'd been encouraged to enter police forensics. He had a pretty good understanding of what was in front of him. While he wanted to maintain respect for the deceased, he was extremely interested himself and also saw this as a learning opportunity for his class.

Constable Ernie Arns was the first officer to arrive at the scene. Alan, who had been taking pictures, gave his film to Ernie and offered the video tape as well—but first wanted to copy the beginning of the tape. It contained footage of his young son and Ernie agreed to the request. A team of investigators arrived later that afternoon.

"We thought this was going to be boring looking for fossils," said one student on the way back to Ashern, "but there is no way we'll ever top this field trip."

"I know," Alan said as the students prepared to leave the bus, "and no matter what comes of this, I want you to remember that you have done some family a huge favour by finding their lost relative."

As Alan watched the students depart, he remembered that he'd taken a group of grade 12 students to the same spot two weeks before. They'd walked past the site and even commented on the same shoe.

News spread quickly through the region that Mike Kalanza's body had been discovered. There was some criticism of the teacher because of the way he'd handled the situation. Some people believed he should have stopped the students from removing rocks as soon as he knew a body was buried beneath the pile. Others believed there was no harm done—how was he to prepare in advance for such a grisly discovery?

There were parents who feared their children might be traumatized by the event. A few students were critical of Alan's actions but many shared in his excitement and some saw it from a purely scientific point of view.

It had been nearly 12 years since Mike's disappearance and now the RCMP had a body. A DNA sample was sent to a laboratory in Ottawa, Ontario to confirm the identity of the remains. But because of the layers of clothing, plus items found in the pockets and the one hand with a partially missing finger, there was little doubt that Mike had been found.

The investigation began immediately.

Speculation over what had happened to Mike spread through the north Interlake. Old rumours and stories resurfaced. People were now under intense scrutiny within the community. Few wanted to admit they even knew the man for fear they'd become a suspect. It was unsettling for everyone to think that a murderer might be living in the close-knit community.

A police cruiser arrived at Elm Point to interview Alan Thomson.

"When did you move to Manitoba?" an officer asked Alan after introducing himself.

"1991," he replied.

"Where did you work when you first came here?" he quizzed.

Alan said that he'd worked in a northern First Nations community.

"What year did you buy Elm Point?"

"1995," Alan said.

"Had you ever been out here before the 1990s?" the officer asked.

"I was living in Ontario when Mike disappeared, if that's what you're wondering," the teacher replied.

"Don't you think it's a bit of a coincidence that you own the place that Mike used to own," the officer asked, "and that you found his body?"

Alan laughed.

"What's even more coincidental is that on this large piece of land, you've parked your car in the exact spot where Mike's house used to be," Alan said. "So a coincidence is just that—a coincidence."

Alan didn't mention that it had occurred to him that Mike's body could be somewhere in the quarry after a conversation he'd had the year before. The fact that he and his students found it had been purely accidental.

The subject had come up naturally when Alan began discussing the book about the Pischke twins with Gus.

"That's quite the story," Alan had said.

"A lot of it can't be true," Gus had replied. "I knew Domko."

"Well, it must be true to a certain extent, otherwise there would be credible people out there disputing it," Alan replied.

Gus snorted. “Not everyone believes what those Pischkes have to say.”

The conversation wound itself around to Mike Kalanza’s disappearance.

“Mike would have to have been buried in a quarry or gravel pit,” Gus had said. “He disappeared at a bad time of the year to bury someone. The ground was frozen, so he must have been put where the digging was easy. And they couldn’t have hauled the body out to the lake because it wasn’t completely frozen. They couldn’t get out very far without falling in themselves.”

Gus told Alan that he’d called Karen to tell her who, in his opinion, had murdered Mike.

“I know who the murderers are,” Gus told Alan. “In due time, it will all come out.”

A call was made to the Manitoba Crimestoppers saying the Pischke twins had been responsible for the disappearance and subsequent murder of the old man. The RCMP contacted David and Dennis about the allegation and asked them to submit to a polygraph test.

Dennis took the test on November 26, 1997. It confirmed his innocence and eliminated him as a suspect in the Kalanza murder.

Around the same time, an anonymous typewritten letter was received at the Ashern detachment. It alleged that Lorne Park was responsible for Mike’s murder. Lorne was contacted and told about the letter. He wondered who in the area would despise him enough to write such a slanderous letter. He was also asked by the RCMP to take the polygraph.

“When can you come in?” Ernie asked.

“When do you want me there?” Lorne said. “I’ll come right now if you like.”

Lorne Park took the test November 27 and also passed, eliminating him from the list of suspects. When asked if he thought the Pischke twins would be capable of committing such a crime, he’d replied, “Not a chance.”

David heard the accusation about Lorne and thought it was ludicrous.

To those who knew the three men, it seemed that police were grasping at straws as they looked for clues in what was now a 12-year-old murder investigation. It was discovered that they had also polygraphed three other people. One was Gus Breitkreitz. The other two remain anonymous.

When the file shifted from a missing person to a murder investigation, police became tight-lipped about details. They would neither confirm nor deny any suspicions or allegations as they looked for Mike's killer.

One afternoon, Ernie and Lorne were having coffee together. They began talking about how rumours spread in a small town.

"Rumours . . . you wonder how many people's lives and reputations have been ruined by malicious rumours," Lorne said, still smarting over the nasty letter. "I can't believe the things some people will say."

Ernie chuckled, then turned serious. "And the things they won't say. Somebody in this community knows what happened to Mike Kalanza and they just aren't talking."

Chapter 28

SERGEANT MCMILLAN HESITATED.

"You seem to be having difficulty with one of these questions," he repeated.

"Which one?" David asked.

"Which do you think?" McMillan said.

The two men stared at one another.

This was the part of the test that McMillan hated the most, but it was necessary. He felt particularly bad to cast doubt on David's innocence this late in the test, but it had to be done. McMillan had to be sure that David was telling the truth.

"All I know is I n-never killed Mike Kalanza," David said firmly. "And I don't know who did."

He sat straight in his chair and his eyes bore into the officer's.

"My wife checked our records, not that you'd believe us anyway," he continued. "We weren't even home that weekend. We were in W-winnipeg."

McMillan turned back to his screen to complete a few calculations.

It took a few minutes, but finally he looked at David then smiled. "Your test shows no deception indicated," he said. "As you said, you are an honest man."

David stared at him. "That's it?" he asked.

"That's it. You're free to go," McMillan said. "I'll tell the officers downstairs they have no reason to suspect you."

David stood up and stormed from the office. He left the detachment angry and insulted. Having to admit all his wrongdoings had brought back a lot of terrible memories. These were things he'd worked hard to overcome and even harder to forget.

"I want to do something," David said one afternoon as he sat at his kitchen table. It had been nearly a year since he'd taken the polygraph, and David was still insulted that he'd been implicated in the murder of Mike Kalanza. The case was still unsolved and, like before, most people had forgotten about it.

"I want to do something con-structive," he said. "I want to raise money for kids who are having a tough time."

David had been busy during the past year attending book signings and giving tours of the old farm site. He even began accepting speaking engagements at small events that addressed the problem of family violence. He recognized that because of his experiences he might be able to offer support to others.

A few months passed before David raised the subject again. This time he mentioned going on a walk to raise money and awareness. Friends told him that if he were serious about doing this, they'd help him put together an organizing committee. He said he was, but first had to find out if he could get the needed time off work.

The committee sent a letter to Continental Lime (formerly Winnipeg Supply and Fuel) asking that David be given a three-month leave of absence so he could go on the road to heighten awareness of child abuse and raise money for victims.

A letter came back to the committee saying that his employers would grant him the three months needed to complete the walk and that they would give it to him *with pay*. The letter described David as an exemplary employee who'd never had a black mark on his work record. They said they would be honoured to contribute to such a worthwhile cause.

In a whirl of activity, planning the fundraising walk began. A route was mapped out and David started physically preparing for the 2000-kilometre trek. The committee decided that they'd rent a motorhome for him that Lynne could drive.

David knew that before he left he'd spend most of the three months walking alone. Organizers and friends promised to meet them along the way as often as they could—to offer moral support.

David and Lynne started out from Banff, Alberta on May 6, 2000. The plan was to walk all the way home to Steep Rock. In a remarkable display of fortitude, the 51 year old walked every step of the journey covering up to 35 kilometers a day. The distance was traveled in three months. David and Lynne arrived in Steep Rock August 6, 2000. The community held a wonderful homecoming in his honour and hundreds of supporters turned out for the event.

The Foundation established in his name collected approximately $34,000 during the three months. The majority of David and Lynne's traveling expenses were covered by a separate fund—supported mostly by local businesses, organizations and citizens. David used at least $3,000 of his own money and the organizers paid all their own traveling expenses.

Unfortunately, all corporations except Continental Lime turned down the opportunity to sponsor the walk. This lowered the event's profile and limited its financial success. David donated most of the funds raised to a family shelter in Lloydminster, Alberta and to several shelters in Manitoba.

The Ashern RCMP detachment organized a fundraising event in David's honour. Spearheaded by Constable Arns, police constructed a makeshift jail on Main Street and citizens paid to have a friend "thrown in jail." The RCMP drove around all day in a police car, picking up people and putting them in the cage. Family members had to pay to bail them out. The event raised more than $400 for David's cause. It was a wonderful gesture of support and symbolic on many levels. Police presented David with the donation when he walked into Ashern.

Time alone on the road between Banff and Steep Rock gave David the opportunity to reflect on his life. He thought about his job, friends and family. Solitude allowed David to go inside himself in an effort to come to terms with what happened to him as a child. He'd begun the walk in an effort to help others, but there came an unexpected twist—he was able to let go of his own pain, much of which he'd been carrying for decades.

David met many broken souls on his journey. He discovered that his family was not the only one that had suffered. He heard first-hand accounts of similar abuse, some even worse than what he'd endured. As people joined him on the road, he laughed and cried. Sometimes all he had to do was listen.

And then the walk finished where it all began.

On David's final night on the road, he and Lynne slept at the old farm. It became a wonderful evening of storytelling, with plenty of food and singing around one of David's campfires. Those who wanted to join in the festivities were invited to bring their campers and tents. David greeted loved ones, friends and strangers alike.

When David woke the next morning and stepped out of the motorhome, all was still at the farm. The grass was heavy with dew and a light mist hung in the air. Through the trees, he could see the St. Thomas Lutheran Church—the haven where he and his twin had spent so many nights as children—a stark reminder of the past. Between it and the old farm house, sat the motorhome, a valiant emblem of the present. Both represented David's journey and suddenly the old house didn't seem so frightening anymore.

When David walked away from the farmyard that morning, he did so with the same bold determination he'd shown 36 years earlier when he'd climbed into Norman's car and began a new life. David was facing the future again—but this time with certainty. And on this glorious morning, the wind that he'd walked against so many times was to his back. Within minutes, the sun appeared and it shone bright and warm on his smiling face. It had rained the day before and the shoulder of the road was soft. As David walked towards home, he left behind tracks for all to see. It was then he realized that his journey was nearly over and he can live in the present—happy and content in the knowledge that he is worthy. David has nothing to hide from and nothing more to fear.

He's arrived at a place he's longed for his entire life.

And it is better than he ever imagined.

Epilogue

Stephen Pischke - Stephen is living in British Columbia. He and David visit regularly and their childhood squabbles are long forgotten.

Mark Domko - Mark married Eileen Niemczyk and is living in Winnipeg.

Gus Breitkreitz - Gus died March 3, 1999.

The Matheson Family - Mrs. Matheson died in the winter of 1995/96. Her sons Johnny and Jimmy are living and working in Winnipeg.

Nick Kolansky - Nick is living in Portage la Prairie. He has since sold Nick's café.

Sergeant Dave Asmundson is retired from the RCMP and living in Gladstone, Manitoba.

Constable Helmut Neufeld is posted in Amaranth, Manitoba.

Sergeant Robert McMillan is still the polygraph examiner for Manitoba.

Lorne Park is the Reeve of the R.M. of Siglunes.

Emma Harwart and Ruby Ratz - Emma Harwart died April 25, 1984. Ruby (Deighton) Ratz died October 31, 1991.

George Rentz and Jack McGuiness - Both are now deceased.

Bryan the bully - David was happy to never see him again.

"Being truthful, when you know it will cost you, is the true test of honesty."

- Dave Weinbaum.

Author's Note

Do I know who killed Mike Kalanza?

No. My greatest fear in writing this book is that readers will believe it is a murder mystery—thinking that clues about who the murderer is, can be found hidden within the pages. If that is the case, any connection is purely coincidental.

The real challenge in writing this story was to not further perpetuate rumours. Of course each time a rumour is mentioned, it is given life so I tried to only include what I believe was relevant and furthered the story. Discussions about Mike Kalanza as illustrated here, took place in many homes and coffee shops in the area.

Because the Kalanza murder investigation is still ongoing, details here are incomplete. Also, I did not include a lot of the second-hand information I came across about Mike's disappearance in this story. I wanted to avoid generating too much speculation or cast a shadow over innocent people. All I wanted to do was explain who victim was, a possible motive for the murder and Mike's connection to the Pischke family.

As far as Mike Kalanza is concerned, this is all I have to say.

For now.

About the Author

Karen Emilson began her professional writing career in 1993 when she began as a reporter with the Interlake Spectator newspaper. She wrote, *Where Children Run* in 1996 and since then has been freelance writing and working on numerous other writing projects.

Karen lives with her husband Mark and their son Laurie on a ranch in Manitoba's Interlake Region.

Bibliography

Published Sources

Gzowski, Peter. The Sacrament. Toronto: McClelland and Stewart Limited, 1980.

The Moosehorn-Gypsumville History Book Committee. Northwest Interlake Heritage Museum History Book, Moosehorn: The Committee, 1991.

Archival Sources

Lakeshore School Division

Ashern School registers, Sept. 1961-June 1985

Moosehorn School registers, Sept. 1961-June 1985

Manitoba Public Archives

Carn Ridge School registers, Sept. 1938-June 1955

Steep Rock School registers, Sept. 1935-June 1955

Winnipeg Land Titles Office

Property searches

Selkirk Mental Health Centre

Register Data Sheets for patient Boleslaw Domko, Feb. 6, 1961, May 19, 1962, Feb. 23, 1966, July 5, 1966, Oct. 3, 1967, June 28, 1968, Sept. 7, 1968, Dec. 9, 1968,

CJOB Radio

Transcript, April, 1995.

CBC Radio

Transcript, Dec. 8, 1997

Interlake Spectator

Nov. 27, Dec. 4, 1985; Aug. 22, 1990; Jun 16, Jun 23, Jul 14, 1997.

Winnipeg Sun

Jul 22, 1997.

Environment Canada Climate Services

Weather data, 1961-1985

Arnason Funeral Home, Ashern.

Anderson Family Funeral Home, Ashern.

Funeral Home, Lumsden, Saskatchewan.